What You Need

TO LEAD

an Early Childhood Program

Emotional Intelligence in Practice

Holly Elissa Bruno

National Association for the Education of Young Children
Washington, DC

naeyc®

National Association for the
Education of Young Children
1313 L Street NW, Suite 500
Washington, DC 20005-4101
202-232-8777 • 800-424-2460
www.naeyc.org

NAEYC Books

Interim Editor in Chief
Derry Koralek

Director of Creative Services
Edwin C. Malstrom

Senior Editor
Holly Bohart

Design and Production
Malini Dominey

Assistant Editor
Elizabeth Wegner

Editorial Assistant
Ryan Smith

Permissions
Lacy Thompson

Through its publications program, the National Association for the Education of Young Children (NAEYC) provides a forum for discussion of major issues and ideas in the early childhood field, with the hope of provoking thought and promoting professional growth. The views expressed or implied in this book are not necessarily those of the Association or its members.

**What You Need to Lead an Early Childhood Program:
Emotional Intelligence in Practice**

Library of Congress Control Number: 2011943664
ISBN: 978-1-928896-80-7
NAEYC Item # 363

About the Author

Holly Elissa Bruno, MA, JD, attorney and keynote speaker, hosts the online radio program *Heart to Heart Conversations on Leadership: Your Guide to Making a Difference* on bamradionetwork.com. She teaches graduate leadership and law courses at Wheelock College and National Louis University's McCormick Center for Early Childhood Leadership. Having served as assistant attorney general for the state of Maine, assistant dean at the University of Maine School of Law, and dean of faculty and associate professor at University of Maine–Augusta (UMA), she was named UMA's Outstanding Professor.

Holly Elissa's keynotes engage and inspire audiences from Reykjavik, Iceland, to Budapest, Hungary, and from Honolulu, Hawaii, to Anchorage, Miami, Chicago, Austin, San Diego, Tulsa, and Spearfish, South Dakota. She believes early childhood leadership is one of the most powerful positions anyone can hold.

Acknowledgments

Thank you to my mentors: Michael Gonta, Nelle Smither, Arthur LaFrance, Madeline Birmingham, and each of my students from West Charlotte Senior High School.

With appreciation to the guests on my radio program, *Heart to Heart Conversations on Leadership: Your Guide to Making a Difference*, beginning with Louis Cozolino in 2010.

Thank you, inspiring and steadfast colleagues: Kay Albrecht, Lorna Backus, Sue Baldwin, Ruth Ann Ball, Paula Jorde Bloom, David Bloomfield, Joanna Booth-Miner, Pam Boulton, Suzi Brodof, Beverlyn Cain, Vicki Calderone, Mary Cecchinato, Hooray Childers, Neila Connors, Doreen Dubuque, Bess Emanual, Virginia Epps, Marcia Farris, Robin Fox, Cynthia Gamez, Janet Gonzalez-Mena, Marsha Hawley, David Heath, Luis Hernandez, Joyce Holman, Gwen Hooper, Cathy Jones, Liz Kendall, Otto Kroeger, Marie Ellen Larcada, Dawn Lui, Michelle Manganaro, Evette McCarthy, Kiki McWilliams, Barb Milner, Gladys Montes, Gwen Morgan, Bonnie and Roger Neugebauer, Sue Offutt, Kyra Ostendorf, Bjork Ottarsdottir, Sandy Owen, Betty Pearsall, Rae Pica, Peter Pizzolongo, Helen Post Brown, Donna Rafanello, Hile Rutledge, Jorge Saenz De Viteri, Alicia Smith, Errol St. Clair Smith, Jo-anne Spence, Debra Sullivan, Barbara Tacchi, Alan Taylor, Julie and Larry Thorner, Ann Terrell, Kim Tice & team, Nancy Toso, Susan Twombly, P. Gail Wilson, Vernon Wilson, and Nancy Witherill.

With gratitude for the support of Adrienne Beaupre, Catherine Cauman, Marina Colonas, Judy Conway, Joyce Dattle, Gita Devi, Douglass College alumnae, Wendy Dunning, Akimi Gibson, Jane Gottko Marcozzi, David Hoffman, Derry Koralek, Jay Manning, Jo Obin, Jan Patten, Cindy Popp-Hager, Jacqueline Raicek, Brian Roach, Ronni Rowland, Karen Vivieros, Brandy Ward, and Caitlyn Williams.

With a smile to *mia famiglia*, Nick and Lily Bruno-Hymoff, Richard Harrison, Lynne Bissonnette Pitre, Louise Riggs Bruner, Vincenzo Bruno, the Gorg family, Karen Bruner Hull, Art and Concetta Bruno, Susan Bruno, Toby Grapelli, and Walla.

*For Michael Gonta, who, in two months, 56 years ago,
made this moment possible.*

Contents

Preface

What do you need to succeed as a leader?

- Proper academic credentials
- Solid business plan
- Articulated vision and mission
- Budgeting expertise
- Knowledge of the latest leadership theory
- Well-designed buildings with green play areas
- Mastery of health and safety standards
- Time management expertise

You may have all of these capacities and still be struggling as an early childhood leader. What are you missing?

You know the answer: Relationships.

Unless we can build and maintain honest, productive, and dynamic relationships with everyone we encounter, we cannot be excellent leaders. Unless we can build effective teams, our carefully crafted vision statement will gather dust. Unless we inspire our staff's trust, we cannot bring out their best. Unless we earn the respect of families, our business plan will never be fulfilled. Without people skills, even the most stellar academic credentials are just capital letters after our name.

"I've learned that people will forget what you said, people will forget what you did, but people will never forget how you made them feel." With these words, poet Maya Angelou reminds us of how invaluable it is to build connections with the people we encounter. This ability to put people at ease, earn their trust, and inspire their dedication to quality is called emotional intelligence (EQ).

What You Need to Lead an Early Childhood Program: Emotional Intelligence in Practice is the first and only early childhood leadership book anchored in what matters most: EQ, the art and science of building relationships. Emotional intelligence is the ability to read people as well as you read books and to know how to use that information wisely. Each chapter begins with a case study that features richly complex, everyday challenges facing early childhood program directors. Alongside case studies are EQ theory and principles, pointers and problem-solving steps to help you practice and hone your leadership skills.

To lead with EQ is to read the story behind the story. Can you hear the cry for help beneath a parent's outburst? Or the unstated fear that sabotages a teacher's openness to a new approach? Leading an early childhood program requires learning the unspoken language of every individual and team. Valuable as rational analysis is, logic cannot translate these languages. Author Antoine de Saint-Exupéry's Little Prince explains: "It is only with the heart that one can see rightly; what is essential is invisible to the eye."

Emotional intelligence is not magic, nor is it "soft" science. EQ can be measured and learned. Current research in the growing field of neuroscience documents the physical, neuron-to-neuron impact we have on one another. For example, without one word being spoken, the human heart electromagnetically communicates a "Great to see you" or "Keep your distance" message to people within five feet of us. In addition, research shows that the brain's ability to make effective consecutive decisions declines after three or four hours. Yet, how many of us forge ahead, unaware that our brain has hit the snooze button? Sixty-five to ninety percent of human emotion is communicated without words. Leaders need to listen with the heart as well as the mind.

Our leadership practices, informed by neuroscience research, can be sharpened and polished to greater effectiveness. Thanks to *f* MRI (functional magnetic resonance imaging), research on the adult brain is now as compelling as research on the newborn to three-year-old's brain. Knowledge liberates. When we know how the brain functions, we can partner with its idiosyncrasies and not feel restrained by uncomfortable thoughts and reactions. To lead with EQ is to lead with confidence and integrity. As we build and refine our EQ capacities, our confidence as leaders grows commensurately.

What You Need to Lead an Early Childhood Program: Emotional Intelligence in Practice covers the entire realm of a leader's responsibilities, from financial management to marketing, supervision to assessment, and health and safety to preventing legal troubles. What makes this book unique and engaging is the human focus in each of these areas.

What You Need to Lead is the new edition of *Leading on Purpose: Emotionally Intelligent Early Childhood Administration*. This edition incorporates the latest research, theories, and practices a leader must know, while retaining the best of the original book.

Examples of new and updated topics include:

- Research findings by Adam Bryant on the five essential skills of successful leaders

- How to avoid legal troubles in the age of social networking

- Courage: What is it, where do we find it, how do we use it?

- QRIS: New evaluation tools to assess our leadership and our programs

- Using the brain to stay cool under pressure—the neuroscience of button pushing

- Eliminating whining in the workplace

- New practices to comply with the Americans with Disabilities Act, as Amended (enacted January 1, 2009)

- Working with immigrant families, legally and culturally

- Gender issues in leadership

- When should a leader apologize?

- What do you do if your boss is the problem?

- Managing Millennials, Gen-Xers, and Baby Boomers in the same workplace

- Building teams where women predominate

The new edition also features podcasts of interviews with a variety of early childhood professionals. Starting in 2010, as the host of the online radio program *Heart to Heart Conversations on Leadership: Your Guide to Making a Difference* (bamradionetwork.com), I have had the pleasure of conducting live interviews with experts, authors, practitioners, and futurists in the field of educational leadership. Interviews with Neila Connors (*If You Don't Feed the Teachers, They Eat the Students*), Meg Wheatley (*The New Science* and *Walk Out, Walk On*), Adam Bryant *(The Corner Office)*, Phyllis Chesler (*Woman's Inhumanity to Woman*), Robert Sutton (*Good Boss, Bad Boss*), Stephanie Feeney (*Professionalism in Early Childhood*), Roy Baumeister (*Willpower*), and Rick Kirschner (*Dealing with People You Can't Stand*) are a click away! Their answers are revealing and thought provoking.

Thanks to those interviews, *What You Need to Lead* shimmers with direct quotations and insights not found anywhere else. I ask the questions most of us want to ask but feel we shouldn't; my guests open up and tell the truth. The links to the podcasts of these interviews are noted in the page margins, so you can follow them online.

Telling the truth is the core of *What You Need to Lead*. As you turn each page, you are invited to resolve sticky dilemmas, identify your underlying gifts, activate your sense of humor, illuminate your blind spots, apply the latest leadership theories, and be the best leader you can be.

This book honors your individual learning style through a variety of print, online, and hands-on resources. The following resources are conveniently featured in the margins and highlighted in the text:

- Opportunities to assess where you stand on issues
- Case studies to ponder and resolve
- Quotations to inspire you
- Podcasts featuring interviews with leadership experts
- Invitations to reflect on what you have learned from your own experience
- Choices about which steps you will take next

In addition, if you lead workshops or are a teacher educator, at the end of each chapter there are questions for reflection and team projects to engage participants in professional development sessions and to extend the learning of students in early childhood education courses.

Finally, as an attorney, I have given special attention to the legal conundrums early childhood leaders face: providing and acquiring authentic references for job applicants; handling custody disputes at pickup time; instituting no-babysitting policies; allowing smokers to work with young children; facing an intoxicated parent walking out the door with her infant; and preventing confidential or otherwise damaging material from appearing online. The text includes policies, procedures, and, above all, clear (nonlegalese) and direct information. With emotional intelligence and accurate information, you will find *what you need to lead* in each page you turn.

Your response to *What You Need to Lead* matters to me. I value your feedback, insights, questions, and ideas for change. Contact me at hollyelissabruno.com.

Now, read on to explore the uncharted territories of original leadership!

PART I

Forming

Setting Up the Program and Yourself for Success

1 Five Essential Leadership Competencies: You Heard It Here

Case Study—Vanessa

Director Vanessa is in a bind. She's been nominated for president of her AEYC affiliate organization and is scared she will fail. Vanessa works well behind the scenes, loves getting results, and seems to please everyone. She knows, however, that as president she will have to address long-standing organizational power struggles and speak in front of hundreds of people. Both of these prospects scare her silly. At times, Vanessa feels like an imposter: "Everyone thinks I have it all together. If they knew the terrible mistakes I've made, they would kick my sorry self to the curb!"

Should Vanessa run for president, given the internal and external challenges she is sure to face? Do leaders have to present a false image of perfection in order to succeed?

Would you believe me if I told you that early childhood leadership is one of the most important jobs anyone could ever hold? Who else inspires children to love learning for the rest of their lives? Who else welcomes and embraces every child's family—newly arrived immigrants, single dads, elderly grandparents, two moms, and teen parents? Who else squarely faces and addresses legal issues that set the precedent for every educational institution that follows? Who else goes home at the end of the day, exhausted for sure but knowing without a doubt that she or he has made a difference in someone's life?

Effective leaders are forever learning, both about their own strengths and challenges and about what makes relationships work. Not every lesson we learn is neat or pretty; supervising resistant staff members can put us face-to-face with our own blind spots. We may not be able to help every child with special needs or prevent our budget from being cut to the bone. We can, however, choose our own attitude, whatever comes our way.

In early childhood, we lead through relationships. We touch other people deeply, just as they touch us. Building healthy, happy relationships is both an art and a science.

Beginning right now, shall we set off on a treasure hunt to discover what we need to lead, humbly and elegantly, powerfully and gently? We'll stop to explore eye-popping neuroscientific studies, liberating theories of leadership, and the hard-earned wisdom of seasoned colleagues. Our quest? To uncover the hidden dynamics of effective relationships so we can lead with savvy and authenticity, never leaving home without our sense of humor. Are you ready? Here's the first clue.

> Leaders aren't necessarily the smartest people in the organization, but they are the best students of human nature. . . . A leader's real job is to ask questions, not to have the answers.
>
> —Adam Bryant
> (podcast)

Heart-to-heart conversations on leadership

Did you intend to become a leader? Some of us, without our planning it, discover we have to make a choice: Step up to lead, or forever after wonder what we might have missed.

Late in 2009, I received a curious e-mail with an even more curious question: Would I create and host an online radio program for education leaders? BAM radio network's Emmy award-winning executive producer, Errol St. Clair Smith, promised I could interview anyone I wanted and ask whatever questions I chose. Join us, he said, in pushing the envelope in educational journalism.

Who likes to fail, especially publicly? Not me, that's for sure. Yet how else would I learn unless I risked failure? Despite the steepest of learning curves, I knew I needed to step up. I accepted Errol's challenge. As I often say, "Life's too short to be boring."

Heart to Heart Conversations on Leadership: Your Guide to Making a Difference "went live" in 2010 on the Leaders Channel. Now, with one quick click at your computer to http://bamradionetwork.com, you can tune in to podcasts and hear leaders, experts, authors, and colleagues tell their truths and share their latest research on what leaders need to succeed.

> All sorrows can be borne if you put them into a story or tell a story about them.
>
> —Isak Dinesen
> *Out of Africa*

When people are asked to share what matters, they generally do. Each of my guests levels, "heart to heart," about his or her hard-earned leadership lessons—what we need to leave behind and what we need to undertake. Those leaders' experiences, research, and insights prove that effective leaders manage through relationships, not control. In fact, leading *is* relating.

This book is for smart, heart-to-heart, everyday leaders—the relationship builders. It shines a light on the qualities of the best leaders and guides us in making our own light shine a little brighter.

Indispensable and unexpected lessons

Pulitzer Prize–winning *New York Times* journalist Adam Bryant wanted answers about what makes a leader successful. For his book *The Corner Office: Indispensable and Unexpected Lessons from CEOs on How to Lead and Succeed* (2011), Bryant taped more than 70 interviews with leaders from disparate fields. Among them are Teach for America's

---

Bryant's Five Traits of Successful Leaders

Passionate curiosity: Deep sense of engagement with the world; burning need to know "What's it all about?"

Battle-hardened confidence: Track record of facing down, learning from, and growing stronger through adversity.

Team smarts: Bringing the best out of staff teams, by using or altering the organization's unwritten rules.

Simple mindset: Ability to see through information overload to the heart of the matter.

Fearlessness: Willingness to think differently, despite pressure or inertia, and risk making changes for the better.

---

founder and CEO, Wendy Kopp; the Alvin Ailey American Dance Theater's artistic director, Judith Jamison; Harvard University's president, Drew Gilpin Faust; and Disney's CEO, Roger Iger. In his interviews Bryant booted out the usual questions, like "What are the most important competencies leaders need?" Instead, he asked soaring questions: "How do you do what you do?" . . . "How did you learn to do what you do?" . . . "What lessons have you learned that you can share with others?"

> He is educated who knows where to find out what he doesn't know.
> —Georg Simmel

Bryant found the results—the five traits of successful leaders listed above—both "indispensable and unexpected." As you manage through relationships, these strengths will serve you well. Let's dive for pearls in each of Bryant's findings.

▶ EXERCISE YOUR EQ   ▦   Which traits describe you? Which is your greatest strength? Which is an area for improvement?

Passionate curiosity

Do you love learning more than you fear failing? Are you willing to set aside presumptions and challenge your own thinking? Passionately curious leaders

> wrestle with tough issues. . . . They ask big-picture questions. They seem like eager students who devour insights and lessons, and are genuinely, enthusiastically interested in everything going on around them. . . . They wonder why things work the way they do and whether those things can be improved upon. They want to know people's stories, and what they do. (Bryant 2011, 13)

The leader doesn't have to be the smartest person in the organization, Bryant noted when I interviewed him. Instead, effective leaders are the "best students of human nature" (podcast).

Bam!radio
"The 5 Traits of Successful Education Leaders" Interview with Adam Bryant
Heart to Heart Conversations on Leadership
http://bamradionetwork.com

The mental agility fostered by boundless curiosity allows a leader to take risks and envision alternatives, even when the proven approach still works. Motivated by the desire to stay fresh and be more effective, passionately curious leaders question what others take for granted. They often lead first and analyze later. In his book, Bryant quotes the CEO of technology company Nvidia, Jen-Hsun Huang, as saying, "I actually like making decisions with intuition. I like to validate the decision with analytics. I don't believe you can analyze your way into success. I think it's too complicated. You have to use intuition, which is everything—your artistic sensibility, your intellectual sensibility, experience" (2011, 15).

Roger Neugebauer, cofounder with his wife, Bonnie, of the World Forum Foundation, carries his passionate curiosity to a global level. About wanting to see with his own eyes and hear with his own ears what early educators around the globe are doing for children, Neugebauer observed,

Children in our care right now will inherit a vastly different world. My grandparents grew up in South Dakota and never left their county. My parents didn't travel outside the country until they were in their 60s. Bonnie and I didn't travel internationally until we were 22. Our children, before they were 21, had traveled to Estonia, India, Turkey, Russia, China, and New Zealand. I can't fathom what the world will be like for our grandchildren. (podcast)

Each time Roger and Bonnie prepare for the next World Forum, they travel the world, meeting and dialoguing with educators . . . from Afghanistan, Kenya, South Africa, Malaysia. In their travels, they are endlessly curious, passionate about discovering leaders who are making a difference and, as a result, forever learning.

▶ EXERCISE YOUR EQ   ■ What sparks your curiosity? Are you always on a quest to learn and understand more? What compels you to remain a lifelong learner?

Battle-hardened confidence

Vanessa, in the chapter case study, has a track record of getting results. She is well respected enough by colleagues to be nominated for a vital leadership position. Yet Vanessa doubts herself and feels like "the great pretender." What would it take for Vanessa to overcome her self-doubt and confidently lead her affiliate?

There is no education like adversity.

—Benjamin Disraeli
British prime minister

Bryant discovered that successful leaders share a second trait: hard-earned confidence in their ability to learn from and face down adversity. Confidence is rarely the same as cockiness. Self-doubt, unlike humility, is not always productive. What kind of confidence in their abilities must leaders have? In his book, Bryant says of these leaders, "They have a track record of overcoming adversity, of failing and getting up off the mat to get the job done. They have battle-hardened confidence" (2011, 24). They may have faced adversity in their professional lives or their personal lives, or both. Wherever the difficulty is, leaders don't run from it. Bryant quotes Nvidia's Huang as observing, "There are some people who, in the face of adversity, become more calm" (25).

Teach for America founder Wendy Kopp wanted to know the "personal characteristics that differentiate the people among our teachers who are the most successful" (Bryant 2011, 30–31). Kopp's researchers discovered perseverance is a successful teacher's most important trait. Kopp describes persevering teachers as

people who, in the context of a challenge . . . have the instinct to figure out what they can control, and to own it, rather than to blame everyone else in the system. And you can see why in this case. Kids, kids' families, the system—there are so many people to blame. . . . And it's so much about that mindset—the internal locus of control, and the instinct to stay optimistic in the face of a challenge. (Bryant 2011, 31)

The wise don't expect to find life worth living; they make it that way.

—Anonymous

Perhaps bleeps and bumps on a résumé indicate more depth than a résumé with a perfect record. Facing the worst and squeezing out the best hones a kind of battle-hardened confidence. Having survived battles, a leader knows that each new problem is one more in a line of challenges that can be dealt with and learned from. After all, as the folk saying goes: "A diamond is a chunk of coal that made good under pressure."

Gus Lee, ethics faculty member at West Point, summarizes battle-hardened confidence in one word: courage. Lee defines courage as the "ability to identify your highest possible moral action and then to do it without worrying about risk to self" (podcast). To act with courage, Lee says, leaders need discernment along with critical thinking. To discern what to do when facing adversity, Lee recommends a three-part process. Ask:

- *What's the most selfish thing I can do?* (The answer is always obvious, Lee says.)
- *What is the most pragmatic thing I can do, that would solve the problem and in the process make me look good?* (Again, Lee notes the answer to this question is often easy.)
- *What's my highest possible moral act? What's my purpose, my highest goal, and what must I do, regardless of fear?* (With battle-hardened confidence, choosing the highest moral act becomes more natural.)

Lee warns that we tend not to use this resource—our ability to discern—enough.

Equipped with battle-hardened confidence, we are more likely to stand alone, when we have to, to do the right thing. Otherwise, lacking battle-hardened confidence, we make fewer courageous decisions. Lee observes: "The moment my staff senses I am acting out of self-interest, fear, or cowardice, I can no longer lead. Leaders must inspire others to be their best selves. If a leader doesn't inspire that, he's just a manager" (podcast). In keeping with Bryant's observations about risk taking for the greater good, Lee adds, "Once we decide holding our job is our top priority, we sacrifice courage."

> Think about yourself and the people you work with. What have you each been through in your life? What got you here? What makes you worth knowing—and trusting? What fires your creativity? What makes you real—and valuable? If I can't know what you feel, what matters to you, then . . . we are little more than a face and a name to each other; you are not deep or alive to me, nor I to you.
>
> —**Robert K. Cooper and Ayman Sawaf**
> *Executive EQ: Emotional Intelligence in Leadership and Organizations*

Team smarts

Team smarts begins with an "understanding that teamwork is built on a foundation of one-on-one interactions among people, an unwritten contract that has nothing to do with business cards, organizational charts, or titles" (Bryant 2011, 41). With team smarts, leaders "know how to create a sense of mission and how to make people feel like everyone's getting credit. They know how to build a sense of commitment in a group" (40–41).

Much of team smarts sounds like using EQ—*emotional intelligence,* or the ability to read people as well as we read books—and then acting wisely on that information. Bryant quotes Susan Lyne, CEO of Gilt Groupe: "I think that I now have a very strong antenna for someone who is going to be poison within a company" (2011, 50). Trusting our gut instinct about an employee often pays off. How many of us have held on to an employee either because we hoped she might change or because we feared we wouldn't find anyone better? Team smarts adds up to trusting our gut to say goodbye to the poor performer, opening the door to a more qualified applicant.

Bam!radio
"Do You Have the Courage to Be an Effective Educational Leader?"
Interview with Gus Lee
Heart to Heart Conversations on Leadership

"Leadership Styles: What Works, What Works Better"
Interview with Liz Wiseman
Heart to Heart Conversations on Leadership
http://bamradionetwork.com

In our interview, Liz Wiseman and Greg McKeown invited us all to evaluate our team smarts as staff motivators (podcast). Their research shows that 48 percent of leaders fail to bring out the best in their employees. Called "Diminishers," these bosses assume that employees cannot accomplish difficult tasks on their own. A faulty assumption made by Diminishers is to falsely assume that they can involve staff only in low-stakes issues. Lacking in team smarts, a leader may undermine the team's motivation to perform well.

In contrast, the leader with team smarts and emotional intelligence tones down her "enlightened" presence to put the spotlight on her staff's potential.

A leader with team smarts is a "Multiplier," say Wiseman and McKeown. Multipliers devote significant time to listening to and observing their employees. With passionate curiosity, a Multiplier takes the time to uncover what matters to each employee. Does Reginald adore pro football? Ask Reginald how his favorite NFL coach's team smarts might be appropriate to use with young children.

> If you judge people, you have no time to love them.
> —**Mother Teresa**

To develop team smarts, Wiseman and McKeown (podcast) encourage us to:

- Move out of "answer mode" and into "question mode." Effective leaders know that the best questions cause people to think.
- Assess how you might be inadvertently discouraging your staff.
- Operate in a mode of intellectual curiosity: Listen to learn.
- Go beyond what is comfortable. Commit to discovering each employee's hidden value, especially those employees you assume are the team's weak links.

Go to *http://multipliers-book.com/accidental-diminisher* to take a brief quiz.

As Bryant (2011) says, a leader with team smarts not only knows the unwritten rules of the organization but also chooses wisely which of those rules to overthrow and which to honor. One unwritten rule may be: "The director will rewrite everything we do, so don't bother to write well." The leader with team smarts knows to amend that unwritten rule through word and action: "Do your best writing; I appreciate that."

Does your leadership challenge teachers to step up and be leaders in their class-room and beyond? Leaders with team smarts move out of the limelight to let their employees shine. Wiseman tells us even to tone down our billowing enthusiasm to make room for teachers' enthusiasm to bubble up. In doing so, you may discover and multiply employee contributions.

Simple mindset

There's an ocean of data on the Internet we all have access to, just a few clicks away. The leader has the ability to look at that ocean and pull out 13 things that matter. As a leader you need to distill the message.

—**Adam Bryant** (podcast)

Do you feel pressured or distracted by the flurry of data available to you? If you feel overwhelmed, imagine how you might be flooding your own team with "TMI" . . . too much information! Everyone appreciates the person who sees and tells the simple truth. With a no-nonsense, cut-to-the-chase approach, a leader can focus a team's attention.

Bryant (2011) says the best leaders avoid information overload, and instead extract the one or two things that matter. He makes the point, for example, that most people don't pay much attention to PowerPoint presentations that go on and on. All those lists and charts and cute cartoons may entertain, but do they tell you what's important? "Death by PowerPoint" is Bryant's label for such unnecessary complexity. Why deliver an hour-long presentation when five minutes would be more effective? Maintaining a simple mindset is the fourth trait of powerful leaders.

Fear can push us to obfuscate or to cover up our own lack of certainty with long-winded, confusing explanations. Courage allows us to tell it like it is.

What does Bryant mean by "simple"? Consider the presenter who skips the PowerPoint altogether and "simply talks, giving a short pitch for her idea, backed up with three key facts" (2011, 52). We all deal with TMI. Torrents of data flow at us from our computer screens. How can we sort through information overload to pinpoint what matters most? The leader who cuts to the chase clears a path to her staff.

Concise leaders are respected and powerful. Keep it simple. Keep it clear. Business leader Guy Kawasaki complains,

> Schools could do a better job teaching the value of brevity. . . . What you learn in school is the opposite of what happens in the real world. In school, you're always worried about minimums. You have to reach 20 pages and 50 slides. They should teach students how to communicate in five-sentence e-mails and with 10-slide PowerPoint presentations. . . . No one wants to read *War and Peace* e-mails. Who has the time? Ditto with 60 PowerPoint slides for a one-hour meeting. (Bryant 2011, 55)

Author Russell Bishop (podcast) maintains that program staff and family hand-books are frequently weighed down by wordy, tiresome, and often outmoded policies and procedures. Sure, we require new employees to initial that they have read and understand these policies. But can a new employee fully understand what policy B-4.c in

Section IV means? Leaders have the power to use the simple mindset to streamline those policies and make them into living, meaningful guideposts.

Bishop calls his simple mindset approach the "stop, start, and continue" process. Use this process with your team to cut out the fat in long-winded, hard-to-understand policies. Simplify your staff and parent handbooks so everyone is clear on expectations. Imagine that a staff member who initials that she has "read and understood" everything in the staff handbook actually means it!

To initiate the stop, start, and continue process to simplify policies:

- STOP using unnecessary or wordy sections in the policy.
- START writing simple policies.
- CONTINUE using policies that work.

Bishop has seen cumbersome documents reduced to one meaningful cut-to-the-chase statement that everyone understands and can rally behind. For example, let's apply his stop, start, and continue method to policies for online communication. Many Internet policies are pages long, referencing every imaginable social networking site and terms relevant to those sites. For example, a Facebook policy might enumerate who can be "friended" and who cannot. By the time such a policy is posted, three new social networking sites will have leapt into popularity and current sites will have bitten the dust.

To simplify your Internet policy with Bishop's simple mindset approach:

- STOP: Ask, "Why do we need an Internet usage policy?"
- START: Identify what your bottom line on Internet usage should be.
- CONTINUE: Save anything worthwhile in the current policy.

Internet policies require staff to be as professional online as they are in person. A simple professionalism policy (more on this in Chapter 7) will set a standard for online behavior that will outlast today's wordy list.

Pick up your handbook. Do you need to lift weights to do that comfortably? If so, now is the time to "Simplify, simplify," as Thoreau advised us in the nineteenth century.

▶ EXERCISE YOUR EQ   ▮ This simple mindset trait can take time to develop. Can you explain what your work is in one minute? Which of your policies could use a start, stop, and continue overhaul?

Bam!radio
"Silly Teacher Policies: How to Change Them"
Interview with Russell Bishop and Deborah J. Stewart (8/16/11)
Heart to Heart Conversations on Leadership (Leaders Channel)
http://bamradionetwork.com

Fearlessness

Do you see yourself as a fearless leader? Fearlessness is the willingness to do the right thing regardless of the consequences. You may lose colleagues. You may be ridiculed. You may hear: "You're fired!" My Head Start colleague Dennis Ichikawa describes fearlessness as stepping into the dark guided by your inner light.

To assess our level of fearlessness, Bryant asks:

- Are you comfortable being uncomfortable?
- Do you get bored when things seem too settled?
- Do you like situations where there's no road map or compass?
- Do you start twitching when things are operating smoothly, and want to shake things up?

I've missed more than 9,000 shots in my career. I've lost almost 300 games. Twenty-six times I've been trusted to take the game-winning shot and missed. I have failed over and over and over again in my life. And that is why I succeed.

—Michael Jordan

- Are you willing to make surprising career moves to learn new skills?
- Is discomfort your comfort zone? (2011, 62)

Ursula Burns of Xerox describes fearlessness as

Seeing an opportunity even though things are not broken. The company is not headed toward a wall. It's not broken, but there is definitely a way to do it better and someone will actually say, "Things are good, but I'm going to destabilize them because they can be much better and should be much better." (quoted in Bryant 2011, 63)

To be fearless, leaders need to let go of the belief that security is more important than truth. No one said being fearless is easy.

Valora Washington, founder of the CAYL (Community Advocates for Young Learners) Institute and president and CEO of the Council for Professional Recognition, embodies this willingness to take action and shake things up. In our interview, she notes that differences between elementary school educators and early childhood educators can deteriorate into a one-up, one-down impasse: "Historically we've had a lot of prejudices in each sector" (podcast).

Rather than running from this impasse, Washington brought both groups to the table: "We all have to lead by changing. We all have to acknowledge there are performance gaps at both levels. We all need to take collective responsibility for problem solving" (podcast). Elementary teachers can learn more about using developmentally appropriate practices, and early childhood teachers can learn ways to help children successfully transition to elementary school. In Washington's book *Ready or Not: Leadership Choices in Early Care and Education* (2007), she and coauthor Stacie Goffin challenge us to be fearless in creating a more welcoming environment for tomorrow's adults.

> **Bam!radio**
>
> "Can the Pedagogical Divide Between Early Childhood and Elementary Educators Be Bridged?"
>
> Interview with Valora Washington
>
> *Heart to Heart Conversations on Leadership*
>
> "When Leaders Flunk: The Critical Role of Failure to Success in Education"
>
> Interview with Megan McArdle
>
> *Heart to Heart Conversations on Leadership*
>
> http:/bamradionetwork.com

Journalist Megan McArdle takes fearlessness to the next level. In her interview, she asks: Can leaders fail and be successful? To McArdle, failure is an essential part of leadership. We have to model failure, she argues, if only to show children how to learn and bounce back. Being fearless virtually ensures that we will, at some point, fail (podcast).

When asked about the "gotcha" factor prevalent today, McArdle says leaders need to buck the "one strike and you're out" trend to create cultures in which failure is a natural part of learning. Geoffrey Canada, founder of Harlem Children's Zone, encountered failures all along his 20-plus years of improving learning environments for children, their families, and their community. Had Canada quit at his first failure, he would never have been able to uplift the lives of thousands. Fearlessness, although full of risk, creates the change we need.

An unexpected question about power

Adam Bryant's five traits of successful leaders set standards for authenticity, but they do not directly confront the issue of power. What is a successful leader's relationship to power? How does she exercise power? How do employees determine whether a leader is powerful?

Batia Wiesenfeld and her colleagues' research (2011) explores that very question: Can a leader be fair *and* have the power to succeed? As educators, we assume leaders need to be compassionate, participatory, respectful, and fair. In an early childhood program, wouldn't a despot be quickly overthrown, if not directly then by passive resistance?

To the contrary, Wiesenfeld discovered. In fact, leaders who treat employees with fairness and respect actually diminish their own power. "Our results suggest the opposite of intuition," Wiesenfeld says. "Leaders who treat people with dignity and give them opportunities to speak up consistently are seen as being less powerful." Her research shows that leaders perceived to be fairest were not as likely to be promoted into positions of greater power. Wiesenfeld "worries that we don't have the time frame to allow fair leaders to bubble up through the system" into powerful positions.

Wiesenfeld and her colleagues' research might appear to focus on how a leader's own boss views the leader. In other words, an executive director may promote a "tough" director over a compassionate one. Curiously, the research shows that *employees* hold the same perception. Authoritarian leaders, who show less concern for their employees, are perceived by their employees as having more power. In the end, leaders are measured by their effectiveness, especially by how successful they are at winning funding and favor from higher-ups. Teachers may turn against you if you don't have the power to be effective, regardless of how fair or caring you are.

Wiesenfeld's counterintuitive conclusions may be troubling. Most likely, early childhood leaders need to exercise power with both compassion and toughness. A fair and respectful leader must also maintain integrity steely enough to make those "buck stops here," impossible decisions.

> **Bam!radio**
>
> "The Surprising Role of Power in Education Leadership"
>
> Interview with Batia Mishan Wiesenfeld and Eric Sheninger
>
> *Heart to Heart Conversations on Leadership*
>
> http://bamradionetwork.com

Integrity: "Only a mediocre person is always at his best"

At the heart of effective leadership is integrity. Integrity is that admirable trait of being true to your word, true to your values, and authentic in your actions. A leader's integrity is golden. Authenticity is the touchstone of integrity.

An authentic leader is one of a kind, self-defining, and far from perfect. She embraces and grows through her own history, regardless of how tainted it may be. Every human being who has made a difference has been a flop at one point or another. Most leaders have embarrassing or flawed histories. Who hasn't made a mistake, told a lie, or done something regrettable?

A leader with integrity doesn't pretend to be anyone other than herself, "warts and all." As the 12-step slogan says: "We are only as sick as our secrets." Your secrets and mistakes are out there. Embrace them and be grateful for the lessons they grant you.

> To the extent that we can be emotionally honest—getting out of our head and into the heart, using well-chosen words to say what we truly feel and believe—we find our voice, we become real.
>
> —**Robert K. Cooper and Ayman Sawaf**
> *Executive EQ: Emotional Intelligence in Leadership and Organizations*

You heard it here

Whatever checklists or theories we use to define and understand leadership competencies, we are skating on the surface unless we take a sounding for integrity. Your integrity determines your legacy as a leader. Martin Luther King Jr. knew: "The time is always right to do what is right."

Our treasure hunt is under way: What will you take away? May your strengths be affirmed and your challenges become less daunting.

Reflection questions

1. How fearless are you? Can you name a risk you took that turned out well? If taking the risk led to a failure, how did that experience affect your future actions? When other people are touched by the risks you take, can you be fearless on their behalf, or do you need to be cautious? What is the next risk you need to take but have been avoiding?

2. Do you have a simple mindset that allows you to laser through to the heart of the matter? Is that a skill you had to develop, or is it a skill that has always come naturally to you? If thinking like a laser is difficult for you, what steps might you take to develop a simple mindset? To practice the simple mindset, name the point you found most compelling in this chapter.

3. Would you call yourself "passionately curious"? If so, what drives you? If not, what holds you back? Recall an occasion when you let go of your own assumptions in order to break through to new understanding. Do passionately curious leaders value security? Can they create environments that feel safe to their employees?

4. How do you define integrity? How do you know if someone has integrity? Do you view yourself as having integrity? Is integrity a trait we always have and use, or can we sometimes act with integrity and other times not? Name two people you know, one famous, one from your own life, who have integrity. Does their authenticity differ from their integrity, or is it the same thing?

It is authenticity that will be most effective in marshaling teams to work together to achieve a shared goal.

—**Adam Bryant**
The Corner Office: Indispensible and Unexpected Lessons from CEOs on How to Lead and Succeed

Team projects

1. Where do you stand on whether leaders can fail and still succeed? Find out what directors and other leaders have experienced in bouncing back from failure. Interview at least three directors about their experiences with, feelings about, and lessons learned from failure. Do they think in today's "gotcha" culture that leaders can fail without losing their jobs or careers?

2. Wiseman and McKeown's research reveals that many leaders are unaware of how they may intimidate or otherwise hold their staff back from doing their best work. Read their study and conclusions (see **Bibliography** and **Web Resources** at the end of this chapter). Do you think their findings apply to early childhood leaders? If so, what changes do leaders need to make to uplift rather than minimize employees?

3. Explore the history of a leader you admire. Does this statement from earlier in the chapter describe that leader: "Every human being who has made a difference has been a flop at one point or another. . . . Most leaders have embarrassing or flawed histories. Who hasn't made a mistake, told a lie, or done something regrettable?" How can we embrace our flops and flaws and work them into our understanding of what it means to lead?

4. As a team, decide how would you coach Vanessa, the leader from the case study. What questions would you want to ask her? In your judgment, what will determine whether Vanessa should accept the nomination? Reread the Mr. Rogers quote that opened the chapter: "There is a close relationship between truth and trust." How might that insight help you coach Vanessa?

Bibliography

Bishop, R. 2011. *Workarounds that work: How to conquer anything that stands in your way at work.* New York: McGraw-Hill.

Bruno, H.E. 2010. Creating relational sanctuaries for children who suffer from abuse. *Child Care Exchange* Jan/Feb: 64–68.

Bryant, A. 2011. *The corner office: Indispensable and unexpected lessons from CEOs on how to lead and succeed.* New York: Times Books.

Cooper, R.K., & A. Sawaf. 1997. *Executive EQ: Emotional intelligence in leadership and organizations.* New York: Putnam.

Kellerman, B. 2006. When should a leader apologize—and when not? *Harvard Business Review* 84 (4): 72–81.

Lee, G. 1994. *China boy.* New York: Penguin Books.

Robinson, B.E. 2007. *Chained to the desk: A guidebook for workaholics, their partners and children, and the clinicians who treat them.* 2d ed. New York: New York University Press.

Schwartz, T., with J. Gomes & C. McCarthy. 2010. *Be excellent at anything: The four keys to transforming the way we work and live.* New York: Free Press.

Washington, V., & S.G. Goffin. 2007. *Ready or not: Leadership choices in early care and education.* New York: Teachers College Press.

Wheatley, M., & D. Frieze. 2011. *Walk out walk on: A learning journey into communities daring to live the future now.* San Francisco: Berrett-Koehler.

Wiesenfeld, B., N. Rothman, S. Wheeler-Smith & A.D. Galinsky. 2011. Why fair bosses fall behind. *Harvard Business Review* 89 (7–8): 26–30.

Wiseman, L., & G. McKeown. 2010. Managing yourself: Bringing out the best in your people. *Harvard Business Review* 8 (5): 117–121.

Web resources

Bam!radio: The Voice of the Education Community
www.bamradionetwork.com

Leadership Characteristics That Facilitate School Change
www.sedl.org/change/leadership/character.html

Level 5 Leadership: Achieving "Greatness" as a Leader
www.mindtools.com/pages/article/level-5-leadership.htm

Multipliers: Accidental Diminisher Quiz
http://multipliersbook.com/accidental-diminisher

Principals Identify Top 10 Leadership Traits
www.educationworld.com/a_admin/admin/admin190.shtml

Walk Out Walk On: From Hero to Host
www.walkoutwalkon.net/united-states/a-story-of-citizenship-in-columbus-ohio

To a Robin in Lent

You were the first one back,
the first one back.

You clung to a bare black branch
your habit to choose Sundays in March,
wind whirling around you,
sky grey as a shroud, and wet,
to sing to the flowers, not there yet.

You were not loud.
No, not at all.
But you knew what you were doing.
—Elizabeth Spires

2 Smart Heart-to-Heart Leadership: Honoring Emotional Intelligence

Case Study—Victoria

"You know those tedious classroom portfolios the director wants us to do? I'm not doing mine. Let's all just fake it. She'll forget about them eventually anyway," prods toddler teacher Roxie, just as the director, Victoria, steps into the staff meeting. Roxie, sensing her director's outrage, plasters on a prizewinning smile, and chirps, "Hey, Victoria. I bet you and your gorgeous family had a great weekend!"

All eyes anxiously flick between the beet-faced director and the Cheshire cat teacher. What will Victoria say and do in the face of Roxie's public show of disrespect?

Here's the truth about being an early childhood leader: Each moment of the day is an adventure. You arrive early, optimistic and full of energy, only to find an enraged parent pacing at the door. You cuddle a baby in the infant room just as the baby spits up her breakfast. You get a text message from the cook saying she met the man of her dreams and has eloped to Greece. You determine that accreditation is just what your program needs, then overhear teacher Roxie whipping up discontent. To lead in our field, you have to be "smart heart-to-heart," with a sense of humor that never goes on vacation.

▶ EXERCISE YOUR EQ   ▓ We all have blind spots, times when we didn't see criticism or disagreement coming. When have you been momentarily stunned by someone's behavior? What is a smart heart-to-heart way to prevent or address Roxie's disrespectful behavior?

Day-at-a-time leadership: Perfection is the enemy of the good

We all have our challenges. I have a fear of heights. Not a stop-take-a-deep-breath-and-all-will-be-well fear, but a heart-diving-out-of-my-chest, Jell-O knees, get-me-out-of-here-NOW fear of heights. To complicate things, I cannot predict when the fear will strike. So, I live my life as if I were carefree, staying true to my adventuresome soul.

One September, while exploring the Scottish Borders, I drove up a winding one-lane road unprotected by guardrails. Angling the car around brassy sheep that shot me "Get over yourself, lady; this was our road first" looks, who had time to look down? At the sign for Gray Mare's Tail, Scotland's tallest waterfall, I parked the car at the bottom of hills awash in purple heather. Up the sides of the gorge we climbed, under the spell of the champagne air, called by the water's rumble and the promise of nesting plovers.

Why I turned and looked straight down into the gorge, I do not know. In a heartbeat, my throat closed and my knees melted. I froze until I could, painstakingly, put one foot in front of the other to undo my climb. When the panic released its grip, I stopped again to notice how lovely the heather was close up, and how grateful I was to have climbed so high.

I learned from that bittersweet, blindsiding experience. Leadership can be like that hike in Scotland . . . or the encounter in the case study with Roxie. We aim for the mountaintop. Keep our eyes on the prize. Breathe in the view. Yet, even when inspired by the loftiest of goals, we can still be blindsided by the unexpected.

Success isn't measured by being the "perfect" leader. Perfection is for the gods. Success is measured through our everyday heart-to-heart interactions. Everyday leaders sometimes blow it, sometimes succeed. We stumble and get it wrong, but we still work our hearts out to make a difference. Everyday leaders, always in process, learn as we go—we learn especially to forgive ourselves for not making it to every mountaintop. This chapter is a guide to triumphing over your blind spots and enjoying your accomplishments in a field that is not your typical, everyday business.

> The only way out is through.
>
> —Robert Frost

Early childhood education: Not your typical business

Describing everything an early childhood leader does during her day can be dizzying. We negotiate contracts, oversee building projects, master QRIS (quality rating and improvement systems), plunge toilets, listen to aggrieved teachers, calm angry parents, and advocate with legislators for better education budgets. And we do all this before 11:00 in the morning!

Your typical business has separate departments such as human resources, marketing, development, operations, quality assurance, and finance. An early childhood leader *is* all those departments rolled into one person. Later in this book, we will examine what it takes to perform these functions well. For now, let's acknowledge the direct applicability of the slogan made famous by the sign on President Harry S. Truman's desk: "The buck stops here"—with the early childhood leader.

> Few will have the greatness to bend history itself; but each of us can work to change a small portion of events, and in the total of all those acts will be written the history of this generation.
>
> —Robert F. Kennedy

Our "products" are not jet engines or computer screens. We support and nurture each child and adult to become who he or she is meant to be. We do this even when funding is slashed or our infant room floods. The needs of children and their families come first. The stakes are high, even if the pay or status is not.

We work with intangibles, and often the indefinable. What's a toddler's smile worth? Can you quantify how deeply your heart is touched when a difficult child, now grown into a beaming adult, returns to say, "Thank you, you made a difference in my life"? At the end of the day, despite our to-do lists crabbing at us, we sleep well after we count our blessings.

We work with children at a time when their young brains are most receptive to learning. Our curricula help children explore and make sense of their world. We witness miracles. The silent child sings. The shy teacher takes a stand. The immigrant father observes his son making new friends. We are in the business of opening the door to every educational experience that follows.

All educators are in the business of children's learning. But early childhood educators set the standard for the learning a child will undertake for the rest of his or her life. Nurture a child's curiosity. Help her formulate questions. Help him believe in his gifts. Model how to live peaceably with people who are not like you. The child will carry these lessons with her, and in turn, the lessons will carry the child through hard times.

We cannot be mediocre and lead organizations that accomplish all of this.

When we see ourselves as others see us

Being in the business of early childhood care and education brings another distinction. Only early childhood educators suffer being called "glorified babysitters." We hear a lot, "It must be nice to get paid for playing with children." Rodney Dangerfield got it right: We don't get no respect. We do well to remind ourselves: "What other people think of me is none of my business."

Leading in a field that is, in some people's eyes, low in status and, in everyone's eyes, low in pay brings serious challenges. Our graduates choose professions that pay more money. Our employees struggle to support their families. Elementary schools hire away our best teachers. And those are just the visible consequences.

Invisible consequences are often more hurtful. Even the most gifted teachers, if they do not have degrees, see themselves as second rate. Staff turnover is high, especially when the economy sags. To keep our ratios in compliance with regulations, we might hire people who are not as qualified as we want, and in whom we end up investing inordinate amounts of time. We expend additional time and energy, precious resources we can't afford to squander, explaining what we do and how valuable our work is, to people who may never understand. The worst consequence of being in an undervalued field is when we begin to believe the naysayers. We doubt ourselves. We feel like imposters when others look to us for expertise.

When the world's values seem upside down, keeping our confidence right side up takes courage. For us to succeed, our esteem needs to come from the inside out, rather than the outside in.

Claiming our own brand of leadership

Fortunately, small-minded prejudices are being challenged, and unproductive institutions are being toppled. Knowledge is evolving and disseminating more rapidly than a frog can leap. Scientific studies are debunking long-held beliefs. Deep-rooted definitions

> What concerns me most these days are those people who think that we must (or even *can*) bypass feelings in order to develop the great national resource called children.
>
> —**Fred Rogers**
> *You Are Special*

> It is only with the heart that one can see rightly; what is essential is invisible to the eye.
>
> —**Antoine de Saint-Exupéry**
> *The Little Prince*

Neuroscience has discovered that our brain's very design makes it *sociable*, inexorably drawn into an intimate brain-to-brain linkup whenever we engage with another person. That neural bridge lets us affect the brain—and so the body—of everyone we interact with, just as they do us.

—Daniel Goleman
Social Intelligence

of intelligence and self-worth that have set the standard for more than a century are falling to new definitions. Scientists in burgeoning, brand-new scientific fields such as neurobiology and neuroendocrinology are conducting research that cannot be ignored.

For early childhood leaders, one of the most liberating discoveries is something called "emotional intelligence." Thanks to emotional intelligence research and principles, we early childhood professionals have upliftingly fresh:

- affirmations of the importance of our work,
- views of leadership,
- skill sets to improve our effectiveness,
- strategies to keep our heads when all about us are losing theirs and blaming us, and
- ways to keep our sense of humor and creativity at the forefront.

What is emotional intelligence, and how can it be so helpful? Let's take a look.

What is emotional intelligence, or "EQ"?

In a phrase, *emotional intelligence* (EQ) is the ability to read people as well as we read books, and to handle that information wisely. EQ is paying attention to the power of everything that takes place beneath the surface of our words and behavior. Up to 93 percent of human emotion is communicated without one word being spoken (Borg 2008). If you have ever been given "the look," you know the impact of unspoken communication. We cannot be in someone else's presence without affecting that person's physical and emotional state. Mastering how to read and wisely deal with these moment-to-moment, shifting dynamics and messages is what it means to be emotionally intelligent.

Neuroscientist Louis Cozolino, in his seminal book *The Neuroscience of Human Relationships,* encourages us to realize that "even though we cherish the idea of individuality, we live with the paradox that we constantly regulate each other's internal biological states" (2006, 3). He adds, "As a species, we are just waking up to the complexity of our own brains, to say nothing of how brains are linked together" (3).

To be emotionally intelligent, leaders need to not only read the flurry of unspoken messages in steady transmission between people, but also practice savvy ways to communicate through these channels. To help us with this process, we will check out new research on how the adult brain works. But first, let's get clear on the comparative definitions of intelligence, so we can distinguish EQ from the predominant definition of intelligence, IQ.

Defining EQ

John D. Mayer and Peter Salovey (2004), pioneers in the field of emotional intelligence, define EQ (also referred to as EI) as the ability to:

- Perceive emotions accurately
- Appraise and express emotions
- Access and/or generate feelings when feelings facilitate thought
- Understand emotions and emotional knowledge
- Regulate emotions to promote emotional and intellectual growth (35)

Howard Gardner (2011) includes "personal intelligence" in his multidimensional definition of intelligence. Gardner incorporates both "intrapsychic capacities" and "interpersonal skills" in his list of multiple intelligences.

Reuven Bar-On, creator of the first standardized EQ test, provides the most common-sense definition of EQ: "Emotional intelligence is concerned with understanding oneself and others, relating to people, and adapting to and coping with the immediate surroundings to be more successful in dealing with environmental demands" (2004, 1).

Psychologist and science journalist Daniel Goleman, who did much to bring the concept of EQ to the world's attention, explains, "In a sense, we have two brains, two minds—and two different kinds of intelligence: rational and emotional. How we do in life is determined by both—it is not just IQ, but *emotional* intelligence that matters. Indeed, intellect cannot work its best without emotional intelligence" (2006a, 28).

Before the emergence of the EQ concept, separation of head (intellect) from heart (emotion) was assumed to be essential. The common way of viewing intelligence was to value intellect unfettered by emotion. We now have evidence that without emotion, the intellect is limited and often ineffective.

> Too little emotion can thwart or paralyze reasoning.
> —**Antonio DiMasio**
> *Descartes' Error*

Defining IQ

The term IQ, or *intelligence quotient*, is a familiar one. Since the early twentieth century, IQ has been the accepted measurement of our capacity to think. IQ measures our abilities to:

- Combine and separate concepts.
- Judge and reason.
- Engage in abstract thought.

Think of a judge's responsibility in a court of law: he or she articulates the law or legal standard, listens to the facts of the case, and reaches an objective decision by applying the law to the facts. The ancient Greek philosopher Socrates summed up the process in this way:

1. To hear courteously.
2. To answer wisely.
3. To consider soberly.
4. To decide impartially.

Impartial is the operative word. To be impartial is to be impersonal. Impersonal thinking is logical thinking unswayed by emotion. Without emotion, we have the purely rational. "Thinking with emotions" sounds like a contradiction in terms. It's easier to prize pure logic and disdain emotion. Such was the case for centuries.

IQ testing has been and continues to be the accepted way of measuring human intelligence. Most schools test students for IQ in high school, and sometimes earlier. The PSAT and SAT examinations for college admission are forms of IQ tests. The LSAT, a prerequisite for admission to law school, is another form of IQ test.

"The old paradigm [of intelligence] held an ideal of reason freed of the pull of emotion," notes Goleman (2006a, 29). This led to those who listened to their emotions being stereotyped as "bleeding hearts," "wishy-washy," "soft," or "overly sensitive." They were deemed to have "eggshell skulls," because they might break down easily. Under the old paradigm, only the hard-headed, logical thinkers should be trusted with making major decisions.

Comparing EQ and IQ

EQ is IQ that takes feelings into account. "The new paradigm urges us to harmonize head and heart. To do that . . . we must first understand more exactly what it means to use emotion intelligently," Goleman advises (2006a, 29). If ever there was a field that required us to "use emotion intelligently," early childhood leadership is it.

Neither intelligence is superior to the other. Historically, however, many of us have been labeled as intelligent or not based solely on our IQ scores. In everyday reality, IQ prepares us for academic tests; EQ prepares us for the tests of life. Interestingly, by some estimates, our IQ works in only 20 percent of the decisions we make (Goleman 2006a). The vast majority of our daily decisions and interactions requires EQ. A person with a high EQ is also a genius, albeit an unsung one.

Consider the gifted practitioners you know in early childhood. Would you say their IQ scores are responsible for their gifts? What about their superior ability to make impartial, logical choices? Or would you describe these gifted practitioners as being able to read people well and use that information wisely? Until EQ was identified and backed up by scientific studies, people with "people smarts" or "street smarts" were often looked down upon or considered inferior to those with "book smarts." Today, that bias for IQ over EQ needs to be retired along with eight-track tapes and phonographs. Gifted practitioners need both EQ and IQ.

Scoring EQ: The Emotional Quotient Inventory

Can EQ be measured? According to Reuven Bar-On, the answer is yes. According to Bar-On's research (2007), his standardized test, the EQ-i® (Emotional Quotient Inventory, available at www.mhs.com), measures six components of emotional intelligence:

- Emotional self-awareness
- Assertiveness
- Empathy
- Interpersonal relationships
- Stress tolerance
- Impulse control

The test is self-reporting and requires the taker to describe him- or herself in a range of areas on a 5-point scale, from "Not true of me" (1) to "True of me" (5). I have both taken and been certified in administering the EQ-i® test. The results are highly informative and compelling, for leaders especially. And there's more good news. According to psychologist Steven Stein and psychiatrist Howard Book, "EQ can be accurately determined and effectively improved upon on an individual basis" (2011, 4).

As leaders and practitioners, we continuously hone our people skills. Anyone who has valued and exercised IQ can also become a student of emotional intelligence. The prerequisite is humility. To be emotionally intelligent and arrogant is a contradiction in terms. (In Chapter 4, we will identify additional characteristics of effective leaders.)

As we begin our study of how EQ can prepare us for situations that will test our leadership, let's review first current neuroscientific research on the adult brain. *Neuroscience* is the study of how relationships affect every cell in the body and how the brain and the rest of the nervous system affect relationships.

The neurobiology of emotional intelligence

Director Victoria in the chapter case study finds herself under fire. Leadership requires acting wisely under fire as well as in quiet, reflective times. As the core values in NAEYC's Code of Ethical Conduct (2005) reflect, respect is the heart of professionalism. Curiously, our biological makeup can work against our ability to act wisely, despite our best intentions. Recent research on brain functioning has identified factors in our neurobiology that both help and hinder us in acting professionally.

Biological mechanisms activated by threat

We all know certain people who get under our skin. Like Roxie's divisive behavior in the case study, some people's actions offend what we hold dear. Since early times, human beings have been hardwired to respond without thinking to perceived threats (Cozolino 2006). Wolves, tigers, and fires were all threats to our forebears. Few of us today face real wolves, tigers, or raging fires on a daily basis. However, in metaphorical terms we do. Our brain still registers perceived threats with similar intensity. Feelings of abandonment, shame, or humiliation can activate the same parts of our brain as a slap in the face does.

Director Victoria expects to walk into just another weekly staff meeting until she overhears Roxie denigrate the NAEYC Accreditation process, to which Victoria is passionately committed. Before Victoria can help herself, her face turns red and her jaw clenches.

Let's look at the physiological effect that Roxie's "threat" has on Victoria. Thanks to the evolving field of social neuroscience, we now know more about what causes blow-ups and what we can do to prevent and ease out of them.

Amygdala: The reptile within

Imagine peering inside your own brain. Deep in its center you would see four almond-shaped glands called the *amygdala*. The amygdala's job is to keep us safe from harm by triggering the release of heart-pounding *adrenaline* from the adrenal glands above the kidneys into the bloodstream. Your heart beats faster, your blood pressure jumps, and your blood rushes into your muscles (away from your brain). That adrenaline rush, like a tidal wave, wipes out our thinking as it prepares our body for action. This is our fight-or-flight response.

The amygdala is the hot button when your buttons get pushed by someone or something in your environment. It triggers us to protect and defend others and ourselves. If we see a 2-year-old about to chomp down on another child's arm, we rush to separate the children. Researchers from the University of Southern California termed this the "tend-and-befriend response," because individuals quickly circle the wagons to help one another in a crisis (Taylor et al. 2000).

Whatever terminology you use to describe the amygdala's effect, the result is the same—the impulse for instant, passionate action. In Cozolino's words, "The amygdala works so fast that it can pair stimuli and a fear response far ahead of conscious awareness" (2006, 60).

Mirror neurons: How we catch each other's feelings

We also have nerve cells called *mirror neurons* that allow us, without thinking, to mimic the feelings and movements of people around us. To envision how mirror neurons work, picture a glittering school of fish darting and rising as one in perfectly synchronized motion. A biological force compels that perfection. Similarly, if you have felt the rippling exhilaration of a crowd at a sports event, you have experienced mirror neurons in action.

For better or worse, mirror neurons can cause us to imitate the feelings and body movements of those around us. If you are upbeat at a staff meeting when everyone else is dour and negative, your optimism will likely be pulled down as you mirror the soggy mood. Similarly, if everyone is looking up at the sky, you will find yourself looking up.

Mirror neurons can have positive or negative effects in group situations. They can contribute to a feeling of team spirit and joie de vivre or allow us to deeply empathize with others. But mirror neurons can also allow the corrosive negativity of a few to shred team morale.

Amygdala hijack is Goleman's term for times when our buttons get pushed and our body prepares to rush to action (2006a). If Victoria's amygdala is hijacking her composure, her employees' mirror neurons are likely to pick up the intense, often frightening, feeling coming from her.

What does this have to do with leadership? "In the interpersonal flow of emotion, power matters," Goleman explains (2006, 24). Employees are hardwired to pay more attention to a leader's messages than to a peer's (unless that peer is the group's de facto leader). Just as leaders can positively influence staff's attitudes and actions, adult bullies can have a negative impact. A rampant gossiper, for example, wields considerable power to nonverbally broadcast her threat to others. People begin to think, "If she gossips to me, she will gossip about me." The most powerful person in a group, with or without the leadership title, will have the greatest effect on team members' mirror neurons.

Mirror neurons are heavily responsible for a leader's communication with his or her staff, too. Cozolino reminds us that "we greatly underestimate the degree of information we are communicating to those around us . . . and how much our unconscious processes, while invisible to us, are often apparent to others" (2006, 112).

The effects of mirror neurons and the amygdala can be a blessing or bane. They can let staff members feel deeply the encouraging and visionary messages of their leader. This gives her power to promote positive change and soothe raw feelings. However, if a leader loses control of her emotions (experiences an amygdala hijacking), her unleashed feelings may swiftly knock down staff morale.

How can we avoid losing it?

Brain capacities that help restore sanity

When my son Nick, at 2 years old, couldn't persuade another child to let him play with a coveted toy, he sometimes resorted to biting. Nick's teachers and I would intervene, saying, "Use your words, Nick." As Nick's brain matured, problem-solving capacities replaced impulsive reactions. We can count on diverse parts of our brain to restore our sanity, even under threat, as they did with Nick.

Calling on the executive function

A useful development occurred in the evolution of the human brain. Slowly, the front, top area of our brain (*prefrontal cortex*) grew, and with it our capacity to back off and regain perspective in the midst of threats. These capacities such as planning, attending, problem solving, inhibiting, and monitoring are called collectively our *executive function*. Although our amygdala can still override the executive function, our prefrontal cortex lets us take conscious steps to reactivate the calmer part of our brain, especially the part that controls decision making (*orbitofrontal cortex*, or OFC).

Emotional intelligence, that ability to read people as well as we read books, can be called on to help us stay cool under pressure. Emotional intelligence helps us acknowledge and learn from our feelings. We need emotional intelligence to understand others and ourselves accurately. Rather than being ruled by unconscious biological forces, such as amygdala hijacks or mirror-neuron mimicry, we can hone our emotional intelligence to:

- **Acknowledge and listen to our feelings:** "What's going on in my body right now?" or "What feelings am I picking up from others?"

- **Accept that feelings offer useful information:** "What are these sensations and feelings telling me?"

- **Step to the side to regain perspective and identify options:** "If my heart weren't pounding, what might I do?"

IQ is often associated with the brain's executive function. As mentioned earlier in this chapter, IQ was considered intellect untainted by emotion. Purely logical analysis was thought to be superior to the "muddled thinking" caused by feelings.

Logical thinking is still critical; however, the executive function by itself is rarely enough. We need emotional intelligence to help us call on that executive function. The data from our emotions can significantly serve our rational analysis. Goleman (2010) suggests that 80 percent of major life decisions require EQ, not IQ.

Thanks to our mirror neurons, we cannot hide our emotions from others, who can sense when we are discouraged, nervous, or happy. Our heartbeat communicates messages to people within five feet via electromagnetic pulses (McCraty, Atkinson, & Bradley 2004). A quickened heartbeat may communicate "Welcome!" or "Back off!" Although we cannot stop our emotions from communicating, we can pay attention to several indicators of emotions, as outlined in the table **How Do We Identify Emotions?**

In the introductory vignette, Victoria's red face communicates her anger to the staff. Her sweating palms tell her she senses fear in the environment. In that moment, armed with valuable emotional information, Victoria can take a deep breath, pull her shoulders back, and call on her executive function for help.

To envision executive function at work, picture a practitioner of tai chi, a martial art of self-defense. When an attacker strikes out, a tai chi master *steps to the side*. This causes the attacker to plunge off balance, deflecting the violent energy. Our emotional intelligence, like tai chi practice, allows us to step aside emotionally to stay out of harm's way. Executive function allows us to stay cool. If you can recall a time when something that should have pushed your buttons didn't, your prefrontal cortex was probably behind it.

Trusting intuition or our gut feeling

Sometimes, when our amygdala puts the executive function out of commission, we need to rely on other parts of the brain. Fortunately, there are other brain capacities that allow us to act appropriately, especially in the face of danger. Journalist Malcolm Gladwell calls one of these intuitive processes "thin-slicing" (2005, 23). Thin-slicing occurs when we judge situations or individuals based on the thinnest slice of experience. Gladwell explains, "We thin-slice whenever we meet a new person or have to make sense of something quickly or encounter a novel situation. We thin-slice because we have the ability to, and we come to rely upon that ability" (2005, 44). Thin-slicing is not rare; it is "a central part of what it means to be human" (44).

How Do We Identify Emotions?	
Emotion	**Your Body's Responses**
Fear	Dry mouth, sweaty palms, and difficulty swallowing; tense muscles, especially at the back of the neck. (Picture a cat with its back arched.)
Anger	Heat in the face, pounding heart, and surge of adrenaline energy; impulse to act immediately ("fight or flight").
Sadness	Lump in the throat, tightness in the chest, eyes "misting" or filling up with tears, loss of energy, pain around the heart. (Scientists have recently documented the "broken heart syndrome," actual physiological changes that squeeze the heart muscles.)
Loneliness	Coldness, yearning for touch/connection, aching heart. Isolation from others, feeling abandoned, rejected, left out.
Guilt	Impulse to look down, away from people; need to shield or defend the body.
Shame	Intense impulse to disappear or alternately the need to strike out against what/who caused the feeling of shame. Feelings of unworthiness, uselessness, being undeserving. Feelings like guilt, but harder to shake.
Joy	Light-heartedness, carefree feeling, uplifted confidence. Head held high, "walking tall," feeling of breathing freely, ebulliency, "bubbling" energy. Sense that "all's right with the world," "attitude of gratitude."

We have all heard of everyday people who act heroically, like the man who leapt like a gazelle to save an ailing person who had fallen onto New York City subway tracks. Or US Airways pilot Chesley "Sully" Sullenberger, who relied on thin-slicing to guide his aircraft to a safe landing in the Hudson River. Most of these heroes say simply, "I was just doing what anyone would have done."

Trusting our intuition, our gut decisions, in dangerous situations is reassuring. Gut decisions are far more than irrational acts; they use all our learning from prior difficult experiences. Each time we redirect a toddler from biting to another activity, we rely on our instinct to protect children from harm.

Studies of brain activity do not show the OFC "lighting up" when we make gut decisions. Instead, three parts of the brain linked to emotion and intuition are activated to help us make such instantaneous, intuitive decisions:

- **Insula:** Is instrumental in emotional processing.

- **Anterior cingulate cortex:** Allows us to make decisions based on our experience with and assessment of prior outcomes.

- **Superior temporal sulcus:** Helps us anticipate other people's thoughts and emotions by reading their, and our own, sensory stimuli, including what we see, hear, touch, and smell.

In a layperson's terms, in making a gut decision, we heed the wise voice within. The executive function by itself cannot produce our best problem solving (Gilkey, Caceda,

& Kilts 2010). Paying attention to our gut responses and intuition leads to holistic, effective decision making.

Gladwell describes this work of the "adaptive unconscious" as "a kind of giant computer that quickly and quietly processes a lot of the data we need in order to keep functioning as human beings" (2005, 11). Rudyard Kipling called it keeping "your head when all about you are losing theirs and blaming it on you."

How can I make wise decisions under pressure?

Thanks to recent research in neuroscience, we now know we can call on both rational processes *and* gut instincts when we are under pressure. For example, recall a time when you stepped up to "do the right thing" regardless of fearsome pressures from within and without.

What can we learn from colleagues and other experts about acting wisely under pressure?

Take a deep breath: Tune in to your rational self

I have had the honor of interviewing early childhood leaders and other experts on Kipling's question. Here are some of their insights on engaging healing parts of the brain when under pressure:

> I check in with myself: Am I angry? Upset? Worried? I acknowledge those feelings as parts of myself. Then, I dialogue with those feelings: "I know you're upset. How can I help?" (Bryan Robinson, podcast)

> As we tell children, "You can be angry, but your actions don't have to be done in anger." (Debbie Sullivan, podcast)

> Turn quacking ducks into eagles that soar above. Find out what's going on: A lot of people have "stuff" in their lives. Tell them, "Talk to me. Why are you so against this?" Develop an action plan together that gets them involved. (Neila Connors, podcast)

> Listen one time really well to capture their main point. Drill down on the main point. Redirect the person's attention to problem solving. Ask, "What do you think we should do? What do you think I should do? I want to help you, but I need your help, too." (Rick Kirschner, podcast)

Bam!radio

"Overworked Educators: Dedicated, Fearful, or Addicted to Work?"
Interview with Bryan Robinson
Heart to Heart Conversations on Leadership

"Dealing with the Death of a School or School Program"
Interview with Debbie Sullivan
Heart to Heart Conversations on Leadership

"Teacher Negativity: Turning Naysayers into Hooraysayers"
Interview with Debra Viadero and Neila Connors
Heart to Heart Conversations on Leadership

"Dealing with People You Can't Stand"
Interview with Rick Kirschner
Heart to Heart Conversations on Leadership
http://bamradionetwork.com

Use humor: Emotional intelligence's powerful partner

Humor can lighten up the heaviest situation. When I laugh at myself, I stand a better chance of "getting over myself" in the moment. Stuart Brown advises, "When people are able to find that sense of play in their work, they become truly powerful figures" (2009, 154). Laughter and playfulness allow our reptilian amygdala, our purely logical OFC, and our thin-slicing ability to work in collaboration.

Case Study—Lily

When my daughter Lily was in preschool, she and I went to a birthday party for one of her friends. Lily looked adorable in her favorite polka-dotted bathing suit.

Without warning, one of the fathers got right in my face: "What did you do to your daughter?" he exclaimed so loudly everyone turned to watch. I was so offended. I wanted to get right back in his face. Somehow, I paid attention to that quiet, sane voice within and said, "Thank you for your concern for my daughter. Lily is Korean. Some Korean children have Mongolian spots that look like bruises. Lily is not bruised. Her skin's pigment on her back is black and blue for now. That will pass." . . . And then I said something to lighten up the situation.

People laughed and children went back to playing. My heart still pounded in my ears; however, I didn't lose it. To this day, I recall the incident like a Technicolor video. Although I felt like yelling back, a gentler internal voice spoke. I listened. And that made all the difference.

Consider how Victoria could employ humor as she calls on all of her brain's resources to deal professionally with Roxie's affront:

Bam!radio

"Three Keys to Understanding People Who Push Your Buttons."

Interview with Louis John Cozolino

Heart to Heart Conversations on Leadership

http://bamradionetwork.com

Roxie's undermining comment speeds at Victoria like a poisoned dart, but Victoria steps to the side and lets it go by. She pauses, breathes deeply, and firmly meeting Roxie's gaze, she says, "It sounds like we need to have a frank discussion about classroom portfolios."

Then, heaving a theatrical sigh, she continues: "You all know, I will never win the prize for most organized director" . . . the other teachers relax, and several give her a smile. "However, if I can pull off the organizational portfolio with your help, I believe we can work together so each of you can complete your classroom portfolio."

"Trust me, faking it is not an option. Roxie, level with us. What's your real issue with portfolios, and what do you need to get the job done?"

Intelligent early childhood leadership

Last, but by no means least, courage—moral courage, the courage of one's convictions, the courage to see things through. The world is in a constant conspiracy against the brave. It's the age-old struggle—the roar of the crowd on the one side and the voice of your conscience on the other.

—Douglas MacArthur

The next time your buttons get pushed, know that your brain has powerful capacities to help you act wisely. Cozolino says, "As we mature, our amygdala matures with us. It seems to be much more gentle with us and is much less activated by fear and anxiety" (podcast). Perhaps leaders have always sensed this.

Early childhood leaders need a complex set of capacities to lead effectively. We need to read people and know what to do with that information. We need to logically and impartially assess software packages and construction bids, and maintain flawless budgets. We need to supervise staff (more to come on this in Chapter 9) with gentleness (*reflective supervision*) and resolution (*directive supervision*). We need to uphold quality in the best interests of children and families, while surviving deep funding cuts. And like the fearless spring robin buffeted by chilling winds in Elizabeth Spires' poem, we need to have the faith "to sing to the flowers, not there yet."

This is all part of what we need to lead.

Reflection questions

1. Looking back at your mentors, bosses, and teachers, describe the ones who showed the greatest degree of emotional intelligence. What are some outstanding examples of ways they were smart heart-to-heart? What knowledge or life lessons have stayed with you as a result of your time with these people?

2. List five skills you believe an early childhood leader needs. Once you have written your list, go back over it and describe how emotional intelligence is or is not part of each skill.

3. Consider a time when your buttons got pushed. Who or what pushed your buttons? How did you respond? In retrospect and in light of the information in this chapter, what might you have done differently?

4. We all have shortcomings. Looking back at my story about freezing on the way up the Scottish gorge, have you faced any similar challenges brought on by your shortcomings? How much of leadership, in your opinion, is forgiving ourselves for not being perfect? Have you been successful at forgiving yourself? As Fred Rogers said, "The hardest thing is to forgive someone who has harmed us, especially if that person is ourself."

Team projects

1. With the help of the **How Do We Identify Emotions?** chart (p.24), read the case study that follows and answer the questions below:

   Portia has a "soft spot in her heart" for children with special needs. Portia served as special needs teacher for eight years before she transitioned to the directorship. Sometimes she "takes over" in Inez's classroom, which has a number of children with attention deficit hyperactivity disorder. Although Portia thinks she is helping her, Inez seethes from being "put down" and "edged out" by Portia. Portia often procrastinates in her other administrative responsibilities, such as placing orders for supplies and working on the budget. She says she "just loves those children."

   a. Describe the steps Inez can take to use her EQ to work through this challenge with Portia.

   b. What are the possible emotional clues Portia is denying, both from Inez and within herself?

   c. If Portia, feeling something might be wrong, turns to you for advice, what would you say to her? How do you think Portia can use her feelings as data? What steps do you recommend for Portia to take?

2. Interview child care directors about their successful experiences dealing with challenging people: families, staff, or community members. First, create with your team a list of three to five questions you would like the directors to answer. Interview a director (each team member chooses a different director). Discuss with your team what each of you learned. Specifically, how did the directors use EQ to deal with their dilemmas?

3. Consider the concept of "genius." How do you and your teammates define it? Can an early childhood leader be a genius? If so, how? Are there any early childhood professionals you know who, in your experience, qualify as geniuses?

4. Leading in a profession with low pay, and some would say low status, can be daunting. Share with your team members ways in which you have experienced our profession being undervalued. Identify savvy strategies for:

a. Directly addressing people with condescending attitudes.

b. Dealing with your own feelings about being labeled "a glorified babysitter."

c. Ensuring that our field is professional.

Bibliography

Borg, J. 2008. *Body language: Seven easy lessons to master the silent language.* Upper Saddle River, NJ: Pearson Education.

Bar-On, R. 2004. *Emotional Quotient Inventory: Technical manual.* Toronto, Ontario, Canada: Multi-Health Systems.

Brown, S. 2009. *Play: How it shapes the brain, opens the imagination, and invigorates the soul.* New York: Penguin Group.

Bruno, H.E. 2011. The neurobiology of emotional intelligence: Using our brain to stay cool under pressure. *Young Children* 66 (1): 22–26.

Cozolino, L. 2006. *The neuroscience of human relationships: Attachment and the developing social brain.* New York: Norton.

Gardner, H. 2011. *Frames of mind: The theory of multiple intelligences.* 3rd ed. New York: Basic Books.

Gilkey, R, R. Caceda, & C. Kilts. 2010. When emotional reasoning trumps IQ. *Harvard Business Review* 88: 27.

Gladwell, M. 2005. *Blink: The power of thinking without thinking.* New York: Little, Brown.

Goleman, D. 1998. *Working with emotional intelligence.* New York: Bantam.

Goleman, D. 2006. *Social intelligence: The new science of human relationships.* New York: Bantam Dell.

Goleman, D. 2010. *Emotional intelligence: Why it can matter more than IQ.* New York: Bantam.

Mayer, J.D., & P. Salovey. 2004. What is emotional intelligence? In *Emotional intelligence: Key readings on the Mayer and Salovey model,* eds. P. Salovey, M.A. Brackett, & J.D. Mayer, 29–60. Port Chester, NY: National Professional Resources.

McCraty, R., M. Atkinson, & R.T. Bradley. 2004. Electrophysiological evidence of intuition: Part 2. A system-wide process? *The Journal of Alternative and Complementary Medicine* 10 (2): 325–36.

NAEYC. 2011 [2005]. NAEYC Code of Ethical Conduct and statement of commitment. Position statement. Rev. ed. 2005, updated and reaffirmed 2011. Washington, DC: Author. Online at: www.naeyc.org.

Rogers, F. 2005. *Life's journeys according to Mister Rogers: Things to remember along the way.* New York: Hyperion.

Stein, S.J., & H.E. Book. 2011. *The EQ edge: Emotional intelligence and your success.* 3rd ed. Mississauga, Ontario: Wiley.

Taylor, S.E., L.C. Klein, B.P. Lewis, T.L. Gruenewald, R.A.R. Gurung, & J.A. Updegraff. 2000. Biobehavioral responses to stress in females: Tend-and-befriend, not fight-or-flight. *Psychological Review* 107 (3): 411–29.

Web resources

Consortium for Research on EQ in Organizations
   http://eiconsortium.org
Directory of EQ Web Sites
   http://eq.org
Emotional Intelligence Information
   www.unh.edu/emotional_intelligence
EQ Online Test
   www.queendom.com/tests/access_page/index.htm?idRegTest=1121
EQ-i® Emotional Quotient Inventory
   www.mhs.com/product.aspx?gr=io&prod=eqi&id=overview
Society for Neuroscience
   http://apu.sfn.org

When you combine your own intuition with sensitivity to other people's feelings and moods, you may be close to the origins of valuable human attributes such as generosity, altruism, compassion, sympathy, and empathy.

—Fred Rogers, *You Are Special*

Determine what is most important in your life and make your decisions based on those very important criteria....truly become the creative force of your own life.

—Stephen Covey, *The 8th Habit: From Effectiveness to Greatness*

3 Making Tough Decisions: The Art and Science of Decision Making

Case Study—Magda

Everyone knew it was coming; legislators had already cut education budgets way back. Director Magda thought she had faced the worst already. Breadwinners in more than half of the children's families were laid off when local businesses relocated overseas. Magda had scrambled to tap into every possible resource to keep those workers' children in her preschool.

When the evening newscaster announced, "Legislators voted today to cut state voucher monies for child care slots; local preschools to close their doors," Magda gasped. Next she heard the voice of Soledad, a director across town, speaking into the newscaster's microphone, lament: "Last time they cut child care services to the bone. This time they cut through the bone. How can a parent without a job find a job if we can't care for his children?"

Magda knew she would have to choose

which of her loyal teachers to lay off and which struggling families to terminate. With shoulders slumped and her guard down, she let the tears fall as she dialed Soledad's home phone.

If Magda and Soledad invite you to an emergency meeting to help with this crisis, with three months before the law takes effect, what ideas could you offer? Have you faced decisions where you "hit bottom" and could see no easy way out? What helps guide you through impossible choices?

Making tough decisions

One of my staff members, a teacher with more years under his belt than I had at the time, confessed, "Hope springs eternal. But how many times can you get knocked down and get back up?" Leading through threadbare times is wrenching. To have confidence in our choices, we need insights into what makes a good, or good enough, decision. In Chapter 2, we looked at how to act wisely in the moment. In this chapter, we will take on decision making when you have the luxury (or bane) of time to reflect.

I took the question "How do we make difficult decisions wisely?" on a quest as I interviewed experts, read research studies, and listened to colleagues. Here is what I found.

Cut yourself some slack

When tackling the question "How do we make good, or good enough, decisions when stakes are high and the decisions are tough?" I discovered a new and simple guideline: cut yourself some slack. As we'll see, the brain has a finite time each day—a window of opportunity—for making productive decisions that require a measure of self-control. We need to identify that "best time" and then, when our brain hits overload, rest or take on a repetitive task. We simply are not hardwired to handle a full day of continuous decision making, regardless of what the job may require.

John Tierney (2011), in his *New York Times* article "Do You Suffer from Decision Fatigue?" reveals useful research on making tough decisions. Let's examine how we can benefit from these discoveries.

Decision fatigue

Tierney observes, after examining the research of Roy F. Baumeister (see Baumeister & Tierney 2011), that "the very act of making decisions depletes our ability to make them well" (Tierney 2011, 1). Baumeister's research shows that during the day, the more decisions we make that require self-control, the less able we become to make decisions to resist other temptations as the day goes on. Can we monitor ourselves accurately enough to know when our brains are clicking well and when they have run out of steam?

The challenge is in knowing our limitations. At what point in the day do we slip from being alert and self-controlled into mental exhaustion that stops us from making wise choices? As Tierney puts it, "No matter how rational and high-minded you try to be, you can't make decision after decision without paying a biological price" (2011, 1). At some point, our willpower caves to temptation, and our decision-making process winds down to sloppy and careless.

To understand the brain's capacity to make wise decisions throughout the day, Jonathan Levav and Shai Danziger studied several judges' parole decisions. They discovered that the chances of a prisoner being released did not depend on the merits of the case or "the men's ethnic backgrounds, crimes or sentences" (Tierney 2011, 1). Instead, prisoners whose cases were heard by judges early in the morning received parole about 70 percent of the time. On the other extreme, prisoners whose cases were heard late in the day had a far lower likelihood of parole—less than 10 percent. Despite the judges' training or prowess, the prisoners' "probability of being paroled fluctuated wildly throughout the day" (1).

Decision fatigue is not the same as normal physical fatigue. We can be otherwise full of energy yet still mentally exhausted. We inevitably reach the point of having made so many decisions in a row that we become low on mental energy. The effect of making decision after decision is reckless decision making. Without intending to, we end up too mentally depleted to decide wisely.

Our brains look for shortcuts. This is why a dieter can follow her diet rigorously all morning and even through dinner, but in the evening, when her brain is weary of decision making and self-control, the candy bar looks like a good choice. Have you ever been holiday shopping and felt like everything in the store looked good? That's decision fatigue. Our ability to discern caves to our brain's need to take a break from making difficult decisions.

Ego depletion and decision making

Decision fatigue is connected to a similar phenomenon that affects leaders' capacity to continuously make their best decisions. That second phenomenon is known as "ego depletion" (Tierney 2011, 1). Ego depletion happens when we lose enough of ourselves to weariness that we commensurately lose our self-control. Humans have a "finite store of mental energy for exerting self-control" (2). Early childhood leaders need a deep store of self-control to see through a parent's anger to her underlying sadness, or to keep the faith that a teacher who fears going back to college can complete one course at a time toward her degree.

Once we are fatigued mentally, our sense of self is vulnerable to ego depletion— loss of willpower to continue doing the right thing. When ego depletion sneaks up, we become reluctant to negotiate. We settle for less than the best and become susceptible to self-indulgence. More candy bars, please.

Tips for making good decisions

So, what is a decision maker to do? We have to make decisions, often one after another throughout the day. Berating ourselves for making a sloppy decision doesn't help. Our brains can do only so much.

According to a study led by Wilhelm Hofmann, human beings today resist temptation three to four hours a day, during which time we are fit for making sound decisions (Tierney 2011). After that, "when the brain's regulatory powers weaken, frustrations seem more irritating than usual. Impulses to eat, drink, spend and say stupid things feel more powerful (and alcohol causes self-control to decline further)" (7). How do we make tough decisions once that window of self-control and brain alertness passes?

Baumeister and Tierney (2011) suggest the following practical pointers in their book *Willpower: Rediscovering the Greatest Human Strength:*

- Don't schedule back-to-back meetings. Take some kind of a mental break even if only a brief one.
- Establish habits, like scheduled walks or workouts, to eliminate the mental effort of making choices.
- Keep your glucose levels up without relying on hollow calories like marshmallows or candy bars.
- Avoid temptations like all-you-can eat buffets and happy hours.

Perhaps the best advice on how to consistently make difficult decisions comes from Baumeister at the close of Tierney's article: "The best decision makers . . . are the ones who know when *not* to trust themselves" (2011, 7).

▶ EXERCISE YOUR EQ   ▨   What indicators tell you when you ought to postpone making a decision? Can you sense when your brain has reached its limit for making wise decisions? What temptations (we all have them) can knock you off balance? What habits can you establish to eliminate ego depletion and decision fatigue?

Moving forward with impossible decisions

Many things seem impossible until they are done.
—Kimberly Wiefling

Now that we know to take breaks from decision making—or else sacrifice our ability to make tough decisions wisely—we can beware of decision fatigue and ego depletion. How can we make wise decisions when facing another threat: impossible choices due to devastation of one sort or another?

After the 2011 tsunami on the coast of Japan, Japanese leaders had to make impossible decisions. I asked international business consultant Mei Lin Fung and author Kimberly Wiefling for the secret of making impossible decisions in the worst possible circumstances (podcast). Fung stressed, "Conflict is a tremendous opportunity to see what you may not have seen before." Conflict and crisis may appear to be our adversaries, but when viewed differently, they become our allies. In the jaws of the conflict, we see more clearly because our choices are limited. We cannot delude ourselves when the sky is falling on our heads or the tsunami is looming.

Bam!radio
"Facing Overwhelming Leadership Challenges"
Interview with Kimberly Wiefling
Heart to Heart Conversations on Leadership
http://bamradionetwork.com

Wiefling (podcast) added: When stuck making a decision, begin. When stuck again, keep going. See resistance as a kind of movement. In her experience, Wiefling has found these pointers valuable:

1. Language and thinking influence reality. Think in the language of possibility, not failure. What resources do we have, rather than what is lost forever?

2. Start in the future and think backward. Envision that the problem is resolved and what the world would look like then. Make decisions to help move toward that vision.

3. Ignore cynics who criticize you. Put them behind you and take your next step. "Many things seem impossible until they are done," Wiefling stresses. Begin, keep going, and see resistance as a part of the path forward. Decide and get on with it.

Asking questions first

Daniel Kahneman, Dan Lovallo, and Olivier Sibony (2011) offer a set of questions to ask ourselves to ensure that our decisions are our best. (These questions actually pertain to financial decisions but can be adapted to fit any kind of major decision.) They warn that dangerous biases can creep into every decision. Therefore, they urge us to conduct an audit of our motivation and preparation before coming to a conclusion with 12 steps. Here are three of those steps:

- Have I fallen so in love with my own idea that I can't see the flaws? When assessing something we like, we are all prone to minimizing the risks and exaggerating the benefits.

- Have I been open to hearing dissenting opinions?

- Am I limiting my decision by being overly cautious? (Kahneman, Lovallo, & Sibony 2011)

Looking back on Magda's challenge in the chapter case study, which of the items on this checklist might help her? Consider the third question: Am I limiting my decision by being overly cautious? Magda's past experience of feeling she has exhausted all her resources may make her reluctant or cautious about trying anything new. Magda appears to be in the state described by Baumeister as "ego depletion" if not "decision fatigue." She may even be ready to give up. Besides throwing in the towel, what choices does she have? Sometimes if we ask about or are at least open to new possibilities, we find help in unexpected places.

The anatomy of an impossible decision

In response to Magda's dilemma, the Ohio AEYC (OAEYC, the Ohio State NAEYC Affiliate), under the leadership of Kimberly Tice-Colopy, created a solution that threw caution to the wind. The state legislature had again taken its machete to early childhood funding, and providers were shaken. Rather than assume the worst and commiserate with one another, the OAEYC leadership team decided instead to bring all the best problem solvers in the state together. They called a summit on the topic "Making Difficult Decisions in Difficult Times." I was invited to facilitate the summit.

The summit began with "just the facts"—that is, getting out on the table everything that was known about the changes. A high-ranking representative of the state education department shared everything she knew. She answered questions until everyone was up-to-date with the new legislation and its probable ramifications. We felt it was important for everyone to have all possible information.

Next, we took time to grieve our losses by individually expressing feelings and thoughts. Participants formed small groups to share how each person and her program would likely be affected. Some participants were certain they would have to close their programs, putting out needy children and losing their livelihoods. Although compassion from colleagues couldn't take away the pain, hurting people felt cared for and soothed. Feeling the support of a compassionate community bolsters our strength for decision making.

Our working lunch was held in affinity groups. Single-site center directors, family providers, franchised programs, Head Start, multi-site programs, and research and referral agencies met separately to discuss how they could help one another and to formulate questions for the upcoming panel of experts.

The panel had been carefully selected to represent both constituent groups and people who had successfully faced budget cuts. As panelists shared what had worked for them, participants chimed in with other suggestions. No one felt alone, and most everyone heard something valuable to take away.

At the end, we affirmed our commitment to do all we could to bring quality care and education to all children, especially in the worst of times. The OAEYC team created a listserv to keep the discussion going. To this day, when participants from that summit get together, we hold the day in respect. Together, we did the best we could to face the daunting challenge. One outside-the-box decision by one dedicated AEYC Affiliate made all the difference.

Consider whom you trust for help when you face a tough decision. With their support, you are likely to find the decision-making process less burdensome.

The workshop gave members an opportunity to:

- Develop a network of support and identify practical strategies to address the challenges;
- Learn from and engage in conversation with a variety of people with expertise in program management and financial issues; and
- Partner with colleagues from across the state to strategize about the management of budget challenges.

—**Kimberly Tice-Colopy**
"Investing in Members: Ohio Redefines Its Purpose and Services"

Admitting vulnerability in decision making

Even in optimal times, we can make decisions we regret. Those decisions might be unwise or just plain wrong. Fear of making bad decisions can nibble away at our confidence. Second-guessing ourselves jams our brain with chattering static. Attacks of shame for failing to make the right call derail our courage.

Because we will inevitably make disappointing decisions, we would do well to think ahead about how to clean up after a poor decision and how to use that experience to make better decisions in the future. As we continue our discussion of how to make tough decisions, let's also look at how to handle decisions that go wrong. Another way to describe this part of the decision-making process is "damage control."

▶ EXERCISE YOUR EQ   ▨ Recall a time when you blew a decision. You just plain got it wrong, and people may have been adversely affected. Afterward, what internal conversation did you have with yourself? What did you decide to do to address your mistake? What did you learn from that experience?

How forgiving are people when leaders fail? Do leaders have the option of making mistakes and learning from them? Or does a "gotcha" mentality prevail, and because of that one strike against you, you're out? Unlike movie stars, education leaders rarely gain instant forgiveness for checking into a rehabilitation facility. What can an apology by a leader accomplish, and what is the best way to apologize for mistakes? Most important, how can failing to make a good decision transform us into better decision makers?

How to apologize

Barbara Kellerman (2006) spells out clear guidelines for making effective, compelling apologies. Authenticity is Kellerman's standard. A leader has to mean what she says, learn from her mistakes, change her behavior for the better, and take action to remedy the wrong for everyone harmed. Kellerman (podcast) explains that an effective apology for a poor decision embodies these actions:

> **Bam!radio**
> "When and How to Say, 'I Was Wrong'"
> Interview with Barbara Kellerman
> *Heart to Heart Conversations on Leadership*
> http://bamradionetwork.com/

- Acknowledge your mistake.
- Express responsibility; no pointing the finger elsewhere.
- Express regret and mean it.
- Time your apology to define the story rather than to be a forced or late reaction to criticism.
- Commit publicly to not making the same mistake again.
- Roll up your sleeves and take action to ensure the problem does not reoccur.
- Do all you can to restore the parties harmed to wholeness.

The benefits of apologizing far outweigh the costs, notes commentator Justin Snider (podcast). Thinking backward from the future, we might picture what we would say in our apology if we blow it when making a major decision. Heartfelt remorse goes a long way toward restoring trust.

When to apologize

To decide if you need to apologize for a poor decision, Kellerman (podcast) suggests you ask:

1. What function would it serve?

2. Who would benefit?

3. Why would it matter?

4. What might happen if you apologize?

5. What might happen if you decide not to apologize?

By schooling ourselves in how to apologize, we can set ourselves up to make better and better decisions by learning from and being accountable for our poorer decisions.

Learning from legal history

By the time I had researched this input on making (and dealing with the fallout from) tough decisions, I decided I was experiencing decision fatigue, or at least information overload. At times like that, I find that stepping back to take the long view historically can help. Let's consider the history of how tough decisions have been made.

Case Study—William

Imagine yourself as a twelfth-century judge presiding over a court of law in the verdant, rolling countryside of feudal England. William, a tenant who rents his farmland from a local lord, appears before you, asking that he and his family be permitted to stay on his property.

The law says: Tenants who rent property from the landlord must pay their rent on time each season. Failure to pay on time will result in forfeiture of the land. William's rent is due on April 15. William paid his rent on April 20. What say you?

Twenty-first century early childhood professionals, like twelfth-century judges, are called upon to make decisions as often as they take a breath. Decision making is both an art and a science. Examining legal history (how judges have made decisions) can offer perspective on how to make "good enough" decisions.

What constitutes a "fair" or "just" decision?

As the story goes, the judge's decision in William's case was that William should "forfeit the property and quit the land." William had failed to obey the law, and breaking the law had a clearly articulated consequence—forfeiture. The judge did not take into account William's personal circumstances. He used a logical, legal, and "scientific" approach.

Would it matter that William had paid on time for five years and was responsible for a wife and 11 children? What if William had traveled night and day to find a bridge that was still standing after March floods had washed out other bridges William usually used to deliver his rent? The "letter of the law" does not concern itself with individual circumstances. In a letter of the law decision-making process, "the law is the law." Fairness is demonstrated by applying the law the same way to every person.

Legal decisions or equitable decisions?

Letter of the law decisions mete out evenhanded, often impersonal justice. Each person gets the same treatment under the law. "Spirit of the law" decisions, which take into account an individual's circumstances, are called "equitable" decisions. Equitable decisions require viewing each person on a case-by-case basis as a unique individual.

Making equitable decisions can be more of an art than a science. No one-size-fits-all template exists for spirit of the law decisions.

While letter of the law (legal) decisions are expedient, spirit of the law (equitable) decisions require time and reflection. Similarly, legal decisions call more upon our IQ, while equitable decisions require us to use both EQ and IQ. Discerning which type of decision-making process is more appropriate calls for a leader's intellectual savvy and skillful ability to perceive nonverbal messages. We make both types of decisions by grounding ourselves in the deeper goal—doing what is best for children and families.

Spirit of the law decisions may be more appropriate and humane than invoking the letter of the law. When you make a spirit of the law decision, you take into account the totality of the individual's circumstances. You look more deeply to find the root cause of the problem, to make a decision tailored to best deal with each person's situation.

Think how efficient your work would be if you could make all your decisions like a twelfth-century judge. William was out the door, without recourse. As emotionally intelligent twenty-first century professionals, we devote hours to accommodating individual needs. Is there a "middle path" between law and equity? Can equitable decisions take less time? Come back to the twelfth century with me to find some answers.

Recourse for questionable decisions

In London, the Chancery Court (later called the Court of Equity) was a place where controversial cases like William's could be appealed. There, the ecclesiastical member of the king's cabinet, appointed to represent the Church, decided cases using the spirit of the law. The Chancery Court was also called the Star Chamber, because the ceiling paint was resplendent with stars. Under those stars, the Lord Chancellor, or Chancellor of Equity, overturned the decision of the law court (lower court) and returned the property to William for having made a "good faith effort" (traveling night and day) in the face of an "act of God" (springtime flooding). As the Chancellor of Equity acted on William's claim, he used an artful decision-making process, drawing from an alternative definition of fairness. The spirit of the law became legitimized as an official decision-making process.

Decision-making processes

Decision making by spirit of the law

Maxims created in the Chancery Court, such as "making a good-faith effort," are still in common parlance today. Equitable principles evolving from the Chancery Court include:

- ✓ Equity will not allow a wrong to be without a remedy.
- ✓ Equity regards substance rather than form.
- ✓ One who seeks equity must do equity.
- ✓ Equity acts *in personam* (takes into account the individual's circumstances).
- ✓ Equity delights to do justice, and not by halves.

William and countless others over the centuries have benefited from this "softer" decision-making process.

In the swirl of twenty-first century complexity, early childhood leaders stand as if holding the scales of justice, seeking to balance what is equitable with what is just.

Often we feel blindfolded, unclear on the standards to use and troubled by the thought of unforeseen consequences. We may yearn to be back in the day when decision making was simpler. When the law was the law.

In fact, things were never simpler, nor were they ever so difficult. We often must weigh two competing realities: Fairness means taking individual circumstances into account while also upholding professional standards. In some situations, the objective, analytical decision-making process is appropriate. In other situations, the compassionate, individualized process is more fitting. How can we tell the difference?

Decision making by weighing the pros and cons

Letter of the law decisions are made by weighing the benefits and detriments (pros and cons) of each option. Traditionally, decisions were made using a process that involved:

1. Listing the pros and cons of the situation objectively.

2. Analyzing the list: Which side has the more substantial factors?

3. Making a logical decision in favor of the weightier side.

At times, this process works well. Administrators pressed by an onslaught of decisions to be made find the objective approach useful. When a leader makes an impartial decision, he can decide quickly. He does not have to consider the complexity of human emotion. The leader bases his decision on established policies and procedures, and in following precedent or upholding tradition, he furthers predictability and stability. Expectations are met with consistency.

More often than not, however, a director's impartial decision will be challenged. The administrator may hear complaints that she failed to ask everyone's opinion before deciding or did not notify staff about an impending change. Letter of the law decisions often meet with resistance if social intelligence savvy is not part of the decision-making process. Consider the following example.

Preschool teacher Joanne decided to tell Aliesha's mom that her daughter needed an evaluation for learning disabilities. Joanne had painstakingly documented all of Aliesha's behaviors warranting an evaluation. Joanne found very few "cons" in her decision: All factors pointed to Aliesha's needing help.

When Joanne shared her rational decision with Aliesha's mom, Joanne was stunned that her decision was immediately rejected. "Aliesha never behaves like that at home! You must be upsetting her!" the distressed parent cried. Joanne's decision was purely rational and emotionally blind. She did not use her EQ to discover and understand the parent's way of looking at her world—especially the parent's feelings about Aliesha.

In the future, Joanne will pay more attention to building a relationship with parents while continuously sharing information with them. Joanne will practice putting herself in parents' shoes to gain empathy for their situation.

Partnering with family members like Aliesha's mom is not just a science, but also an art. Parents' feelings of pride, fear, denial, outrage, and shame all need to be factored into a teacher's decision about how best to help the child and the family.

A leader needs to develop skill at both types of decision making and, even more important, at discerning when to use each type. Cut-and-dried decisions that do not directly affect people are often best determined by using the letter of the law process. For decisions that touch people directly, a leader will likely do better to use the spirit of the law approach. Both approaches require EQ and IQ—they require us to read people.

Neither decision-making process is superior to the other. Myers-Briggs (MBTI) personality type data (in Chapter 4) help us understand why staff and others have strong feelings about which process to use. People who are (*Feelers*) tend to expect individualized treatment. They are more likely to identify fairness with compassion. Those who are (*Thinkers*) tend to expect consistency and are not as bothered by making impersonal decisions. Leaders who call upon their knowledge of MBTI preferences will be better able to foresee the consequences of the decision-making style they choose.

▶ EXERCISE YOUR EQ   ▨   Recall one of your recent decisions. Was that decision a letter or spirit of the law choice? Do you lean one way more often than the other when you make decisions? Do you see limitations to either process? What is your personal standard for using one decision-making process over another?

Let's look at some other decision-making processes.

Decision making by intuition (thin-slicing)

New research on decision making invites us to take a twenty-first century approach to this age-old dilemma. Malcolm Gladwell, in his book *Blink: The Power of Thinking Without Thinking* (2005), states that our best decisions are made intuitively, in the "blink of an eye." According to Gladwell, rumination, or going back and forth second-guessing ourselves, can be counterproductive. Instinctively, we know what needs to be done. Our job is to trust our intuition and take action without dilly-dallying.

As discussed in Chapter 2, Gladwell calls this decision-making process "thin-slicing." We thin-slice when our "brain reaches conclusions without immediately telling us that it's reaching conclusions" (2005, 10). The part of our brain that thin-slices is the "adaptive unconscious . . . a kind of giant computer that quickly and quietly processes a lot of the data we need in order to keep functioning as human beings" (11). Thin-slicing is the act of listening to our inner voice over the cacophony of self-doubt.

How do you discern the sound of your inner voice over the thunder of other voices? Gladwell says we can "teach ourselves to make better snap judgments" (2005, 16).

Decision making by "gifted improvisation"

In addition to the problem of second-guessing, thin-slicing raises another red flag—prejudice. For thin-slicing to work well, a decision maker needs a richly developed inner landscape. An inner landscape is the sum of our life experience and decisions to date. Our inner landscapes grow lush when nourished by our interactions with people who differ from us, and by taking risks to grow. Otherwise, we tend to see the world in our own image, expecting others to hold similar values and perspectives. An accurate word for this is *solipsism,* the false belief that we are the center of the universe. To let go of solipsistic, biased attitudes, we need thoughtful and heartfelt openness and exposure to diverse people, cultures, and environments.

Nourishing our inner landscape is a lifelong process. At Harvard University, doctoral students were asked to participate in a study that required them to thin-slice. Each student was shown photographs and asked for an immediate response to each image. These students, both black and white, consistently indicated their preference for images of white people. The students were stunned when told the results.

What if our immediate world is not large enough to embrace, witness, and experience others' cultures? What do we do when the larger world, as evidenced in the Harvard study, holds covert as well as overt bias? Our thin-slicing capacity is limited by the boundaries of our experience and the barrage of unstated messages.

When I hear I see, when I see I hear.

—**Zen koan (parable)**

Thin-slicing is not an exotic gift. It is a central part of what it means to be human. We thin-slice whenever we meet a new person or have to make sense of something quickly or encounter a novel situation. We thin-slice because we have to, and we [have] come to rely on that ability.

—**Malcolm Gladwell**
Blink: The Power of Thinking Without Thinking

Gladwell presents a refreshing recommendation for moving beyond this type of bias. He invites us to look beyond our own profession to another profession—improvisational theater. Gladwell studied the ground rules for successful improvisation, or "improv." Improv, he discovered, works only when each actor builds on the previous statement of his or her fellow actor, no matter how absurd that statement appears to be. If the second actor criticizes the first actor's statement, the moment is lost. However, if the improviser finds a creative way to "run with" the statement, magic happens. Energy builds, the audience is engaged, and innovation occurs. Life problems are worked through with humor and originality. The next time you have the opportunity to experience improvisational theater or television, observe in action the principle of building on another's statements.

To support this principle, Gladwell quotes improv expert Keith Johnstone. "In life, most of us are highly skilled at suppressing action. All the improvisation teacher has to do is to reverse this skill and he creates very 'gifted' improvisers. Bad improvisers block action, often with a high degree of skill. Good improvisers develop action" (2005, 114–15). In the blink of an eye, we can find value in what is being offered, or we can turn away and lose the opportunity.

Consider the ramifications of this improv principle for our profession. When a Hmong father describes his practice of healing his child's chest coughs through "coining"—quickly running hot coins in a line down a person's back—what is our response? Do we greet the moment with wonder or judgment? If we judge the parent, we lose the opportunity to learn about Hmong culture, the family, and the child. If we build on the moment, trust and knowledge are shared.

To grow away from bias as a decision maker, leaders can explore and build on differences rather than deny them. Janet Gonzalez-Mena (2001) recommends, "Be a risk taker. If you are secure enough, you may feel you can afford to make mistakes. It helps to have a good support system behind you when you take risks and make mistakes. Ask questions, investigate assumptions, confess your curiosity—but do it all as respectfully as possible" (42–43).

Early childhood professionals are skilled at improv. "Multitasking" is our middle name. Each time a teacher practices the emergent curriculum approach, she improvises by building on the potential of the moment. Children respond with fascination and hunger to learn more. The teachable or learning moment is captured. As a director listens to the meaning beneath the words of a parent, the director may abandon one pathway of working with that parent and spontaneously start down another, better suited path.

To improvise better decisions like this, we benefit from getting out there in the world more and exposing ourselves to things we do not know, to the people we have avoided, to the life experience we have yet to live. In the process, as we deepen our experience and shine light on our blind spots, we find the conviction of our inner voice. We achieve at last that richly developed inner landscape.

As early childhood professionals, we resolutely encourage children to value themselves and trust their own unique worth. What if we practice what we tell our children? Gavin de Becker (1997), a security specialist, counseled: "We have the gift of a brilliant internal guardian that stands ready to warn you of hazards and guide you through risky situations" (13). Develop trust in yourself as a leader. Accept that you are a good enough decision maker. Perhaps, by thin-slicing, the spirit and letter of the law can join hands at last.

Dealing with self-doubt

When making decisions, ruminating too long or second-guessing ourselves about how others will perceive us can detract from our ability to take action. We worry, "What if I'm wrong? What if people misunderstand my intention? What if someone's feelings get hurt?" Ruminating like this wastes time, and worrying devours confidence. While some questioning is productive, too much second-guessing harms our capacity for decision making. Staff will wonder whether such a director can make decisions. Gladwell cautions, "I think that approach [requiring extensive documentation] is a mistake, and if we are to learn to improve the quality of the decisions we make, we need to accept the mysterious nature of our snap judgments" (2005, 52).

I am perfectly imperfect.
—Pia Mellody

How do we step out of the trap of debilitating self-doubt? An answer lies in positive self-talk. When repetitive, worrisome voices impede your decision-making ability, quiet down those negative voices with words of self-confidence.

▶ EXERCISE YOUR EQ   ▪ Each of us can develop our own phrases or affirmations to repeat when we find ourselves slipping into second-guessing. Reflect on situations that erode your confidence, and then say these affirmations aloud:

- Every decision is the right decision, because I learn from each one.
- I make snap decisions with children, and my judgments are good. I can do the same with adults.
- "Once you make a decision, the universe conspires to make it happen." (Ralph Waldo Emerson)
- What other people think of me is none of my business.

Create your own positive affirmation: _____.

Positive self-talk replaces self-doubt with faith in our ability to make "good enough" decisions. Second-guessing is a rut, a well-established brain pathway. Positive self-talk, with regular practice, helps us climb out of that rut. You can build new brain connections when you remind yourself, "I am a good enough decision maker." Do your best for today and move on.

Here are tips directors recommend:

1. **Set a firm deadline** for making the decision. Honor that deadline and move on.
2. **Sleep on it**. Make a tentative decision by the end of the workday. Sleep on that decision overnight. You are likely to wake up resolved in your decision.
3. **Stop second-guessing** by choosing to thin-slice your decision in the moment. Write down your snap decision. Walk away and get involved with something else. Come back later to read what you wrote. You may find your decision has been made.

The right or good enough decision is often already inside us. This process of defusing self-doubt helps directors cut to the chase to uncover that decision. Leaders have many opportunities to replace worry with positive self-talk. Many directors find they need to let go of the impossible or perfectionist standard they set for themselves—the standard to make infallible decisions that will never be questioned. Good enough decisions allow us to move on to the next challenge that awaits us.

Involving others in the decision-making process

In studying how leaders make decisions, we need also to look at involving others in making important choices.

Mine, ours, yours

Early childhood leaders work within a community of stakeholders. Stakeholders are people who have an interest, or stake, in the outcome of a decision. Teachers, parents, board members, cooks, and bus drivers can all be stakeholders in early childhood programs. People whose lives are affected by a decision expect to be consulted before that decision is reached. Stakeholders demand "due process" (discussed later, in Chapter 7), the right to speak up and have their opinion taken into account.

For this reason, effective directors need to level up front with staff about who will make the decision. Before a director makes a decision, he needs to determine: Will this decision be mine, ours together, or yours to make? A leader who sets clear expectations about who has the authority to make decisions prevents many misunderstandings.

Decisions that involve groups of people fall into three categories: mine, ours, and yours. To set clear expectations about who has the authority to make decisions in each situation, inform everyone about which group or person that is. Here are some suggestions for letting staff know whose responsibility a decision is.

Mine:

- This decision is my responsibility. I'll let you know as soon as I come to a decision.

- I would appreciate your input before I make my decision.

- Give me a list of your top three suggestions. I will take those into account as I make my decision.

Ours:

- This decision is ours to make as a team. Let's come to a consensus. We'll start by going around the circle to hear how everyone feels.

- We all will have an equal vote in this decision. Would you prefer a show of hands or a written ballot?

Yours:

- You can decide how you want to handle this situation. I will back you up.

- Your team will be the final decision maker on this question. Let me know what you decide.

▶ EXERCISE YOUR EQ   ▨   Think of a decision you are currently facing that involves other people. Which of these three categories best describes who will make the decision? Do you think everyone is clear on who has the authority to make this decision?

Making group decisions

Staff members are more likely to feel responsible for carrying out decisions they have taken part in making. Just as individuals need to understand their personal decision-making process, teams need to be clear on the group decision-making process. Teams reach decisions by one of two methods—consensus or majority vote. Leaders will want to ensure that everyone understands which process will be used.

Groups reach consensus when they come to a meeting of the minds about what action to take. The group gels and is ready to act as one, needing no further debate. With a consensus, no vote is necessary. A consensus is best reached after everyone has spoken on the issue. Before reaching consensus, make sure that concerns and doubts are voiced and resolved. Use your EQ to sense when the group is ready to reach a

Due process is guaranteed by the 14th Amendment of the United States Constitution. Due process consists of giving stakeholders:

1. Notice of a possible change that will affect their rights, and

2. Opportunity to be heard, to speak their minds about the proposed change.

When an administrator fails to give her staff due process, she can expect resistance. "You never told us about that!"

consensus. Rushing a consensus can result in a lukewarm commitment or sabotage the decision.

Voting on an issue allows the majority to decide for the whole team. This can lead to a disgruntled minority. For this reason, decision making by consensus is usually more unifying. However, if your team's maturity level is high, voting can work. Those who lose the vote "let go," move on, and support the outcome. Make sure again that everyone who participated in the vote agrees to support the decision. Ask: "Does anyone anticipate a problem carrying out this decision? If so, let's talk that over before we leave the room. We all need to be on the same page."

Decision-making structures

Your decision-making style predicts how you will structure your organization. Directors "structure" their programs internally to let every employee know where she or he belongs in the organization by knowing how decisions will be made that affect them. The clearer the expectations, the fewer the power struggles. Power struggles often come about because decision-making authority is ambiguous.

The structure you choose indicates your chain of command. In a chain of command, each person is a link in the chain of decision making. Each teacher knows her supervisor. She also knows to whom her supervisor reports. This chain of command tells us who is responsible for what decision.

An organization's chain of command clarifies who reports to whom. A "floating" teacher especially needs to know to whom she reports. Every teacher wants to know who will perform her annual evaluation. The personnel committee of a board is appointed by and responsible to the board chair. A clear chain of command provides security and predictability on who will make important decisions.

With a clear chain of command, a leader has choices about the organizational structure she wants to use. Three types of organizational structures are:

1. Hierarchy

2. Flat structure

3. Hybrid (combination of hierarchy and flat).

▶ EXERCISE YOUR EQ   ▦   As you study each of these structures, pay attention to your response to each one. Do you find you have a preference for one form over another?

Hierarchy

Directors who make decisions by themselves tend toward "top-down" structures, or hierarchies. In a hierarchy, the chain of command begins with the director at the top, and every other employee reports to the director in some way. In a hierarchy, the person at the top of the organization makes the important decisions. A military general issues a command, which everyone must follow.

Flat

In flat organizations, teams make decisions. Juries, Quaker meetings, and 12-step groups are examples of flat organizations. Flat structures rely on building consensus among team members. Participation and ownership of decisions are highest in flat structures.

Hybrid

In hybrid organizations, the leader makes some decisions and teams make other deci-sions. For example, directors make budget decisions (hierarchical), and teams decide how to plan activities that involve parents (flat).

▶ EXERCISE YOUR EQ   ▓   What is your perception of how decisions are made in your organization? Draw a representation or chart of how your program would look to an outsider.

Use circles to represent a team that makes decisions. Draw a vertical line from the top of each team's circle to the person to whom the team reports. Write the position and name of the decision maker at the top of each vertical line. For example, draw a circle for the infant/toddler teaching team. Next, make a vertical line upward from that circle. At the top of the line, create a box with the relevant supervisor's title or name. Continue doing this until every individual and team is included in the representation.

Once you have drawn your representation of how decisions are made in your organization, compare it to your program's organization chart, or "org chart." These charts are often required for grant applications. Each director should have an org chart available for you to view. Is your drawing in line with the official chart? Differences in perception can lead to lively, informative discussions.

The dynamics of decision making in hierarchies, flat organizations, and hybrids

Hierarchies: Decision making by Tops, Middles, and Bottoms

In hierarchies, the top-down decision-making process has a strong effect on morale. Middles and Bottoms may feel insecure and slighted because the director can hire and fire staff at will. Lower-level staff members sometimes have little loyalty to the organiza-tion. They see themselves as working for the children and the paycheck. Only a charis-matic leader, or an engaging mission, can inspire loyalty to a hierarchy.

Authoritarian structures like hierarchies have strengths and weaknesses. Strengths include expedient decision making, a clear chain of command, and role clarity. Deficien-cies can include rigidity; stagnation; and restricted, top-down communication.

Management consultant Barry Oshry (1986) describes the predictable dynamics in hierarchies. Oshry labels employees in hierarchical organizations as Tops, Middles, and Bottoms.

Tops

The executive decision maker, or Top, wields a great deal of power. Tops (owner, director/owner, director, or board) make decisions with little input. Tops often take a letter of the law approach. Due process, taking time to get employees' input, slows down a Top.

According to Oshry, Tops are perceived as "numbers-oriented, distant, arbitrary, out-of-touch, and thinking of people as things not as people" (1986, 21). Tops appear to be dedicated to their own interests, rather than the interests of others in the organization.

Middles

Middles (assistant directors, site directors, and curriculum coordinators) report to Tops. Middles are limited in the decisions they can make. The job of the Middle is to negotiate between the Top and the Bottoms of the organization. If you have ever felt "stuck in the middle," you know what a middle manager's position feels like. Others see Middles as diligent, responsible, well-intended, but also turncoats, weak and unable to make decisions that stick (Oshry 1986). Decisions made by Middles are often tentative, pending approval from above. A middle manager says, "I'll have to get back to you on that" or "I'll see what I can do."

Bottoms

Bottoms (teachers, teacher's aides, bus drivers, and family support workers) feel least empowered to make meaningful decisions. Bottoms unhappily label themselves as "pawns," "peons," and "worker bees" at the mercy of those in power. Tops are not required to pay attention to what Bottoms want or need. Bottoms' decision-making power is to strike or quit. Bottoms can drop everything and walk out the door. Frustrated Bottoms resist authority by saying, "That's not in my job description; you don't pay me to do that."

Flat structures and decision making

In flat structures, everyone takes part in decision making. The director knows everyone, and everyone has access to the director. Employees are maximally involved. Everyone is kept informed. Pathways are in place for transmitting information rapidly to everyone in the organization. Due process is at the heart of flat structures. Leaders rarely act unless everyone has been informed and has spoken on each issue. Early childhood organizations almost always include some form of flat, or team, structure.

Flat structures, like hierarchies, have endured through the ages. The Native American process of using a "talking stick" ensures that everyone has the right to speak. Juries sit around a table together for as long as it takes to reach often heart-wrenching decisions. Our legal system assumes that a jury's flat structure ensures that the "voice of the people" will be heard.

Early childhood organizations are imbued with flat structures. Parent advisory committees, team teachers, and other collaborative efforts are often the preferred mode for making decisions. Flat structure strengths include a high level of staff commitment, ownership, empowerment, and involvement.

Flat structures present challenges, however, especially to those who grew up in hierarchical systems. Decisions made by consensus require that each team member be mature and accountable. Without maturity, individuals in flat structures can slide into power struggles, manipulating others into following their lead. Unlike hierarchies, in flat structures, jobs may not be clear. The chain of command can be foggy. Decision making by teams often takes more time than anyone has. Directors are likely to hear the cry, "Not another meeting!"

Hybrid approach to decision making

As you may have imagined, few organizations are purely hierarchical or purely flat. Most early childhood leaders institute team decision making. Directors who want to develop future leaders encourage employees to make decisions for themselves. Reflective supervision (discussed in Chapter 9) is an example of hybrid decision making. Employees are mentored to become more confident and competent in making daily decisions. The supervisor retains the authority to evaluate the staff member.

Team teaching is another example of a hybrid decision-making structure. Both teachers have an equal voice in how the classroom will function. Aides and assistants are encouraged to share their views. Even lead teachers often act as just another voice in the classroom decision-making process. Nonetheless, each teacher is ultimately responsible to the director. Directors decide whether to retain or terminate employees.

Who would want a committee to perform his brain surgery? Surely, we want one competent person in charge. Similarly, most directors would not want to change the staff handbook without listening to teachers' ideas and feelings first. Crystal clear, no questions asked, emergency evacuation plans are essential. However, without staff input in developing the plan, that plan is less familiar.

The buck stops here

Directors have the opportunity to decide how much decision making to share and how much to retain. As a leader, regardless of the decision-making approach you choose, remember to inform your staff if the decision is mine, ours, or yours. Staff will thank you, and the program will run more smoothly.

How we make decisions affects the morale, efficiency, and structure of our programs. Now that you know your options, what works best for you? Are you more likely to make letter of the law or spirit of the law decisions? Would you weigh the pros and cons of each choice before making a decision? Or are you more at ease thin-slicing, calling upon your intuition? Many administrators are most comfortable using a combination of these approaches, depending on the situation. The choice is yours.

Along the way, remember that leaders can suffer from decision fatigue. Give yourself a break from decision making when you can. That act of kindness to yourself will clear the fog and make your next decision-making marathon more powerful.

Reflection questions

1. Complete the organizational chart for your program, as discussed on page 44. Would you say your organization is hierarchical, flat, or a hybrid? Is the chain of command clear? Do you see yourself as a Top, Middle, or Bottom in that structure? If you were to change one thing about your organizational structure, what change would you make? What effect would this have on your program? Include your org chart and reflections in a paper on these questions.

2. Reflect on an important decision you have made. For example, how did you decide where to go for your schooling, how to resolve a recent conflict, or who would be your closest friend? Which of these decisions did you make by using the letter of the law (pros and cons) process, and which did you decide by the spirit of the law approach? Do you see a pattern emerging in your decision-making preference? Are letter of the law or spirit of the law decisions more successful with young children?

3. Describe in an oral presentation or in writing what you have learned about yourself. How comfortable are you with thin-slicing your decisions? Give an example of a decision you thin-sliced successfully and a thin-sliced decision that was not so successfully. Gladwell suggests that we get better at thin-slicing the more we expose ourselves to the unfamiliar and unknown. Write a list of steps you might take to deepen your experience and your ability to thin-slice. Be as concrete as you can.

Team projects

1. Compare your organizational chart with those of your teammates. What decision-making structures do early childhood organizations appear to have in common? Research and share at least one article apiece on what makes early childhood teams effective. What three changes would you make to ensure that team decisions are made effectively in your organization?

2. Morale can be enhanced or harmed by the degree and quality of staff involvement in decision making. Discuss which decisions should be "mine" (the director's and/or administrator's), "ours," or "yours" in early childhood programs. Are staff members in your programs clear about who has responsibility for each decision? Does your program include Tops, Middles, and Bottoms? If so, how does that structure affect morale? As a group, identify three ways morale in your program could be uplifted by making changes in the decision-making process. Lead small group discussions with colleagues on this topic.

3. Find a local improv group or performance, or view one online or on television. One example of an improv television show is *Whose Line Is It Anyway?* Attend or watch the improv performance together. Meet afterward to share your observations in the light of improv theory discussed in the chapter. Finally, practice doing improv within your team by quickly adding on to what another person has said. Record or video highlights of your team's efforts in learning about the relevance of improv to our daily decision making in early childhood.

Bibliography

Americans with Disabilities Act of 1990, as Amended, 42 U.S.C. 12101 et seq (2008).

Baumeister, R.F., & J. Tierney. 2011. *Willpower: Rediscovering the greatest human strength.* New York: Penguin.

Bruno, H.E., & M.L. Copeland. 1999. Decisions! Decisions! Decision-making structures which support quality. *Leadership Quest* (Spring).

Bruno, H.E., & M.L. Copeland. 1999. If the director isn't direct, can the team have direction? *Leadership Quest* (Fall).

Buchanan, L., & A. O'Connell. 2006. A brief history of decision making. *Harvard Business Review* 84 (1): 32–41, 132.

de Becker, G. 1997. *The gift of fear: And other survival signals that protect us from violence.* New York: Dell.

Dobbs, D.B. 1993. *Law of remedies.* 2nd ed. St. Paul, MN: West Publishing.

Gladwell, M. 2005. *Blink: The power of thinking without thinking.* 2nd ed. New York: Little, Brown.

Goleman, D. 2010. *Emotional intelligence: Why it can matter more than IQ.* New York: Bantam.

Gonzalez-Mena, J. 2001. *Multicultural issues in child care.* 3rd ed. New York: McGraw-Hill.

Greenspon, T.S. 2002. *Freeing our families from perfectionism.* Minneapolis, MN: Free Spirit Publishing.

Kahneman, D., D. Lovallo, & O. Sibony. 2011. The big idea: Before you make that big decision … *Harvard Business Review* 89 (6): 50–60, 137. www.hbr.org/2011/06/the-big-idea-before-you-make-that-big-decision/ar/9

Kellerman, B. 2006. When should a leader apologize—And when not? *Harvard Business Review* 84 (4): 72–81, 148.

Oshry, B. 1986. *The possibilities of organization.* Boston: Power & Systems.

Senge, P.M. 2006. *The fifth discipline: The art and practice of the learning organization.* Rev. ed. New York: Doubleday.

Tice-Colopy, K. 2010. Investing in members: Ohio redefines its purpose and services. *Young Children* 65 (5): 66–68.

Tierney, J. 2011. Do you suffer from decision fatigue? *New York Times,* August 17. www.nytimes.com/2011/08/21/magazine/do-you-suffer-from-decision-fatigue.html?pagewanted=all.

Web resources

Blink: Thin-Slicing Skills
www.gladwell.com/blink

Create Organization Charts
http://office.microsoft.com/en-us/powerpoint-help/create-organization-charts-and-other-diagrams-HA001132750.aspx

Group Decision-Making Tool Kit
www.extension.iastate.edu/communities/tools/decisions

Improve Employee Performance with Improv
www.marshallgoldsmithlibrary.com/cim/articles_print.php?aid=661

Make Decisions
https://career.berkeley.edu/Plan/MakeDecisions.stm

Overcoming Perfectionism
www.livestrong.com/article/14702-overcoming-perfectionism

Thought Awareness, Rational Thinking, and Positive Thinking
www.mindtools.com/pages/article/newTCS_06.htm

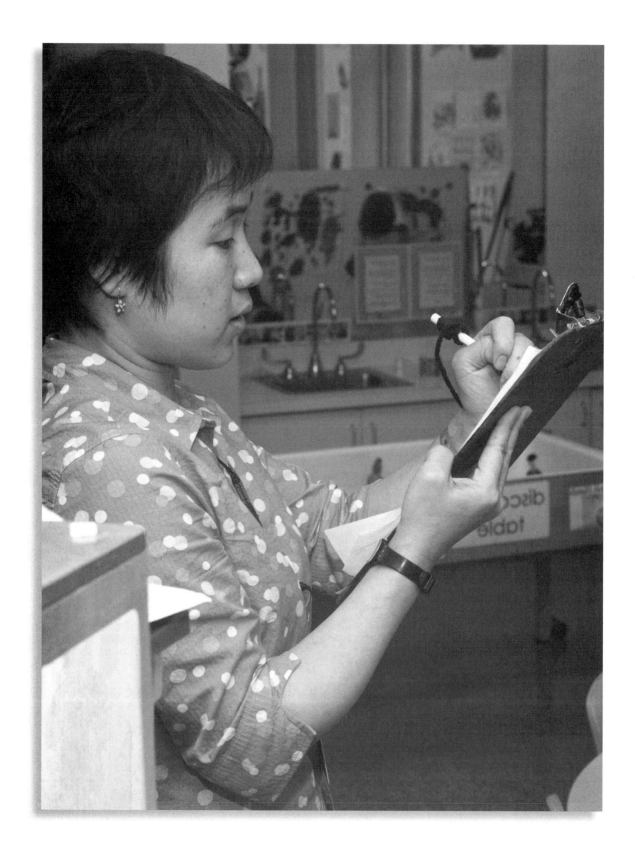

One of our chief jobs in life, it seems to me, is to realize
how rare and valuable each one of us really is—that
each of us has something which no one else has or ever
will have—something inside which is unique to all time.

—Fred Rogers

Two roads diverged in a wood, and I,
I took the one less traveled by,
And that has made all the difference.

—Robert Frost, "The Road Less Taken"

4 Leading on Purpose: The Road to Making a Difference

Case Study—Jamilah

Jamilah's classroom purrs with activity. Senior citizen volunteer Ms. Maisie reads Cassie
her favorite stories; Joshua and Trey paint a solar system awash with glittery pearl and
gold shooting stars; Eliza and Mimi puzzle over where to dig a pond for frogs' eggs.

Although Jamilah is content with her work, she is ready for something more. She dreams of
building her own school. She would name it "Jamilah's Neighborhood."

Looking around her community, Jamilah sees a number of early childhood centers, a
Head Start program, faith-based nursery schools, and family child care providers. "They
all want to help children," Jamilah ponders. "How is my dream any different?" Jamilah asks
you to level with her: "What is all this vision and mission stuff about? All these programs
sound the same to me! I want Jamilah's Neighborhood to stand out and be special."

Before emotional and social intelligence

theory came about, common practice for identifying one's purpose, vision, mission, and core
values was linear and rational. A leader first identified the impact she wanted to make, focused
in on drafting her workplace mission, and whittled down from there. Recent management
theory, however, embraces social intelligence, which includes social awareness—what we sense
about others—and social facility—what we then do with that awareness (Goleman 2006, 84).
Finding our vision and mission is a far more internal, subjective, and individual process. Carter

and Curtis (2010) encourage us to search our heart for what is important. This chapter invites you on an adventure to search your heart for the kind of leader you have the potential to be.

Purpose, the heartbeat of our existence

To lead by inspiration, a leader must first find and tap into her source of inspiration. Purpose is our deepest motivating force. Derived from our life story, purpose is deepened by the difficulties we face. Rather than running from failures or attempting to cover up inadequacies, leaders who do well embrace the hard knocks and disappointments in their lives (Bryant 2011).

> Those who bring sunshine to the lives of others cannot keep it from themselves.
> —Sir James Barrie

Staff will trust leaders who are true to themselves and who remain resilient during challenging times. "It's striking to hear teachers describe the contrast between directors who work with a vision and those who settle for how things are. The word 'vision' isn't always used, but they excitedly describe how their director really inspired them to work at the center, how 'she's usually got a twinkle in her eye,' is always 'showing us pictures or little quotes to expand our thinking,' or 'keeps her eyes on the prize even when the budget comes up short'" (Carter 2000, 99). Purpose gives meaning to our lives and intentionality to our work. Purpose gives us clarity in confusion, hope in discouragement, and courage to do the right thing.

Consider how Jamilah's purpose affects her actions in the chapter case study. If you asked her to define her purpose, Jamilah might tell you that she "was born to" instill happiness, respect, and confidence in children. This purpose will inspire her to leave the comfort of her classroom behind and establish her own school. Later, as she develops her vision, mission, and goals for her center, she will return to her purpose again and again just as a hiker takes out a compass to find her destination. [See **Helpful Definitions**.]

Helpful Definitions

1. **Purpose** is your reason for living, your deepest passion.
2. **Vision** is your dream of how you can change your world.
3. **Mission** is the practical way you will turn your dream into reality.
4. **Goals** are specific milestones for accomplishing your mission.
5. **Objectives** are steps you take, and a way to measure your progress toward accomplishing goals.
6. **Core values** remind us, while making decisions, what we stand for.

Finding your purpose: The "inner longing"

How do you uncover your *purpose*? Author Stephen Covey believes each of us intuitively knows our purpose. "Deep within each one of us there is an inner longing to live a life of greatness and contribution—to really matter, to really make a difference," Covey advises (2004b, 28). Some of us have to dig harder than others do to uncover that longing within, and the discovery process often takes a lifetime. No matter how much effort and time your excavating takes, be gentle with yourself. Your efforts will one day hit paydirt. As Confucius once wisely said, "Choose a job you love and you will never work a day in your life."

▶ EXERCISE YOUR EQ ▦ To gain a clearer sense of your purpose, explore each of these activities:

1. Name three traits you had as a child that you still have today. These traits will help you identify your gifts and strengths.

2. Recall a time in your life when you felt you were doing exactly what you were meant to do. This is what living "on purpose" feels like.

3. Identify a person who noticed your potential. What did that person see in you? Others often serve as messengers to help us see what we cannot yet see in ourselves.

4. Describe a time when you experienced "flow" (Csikszentmihalyi 1991), meaning you did not need to think about what you had to do, you just did it. You may have felt that everything came naturally to you.

5. Ask three people you trust and who care about you: "When have you seen me at my happiest?" . . . "What impact do you believe I can have on the world around me?"

6. What contribution would you most like to make? Some people find it helpful to imagine what they'd like written on their gravestone. Others think about what might be said about them at their retirement party.

Your turn has come. Let go of the need to be perfect or to get it just right, or the mandate to please anyone else. This moment is yours. Complete the following sentence:

My purpose on earth is to: _____.

For some people, a purpose will flow like a stream from the tips of their pens. Others will feel stuck. Still others will find themselves squinting to see a purpose that seems just beyond their view. Be kind to yourself. Wherever you are in this process is where you are meant to be. As children need time to grow, your purpose needs time to unfold. Ask yourself, "What am I meant to do?" This will help you discover your purpose. Then ask, "How does knowing my purpose clarify for me the leader I want to be?"

When our inner longing catches fire with our personal vision, we come into our own as leaders.

As soon as you trust yourself, you will know how to live.
—Johann Wolfgang von Goethe

Vision

Vision is your dream of how your world will be when you are being true to your purpose. Having a vision means taking the long view and looking at the big picture. As you envision the way you want the world to improve, remain true to your purpose as you interact with others and make daily decisions. Leading on purpose is the everyday, lived commitment to make your vision come true. Recall the chapter case study, in which Jamilah's purpose was to instill happiness, respect, and confidence in children. Her next step is to envision a special world where every child feels worthwhile and loved.

Stephen Covey's best-selling book *The 7 Habits of Highly Effective People* (2004a) shares ways to successfully problem-solve in both personal and professional situations, a critically important skill for early childhood administrators. Covey's later book, *The 8th Habit* (2004b), discusses "finding your voice." Covey invites you to cultivate these positive behaviors:

Habit 1: Be proactive.
Habit 2: Begin with the end in mind.
Habit 3: Put first things first.
Habit 4: Think win/win.
Habit 5: Seek first to understand, then to be understood.
Habit 6: Synergize—creatively cooperate.
Habit 7: Sharpen the saw—stay clear and open to possibilities.
Habit 8: Find your voice and inspire others to find theirs (Covey 2004a, b).

Each person's work is always a portrait of himself.
—Samuel Butler

Each of these habits will help you discover and hone your vision.

Everyone has a pathway that is unique. No one else has exactly the same vision you do of how to change the world. As early childhood professionals, our vision often focuses on making the world better, safer, and happier for children and families. When you know your purpose and have a vision of how it will manifest on earth, you are ready for the practical step of articulating your mission.

Articulating your mission

Your *mission* is the practical way in which you will make your dream come true, thereby fulfilling your unique purpose. Jamilah's purpose is to help every child know his or her preciousness. Jamilah's vision is to create an early childhood program where children are treated as precious. Her program's mission is: "Where children learn their worth as they explore their neighborhood and world."

A mission is strong and true when it meets these standards:
- Inspires everyone who hears it.
- Empowers staff to find their own purpose within the greater mission.
- Shines steadily like a lighthouse when storms bluster.
- Sets a standard for quality performance.
- Reflects our deepest core values.
- Informs every decision.
- Remains timeless.

Above all, a mission is personal, and true to one's purpose and vision.

▶ EXERCISE YOUR EQ   ▓ Margie Carter and Deb Curtis, authors of *The Visionary Director* (2010), can help you discover your mission as an early childhood leader. Think about which goal represents your highest priority:
- To provide a service for parents while they work.
- To give kids a head start to be ready for school and academic success.
- To enhance children's self-concept and social skills as they learn to get along in the world.
- To ensure children have a childhood that is full of play, adventure, and investigation.
- To create a community where adults and children experience a sense of belonging and new possibilities for making the world a better place.
- _____

(Add your own words here)

▶ EXERCISE YOUR EQ   ▓ Find and examine the mission statement of your current organization, program, college, or university. To what extent does it actually reflect the goals of its mission statement? Now imagine that you are the director of a child care center; write your own mission statement. How does your mission support your purpose and vision?

The value of "core values"

We all need touchstones. Touchstones keep us grounded. We touch them to remind ourselves of what matters. A touchstone is an object of value we return to again and again for clarity of purpose. Think of a touchstone as a precious sapphire, ruby, or smooth chunk of turquoise. Touching that precious stone can feel reassuring, cool, soothing;

Dreams are the touchstones of our characters.
—Henry David Thoreau

touching might remind you of how you came to find it. Core values are touchstones for your work.

A *core value*, like a touchstone, reminds you who you are and how you want to lead your life. Leaders who live by their core values act with integrity. Integrity is aligning your decisions with your core values.

One example of a core value is honesty. Leaders with this core value look without blinders at their opportunities, challenges, and blind spots. With honesty as a touchstone, leaders cannot hide in denial or procrastination. Lightheartedness, the ability to keep perspective and not take oneself too seriously, is another core value. Lighthearted leaders have an abiding sense of humor and are optimistic and hopeful.

Other core values include:

- Respect
- Courage
- Inclusiveness
- Compassion
- Humility
- Hope and optimism
- Hard work
- Creativity
- Conflict resolution today
- Community involvement
- Families come first

▶ EXERCISE YOUR EQ ▉ I work with an early childhood leader whose *purpose* is "Let people know what is wrong, so we can make it better." As you can imagine, her core values are courage, honesty, and objectivity. What are the core values you could not live without? As you name these, consider your purpose. Your core values and purpose are close companions.

List several examples of your core values:

_____.

Your team's purpose and core values

Teams, like leaders, need a mission and core values. A helpful exercise is for staff members to write down their *individual* core values. They can follow that exercise by brainstorming their *team's* core values together. Teams that are highly functioning typically find that the individual team members' core values align with the team's.

Consultant and former director Ruby Martin leads child care organizations through a process of finding their vision, mission, goals, and objectives:

> The process I use is very simple. It starts with the director of the center holding a staff meeting with all her employees and brainstorming what they would love for their center to look like. Someone during the meeting jots down all they key items the employees would like to see. The director then takes all information pulled from the meeting and places it into a paragraph-long vision statement. All employees receive a copy to review and edit and get their feedback to the director.

> Leadership is the art of getting someone else to do what you want done, and to believe he wants to do it.
>
> —Dwight Eisenhower

Sample Early Childhood Mission Statements

- "Our mission is to provide lots of love to the children whose parents have to work to meet the demands of the society we live in. Our blueprint for this Child Care Center is excellent education, love, guidance, and a home away from home."
  —*Baycrest Academy Child Care Center*

- "'Play with a purpose' guides our unique age-specific programs and curricula, each designed to move your child ahead developmentally, intellectually, and socially in an environment that's warm, nurturing, and fun."
  —*La Petite Academy*

- "A community that shapes and inspires children for the future."
  —*Kiddie Academy*

- "An educated society that contributes to an improved quality of life."
  —*Region 19 Head Start*

- "Provide a safe, stimulating, and nurturing environment in which young children can learn and grow…while focusing on healing from past trauma through love, support, and stability."
  —*The Salvation Army Harbor House Childcare Center*

This vision is then used as a tool at the next staff meeting to develop goals. The goals are pulled from the vision: areas to improve, disband, initiate. Each goal is then divided into Action Steps where employees are empowered to take on the responsibilities for reaching the goals. A timeline is set and the process begins.

I always encourage centers to hold frequent team meetings throughout the action phase to keep on track. After the vision is fully met, I encourage them to go through the process again about once a year to make sure they are always improving, growing, and remaining focused on areas important to them. This process also works to create a vision for each classroom, only it just involves [that teacher] and director. (Personal correspondence, September 19, 2007)

Ruby might also invite the team to annually identify their core values. She could post the team's core values and purpose in prominent places around her building as an inspirational reminder for the staff. Team decisions are far easier to make when choices are based on agreed upon core values. Many potential conflicts can be resolved by the parties referring back to these touchstones.

The S.M.A.R.T. method

The five-step S.M.A.R.T. method of visioning and planning helps leaders turn their dreams into everyday realities. Peter Drucker (1954) is often credited with the concept of "management by objectives," from which the S.M.A.R.T. method has evolved.

The first step is to identify goals related to the mission statement. From there, leaders create measurable action items with timelines for success.

S.M.A.R.T. Method
• What Specifically do I want to achieve?
• How will I Measure success?
• What Actions do I need to take?
• What Resources do I need?
• What is my Timeline?

S: Develop Specific goals that will bring you closer to your mission.

M: Determine how your success will be Measured.

A: Make a list of Action items that will lead you closer to your goal.

R: Identify the Resources you will need.

T: Establish a Timeline for meeting your goal.

Examine the S.M.A.R.T. method in relation to the chapter case study. Jamilah's purpose becomes real by using the S.M.A.R.T. method as follows:

S: Jamilah wants to actively engage community members within the daily operations of her school.

M: She will measure success by monitoring weekly sign-in sheets for parents and community volunteers.

A: She needs to write e-mails and letters to parents and community organizations asking for volunteers.

R: She will read relevant books and articles about establishing effective volunteer programs, and she will enlist the help of program staff in identifying areas of need.

T: She and her staff will establish an ongoing volunteer program within six months.

▶ EXERCISE YOUR EQ   ■ Try using the S.M.A.R.T. method to set and accomplish a goal. You can apply the process to a rainbow of situations, such as a school assignment, a workplace project, or an issue with a classmate or colleague. Using the five steps, identify a goal and mark your pathway to achievement.

Vision, purpose, and leadership

Leaders, confident of the difference they want to make, inspire others to join them on the journey to make a difference. Effective leaders have a vision powerful enough to embrace the vision of others who work with them. Clear on their purpose, leaders inspire the best in others and invite others to live "on purpose" too. As Margie Carter (podcast) advises, "We can't afford to not dream!"

Consider the chapter case study. Now let's say that Jamilah takes her enthusiasm, with her business plan, to her local bank. Jamilah's vision, and her S.M.A.R.T. legwork, inspires the bank's lending officer to grant her requests. That banker will delight in hearing about the progress Jamilah makes and will attend the opening of Jamilah's Neighborhood.

Leaders are everyday, real, "perfectly imperfect" people (Mellody & Miller 1989). A teacher is a leader in her classroom. Parents are leaders in their home. A child is a leader in learning all about his world. Leaders connect with fellow travelers to create environments for growth. In his book *The Fifth Discipline,* management expert Peter Senge (2006) calls these environments "learning organizations," spaces where everyone grows, learns, and supports the growth and learning of others. Does this sound like the early childhood profession? You bet it does.

> The best and noblest lives are those set to high ideals.
> —Rene Almeras

Servant leadership: "Paying it forward"

Consider another valuable management theory in knowing yourself as a leader. This concept is called "servant leadership" (Greenleaf 1970). Understanding servant leadership will help you move from self-knowledge to knowledge of what motivates others, just as your EQ strengthens your social-emotional intelligence.

Servant leaders dedicate themselves to listening to and enhancing the well-being of those around them. Humility is the servant leader's core value. Servant leaders don't concern themselves with self-promotion. They know that helping others grow helps everyone, including them. Servant leaders ask, "Do those served grow as persons? Do they, while being served, become healthier, wiser, freer, more autonomous, more likely themselves to become servants?"

For women and people of color, the word *servant* does not usually have positive connotations. Such groups have a history of being coerced into serving others who have taken the service for granted. When you are a servant, you leave your personal dreams at someone else's door. This term, "servant leader," reveals the complexity of leadership.

People who feel obligated to be leaders are rarely content or effective. When you *choose* to be a leader, however, you are doing what you are meant to do naturally. A servant leader, in the kindest meaning of the term, stands ready to work in service to the greater good. Servant leaders serve by choice, not coercion. Servant leaders acknowledge the value of those they serve. Early childhood servant leaders are committed to bettering the lives of children, families, and staff in their care.

Altruism, looking out for others, can be liberating if free of codependency. Altruism is giving back to the world generously, freely, and without expectation of praise or recognition. Codependency is relying upon others for our self-worth. People who are codependent manipulate others to gain praise and acknowledgment for themselves.

> The privilege of a lifetime is being who you are.
> —Joseph Campbell

Servant leadership is free of obligation and codependency. Servant leadership is altruism at its best. "Paying it forward" is another way to describe servant leadership.

Like paying the toll taker not just for your toll but also the person's behind you, you selflessly brighten another's life. When we are working and living "on purpose," we grace our worlds with our gifts. Servant leaders display heroism by freely offering the best of themselves to children, families, staff, and communities. Altruism leads to an inner sense of serenity and completion.

As you dream, so shall you become.
—Ralph Waldo Emerson

Futurists Margaret Wheatley and Deborah Frieze offer a fresh vision of "servant leadership" in urging us to leave behind the expectation that leaders should be heroes with all the answers. Wheatley notes, "Our current way of solving problems is not solving problems. No one knows what to do; but collectively, we all know what to do" (podcast). Wheatley and Frieze propose leaders serve instead as hosts. Leader "hosts" invite staff to be at the forefront of leading change, while the host steps back to provide facilitation and support. Host leaders make use of resources such as "World Café" (see Brown & Isaacs 2005) to engage all stakeholders. Both servant and host leadership invite us to go deep to find the place where our individual vision aligns with the deepest vision of the community we serve.

Bam!radio
"Rethinking Leadership Expectations: Moving from Hero to Host"
Interview with Margaret (Meg) Wheatley
Heart to Heart Conversations on Leadership
http://bamradionetwork.com

Look back at your purpose, vision, mission, and core values. Articulating each of these clarifies who you are as a leader. Now you can look at your style of leadership. Knowing your style helps you communicate your vision and purpose to others.

Myers-Briggs leadership inventory

Each of us will have a highly individual leadership style. Directors are not fungible (interchangeable, one for the other), they can share similar preferences. You may find it helpful to know what you and others have in common, as well as where you are unique. A study of styles to find where you land on the leadership continuum can be enlightening. Insights you gain by learning about leadership styles will enhance your leadership EQ competencies.

Carl Jung, the Swiss psychologist, traveled the world to live among and observe different cultures and people. He concluded that although we are unique, we also have commonalities. One commonality, for example, is that each of us is either right- or left-handed.

Jung (1961) set about identifying other human commonalities, or "preferences." Some people, he discovered, preferred to lead quiet and reflective lives, gathering their energy from within (*Introverts*). Others preferred to be social, outgoing, and gregarious, gathering their energies from the environment (*Extraverts,* also spelled *extroverts*). Jung placed these preferences on a continuum with two opposite poles. Right- and left-handedness sit at opposite sides of the handedness continuum. Similarly, introversion and extroversion sit at opposite ends of the preference continuum:

Right-handers..Left-handers
Extraverted...Introverted

Mother-daughter team Katherine Cook Briggs and Isabel Briggs Myers translated Jung's work into a highly validated, easy-to-take leadership inventory. Millions of people around the world have taken the Myers-Briggs Type Indicator (MBTI) questionnaire since its inception in 1943. Myers-Briggs research provides us with significant insights into how leaders and their team members function.

Throughout the following sections, you will have a chance to explore your own personal preferences and temperament type. Although this material is not intended to be used as a scientifically validated assessment instrument, it provides an in-depth overview of the MBTI. The following MBTI descriptions are based on my more than 25 years as an MBTI practitioner and certified MBTI administrator. (For additional information about the MBTI and online instruments, visit The Myers & Briggs Foundation at www.myersbriggs.org/.)

Using the following information, you will be able to assess your leadership style and temperament. You also will be able to use this information to grow yourself as a leader, and help others grow.

Your leadership style and temperament

Let's examine the four different preferences that people around the world exhibit (Kroeger, Thuessen, & Rutledge 2002; Myers et al. 1998):

Extraversion (E)..Introversion (I)
Sensing (S)..Intuition (N)
Thinking (T)...Feeling (F)
Judging (J)...Perceiving (P)

As you read along, you may find that you identify with each preference somewhat. An outgoing leader may also need "quiet time," for example. A spontaneous, free-spirited teacher can also meet deadlines. Jung found, however, that most of us have preferences that place us more toward one end of each continuum than the other.

Leaders face situations daily that require them to be real and authentic. Jung called this our "true self." As you study the preferences below, ask yourself, "Who am I when I am not playing one of my roles (teacher/director, parent, student, daughter)?" Take a look now at each of the MBTI types in the **MBTI Overview** (next page) to assess which better describes you.

Introverts and Extraverts

Case Study—Gustavo and Willow

Energetic Gustavo, loved by families, is forever creating new activities for his after-school children. His team teacher, Willow, prefers to stay in the background. Willow is most comfortable helping individual children with their homework. Whenever Gustavo and Willow attempt to plan curriculum together, Willow sits quietly while Gustavo enthusiastically shares one idea after another.

You are asked to help these teachers "speak each other's language." What recommendations could you make to help Gustavo listen to Willow, and help Willow speak up for what's important to her?

Have you noticed a staff member who rarely speaks up? Then, like Willow, when she finally shares her thoughts, she amazes everyone with the depth of her insights? This person is an Introvert. She derives her energy from within. She prefers to think things through quietly.

The latest MBTI data finds that Introverts make up 51 percent of Americans (Myers et al. 1998, 157–58) Extraverts are noted for their energetic, friendly, and talkative nature. They thrive on social interaction and prefer to talk things through with others.

Are you an E or an I? Your E/I preference identifies the source of your energy.

MBTI Overview			
Preference	**Characteristics**	**Strengths**	**Challenges**
Extraversion (E)	Friendly, thrives on interaction, gregarious, welcoming	Enjoys team meetings, brainstorming, shares easily	Impatient with silence, difficulty listening, calls too many meetings
Introversion (I)	Quiet, reflective, forms one or two deep relationships, thrives on solitude	Skilled listener, soothing, concise communicator	Public speaking, misunderstood by others, viewed as aloof
Sensing (S)	Uses the five senses to observe, concrete, down-to-earth, realistic	Notices facts and specifics, documents accurately	Misses the "big picture," doesn't like long planning sessions
Intuition (N)	Visionary, open to possibilities, "eyes on the prize"	Welcomes change, dreams "big"	Overlooks details, less interested in practical approaches
Thinking (T)	Objective, critical, task-oriented	Objective and consistent decision maker, direct communicator	Overlooks interpersonal dynamics, can "blame" others
Feeling (F)	Personal, process- and people-oriented	Is able to "stand in another's shoes," promotes harmonious workplaces	Takes things personally, avoids conflict
Judging (J)	Prefers clarity and order, punctuality, and organization	Makes a plan and sticks to it, meets deadlines, neat	Can judge too quickly, perfectionism, dislikes surprises and ambiguity
Perceiving (P)	Easygoing, open to possibilities, organizes by piling things up	Adept at inventing alternatives, creates a fun work environment	Has difficulty making decisions, disorganized, last minute

Introverts

Leadership strengths. Introverted leaders bring well-thought-out solutions to problems. An Introvert (called "I" in the Myers-Briggs inventory) creates quiet, reflective workspaces where individuals are free to focus on their work or play. Children especially feel soothed by an Introvert's serene approach. Introverts are often skilled listeners. Parents and teachers feel heard by an Introvert director. Introverts often "craft" their words, taking time to choose the most accurate, concise way to communicate. An Introverted director is comfortable with silence.

Leadership challenges. Constant verbal interactions drain an Introvert's energy. Public speaking, even addressing a parent group, can exhaust them. Introverted leaders can seem aloof or uninterested in the ideas of others. Some staff believe Introvert administrators withhold information. Introverts need private time to recharge their batteries. They may avoid brainstorming sessions, when many people talk at once. Introverts sometimes "pretend" to be Extraverts to be able to perform their duties.

Tips for Introverted leaders.
- Take quiet time each day for yourself. Recharge your internal batteries. Take a walk, read a book, close your door to meditate.

- Tell staff: "Thanks for sharing that with me. I need time to consider what you said. I'll get back to you tomorrow morning."
- Distribute agendas for staff meetings in advance. Introverted staff will need time to reflect on agenda items.
- When conducting meetings, invite staff to work in small groups, especially groups of two. This practice ensures that Introverts will have a chance to speak.

Tips for communicating with Extraverts.

- Ask Extraverts questions. Listen for the main points. Let go of expecting yourself to take in every word an Extravert utters.
- Look for an Extravert's strengths, rather than stereotype her ("loud mouthed," "pushy," "a bulldozer").
- Find ways to enjoy an Extravert's upbeat energy. Show enthusiasm for his ideas.
- Communicate as spontaneously as you feel able. Avoid long silences.

Extraverts

Leadership strengths. Extraverts (E) are friendly, gregarious, and welcoming. Extraverted leaders actively engage with everyone and everything, bringing upbeat, positive, sometimes ebullient (bubbling) energy to the workplace. Comfortable expressing what is on their minds, Extraverts talk things out to learn what they themselves are thinking. (By contrast, Introverts think before they talk.) Extraverts are at home at brainstorming sessions, team meetings, and social events. Extraverts thrive in lively environments.

Extraverts gain energy through engaging with people and activity around them. Introverts find their energy inside and by being alone.

Leadership challenges. Extraverts, by virtue of their high energy and need to engage others, can overwhelm Introverts. Extraverts, although slightly in the minority (at 49% of the world's population [Myers et al. 1998, 157–58]), can assume that everyone should be outgoing, active conversationalists. Extraverts can ask questions and not wait for the Introvert's thoughtful response. In fact, Extraverts often answer *for* Introverts. Extraverts call meetings frequently, not thinking of how uncomfortable groups can be for Introverted employees. Extraverts may be impatient with silence and lose energy when separated from others.

Tips for Extraverted leaders.

- Maintain networks of diverse friends and acquaintances outside your program.
- If you work primarily with Introverts, use the phone, e-mail, or instant messaging to keep your energy high.
- Practice your active-listening skills to connect with Introverts. Remember, 65 to 90 percent of emotion is communicated nonverbally (Myers et al. 1998, 157–58).
- Use your social EQ to appreciate Introverted staff. Listening fully to an Introvert helps her trust you.

Tips for communicating with Introverts.

- Count to 10 slowly before you answer a question for an Introvert. Give Introverts time to think.
- Distribute agendas in advance of meetings to allow Introverts preparation time.
- Schedule individual and one-on-one activities, to balance group meetings.
- Devote time to inviting the Introvert to get to know and trust you.

Assessing yourself

▶ EXERCISE YOUR EQ   ▪ Where do you get your energy? Do you prefer to actively engage with others (E) or to quietly reflect by yourself (I)? You may prefer one strongly over the other; or you may be some of both. For purposes of the assessment question below, select the letter that more accurately describes you. If you feel in the middle on this preference, ask yourself: "Which preference could I not live without?" Extraverts must have people around them; Introverts cannot survive without frequent, regular time alone, away from all the bustle.

Question 1: Are you more of an Extravert than an Introvert? E _ _ _ or I _ _ _ ?
Now fill in the first blank below with the letter that indicates your preference:
My MBTI type: ___ ___ ___ ___
You now have determined 25 percent of your MBTI type.

Case Study—**Serena and Maureen**

Serena concentrates on recording every detail accurately for the classroom newsletter, while Maureen keeps coming up with new ideas to include. Serena feels Maureen "upsets the apple cart," and Maureen thinks Serena is a "wet blanket." In fact, Maureen gets bored when she has to focus on details, while Serena feels confused by Maureen's constant innovations.

How can these teachers build upon each other's strengths in creating the monthly classroom newsletter for families?

Sensing and intuition

Jung said we observe the world in one of two different ways. Some of us, skilled at accurate observation, use our five senses to take in facts and details. Others of us prefer using our imagination when observing; we look for meaning, inspiration, or an unfolding story.

Observers who notice specific details are called Sensors (S). Observers who see connections, meaning, and possibilities are Intuitors (N).

Jung's second preference identifies how we take in information and perceive our world. Seventy-five percent of Americans prefer to take in information in the "Sensing" way, noticing facts and specifics (Myers et al. 1998, 157–58). Called "Sensors," they observe the shape, size, smell, taste, texture, color, and sound of their environment. The rest are called "Intuitors," and they use their intuition. Intuitors are like brightly colored helium balloons lifting toward the skies. Sensors are like the strings that hold the balloons in place. Sensors and Intuitors need each other.

Sensors

Leadership strengths. Sensors tend to remember details, including names. Concrete and down-to-earth, Sensors are realistic. They report what they observe in accurate detail. In terms of learning styles, Sensors learn better when information is presented sequentially, in order, detailing the steps involved. Sensors live in the present and use common sense to create practical solutions. Most U.S. presidents have been Sensors.

A Head Start slogan is, "If it isn't documented, it didn't happen!" Documentation records the who, what, when, and where of events; documentation rarely records the why. Describing exactly what happened in a factual way is essential in reporting children's behavior. Sensors perceive the world in this concrete way.

Intuitor students, unlike Sensor students, do not need the instructor to present information sequentially. Intuitors learn when the instructor or the subject matter sparks their imaginations.

Leadership challenges. Because Sensors notice details, Sensing directors can miss the "big picture." Planning for the future is uncomfortable for Sensors. Sensors focus on what is directly in front of them. When a Sensor teams with a non-Sensing teacher, the Sensing teacher can think her teammate has her head in the clouds or "is a space shot." Sensors can be disoriented when given vague or scant instructions. If asked to plan a holiday party, the Sensor will be adrift if she is not given all the details. (Her opposite, the Intuitor, is more likely to "run with" a less detailed request. Intuitors will be intrigued by all the possibilities.)

Tips for Sensor leaders.
- Find ways to enjoy the free-spiritedness of your intuitive colleagues.
- Let them help you see the forest, and not just the trees. Ask them to help you understand how they see things.
- Sensors tend to be pessimistic; Intuitors, who focus on the future, tend to be optimistic. Enjoy the Intuitor's upbeat approach.
- At the same time, value your preference to "tell it like it is" and to accurately observe what is in front of you.
- Documentation may come easier for you than others. Use your preference to create useful templates and report forms.

Communicating with Intuitors
- Summarize your main idea first. Hold detailed explanations for later.
- Identify how your idea will create a brighter future.
- Let go of expecting Intuitors to work methodically; Intuitors thrive on novelty and innovation.
- Allow the Intuitor's imagination to soar; do not insist on detailed, sequential explanations.
- Learn from the Intuitor's ability to see connections that you might miss.

Intuitors

Leadership strengths. Intuitors prefer the big picture, always on the lookout for possibilities. Intuitive leaders keep their eyes on the prize. While Sensors prefer familiar practices, Intuitors welcome novelty and change. Even though only 26.7 percent of people are Intuitors, as visionaries they have major influence (Myers et al. 1998, 157–58). Martin Luther King Jr., Mohandas Gandhi, John F. Kennedy and Robert Kennedy, and Abraham Lincoln were Intuitors who dreamed of making the world better. Intuitor leaders lift an organization out of the doldrums by inviting staff to step back, gain perspective, and envision positive change.

Leadership challenges. If Sensors miss the forest for the trees, Intuitors miss the trees for the forest. Intuitors, looking for deeper meaning, miss the puddle right in front of them and get wet. Intuitors, preferring novelty, can be less suited to taking practical, pragmatic approaches. Intuitors and Sensors hear each other's words differently. A common dispute between an Intuitive teacher and her Sensing team teacher may sound like this: "That's not what I meant," sighs the Intuitor. "But that's what you said," argues the Sensor.

Tips for Intuitor leaders
- Acknowledge that the majority of people do not see things the way you do.
- Pay attention to the details of a situation, and look for the facts.
- Be ready to "speak the language" of Sensors if you want to be understood better.
- Honor your visionary, optimistic approach, even when those around you are less enthusiastic. Remember, moods are catching. Maintain your hopeful view of the future, and you will uplift and inspire others.

Communicating with Sensors
- Be practical and pragmatic.
- Use facts and figures to support your ideas. Give concrete examples.
- Document your experience in detail.
- State the steps to be taken to reach the goal in order.

Assessing yourself

▶ EXERCISE YOUR EQ   What is your preferred way to observe situations? Are you factual and realistic (S), or imaginative and looking for deeper meaning (N)? You may prefer one strongly over the other; or you may be some of both. For purposes of the assessment question below, select the letter that more accurately describes you. Schooled in documentation practices, early childhood educators learn Sensing skills; but being skilled in this way does not make you a Sensor. If you feel in the middle on this preference, ask yourself: "When I look at something new, do I prefer to see details or possibilities?"

Question 2: Are you more of a Sensor than an Intuitor? _ S _ _ or _ N _ _?

First fill in the first blank below with your answer to Question 1. Now fill in the second blank with the letter that indicates your preference to Question 2:

My MBTI type: E/I __ __ __

You now have determined 50 percent of your MBTI type.

Case Study—Phillipe

Like a duck, everything rolls off lead teacher Phillipe's back. Phillipe has no time for gossip, and no problem telling people what he thinks. In fact, when Phillipe has a problem with another person, he walks directly up to that person and says, "We need to talk." Teachers hurt by or uncomfortable with Phillipe's directness avoid or placate him. Raylene refuses to speak with him entirely because he is so "insensitive to people's feelings."

How would you coach these teachers to communicate with one another?

Thinking and feeling

Jung's third preference identifies the different ways we make decisions. Some of us prefer to decide things impersonally, by taking an objective, critical approach. Jung named this preference the Thinking preference. Others of us prefer to make decisions more personally, by taking into account each person's needs, situation, and history. This preference is Feeling. Across the nation 43.5 percent of men and 75.5 percent of women are Feelers, which means 56.5 percent of men and 24.5 percent of women are Thinkers (Myers et al. 1998, 157–58).

Neither Thinking nor Feeling is superior, one to the other. However, as more men than women prefer the Thinking modality, the male-dominated business world can leave women feeling their interpersonal way of making decisions is unappreciated. Thinking directors are likely to hear they have "ice in their veins." Men in the Feeling mode, appreciated in early childhood for their compassion and sensitivity, may be stereotyped negatively outside our profession. Work to become comfortable with both decision-making process modes, so you can call on whichever you need.

Thinkers

Leadership strengths. Thinkers (T) bring objectivity, clarity, and emotional distance to decision making. A thinker can be counted on to treat everyone fairly. That is, the Thinker will not favor one person over another. Thinkers decide things "evenhandedly," that is, with consistency.

Thinkers make decisions quickly, unfettered by second-guessing themselves. Thinkers often are able to make direct statements, without worrying first about whether "the truth" will hurt people's feelings. This is not to say that Thinkers do not have feelings. Thinkers "rise above" their feelings to make objective decisions. In fact, Thinkers are tireless in their pursuit of the objective truth. Thinkers are more task- than process-oriented.

Thinkers use a "letter of the law" process, whereas Feelers use the "spirit of the law" approach. This topic comes up again in Chapter 7.

Leadership challenges. Thinkers, focused on getting the job done, tend to overlook interpersonal data and dynamics. Thinkers, who believe in cause and effect, can "blame" the person they perceive to be responsible. They often fail to notice nonverbal cues of coworkers. Thinkers may not be aware of the subtle dynamics that go into building trust between individuals or in teamwork. They can perceive Feelers as "bleeding hearts." Thinkers, who focus on tasks rather than relationships, can find working with Feelers to be overly complicated.

Tips for Thinker leaders
- You may be perceived as "cold" or "overly analytical" if you are in a field that is highly relational.
- Investigate how to enhance your emotional and social intelligence. Practice noticing and reading nonverbal behavior.
- Praise staff more readily. Acknowledge employees' strengths and contributions.
- Practice active-listening skills.
- Slow down your pace. Colleagues need time to process how they will work together.
- Understand that tasks will be accomplished much easier when you build trusting relationships.

Communicating with Feelers
- Invest time in building relationships. Find out and ask about what matters to them. A Feeler may smile; but if she doesn't trust you, she won't work with you easily.
- Focus on how an idea can improve the quality of people's lives, rather than just focusing on the logic of the decision.
- Acknowledge that the majority of your colleagues are uncomfortable with conflict. Help Feelers focus on common goals in addressing disagreements.
- Pay attention to how you communicate.
- Staff members "take things personally." Give them time to talk about their feelings with you. Honor those feelings.

Feelers

Leadership strengths. Feelers (F) are devoted to building a harmonious, comfortable, and supportive workplace environment. A Feeler automatically steps up to welcome a new person and help her feel at ease. Feelers pay attention to unspoken clues and signs, such as tone of voice and eye and body language. Expect a Feeler to read people on many levels. Dedicated to making decisions that are compassionate, Feelers take everyone's needs and individual circumstances into account.

> **Bam!radio**
> "Handling Criticism: Five Survival Tips for Early Childhood Education Leaders."
> Interview with Cathy R. Jones
> *Heart to Heart Conversations on Leadership*
> http://bamradionetwork.com

Leadership challenges. Conflict is often painful for Feelers, who can get their feelings hurt more easily than a Thinker would (podcast). Feelers try to avoid confrontation at any cost. Being conflict-avoidant leads to misunderstanding, distancing, and indirect behavior such as talking *about* another person rather *to* her directly. Feelers work well with people they trust. Trust is built by sharing personal information, likes, and dislikes.

Tips for Feeler leaders

- Carry a Q-tip as a reminder to "quit taking it personally." Not every problem is about you.
- Don't neglect your own needs by focusing too much on other people's. Take time to do what you love, even if that means not always saying "yes" to helping out. In the end, with your renewed spirit, you will find you have much more energy to share.
- Don't give yourself away; you can end up feeling like a martyr and resentful.
- Practice ways to deal directly with conflicts. Feeling resentment can bring you down from your usual cordial, friendly ways.

Communicating with Thinkers

- List the pros and cons for each idea you present. Thinkers base decisions on objective analysis.
- Make your main point quickly and concisely.
- Back up your point with objective ideas and supporting facts.
- Commit to addressing conflicts directly with others. Set a time limit by which you will step up to face a conflict.
- Use your EQ to identify your feelings, and be open to the data that feelings offer.
- If you find yourself nursing hurt feelings, "step to the side" to look at the situation objectively.
- Practice looking at a problem through the eyes of a Thinker. Analyze the problem critically and impersonally, as if you were a "letter of the law" judge.
- To be successful, leaders need to use both the Thinking and Feeling modalities.

Assessing yourself

▶ EXERCISE YOUR EQ   What is your preferred mode of decision makings? Based on the objective facts (T) or accounting for the interpersonal dynamics (F)? You may prefer one strongly over the other; or you may be some of both. For purposes of the assessment question below, select the letter that more accurately describes you.

Question 3: Are you more of a Thinker or a Feeler? _ _ T _ or _ _ F _ ?

Fill in the first and second blanks below with your answers to Questions 1 and 2.

Now fill in the third blank with the letter that indicates your preference to Question 3:

My MBTI type: <u>E/I</u> <u>S/N</u> __ __

You now have determined 75 percent of your MBTI type.

Case Study—Jeong and Teri

Director Jeong decides he has no choice but to delegate tasks to assistant director Teri from the growing list in his iPhone. Although Jeong believes he can't count on Teri to meet his high standards, Jeong admits Teri gets the job done, if always at the last minute. Teri's "whatever" approach drives Jeong crazy.

Handing Teri a list of phone calls to return, Jeong watches over his shoulder to see how many calls Teri makes. Jeong fears the phone list will get lost in the piles on Teri's desk.

Teri claims she knows where everything is. She is chafing under Jeong's "condescending, holier than thou" attitude. How can Jeong and Teri find ways to build on each other's strengths?

Judging and perceiving

The "lifestyle" preference indicates how we prefer to conduct our lives, either in an organized, planned way (Judging) or a in a spontaneous, "go with the flow" way (Perceiving). According to MBTI data, 54.1 percent of us prefer to be organized, while 45.9 percent of us prefer to take a "why worry, be happy" approach (Myers et al. 1998, 157–58). In early childhood education, many of us would prefer to go with the flow more than a leadership position allows. We may have taught ourselves to be organized, even though our preference is to spontaneously engage with the children.

The majority of senior managers in any profession are Judgers. Improvisational theater professionals and inventors are more often Perceivers. Perceivers benefit from judgers' predictability and reliability. Judgers benefit from perceivers' easygoing, playful manner.

Judgers

Leadership strengths. Thanks to the Judgers (J), accreditation forms are completed, deadlines are met, and airplanes take off from the right runways. Judgers plan in advance. Judgers favor organization and orderliness, avoiding stress by keeping ahead of deadlines. Judgers "cross their t's and dot their i's." Their classrooms are neat, clean, and thoughtfully organized. Clear on where they stand, Judgers make decisions quickly. They take pride in accomplishing everything on their lists.

Leadership challenges. Judgers can be impatient with colleagues who need time to check out all their options. Disorganization and disarray annoy Judgers. Judgers can form opinions too quickly, before gathering all pertinent information. Judgers show up early for meetings and roll their eyes when others arrive late. Preferring decisiveness, Judgers find living with ambiguity uncomfortable. Judgers dislike surprises. Flexibility can be difficult. Perfectionism is the Judger's Achilles' heel. Judging directors often have difficulty delegating because few people will meet the high standard the Judger sets for herself.

Tips for Judger leaders

- You can learn much from living in the moment. Stretch yourself by scheduling and taking some time off.
- Delegate, step back, and *assume* the task will be accomplished, just maybe not in the way you would have done it. Your worry will not help the other person get the job done.
- Realize that unlike you, other people prefer to multitask and are comfortable juggling many balls in the air.

Communicating with Perceivers

- Learn to appreciate the creativity and playfulness of your colleagues.
- Ask a Perceiver to help you identify alternatives and options.
- Show the Perceiver you trust her to get the job done, even if she does it at the last minute.
- Allow time for exploring all possibilities, and for spontaneous changes to be made to plans.
- Incorporate lighthearted, fun activities into staff meetings.

Perceivers

Leadership strengths. Perceivers (P) prefer to keep their options open. Adept at creating alternatives, Perceivers see possibilities. Perceivers have fun at work. An easygoing work environment suits them. Perceivers bring spontaneity and humor to the workplace. They enjoy the journey, not just reaching the destination. Emergent curriculum is often the Perceiver's preferred classroom approach. Perceivers describe themselves as "human beings, not human doings."

Leadership challenges. Wanting to keep their options open, Perceivers put off making decisions. Neatness and orderliness are not a priority. Perceivers organize by piling things up; nonetheless, they know where to find things. Perceivers think meetings start when they get there; this may frustrate on-time and Judger colleagues. Perceivers can resent the up-tightness they perceive in Judgers. They often complete tasks in the eleventh hour.

Tips for Perceiver leaders

- Break assignments into manageable tasks. Set a deadline for each task. Celebrate when you complete a task early.
- Avoid surprising your colleagues when you change your plans. Give them as much notice as possible to adjust.
- Since flexibility comes more easily for you, try something different and structure a task. Making the effort will increase your empathy for judgers.
- Use your sense of humor to help your colleagues lighten up.

Communicating with Judgers

- Be clear about when you will complete a project.
- Make small, inconsequential choices more quickly than usual.
- Demonstrate your ability to complete tasks.
- Volunteer to clean up, put things away, and organize events.

Assessing yourself

▶ EXERCISE YOUR EQ   ▪   Which describes your "lifestyle" preference: Are you more organized and structured (J) or laidback and easygoing (P)? You may prefer one strongly over the other; or you may be some of both. For purposes of the assessment question below, select the letter that more accurately describes you.

Question 4: Are you more of a Judger or a Perceiver? _ _ _ J or _ _ _ P

Fill in the first three blanks below with your answers to Questions 1–3. Now fill in the last blank with the letter that indicates your preference to Question 4:

My MBTI type: E/I S/N T/F __

Which type are you?

Congratulations! You have completed all four letters of your MBTI type. Look for your four-letter type in the **MBTI Type Summary**.

For more complete descriptions of each type, go online to www.typelogic.com, or read *Type Talk at Work,* by Otto Kroeger, Janet Thuesen, and Hile Rutledge (2002). In *The Leadership Equation* (Barr & Barr 1989), you will find in-depth descriptions of each type's leadership style.

To take an abbreviated MBTI, go to www.teamtechnology.co.uk/mmdi-re/mmdi-re. htm. Upon completion of the questionnaire, you will get a description of your type. There also are MBTI professionals who can administer and evaluate a full inventory. This service is often available at a college or university career development office, or from a certified MBTI administrator.

Learning from our shadow preferences

Carl Jung noticed that in addition to our preferences, we all have a "shadow." Our shadow is the least developed part of ourselves, which we keep hidden from most people. Stress nudges us into our shadow. When we have "bad hair days," we fall into using the preferences at which we do not feel as skilled. A friendly person, under pressure, becomes withdrawn. An easygoing person becomes a taskmaster. The more we learn about our shadow side, the more accepting we can become of people who are the opposite of us.

Now that you know your MBTI preferences and type, you can identify your shadow. Write your four-letter type in uppercase letters. Underneath each letter, write the opposite MBTI letter in lowercase. For example:

ESTJ	ISFJ	ENFP	ISFP
infp	entp	istj	entj

The four letters in lowercase are your *shadow preferences*. The shadow of an ESTJ is an INFP. The shadow of an ISFJ is an ENTP. Now, go back to the descriptions of the 16 MBTI types (p. 70). Read the description for your shadow type. Use your EQ to notice your response. When you are in your shadow, do you remind yourself of someone else? Feeling "beside ourselves" is another way to describe being in our shadow (Quenk 1993).

At first we feel cranky and awkward in our shadow. To demonstrate this, sign your name on a piece of paper. Now, place the pen in your opposite hand. Sign your name again. How does that feel and look? When we are in our shadow like this, we are able to complete the task, even though we feel uncomfortable. Consider your shadow as a pathway to learning how to communicate with people who have opposite preferences from you.

MBTI Type Summary

ISTJ	ISFJ	INFJ	INTJ
"Doing What Should Be Done" Organizer • Compulsive • Private • Trustworthy • Rules 'n Regs • Practical MOST RESPONSIBLE	"A High Sense of Duty" Amiable • Works Behind the Scenes • Ready to Sacrifice • Accountable • "Doer" MOST LOYAL	"An Inspiration to Others" Reflective/Introspective • Quietly Caring • Creative • Linguistically Gifted • Psychic MOST CONTEMPLATIVE	"Everything Has Room for Improvement" Theory Based • Skeptical • "My Way" • High Need for Competency MOST INDEPENDENT
ISTP "Ready to Try Anything Once" Very Observant • Cool and Aloof • Hands-on Practicality • Ready for What Happens • Unpretentious MOST PRAGMATIC	**ISFP** "Sees Much But Shares Little" Warm and Sensitive • Unassuming • Short-Range Planner • Good Team Member • In Touch with Self and Nature MOST ARTISTIC	**INFP** "Performing Noble Service to Aid Society" Strict Personal Values • Reserved • Seeks Inner Order/Peace • Creative • Nondirective MOST IDEALISTIC	**INTP** "A Love of Problem Solving" Challenges Others to Think • Absent-Minded Professor • Competency Needs • Socially Cautious MOST CONCEPTUAL
ESTP "The Ultimate Realist" Unconventional Approach • Fun • Gregarious • Lives for Here and Now • Good at Problem Solving MOST SPONTANEOUS	**ESFP** "You Only Go Around Once in Life" Sociable • Spontaneous • Loves Surprises • Cuts Red Tape • Multi-Tasking • Quip Master MOST GENEROUS	**ENFP** "Giving Life an Extra Squeeze" People Oriented • Creative • Seeks Harmony • Life of Party • More Starts Than Finishes MOST OPTIMISTIC	**ENTP** "One Exciting Challenge after Another" Argues Both Sides of a Point • Brinksmanship • Tests Limits • Enthusiastic • New Ideas MOST INVENTIVE
ESTJ "Life's Administrator" Order and Structure • Sociable Opinionated • Results Driven Producer • Traditional MOST HARD CHARGING	**ESFJ** "Host and Hostess" Gracious • Good Interpersonal Skills • Thoughtful • Appropriate • Eager to Please MOST HARMONIZING	**ENFJ** "Smooth-Talking Persuader" Charismatic • Compassionate • Possibilities for People • Ignores the Unpleasant • Idealistic MOST PERSUASIVE	**ENTJ** "Life's Natural Leader" Visionary • Gregarious • Argumentative • Take Charge • Low Tolerance for Incompetency MOST COMMANDING

Although uncomfortable at first, an Extravert can practice meditation. An Introvert can become more at ease with public speaking. A Sensor can become more of a dreamer. A Perceiver can become more organized. A Thinker can demonstrate compassion.

Jung noted that as we embrace our lesser developed, shadow side, we discover our deeper spirituality. The more we find out about our shadow, the more open and accepting we become to different ways of being. To develop our emotional intelligence further, leaders can practice using their shadow preferences. Bad hair days can become opportunities to learn.

Leadership temperaments

The MBTI translates readily into four *temperaments* (Bates & Keirsey 1984) that will help you better understand leadership. Temperaments are our favored ways to behave. When you determined your MBTI type, you identified your temperament, as well. The four temperaments are SJ, SP, NT, and NF.

▶ EXERCISE YOUR EQ ▮ To identify your temperament, write down your MBTI four-letter type again.

Now, write down the second letter of your four-letter type (either S or N). If your letter is S, write the last letter in your type (either J or P) immediately following. If your first letter is N, write the third letter in your type (either T or F) immediately following.

Congratulations! You have identified your MBTI temperament.

Find your temperament in the chart below. Knowing your MBTI temperament's strengths and challenges increases your emotional intelligence. Pay special attention to the tips on how to grow as a leader. To read more about the four temperaments, see David Keirsey's book *Please Understand Me II* (1998).

SJ leadership style

SJ leaders are the traditionalists, the bringers of stability, order, and predictability to an organization. SJs lead with authority, instructing others what to do. SJs value hard work and loyalty, as well as a no-nonsense and "can do" attitude. SJs respect authority and exude responsibility. They are highly skilled at detailed follow through. President George Washington was an SJ.

MBTI Temperaments	
SJ Hardworking Focused Traditionalist Perfectionist Example: George Washington	**NT** Visionary Big picture, systemic approach Independent and scientific Condescending Example: Hillary Clinton
SP Problem solver Negotiator Hands on, action-oriented Avoid paper work Example: Theodore Roosevelt	**NF** Utopian thinker Change agent People first Try to rescue everyone Example: Mohanda Gandhi

© 2012 OKA, (Otto Kroeger Associates) LLC. Used with permission.

Achilles' heel

SJs expect excellence, sometimes to the point of perfectionism. Sometimes forgetting to communicate satisfaction to staff for a job well done, they may focus instead on reviewing mistakes and exhorting staff to do better. Hard workers themselves, some SJs may have little patience with others who do not embody the hard work ethic. SJs can come across like military generals.

To grow

SJs benefit from delegating and letting go of expecting perfect results. If you're an SJ, focus instead on developing your staff's strengths. Observe leaders whose "go with the flow" temperaments produce effective results. Praise and acknowledge staff efforts.

SP leadership style

The SP leader is the creative problem solver. SP leaders negotiate agreements among people with conflicting viewpoints. SPs are at their best when putting out fires. SPs are pragmatists; they thrive on activity and prefer hands-on work. They are fun to work with, easy to be with, and quick to keep the physical work environment functioning smoothly. Children are drawn to SPs' fun-loving, physical, spontaneous ways. "Rough Rider" Teddy Roosevelt was an SP. In fact, of the four temperaments, only the SP is not particularly hard on herself. Every other temperament leads to rigorous self-criticism.

Achilles' heel

If there is no fire to put out, the SP starts a fire. Inactivity is the SP's Achilles' heel, along with paperwork. SPs get bored easily when sitting still and listening to lectures. Detailed follow through is not the SPs strength.

To grow

If you're an SP, step back out of the action to notice other ways to do things. Teach colleagues how to solve problems, rather than always being the person who puts things right. SPs are often artistic, crafty people. SP leaders need to claim time to work on their own craft projects and/or to find ways to involve colleagues and families in these creative endeavors.

NT leadership style

NT leaders are the visionary logicians. An NT leader's quest is competency and mastery. NTs bring objectivity, intellectualism, and the long view to their organizations. NTs conceptualize systems to streamline work. Like SPs, NTs are pragmatic. An NT leader expects others to learn how to do things by watching the NT. NTs are rarely comfortable giving praise. Hillary Clinton is an NT.

Achilles' heel

Their preoccupation with the theoretical makes NT leaders appear aloof and condescending. NTs undervalue interpersonal dynamics. NTs judge whether others are competent enough to earn the NTs respect. NTs have little patience with socializing and team building.

To grow

NTs grow by dedicating themselves to the study and practice of emotional and social EQ. If you an NT, pay attention to how colleagues feel about their work, not just to the work itself. An NT benefits from researching and learning how to read nonverbal communication cues. Consider the rationale for developing highly functioning teams, and find ways to foster the growth of teams in your program.

NF leadership style

The NF leader is a visionary change agent. The heart's desire of the NF early childhood leader is to make the world better for children and families. NFs are utopian thinkers, idealistic and optimistic about changing things for the greater good. NFs lead by encouraging others to fulfill their potential. Unlike authoritarian SJs, NFs are egalitarian, working to bring out the best in everyone through praise and enthusiastic support. NFs are inspiring and charismatic leaders. Mohandas Gandhi was an NF.

Achilles' heel

Guilt and impossibly high ideals can wear an NF down. NFs are conflict avoidant. Confronting inappropriate behavior is difficult for the NF leader. NFs lose optimism when times are conservative and social change is unwelcome.

To grow

If you are an NF, study and practice conflict resolution and effective confrontation skills. Invoke the serenity prayer: "Grant me the serenity to accept the things I cannot change, courage to change the things I can, and wisdom to know the difference." This helps the NF stop carrying the weight of the world on her shoulders. Because NFs take a moralistic approach, they can build unlikely alliances with SJs, who also favor moralistic over pragmatic stances.

> Whatever you are by nature, keep to it; never desert your line of talent. Be what nature intended you for, and you will succeed.
> —Sydney Smith

The power of self-knowledge

Leaders must learn how to communicate with everyone, especially people who are least like them. An early childhood administrator who understands her own MBTI type, temperament, and shadow preferences is better prepared to respect and honor others' differing gifts. The MBTI helps leaders read and understand others, key emotional intelligence competencies.

Leading on purpose, making decisions anchored in core values, and understanding leadership styles empower individuals to be authentic, gifted directors. Self-knowledge, the heart of emotional intelligence, is what you need to lead an early childhood program. Jamilah knows what she wants. What about you? I hope this chapter has helped you be clearer on the difference you want to make as a leader. To paraphrase the motto of another healing profession: "Director, know thyself."

Reflection questions

1. Core values ground us as we make decisions. We can measure our decisions against our core values to ascertain if we are being true to our values. Think of a decision you need to make. Now write at least three of your core values. Next, write your purpose. Now, work through your decision. Use any process that works for you: letter of the law, spirit of the law, or "thin-slicing." Look back over your core values. Is your decision consistent with what you value? Does your decision align with your purpose? Recall another decision you have made recently. How does that decision measure up to your core values and purpose? Write a reflection paper (or record a statement) on what you are learning about your process of making decisions.
2. Put the S.M.A.R.T. method to work for you. This method turns dreams into realities. Reflect on one specific goal you would like to accomplish. For each of the S.M.A.R.T. steps, write the action you will take to reach your goal. Commit to taking the first step by no later than the end of this week. Follow the timetable you set for yourself. Share with your class, or a colleague, how being S.M.A.R.T. can help you as a leader.

3. Investigate how opposites attract. Explore your shadow preferences and type. First, read the information on each of your shadow letters. Next, read your shadow type. How do you feel as you read this information? How do you respond to people who behave like your shadow? Does your shadow behavior show up on your "bad hair days"? Shadow is the lesser known part of yourself. The more you learn about your shadow, the more comfortable you will be with others who have opposite preferences from you. Review how to communicate with your opposites. Write or record a reflection on how understanding your shadow will help you as a leader.

Team projects

1. Go to page 52, where the steps for finding our purpose are listed. Work through this process in pairs, one question at a time. At the end of the process, write down your purpose. Discuss with your classmate the degree to which your work or studies align with your purpose. Brainstorm ways in which you could change your daily activities to fit better with what you are meant to do. Some of us find we need to make career shifts in order to "lead on purpose." If you are one of these people, what are your options?

2. Teams, like individuals, exhibit MBTI preferences. Explain the MBTI to your colleagues. Invite willing team members to take the MBTI online. Ask them if they would be willing to share their MBTI results with you. Collect and tally the results. Does your team have more Extraverts than Introverts? Do more teammates prefer Sensing to Intuition? Continue to list the majority letter for each of the four preferences. The four majority letters indicate your team's preferences and type. Write down the team's four -letter type. Identify the team's shadow letters. Read up on your team's type. Reflect on how accurately (or not) each of the dominant preferences describes your team. How do your own preferences align with your team's type? Report your findings to your team.

3. In a small group, identify each person's leadership preferences, type, and temperament. Discuss the strengths and challenges of each temperament represented. What percentage of the population does your temperament represent? Discuss how your preferences and temperament help and hinder you as a leader. What steps can you take to communicate better with people who are your opposite in preference and temperament? Name five steps you can take to improve communication with team members, by using your MBTI information.

Bibliography

Barr, L., & N. Barr. 1989. *The leadership equation: Leadership, management, and the Myers-Briggs.* Austin, TX: Eakin Press.

Bates, M., & D. Keirsey. 1984. *Please understand me: Character and temperament types.* 5th ed. Del Mar, CA: Prometheus Nemesis Book Company.

Brown, J., & D. Isaacs. 2005. *The World Café: Shaping our futures through conversations that matter.* San Francisco: Berrett-Koehler.

Bryant, A. 2011. *The corner office: Indispensable and unexpected lessons from CEOs on how to lead and succeed.* New York: Henry Holt.

Carter, M. 2000, November. What do teachers need most from directors? *Child Care Exchange* pp. 98–101. Online at: http://www.childcareexchange.com/library/5013698.pdf.

Carter, M., & Curtis, D. 2010. *The visionary director: A handbook for dreaming, organizing, and improvising in your center.* 2d ed. St. Paul, MN: Redleaf Press.

Covey, S. 2004a. *The 7 habits of highly effective people.* Rev. ed. New York: Free Press.

Covey, S. 2004b. *The 8th habit: From effectiveness to greatness.* New York: Free Press.

Csikszentmihalyi, M. 1991. *Flow: The psychology of optimal experience.* New York: Harper Perennial.

Drucker, P. 1954. *The practice of management: A study of the most important function in American society.* New York: Harper & Row.

Greenleaf, R. 1970. *The servant as leader.* Published essay. www.greenleaf.org.

Jung, C.G. 1961. *Memories, dreams, reflections,* ed. A. Jaffe. New York: Vintage Books.

Keirsey, D. 1998. *Please understand me II: Temperament, character, intelligence.* Del Mar, CA: Prometheus Nemesis Book Company.

Kroeger, O., J. Thuesen, & H. Rutledge. 2002. *Type talk at work: How the 16 personality types determine your success on the job.* Rev. ed. New York: Delta.

McCaulley, M.H. 1982. *Jung's theory of psychological types and the Myers-Briggs Type Indicator.* Gainesville, FL: Center for Applications of Psychological Type.

Mellody, P., & A.W. Miller. 1989. *Breaking free: A recovery workbook for facing codependence.* San Francisco, CA: HarperOne.

Myers, I.B., & P.B. Myers. 1995. *Gifts differing: Understanding personality type.* 2d ed. Boston: Nicholas Brealey.

Myers, I.B., M.H. McCaulley, N.L. Quenk, & A.L. Hammer. 1998. *MBTI manual: A guide to the development and use of the Myers-Briggs Type Indicator.* 3d ed. Palo Alto: Consulting Psychologists Press.

Quenk, N. 1993. *Beside ourselves: Our hidden personality in everyday life.* Mountain View, CA: Consulting Psychologists Press.

Senge, P.M. 2006. *The fifth discipline: The art and practice of the learning organization.* New York: Doubleday.

Thoreau, H.D. 1854. *Walden; or, life in the woods.* Boston, MA: Ticknor and Fields.

Wheatley, M., & D. Frieze. 2011. *Walk out, walk on: A learning journey into communities daring to live the future now.* San Francisco: Berrett-Koehler.

Web Resources

The 7 Habits of Highly Effective People
www.stephencovey.com/7habits/7habits.php

ExchangeEveryDay: Free E-Newsletter
www.ccie.com/eed

How to Write Your Mission Statement
www.entrepreneur.com/management/leadership/businessstrategies/article65230.html

Personal Goal Setting
www.mindtools.com/page6.html

Setting S.M.A.R.T. Objectives
www.thepracticeofleadership.net/setting-smart-objectives

Team Technology Personality Test
www.teamtechnology.co.uk/mmdi/questionnaire

TypeLogic
www.typelogic.com

The World Café
www.theworldcafe.com/book.html

PART II

Storming

Identifying, Preventing, and Addressing Resistance to Change

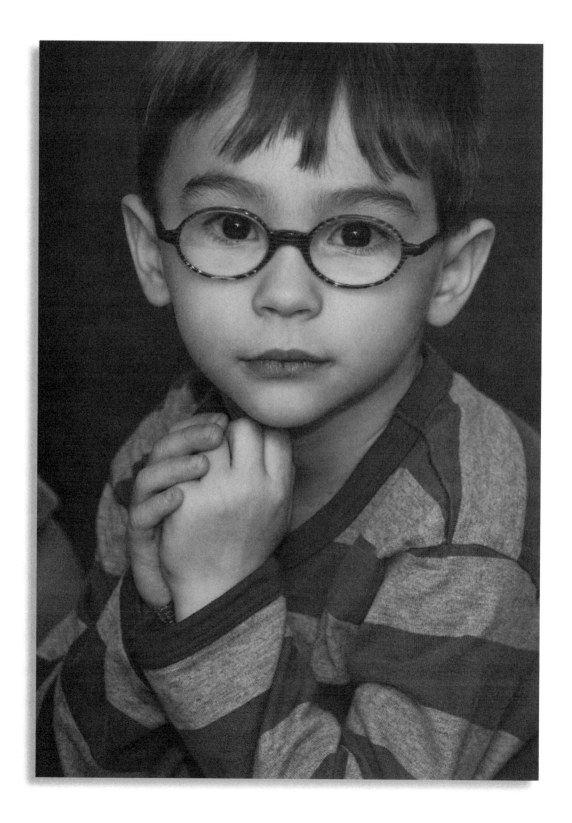

Courage is the main quality of leadership, in my opinion, no matter where it is exercised. Usually it implies some risk—especially in new undertakings.

—Walt Disney

5 Getting Started: Wherever You Are Is the Place to Begin

Case Study—Sergio

Sergio's mother names him to direct one of her centers. Sergio immediately discovers errors in voucher reporting, expenditures, and licensing reports. Some errors are serious enough to approach illegalities. Sergio's mother, the founding director, sees no problem in her record keeping. She says Sergio should just be a good son and follow her lead.

If Sergio asks you for help, what would you advise him to do?

Taking the first step **is both thrilling and** daunting for the new administrator. Although he can hardly wait for that lemony pastel infant room to be completed, he worries about infant care costs. Excitement wells up with his first opportunity to lead a center; however, his heart may still be with the children back in the classroom. Combinations of feelings such as these occur frequently as we take on new challenges. To stay grounded, use your toolkit of social and emotional intelligence skills. Allow yourself to stay energized by your purpose and the vision of the difference you want to make.

Practical tools will support you. In this chapter, checklists and guidelines will help you chart your course into early childhood administration. As each potential challenge or dilemma of getting started is discussed, remember the joys of leading on purpose can far outweigh the difficulties. You will make a difference in children's lives.

Approximately 90 percent of directors have been classroom teachers, but only one-fifth report that they always knew they wanted to become a director of a center and actively pursued the position.

—Research Notes
McCormick Center for Early Childhood Leadership

From teacher to director

Nine out of 10 directors first serve as teachers (McCormick Center 2011). Experienced in the classroom with children, teachers learn how to work with families and colleagues. By taking on additional roles, such as mentor, lead teacher, event planner, union representation, or teachers' representative on the center's board, teachers gain administrative experience. Teachers can gain additional administrative experience by helping with scheduling, overseeing classroom teacher/child ratio maintenance, updating immunization records, and filling in to "get their feet wet" as assistant director when the director takes vacation. Many teachers view administration as their opportunity to make systemic changes they cannot make by remaining in one classroom.

Nonetheless, most teachers transitioning directly to administration feel underprepared for management. Fully three-fourths of directors "report they were not prepared for the issues they encountered when they became directors" (McCormick Center 2011, 1). Dynamics shift overnight, like tectonic plates under the earth's surface. Becoming a leader changes things.

Suddenly, teachers who were your friends steal wary glances at you. Others expect special favors. Some refuse to accept your new authority. They may want you to remain one of them, a rubber stamp for their desires. Some may feel jealous and even attempt to sabotage you indirectly. Phyllis Chesler's research (2009) substantiates that most women in leadership positions face sabotage from another woman.

To prepare yourself for potential challenges, take steps to deepen your confidence and convictions before starting your new role. Teachers who become directors of existing organizations may find the checklist titled **Steps for Transitioning from Teacher to Administrator** to be useful. These steps will strengthen your credentials, help you assess your administrative talent, give you a broader perspective, and encourage you to build your external support system. As you deal effectively with each challenge to your leadership, you will gain your new team's respect and support. As your confidence grows, the team's confidence in you deepens.

Steps for Transitioning from Teacher to Administrator

- List administration functions you have performed as a teacher; identify the "transferable skills" you have gained.
- Assess your administrative strengths and shortcomings; plan how to address these shortcomings. The Myers-Briggs Type Indicator will help you.
- Ask directors, especially those who took similar paths to yours, to share their experience.
- Research how to meet your accrediting agency's and state's requirements for director credentialing.
- Enroll in early childhood administration courses through local colleges or online.
- Seek out and participate in workshops and conferences on leadership and administration.
- Read at least one article or book each week about leadership. (Check the bibliography at the end of this chapter for ideas.)
- Seek out a mentor or coach. If appropriate, ask your own director to mentor you.
- Invite trusted colleagues and friends to serve as your transition support team.

Facing and embracing resistance to new leadership

▶ EXERCISE YOUR EQ   Tanya, toddler lead teacher, is well respected by the other teachers. Tanya and Maggie, your predecessor in the position of director, did not see eye to eye. Tanya has come to expect that directors cannot be trusted to pay attention to teachers' suggestions or needs. When Maggie first introduced you to Tanya, you sensed Tanya's reluctance to connect with you. Maggie whispered to you, "Tanya is a troublemaker." However, families tell you that Tanya's reputation as a great teacher is one of the reasons they selected your school. What steps would you take to win Tanya's trust? What process would you set in motion with Maggie to ensure a productive transition of power?

To defuse the situation, you will need something more than administrative strategies, however. That something more is "political" or "street savvy" EQ to address the volatile power struggles that often heat up when leadership changes. "Excellence in people management cannot ignore these subterranean affective currents: they have real human consequences," Daniel Goleman stresses, "and they matter for people's abilities to perform at their best" (2006, 456).

Much as early childhood programs can be deeply caring environments, they are also especially susceptible to clandestine catfights. Conflicts in women's organizations traditionally are dealt with indirectly, beneath the surface (Chesler 2009). Remind yourself not to take resistance personally by saying, "It's not about me." Anyone stepping into leadership is likely to face some resistance to her authority. Change is challenging. Our neural networks struggle with newness. To be successful:

1. Hold reminders of your purpose close to your heart.

2. Knit together and utilize your internal and external support systems.

3. Introduce a process to transform power struggles into productive action.

4. Follow through on that process.

Picture an organization running smooth and clear as a mountain stream. In addition to being a "great place to work" (Bloom, Hentschel, & Bella 2010), early childhood organizations can stand at the forefront of positive social change. Face your fear about confronting problems as soon as problems arise. President Franklin Roosevelt reminded us that in times of greatest challenge, "We have nothing to fear but fear itself." Your team will thank you for your courage, although perhaps not immediately. Integrity is your reward. Settle for nothing less. Leading on purpose is liberating.

Winning over opinion leaders

To knit together your internal support system, assess first who the opinion leaders are. Opinion leaders have a following in the organization. An opinion leader's "say" influences how others think. Build strong, positive relationships with opinion leaders by connecting with each one individually, preferably off site. Take her out for coffee at a neutral site, away from peers' observing eyes, to start anew with her.

Once you have made a personal connection with opinion leaders like Tanya, you will be more able to talk over concerns with them. Listen closely to the responses as each opinion leader answers these questions for you:

1. What do you feel is important for me to understand to lead this organization effectively?

2. What else would you like me to know about the history/challenges of the organization?

3. What is your dream for the organization? What is your personal hope?

4. In what ways can I count on you to work with me in fulfilling the promise of the organization? What might get in the way of your support?

Opinion leaders' answers to these questions, both verbal and nonverbal, gush with information about whom you can trust, what difficulties need to be addressed, and how your vision aligns with others' hopes for the program. These data will give you much to build on.

Be honest with yourself about the consequences and rewards of leaving the classroom…because there are both. If you wish you were in the classroom every day, then go back to it! The truth is the job never ends (just like being a teacher), so you need to set limits that are respectful of yourself and your life outside of school. And someday, you will have to give away all those curriculum materials you store in your attic.

—**Wendy**
Director and former teacher

Yesterday is history. Tomorrow is mystery. And today? Today is a gift. That's why we call it the present.

—Babatunde Olantunji

Bam!radio
"Dealing with the Unspoken Challenges Women Educators Face"
Interview with Phyllis Chesler
Heart to Heart Conversations on Leadership
http://bamradionetwork.com

If you find resistance to your leadership, welcome it. Often, an employee of the organization harbors resentment that you were chosen and she or he was not. Look for the strengths that person can offer. Consider that person to be a candidate to become one of your strongest supporters. Let her know how you plan to help develop and use her leadership skills in return for her active support of your vision.

Be respectfully direct in telling Tanya that you expect her to come to you first when she disagrees with you. Let her know that you believe differences lead to creative solutions, whereas buried disagreements lead to work disruptions. You and Tanya, after all, are working toward the same worthy goal—quality care for children and families.

Bam!radio

"Teacher Negativity: Turning Naysayers into Hooraysayers"
Interview with Neila Connors
Heart to Heart Conversations on Leadership
http://bamradionetwork.com

I have been through many challenges as a director. What has helped me? Having at least one person you can rely on to tell you the truth, surrounding yourself with people who are willing to follow your dream and help shape it as you all go, hiring people who are committed to early childhood education and their own professional development, understanding that you can't make everything happen at once, and having an absolute ball, enjoying all the children, families, and relationships. Eating breakfast daily with 3–5-year-olds is the best!

—Lori
Early childhood program director

Anyone who proposes to do good must not expect people to roll stones out of his way, but must accept his lot calmly if they even roll a few more upon it.

—Albert Schweitzer

Problem solving with resistant staff

Work through each difference that a resistant staff member brings to you by asking him or her to:

1. Describe the nature of the problem. "Step to the side" to listen objectively for the underlying issue, while using your other EQ skills to read the emotional data.

2. Tell you what he or she needs in order to resolve this problem constructively.

3. Discuss solutions that honor the organization's mission, your vision, and, when in alignment, his or her needs.

4. Find and implement points of agreement when you can.

If an opinion leader acts in ways that sabotage your leadership, call her in immediately and use progressive discipline steps (see Chapter 8). If she fails to come to you directly to voice her concerns, call her in. Remember, courts hold insubordination as a legitimate cause for terminating an employee. The "directive supervision" process (see Chapter 9) gives you a respectful and firm step-by-step approach for holding staff accountable for unprofessional behavior.

Pay attention to cultural differences. Staff whose cultural heritage promotes saving face may not directly share concerns with you. Others may say they agree with you but secretly harbor misgivings. Many people may be uncomfortable telling you directly that they disagree with you. Take time to observe and listen to each staff member and teaching team. Use your social EQ to notice where their hopes and your vision differ. Suggest possible ways to promote alignment of employees' hopes with your vision, and ask for ideas about alternative ways to do things. When honoring individual and cultural differences, leaders grow professionally and build a team that better reflects their community.

Waiting out the transition period

Organizations are organisms. Organisms tend to reject a "foreign object" before adapting to embrace that change. Once you have taken these essential steps to clear the pathway, you can build individual and team relationships with all your staff. Remember, early childhood organizations are relational. By using EQ to build and maintain relationships, you open a clearing in which to introduce your organizational vision. Be sure to relate how your overarching vision embraces the individual missions of staff members.

Use these guidelines to clear the path relationally so that all the other organizational systems can work properly. Fiscal, physical plant, marketing, and curriculum systems all depend upon your personnel system's effectiveness. Your entry as a new leader can take time, patience, and the long view. Your transition period can feel lonely, especially in comparison with the comfort of the classroom you left behind. Keep your eyes on the prize.

Three paths to leadership

Walking the "inside path"

Insiders—people who become directors in the organizations where they already work—take the "inside path." This path has pros and cons. Insiders benefit from knowing and being known by the organization, the families, and the community. But peers sometimes resent the promotion of an insider into a management position.

To move up successfully in an organization, consider these guidelines for insiders:

- Before you accept the offer to become director, pay close attention to the hiring process. How participatory was the process? Who were other internal applicants? What was the "scuttlebutt" among the teachers during the process?

- Work with the current director to plan and hold staff meetings to outline and discuss the transition to new leadership. At that meeting, form small heterogeneous groups to bring to the surface staff's fears, hopes, and practical questions. Address directly whatever concerns emerge.

- Meet individually with former peers. Ask them to describe what they will need from you as their boss. If that question is too direct, ask instead, "When I become director, what will you miss about the way things are now? What can we do to continue to work together as a new team?"

- Be clear about and explain the difference professionally between being a boss and being a colleague. You will make decisions differently, focusing first on the needs of the organization. Friendships at work will become more professional. This does not mean that you will stop caring about each person.

Insiders who have been successful at stepping into leadership positions tell me that accompanying former peers through their discomfort in a professional way helps confirm your leadership.

Taking the "outside path"

Being an outsider brings another set of opportunities and challenges. You may have heard the adage, "The devil you know is better than the devil you don't know." Like clans, organizations tend to favor insiders and suspect outsiders. Again, a "foreign body" may have to endure an uncomfortable initiation process before the clan adapts to the new leader. Initiation rites usually involve testing and some discomfort. Patience, difficult as that virtue can be to come by, sustains outsiders most. Keep the long view while waiting out the adaptation process.

Being an outsider feels painful, as does any experience of rejection or abandonment. Call on your external support network. As your feelings and frustrations emerge, share them with trusted colleagues. At the same time, be proactive. Your staff may be grieving the loss of their former director, and this emotion can take the face of anger as well as sadness. Connect with one person at a time. Word about your integrity will begin to spread.

Insider Susan describes her transition in this way: "Meeting continuously with board members was invaluable. Having the support of the board helped me through what might have been a lonely transition period. Keeping my sense of humor and letting others know I could laugh at my own mistakes also eased the tension. It took three years before my leadership was fully accepted."

Founder's syndrome

Founders, like parents, stamp organizations with personal patterns and expectations. The founder's vision, identity, and style form the organization's vision, identity, and style. Replacing a founder can be one of the prickliest pathways to leadership.

Early childhood programs usually spring like lilac buds from the stem of one person's dream. Creating a promising new program requires a deeply felt life passion. The creator of the program becomes the founding director. This founder, acting like the mom or dad of the organization, perceives the program to be "my baby." Original staff members feel more like family members than employees. Fierce loyalties form. Memories of the good old days when everyone worked tirelessly creating the organization evoke wistful expressions and damp eyes. An "inside" group, with strong attachments, forms. Anyone not involved in the founding of the organization can feel like an outsider.

When you take a director position replacing the program's founder, you may experience a pattern of behaviors, expectations, and events described as "founder's syndrome." In this situation, the departing director's style has firmly established expectations, written and unwritten, about the way the next administrator should function. Founder's syndrome can be a setup for failure. No subsequent leader can be a founding director. Saying goodbye to the founder can be disruptive for staff. Employees may feel they are losing a family member and, in particular, a caring parent. Grieving for their loss is essential. The departing director can do much to clear the pathway for her replacement by creating rituals and holding forums with the staff for closure and moving on.

Should you accept a position in which you follow a founder, you will find these pointers useful:

• Observe organizational dynamics while the founder is still director.

• Assess whether your personal style and vision align with the founder's style and vision. Your new vision must closely align with the founder's vision to be acceptable to staff.

• Dialogue with the founder about activities she plans to ease her departure.

• Ascertain what ongoing relationship the founder wants to have with you and the center. Be clear on how much contact you feel is appropriate.

• Create activities with the founder, including staff, family, community, and team meetings that will signal the change in leadership.

• Acknowledge that your leadership of the organization will initiate a different but essential phase of organizational life.

Stages of organizational development

As you step into leadership, whatever the pathway, an understanding of organizational dynamics will be a helpful EQ tool. Here, we look at two theories of an organization's evolution.

Forming, storming, norming, and performing

Bruce Tuckman proposes that organizations, from classroom teams to families to early childhood programs, progress through predictable stages. Tuckman identified the stages as *forming*, *storming*, *norming*, and *performing* (1965). Each team or program in which you participate, in one way or another, works through similar dynamics. Leaders can gain perspective on the "growing pains" of their organization by identifying its current phase and guiding the organization on to the next phase. Understanding the stages of organizational development is a useful social EQ tool for directors.

Forming

In this "honeymoon" period, everyone is at his or her best—looking good, feeling hopeful, and expecting the best. Team teachers greet one another, eager to share their dreams and ideas for the children.

Storming

When the honeymoon is over, all those little things that seemed so charming before begin to bother us. Staff who may have smiled when welcoming a new director, return to "business as usual," resisting any changes. In organizational terms, certain predictable dynamics need to be resolved to free team members to move on. They include:

• Leadership (who is in charge)

• Task (what our work is)

• Ground rules (clear, written expectations for working together, especially how decisions will be made and by whom)

• Membership (who is on the team, and who is not)

• Time frame for accomplishing the task (goals and measurable objectives)

Norming

The resolutions agreed on in the storming phase now are put in place as the norms of the organization. Expectations about who does what become clear.

Performing

With systems in place and problems addressed, everyone is ready to get down to doing the work of the organization.

Re-forming

In reality, a fifth stage occurs: re-forming. When new issues pop up, new people are hired, or changes to policies or practices are proposed, the organization can return to the beginning stage. The team is re-formed with fresh players; new challenges can bring on thunderclouds and ice storms; and the same list of issues needs to be resolved before the new group can function effectively.

> **Bam!radio**
> "Dealing with the Death of a School or School Program"
> Interview with Debra Renetta Sullivan
> *Heart to Heart Conversations on Leadership*
> http://bamradionetwork.com

Adjourning

Some years later, Tuckman and Jensen (1977) added another likely phase: adjourning. Not every team, partnership, or program is meant to last. When a committee finishes its work, the committee disbands. As new teachers are hired, teaching teams change. Directors move on. In some cases, schools and programs close down. Adjourning is similar to re-forming in that a new phase takes place. However, adjourning is the final phase in the life of some organizations. As with any change, leaders need to pay attention to the feelings of individuals and the mood of the whole organization to better guide them through the transitions.

▶ EXERCISE YOUR EQ ▨   Reflect on a long-term friendship, relationship, or team you have been part of in the context of the stages above. Did you experience the honeymoon? How did you address the storming times? Which stage are you in now?

Initiation and administration

Here is a more descriptive take on how organizations evolve through the forming, storming, and norming stages. It provides insights about a leader's job during these periods (Greiner 1998).

Beginning organizations will grow through initiation and administration. *Initiation* is another way to describe the forming stage or honeymoon stage. It is followed by the *administration* phase, which covers what must happen in order for the organization to flourish in the long run, after the honeymoon is over. As you can imagine, not all organizations survive to reach the administration phase when a new director replaces the founder/director. Some organizations collapse when the founder departs.

Initiation phase

The founding stage is the birth of the organization. This initial phase is characterized by high energy, strong feelings of commitment, and role fluidity. Everyone is caught up in the excitement of creating something new. The founder's words and spontaneous actions become the living core of the organization. Staff pitch in to perform necessary functions, and roles and responsibilities are uncharted. Procedures and policies, forms, and job descriptions are created as needed. Decision-making and problem-solving processes are worked out on the spot. The initiation phase suits a visionary, flexible, and dynamic leader. Staff members often report that they feel like part of the founder's family.

Administrative phase

Stabilizing the organization for ongoing survival after the founder's departure is essential. This is the "cleanup" phase for the organization. Every important task that was done spontaneously now must be set down in writing. Policies and procedures need to be codified. Job descriptions are written. Staff and parent handbooks are created or significantly rewritten. Meeting schedules with agendas are set well in advance. A chain of command replaces ad hoc (or on-the-spot) decision making. The administrative phase best suits a leader who enjoys stability, predictability, and structure.

Your knowledge of organizational development dynamics will serve you well as a leader. By understanding the predictable stages of any group or organization's growing pains, you can offer the light of perspective as well as practical tools for moving on more gracefully to the next phase.

With these principles in mind, let's look at additional pathways into leadership.

We are family: Becoming the director of a family organization

Directors who take over a family-run organization face another set of concerns when getting started. Have you noticed the number of sisters and brothers, aunts and uncles, cousins and in-laws, who work for the same early childhood organization? Families often employ people they know best and trust most. Stepping up from family member to director of a family-run business presents its own set of opportunities and challenges.

Family succession planning, intended to keep the business "in the family," can work. What makes one family succession plan work when others fail? Most families, as human systems, have functional and dysfunctional characteristics. Dysfunctions

The job of the new director in a family enterprise is to build upon the functional and address and/or diminish less functional family dynamics.

can carry over into the program and undermine its quality and day-to-day operations. By emphasizing professionalism, a new director can focus the family organization on enhancing quality.

Tips for taking leadership in a family organization

- Begin by inviting everyone to a family business meeting.

- Bring in an outside facilitator to keep discussions productive.

- Ask participants to reflect on these questions: "What are the organization's strong points to build on? What are the ways in which we need to reinvent ourselves?" Go around the circle, inviting each family member to share his or her experience.

- Use your EQ to "listen" for what is unsaid as well as what is verbalized. Whose contribution commands the greatest attention? Chances are good that the family has one or two members whose opinions matter most. Your job is to work with that person(s) to ensure the optimal transition of leadership to you. If you use the services of a facilitator, be sure to ask for that person's observations and recommendations.

- Discuss professionalism with family members. How can objectivity and fairness be maintained when making decisions? If family meetings are not part of the program's culture, meet individually and follow similar processes.

- Finally, pay attention to "insider versus outsider" dynamics. Nonfamily employees may feel like outsiders. Meet individually with employees to discuss their hopes and goals for the organization and for themselves. Honor legitimate hopes by incorporating them in the organization's evolving mission. Mentor promising staff. Introduce an employee evaluation system and apply it consistently to everyone.

Above all, keep a sense of humor. Humor brings perspective and relief to sticky family situations.

Founding directors: Creating a child care organization

Each year, a small but dedicated number of my students envision opening their own centers. This trend is reflected nationwide. If you become one of those dedicated founders, the **Checklist for Starting Up a Program** can guide your steps. Remember, you will not have to reinvent the wheel. Benefit from the experience of others who have taken the same path. They would want you to stand on their shoulders.

Every new director can benefit from knowing the bases that must be covered to create programs. Not all founders have had classroom teaching experience. Founding directors often leave behind another career to follow the dream of starting their own business. Retailers, accountants, parents, attorneys, financial planners, and musicians have all founded early childhood programs. Many skills are transferable to early childhood.

> All three of my sisters are on my teaching staff. We work pretty well together because we all have a sense of humor. Sometimes, though, I think I am harder on them than I am on my other teachers. I do this because I don't want anyone to feel I am showing family favoritism. My sisters let me know when I do this!
>
> —**Theresa**
> Program director

> You have to know your mission, and believe in that mission. That is the most important thing.
>
> —**Gwen**
> Program founder and director (33 years)

Checklist for Starting Up a Program

- Ask yourself, "What is my dream?" Envision your center after 5, 10, and 25 years of operation.
- Contact your state licensing department and legislators for information, regulations, and help.
- Assess the need. How would your center complement current child care programs in the community? Ask your local resource and referral (R&R) agency and other directors, "What needs are unmet?"
- Meet with your local small business association; use their service for setting up new organizations.
- Study accreditation standards.
- Work with a trusted real estate agent. Assess possible sites to construct, upgrade, or utilize.
- Decide, with an attorney's help, what "legal entity" is best for your purposes.
- Create your business plan.
- Seek financing. Which alternative is best for you?
- Join your local chamber of commerce. Ask for assistance, especially in marketing and network building.

Types of early childhood programs

Creators of early childhood programs can choose from a variety of organization types, from nonprofit program to franchised center. Each of these types has been formalized as a legal entity. What does *legal entity* mean? The term *entity* can indicate a person, an organization, or a company set up in order to act as a business; it can enter into contractual agreements (such as renting a site or accepting vouchers), and it can be sued for its actions. Forming a legal entity sets a useful boundary between the personal and professional realms.

Over the years, different forms of child care programs have been (and will continue to be) created. Each type of entity differs from the others. Each legal entity must meet a set of standards developed especially for it.

Our government regulates businesses to ensure that essential public safety standards are met. Your local small business association can help you study your options while you decide what type of organization best fits your goals. Work with an attorney to draw up and file legal forms necessary for the type of program you choose.

In considering your options, ask yourself, do you want to:

1. Undertake the venture by yourself or partner with others?

2. Found your own program or be part of an established program (for example, a franchised corporation)?

3. Report to a board of directors?

4. Sell stock, make annual reports, and hold meetings with shareholders?

5. Qualify for government grants?

Your answers to these questions indicate the type of legal business entity that will fit you best. Descriptions of options follow.

Sole proprietorship

If you create your own program and have responsibility for making all decisions, you are the program's *sole proprietor*. This is the equivalent of going solo as a businessperson. The title "proprietor" signals that you own the business. You do not need to form a board of directors, nor must you accommodate the requirements of a larger, sponsoring agency. Sole proprietors appreciate the freedom to design their program to align with their personal vision. People who like to work without a boss will be happiest as sole proprietors.

Because a sole proprietorship is a business, you must comply with local, state, and federal laws and requirements for such a business. Legal forms must be completed and filed with certain agencies. A sole proprietor has the right to name her organization whatever she likes—that is, after checking first to make sure that name is not already being used. Otherwise, she may be accused of *trademark infringement,* meaning using a name that has been registered to another business. You can contact your small business association and/or attorney for guidance on these matters.

▶ EXERCISE YOUR EQ   ▦   Consider how trademark law could affect Jamilah in the Chapter 3 case study on the opening page. If Jamilah fears that another center may already be named "Jamilah's Neighborhood" before she opens her program, what steps does she need to take?

Sole proprietors may face the challenge of isolation. Independent owners often long for more contact with peers. Meeting other director/owners at conferences and workshops can provide a community of peers. Forming an owner/director support group with other directors can end isolation, too. While a sole proprietor owns his or her program, this individual does not necessarily serve as its director. Owners often hire a director who reports to them. The owner-director relationship works best when job descriptions and boundaries are clear. Otherwise, staff may be confused about who is in charge.

Partnerships

If you do not wish to venture alone into founding a center, consider joining forces with another compatible person (or persons). Two or more people together can form a legal entity called a *partnership*. Partnerships form when people develop a program together or when one person alone cannot afford the costs of setting up the program.

Partners have choices about who holds the most responsibility, both financial and administrative. Some partners split everything equally. Imagine three teachers who want to collaborate, pool resources, and start a new center. They could each be responsible for 33 percent of the partnership they create.

Partners can also designate differing financial interests in the business. Three partners might decide, for example, that one partner will own 60 percent of the center and the other two will own 20 percent each. Another option is having a *silent partner*. Silent partners invest financially, without requiring a voice in the everyday running of the program. Family members often serve as silent partners, providing seed money to get a new program under way.

Franchised centers

If you file your income taxes with the help of a local branch of a national tax preparation service, you are familiar with franchises. Fast food restaurants are often franchises. At a *franchise,* customers can expect consistent service at each location.

An early childhood organization can franchise its program, including its physical design, curriculum design, mission, mottos, and staff and parent handbooks. Others can purchase a franchise and all that comes with it. The purchaser must legally meet and adhere to the practices and standards of the original organization. Additionally, the purchaser of the franchise pays a percentage of his gross profits to the original organization.

Franchising works best for a well-established organization ready to branch out over a greater geographical area. Maintaining quality at each new franchise can be a challenge.

Corporations

Forming corporations can be especially complex due to the challenges of meeting numerous standards. Founding a corporation requires administrators to complete and file articles of incorporation. Bylaws, the rules an organization adheres to, must also be filed with the secretary of state's office. Corporations are required to form a board of directors, with clearly written responsibilities for oversight (making sure everything is done properly) of the program.

Instead of individual owners or partners, corporations have shareholders. A shareholder owns a share in the profits of the corporation, and shareholders elect directors to run the corporation. These directors are not the same as the center directors. Corporate directors select members for the board of trustees, the group of people who are vested with oversight of the organization. Directors may be personally liable for corporate actions and can be sued. If you are thinking of establishing a corporate legal entity, discuss your plans with directors of existing corporate child care centers and learn from their experiences.

Annually, Roger Neugebauer of *Exchange, the Early Childhood Leaders' Magazine* lists the largest corporate early childhood programs. Bright Horizons Family Solutions and La Petite Academy consistently are in the top five corporate programs.

Nonprofits

Nonprofit centers can make a profit! However, nonprofits are required to use their profits to meet organizational goals. For example, imagine that St. Bartelemeo Family Service System brings in more money than it spends. That extra income must be used directly to fund St. Bartelemeo's programs. Teacher bonuses, classroom books or equipment, and expansion to new sites are some examples of where nonprofit early childhood programs place their profits. A board of directors governs and oversees the organization's work.

Examples of nonprofits include:

• Agency-sponsored programs. For example, community agencies such as faith-based groups (St. Bartelemeo) and community service agencies such as CAPs (community action programs).

• Individually sponsored programs. These organizations rely on grant funding and serve the "greater good." An example of this is Project Hope in Dorchester, Massachusetts. Project Hope serves children and families without homes.

Nonprofits are also known as "501c3s," after the part of the federal tax code that sets compliance standards for nonprofits to follow. Applying for and being approved as a 501c3 organization allows you to apply for grants available only to nonprofits.

For profit or nonprofit?

Profit-making organizations aim to do just that—make a profit. If a for-profit organization has $10,000 left over after paying its bills at the end of the fiscal year, that money may be distributed to its owners/shareholders. However, just as often it would be reinvested in the business. Upgrade the playground? Add on an infant room? Or do shareholders take their share of the $10,000 as a bonus?

Stereotyping nonprofits and for-profits is unproductive. For-profits are not "only out for themselves, dedicated only to the bottom line." In fact, for-profits often give back to their communities. Bright Horizons Family Solutions, for example, funds programs to improve quality in targeted areas. Conversely, nonprofits are not "poorly run, bleeding heart" organizations. Nonprofits use sound business practices and can have effective leaders. Both nonprofit and for-profit early childhood programs may have a mission for the greater good.

Are you ready?

Getting started as a new leader means making practical choices while being uplifted by following your dream. Winston Churchill, who led Great Britain through the perils of a world war, advised: "The pessimist sees difficulty in every opportunity. The optimist sees the opportunity in every difficulty." Brain research (Kliff 2007) reaffirms the power of optimism. Where will your optimism take you on your journey toward leadership?

Reflection questions

1. Considering all the pathways to leadership in early childhood and school-age programs, what was or is likely to be your pathway? Describe in a written or recorded reflection what is most (a) challenging, (b) encouraging, and (c) special about your process.

2. Reflect on your leadership style, which you learned about by studying the Myers-Briggs Type Indicator in Chapter 4. Identify ways in which your leadership style will help you get started as a leader. What steps are likely to be the most challenging for you? How might you use the tips for communicating with people of opposite preferences as you picture yourself building relationships with new team members? Write about your reflections on how your knowledge of your Myers-Briggs leadership style can help you get started as a leader.

3. Laws and regulations can be difficult to put into plain language. Review website literature and small business association booklets. Write 3–5 pages explaining in everyday language (a) the different types of organizations or (b) tips on how to choose the legal entity that is best for you.

Team projects

1. Organize with others into small affinity groups, based on which pathway to leadership you have taken or expect to take. Review the section of this chapter that applies directly to your path. Meet with your small-group members to research and discuss common problems and resources available to you. Prepare and present a summary of your findings to the other groups. As you listen to their presentations, look for similarities and differences.

2. To find out more about your entry into leadership, create (with your group) a questionnaire to use to interview current directors. What would you like to find out about their entry into leadership? Then conduct at least one interview apiece. Summarize and report your findings to the group.

3. Discuss either founder's syndrome or family-run program dynamics. Which of these presents more difficulties in your estimation? Create a case study that captures these special situations. Share the case study with your classmates/colleagues, and facilitate a discussion of possible solutions. Compare your case with Sergio's situation (Chapter 5 opening page). Use the NAEYC Code of Ethical Conduct (www.naeyc.org/positionstatements/ethical_conduct) or the National Association of Child Care Professionals Code of Ethics (www.naccp.org/displaycommon. cfm:an=1&subarticlenbr=287) in your presentation.

4. Shakespeare said, "Uneasy is the head that wears the crown." Resistance to change, especially a change in leadership, can be fierce. Research, discuss, write, and prepare a coaching session or video for potential new directors on how to effectively deal with resistance to new leadership. Take into account resistance from within yourself as well as from outside individuals and constituencies. Share your presentation.

Bibliography

Bloom, P.J., A. Hentschel, & J. Bella. 2010. *A great place to work: Creating a healthy organizational climate.* Rev. ed. Lake Forest, IL: New Horizons.

Brinkman, R., & R. Kirschner. 2002. *Dealing with people you can't stand: How to bring out the best in people at their worst.* 2nd ed. New York: McGraw-Hill.

Carter, R.T. 2000. *Addressing cultural issues in organizations: Beyond the corporate context.* Thousand Oaks, CA: Sage Publications.

Chesler, P. 2009. *Woman's inhumanity to woman.* Rev. ed. Chicago: Lawrence Hill Books.

Click, P., & K.A. Karkos. 2011. *Administration of programs for young children.* 8th ed. Belmont, CA: Wadsworth, Cengage Learning.

Goleman, D. 2004. *Destructive emotions: How can we overcome them? A scientific dialogue with the Dalai Lama.* New York: Bantam Dell.

Goleman, D. 2006. *Social intelligence: The new science of human relationships.* New York: Bantam Dell.

Gonzalez-Mena, J. 2001. *Multicultural issues in child care.* 3d ed. Mountain View, CA: Mayfield Publishing.

Greiner, L. 1998. Evolution and revolution as organizations grow. *Harvard Business Review* (May). http://hbr.org/1998/0aa5/evolution-and-revolution-as-organizations-grow/ar/1.

Jordan, J.V., ed. 1997. *Women's growth in diversity: More writings from the Stone Center.* New York: Guilford Press.

Kliff, S. 2007. This is your brain on optimism. *Newsweek* (October 23). www.thedailybeast.com/newsweek/2007/10/3/this-is-your-brain-on-optimism.html.

McCormick Center for Early Childhood Leadership. 2011. Research Notes. http://cecl.nl.edu/research/rn.htm.

Neugebauer, R., & D. Hartzell. 2011. "For profit organizations showing signs of turnaround." *Exchange: The Early Childhood Leaders' Magazine* 197. https://secure.ccie.com/resources/view_article.php?article_id=5019729.

Sciarra, D.J., A.G. Dorsey, & E. Lynch. 2010. *Developing and administering a child care and education program.* 7th ed. Belmont, CA: Wadsworth, Cengage Learning.

Shapiro, A. 2010. *Creating contagious commitment to change: Applying the tipping point to organizational change.* 2nd ed. Hillsborough, NC: Strategy Perspective.

Shoemaker, C.J. 2000. *Leadership and management of programs for young children.* 2nd ed. Upper Saddle River, NJ: Merrill.

Tuckman, B.W. 1965. Developmental sequence in small groups. *Psychological Bulletin* 63: 384–99. www.mph.ufl.edu/events/seminar/Tuckman1965DevelopmentalSequence.pdf.

Tuckman, B.W., & M.A. Jensen. 1977. Stages of small-group development revisited. *Group & Organization Studies* 2: 419–27.

Web resources

Creating the Future
www.creatingthefuture.org
Forming, Storming, Norming, and Performing
www.mindtools.com/pages/article/newLDR_86.htm
Foundation Group
www.501c3.org
Free Management Library
www.managementhelp.org
Internal Revenue Service: Tax Information for Charities and Nonprofits
www.irs.gov/charities
InvestorWords Investing Glossary
www.investorwords.com
The 'Lectric Law Library
www.lectlaw.com
LegalZoom
www.legalzoom.com
Surviving Founder's Syndrome
www.ccfbest.org/management/survivingfounder.htm
Thompson & Thompson Transactional Law Firm
www.t-tlaw.com

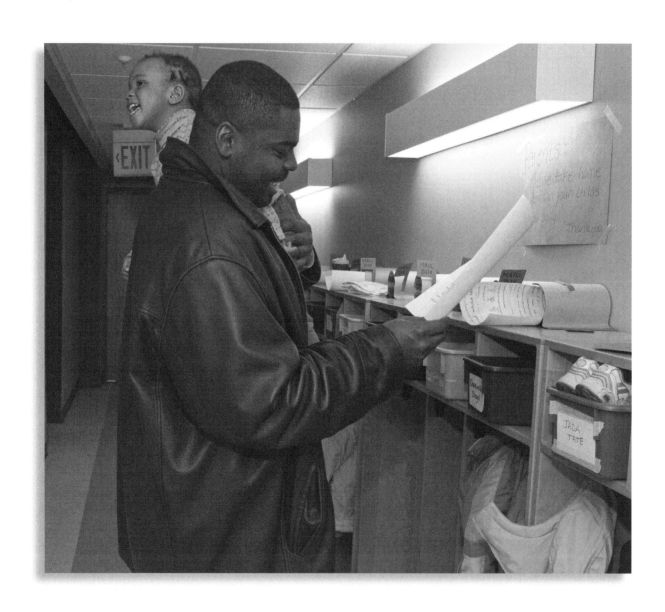

If you don't like something, change it. If you can't change it, change your attitude. Don't complain.

—Maya Angelou

Human growth is full of slides backward as well as leaps forward and is sure to include times of withdrawal, opposition, and anger, just as it encompasses tears as well as laughter.

—Fred Rogers

6 Partnering with Change

Case Study—Amalie

New director Amalie bustles with hundreds of new ideas to enliven Best Friends Preschool. Amalie's heart beats hopefully as she walks into her first staff meeting. "We'll bring in an exciting new curriculum. Research shows children love it," Amalie bubbles.

Looking expectantly around the room for approval, Amalie is shocked to find teachers stiff and still as gravestones. Amalie huffs to herself, "What is their problem?"

Change is many things. For the person who

initiates change, like Amalie, change is energizing. To the person who feels at the mercy of change, change can be threatening and unwelcome. Our attitude toward change derives from the amount of choice we feel we have to create, accept, reject, or modify the change.

We are exposed to change every moment, despite our yearning for stability and security. Heraclites, a Greek philosopher, observed, "You can never place your foot in the same river twice." Rushing river water that flows over our toes can never be called back. Each day as we arrive at work, something changes. A spat over the treasured *Tyrannosaurus rex* toy erupts between preschool pals. Rain splatters drying finger paintings on the playground picnic table. The cook asks to go on maternity leave.

Change is the status quo.
—Gwen Morgan

The river keeps on flowing beyond our view. This chapter provides helpful models for partnering with inevitable changes.

The brain and change

Humans resist change because our brain pathways are wired to click into hyperalert when something new occurs. An innovation may be a threat. Adrenaline revs up our systems in response. We jump from at ease to tensed and itchy discomfort. Adrenaline junkies such as race car drivers and skydivers experience the heart-pounding adrenaline surge as pleasurable. For the rest of us, the physiological effects of change are less appealing. Self-preservation is an ancient motivation: "If it ain't broke, don't fix it."

Anticipate the good so that you may enjoy it.
—Ethiopian proverb

To experience this resistance dynamic for yourself, clasp your hands together like you usually do. This feels "normal." Now, clasp your hands in a different way, lacing your fingers in a new pattern. How does that feel? If even a small change in how we join our hands together feels uncomfortable, imagine our body's reaction to an important change.

Our brain pathways settle into routine patterns. Changes to those patterns can feel abnormal. New brain pathways need to be established for each new pattern. Time and practice are needed for the new pattern to feel as comfortable as the old. Have you moved to a new residence or rearranged your room lately? Do you recall how conscious and alert you needed to be to adapt? Your brain was establishing new connections.

Definitions of change

Change, the noun, according to *Merriam-Webster's Collegiate Dictionary*, is:

a. Alteration

b. Transformation

c. Substitution

d. Passage

e. Menopause

As a verb, *Webster's* defines *change* as "to switch, transfer … to break." Which of these definitions of *change* gets your attention?

For me, "break" and "menopause" call up physical reactions. Ouch! I broke both of my wrists as a child: I broke my left wrist falling from a schoolyard swing; my right wrist in a wrestling match with my best friend's brother. Both wrists now warn me when rain clouds are on the horizon.

Menopause? Oh my! Women talk about "the change" with knowing glances. Have you heard of the Broadway show *Menopause, the Musical*? Writer/producer Jeanie Linders transforms an inevitable (and often disorienting) female life transition into a bevy of humorous songs and dances. Linders is rumored to have written the show "after a bottle of wine and a hot flash." Linders's approach to unbidden change reminds me of the power of humor to bring healing perspective.

Clearly, change, while inevitable, can also be uncomfortable. This dynamic leaves us again holding two opposites in our hands at once. On the one hand, change happens. On the other hand, we resist change. How can leaders, conscious of this paradox, flow with or initiate change in a helpful, functional, useful manner? Are you ready? Let's take a look.

Who is the boss of change?

When I was in elementary school, my mom cautioned me, "The only things you can be sure of on earth are death and taxes." As I looked around, I saw a neighborhood full of predictability. Hadn't our elm tree stood straight as a candle for a hundred years? Didn't snow blanket our hillsides every December so I could sled down at breakneck speeds? Mom couldn't prove that purple lilacs adorning Margery Sage's farm wouldn't bloom every May, or that hot fudge sundaes weren't the yummiest dessert ever. Brownie Scouts "flew up" to become real Girl Scouts. Each September, I regretfully said goodbye to blackberry-picking summer days to trudge my mile to school. As far as my young eyes could see, death and taxes didn't live on my street.

My mom, of course, had a point. My magical-thinking child's mind was not ready to accommodate the concept that just about everything changes. As my colleague Gwen Morgan notes, "Change is the status quo." Even as a young adult, I was ready to make a long list in response to a well-intentioned teacher question: "What do you have control over?" As I ponder that question today, I can place only one thing on my list. How would you answer that teacher's question?

Much as I may like to think I can control outcomes, events, and, I admit, other folks' behavior, I have come to understand that the only thing I can control is my own attitude. I admire author Viktor Frankl. Despite overwhelming agonies as a concentration camp prisoner during World War II, Frankl remained clear about his freedom. He found hope within himself, even though he lacked control over anyone or anything outside of him.

Theologian Rheinhold Niebuhr, who visited war-ravaged Europe, allegedly penned the words, "God, grant me the serenity to accept the things I cannot change, the courage to change the things I can, and the wisdom to know the difference." Twelve-step addiction recovery programs, such as AA (Alcoholics Anonymous) and CODA (Codependents Anonymous), embrace this "serenity prayer" as a daily reminder to keep perspective when problems knock on our door.

▶ EXERCISE YOUR EQ   Think about situations you have tried to change or wish you could change. Write these situations down. Next, consider your list in the context of the serenity prayer: What do you have the power to change, and what lies beyond your power?

Break down Niebuhr's words to find useful leadership insights regarding your "change" list:

• **Serenity** is mine when I let go of thinking I can control others (people, places, or things). These are all "things I cannot change."

• **Courage** is the virtue I need to change my thoughts, attitudes, and actions. The "things I can change" lie within me. My power derives more from letting go of attempting to control than from holding on to the belief that I can control others.

• **Wisdom** evolves from learning to discern what I have the power to change and what I need to let go of trying to "fix," beyond myself.

For managers, directors, and leaders of any sort, control seems essential to authority. They must control budget spending, complete tasks on time, comply with licensing regulations, and maintain positive relationships with boards of directors. If you take a closer look at these functions, however, you will discover that what you can control is *your* action, not others' reactions.

The last of the human freedoms is the ability to choose one's attitude in any given set of circumstances.

—**Viktor Frankl**
Man's Search for Meaning

For example, a director may work hard to build productive relationships with board members; however, she cannot control a board member's response to the director's efforts. Similarly, a director may think he maintains tight control over spending, until the March winds blow down a tree onto the school van. *Crash* goes the transportation budget! The director had placed just enough funds in the account to anticipate rising gasoline costs.

In reality, a manager's control rests, curiously, in acknowledging what is beyond his or her control.

Leadership and control

Who is the boss of change? Back we come to the challenge of leadership: holding opposite realities in each hand. On the one hand, directors are responsible for the budget. On the other hand, they cannot fully predict expenses. On the one hand, directors think they have all the bases covered should the state licensor drop by. Over many years, licensors and directors can develop a strong and collegial working relationship. On the other hand, things change instantly when a new licensor arrives unexpectedly, with an emphasis different from her predecessor's. *Crash* goes the expectation!

Many directors tell me that when they began as administrators they believed, "If I work hard enough and long enough, I will finally get everything in order and under control." New directors work diligently, checking one task after another off their "to do" list. But like mushrooms after a storm, one unanticipated challenge after another pops up. The lead toddler teacher resigns the first week of school; energy costs go through the roof; reaccreditation standards change; cicadas devour luscious leaves on the trees shading the playground.

Andi Genser said of her early days as director, "The hardest and most important lesson for me to learn as a director is that the challenges never end. I went into the position thinking I would work on everything until it got resolved. Eventually, my program would be problem free. I learned to become comfortable with the fact that a new challenge presents itself all the time." [See **Challenges That Come with Change**.]

Here is a helpful principle to keep in mind: "Someone else's action does not have to predict my response" (the Dalai Lama, as quoted in *Life's Journeys According to Mister Rogers* [Rogers 2005, 6]). If a frantic parent loses his temper and yells at a teacher, does the teacher have to yell back? Despite how upsetting the parent's behavior may be, the teacher can choose a professional response. Remember the amygdala hijack in Chapter 2? Adrenaline may flow through our veins, causing us to feel out of control in the moment. Nonetheless, we can choose to wait out that intense, heart-stopping moment before taking action we might regret. In this way, we can be the "boss of change."

Challenges That Come with Change

1. Change is constant.
2. Change happens whether I am ready or not.
3. The only control I have in the face of change is to choose my own attitude and actions.

Knowing when and how to "Focus on Yourself"

"Keep the focus on yourself" may sound selfish. The phrase "it's all about me" signals immaturity. In the survival stage of staff development, for example, teachers cannot see beyond their own needs (see the section **Stages of Organizational Development**, p. 84, in Chapter 5). Imagine a novice teacher who frets so much about preparing for tomor-

---

Walk on the rainbow trail…
Walk on a trail of song…
And all around you will be beauty…

—Navaho song

Keep what is worth saving, and with a breath of kindness, blow the rest away.

—Dinah Mulock Craik

A leader's work is never done. Putting out a fire, reaching a summit, slaying a monster only clears the way for the next and greater challenge, be it organizational or personal.

—Don Moyer
Harvard Business Review

row that he cannot pay attention to parents with questions about their child's day. At that stage, for that teacher, "it's all about me" rings true.

Even directors can get stuck in "it's all about me" thinking. Consider a director who gets tangled up in the fear of confronting staff members who gossip. She cannot see beyond her own fear. Meanwhile, the gossipers, unchecked, spread destructive, untrue rumors. Self-centered "it's all about me" thinking can cause an individual to be unaware of what's going on around her and rob her of perspective. She cannot see her responsibility to address negative behavior if she cannot see beyond her own worries.

A director in New Jersey once told me, "Guilt is a selfish emotion." I was stunned! I always thought feeling guilty was the first step toward accepting responsibility for what I need to change. For that director, prolonged guilty feelings block her from taking action to make changes for the better. Guilt is "all about me" and is paralyzing, in that case. I came to see her point. As Wayne Dyer, author and motivational speaker, observes, "Worry is an attempt to control the future. Guilt is an attempt to control the past." Perspective is a director's best friend.

When it comes to change, "it's all about me" can signal a more positive, mature perspective. Keeping the focus on ourselves, on our power to change the things we can, is an asset. The director who waits for other people to change can wait a lifetime. The director who keeps the focus on herself and the action she can take is the director who makes a difference. Using energy to worry about what others will or won't do wastes precious time. As one of my employees observed, "That's like trying to push a rope." Keep the focus on what you can change. Let go of trying to change others.

When I speak about change to large groups of people, I like to ask, "Who has been either married or in a partnership for a long time?" At first, many people raise their hands. "OK, who has been in a relationship for more than 20 years?" Hands drop. "Thirty years? Thirty-five years?" I continue asking until the number of hands raised has decreased to just a few. The rest of the audience almost always applauds them. I then ask our long-term relationship experts, "Have you been able to change your partner?" "No," they always respond. Some add, "I wouldn't want to" or "Together we have changed." Learning to change together, as director and team, is one of the rewards of leading on purpose.

> When you're stuck in a spiral, to change all aspects of the spin you need only to change one thing.
> —Christina Baldwin

> What other people think about me is none of my business.
> —12-Step slogan

How welcome is change?

Changing what we can and letting go of trying to fix or change others is a powerful director's tool. In your experience, how welcome is a new idea? What percentage of people affected by the new idea "buy in" eagerly? Does "But we've always done it this way!" sound familiar? Let's look at information about how people respond to a change. Does your experience match that of Neila A. Connors (2000, 47), who makes the following observation about a change?

   5 percent of the people will accept it immediately

   25 percent will slowly adapt and accept

   60 percent will take a "let's wait and see" approach and will eventually accept the new idea if it works to their advantage

   10 percent will never accept change

Reflect for a moment on an occasion when another person wanted to change something that affected you. What was your response? Were you instantly enthusiastic, slowly accepting, sitting back with a wait-and-see attitude, or refusing to budge? The answer to this question often depends on who initiated the change and how it was initiated. When we feel that someone else is imposing change on us, then we are more likely to resist.

Many leaders who can inspire staff to buy into new ideas have resisted change themselves at some point. As a result of their own experiences resisting change, these leaders have learned the power of "due process." By involving others from the beginning in developing a change, a leader avoids resistance. Remember Amalie's experience in the chapter case study? When her staff felt left out of the process, they dug in their heels and resisted. If Amalie had first solicited and listened to their ideas about a new curriculum, the teachers most likely would have been more open. In fact, their input might have helped focus, redesign, or otherwise improve her proposal. Buy-in to change depends on an open, engaging, affirming, and appreciative process. (See **The 4 Ps to Remember When Communicating with Staff about Transitions**.)

The 4 Ps to Remember When Communicating with Staff about Transitions

1. Purpose: Why we have to do this.
2. Picture: What it will look and feel like when we reach our goal.
3. Plan: Step by step, how we will get there.
4. Part: What you can (and need to) do to move us forward.

Source: W. Bridges & S.M. Bridges, 2000. "Leading Transition: A New Model for Change." *Leader to Leader* 16: 30–36.

Trauma and transitions

Children and adults who have survived trauma may find change especially wrenching. The child subjected to unpredictable, neglectful, or violent parenting aches for safe places, dependable routines, and soothing relationships. Sadly, statistics show that the younger a child is, the more likely that child is to be maltreated (Center for the Study of Social Policy 2004). In fact, "of the 825,000 substantiated cases of child abuse or neglect in 1999, 14 percent represented children under one year of age; 24 percent represented ages from two through five" (23–24). For steps that childhood professionals can take to help traumatized children, see "Creating Relational Sanctuaries for Children Who Suffer from Abuse" (Bruno 2010).

If you notice that an innovation causes significant anxiety for a staff member, take time to invite that person to talk with you about his or her fears and reservations. When an everyday problem overwhelms adults, we may be reminded of a past problem that remains unresolved. Therapists, not directors, are best suited to help traumatized people. However, listening in a caring way may go a long way to help the staff member relax out of rigidity into flexibility. That staff member may become a strong ally for the change.

Change and "cognitive dissonance"

Driving home from work one day, I listened to a National Public Radio interview with Elliot Aronson, coauthor (with Carol Tavris) of *Mistakes Were Made (But Not by Me): Why We Justify Foolish Beliefs, Bad Decisions, and Hurtful Acts* (2007). Aronson popularized the term "cognitive dissonance"—the internal, squirrely tension we feel when we act in a way that does not honor our value system.

Mistakes were made (but not by me).
—Carol Tavris and Elliot Aronson

Imagine a director whose core value is integrity. When he finds himself favoring one infant teacher over another, he may feel the tension of cognitive dissonance. He may be able to convince himself that he is not showing favoritism. Employees, reading the director's nonverbal cues, sense that he feels guilty and out of sorts, despite the smile on his face.

In early childhood environments, cognitive dissonance is not a secret that can be kept by silence. Teachers' high level of emotional intelligence leads to our discomfort being "read," even when we might prefer our feelings to be invisible. According to Tavris and Aronson (2007), when our anxiety with an internal conflict becomes impossible to bear, some of us pretend or forget we have a problem. Denial is another way to describe cognitive dissonance. For the director who feels she must be flawless, making a mistake ignites cognitive dissonance. That director might feel a mistake was made, but certainly not by her! Denial kicks in when we cannot face the fact that we are not perfect.

> **Bam!radio**
> "When and How to Say, *I Was Wrong*"
> Interview with Barbara Kellerman
> *Heart to Heart Conversations on Leadership*
> http://bamradionetwork.com

Change can be as disturbing as an earthquake. The earth moves under our feet. I will never forget my office chair "walking" across the floor during an earthquake in Augusta, Maine, in 1980! I can picture that chair now. Our brains have a remarkable capacity to recall emotionally powerful changes in living detail.

In the calm that follows an earthquake, some of us get right back to work as if nothing happened. Denial can feel productive at the moment. Denial, however, cannot negate the reality that is taking place. Living in cognitive dissonance or denial takes a toll on our stamina. Consider this:

> Kathy senses that the director is displeased with her telephone etiquette. The director says nothing to Kathy directly, and Kathy tries to brush off the feeling of disapproval. Kathy tries to avoid making phone calls when the director is near, but her denial of the problem does not make it go away. Because neither Kathy nor the director initiates a discussion about the problem, the problem grows between them, like ragweed or skunk cabbage. Trust goes down the drain.

The following model, which I call "partnering with change," offers ways to acknowledge inner conflict, step out of denial, and take action to embrace change. Resistance to change, while inevitable, can be transformed into acceptance and eventually into constructive action. Awareness of the problem must come first, before acceptance and action can follow.

Partnering with change

Have you ever given a new frame to a familiar artwork? If so, you probably discovered that reframing it showcases colors and shapes previously unnoticed. In the past, organizational development consultants commonly presented "managing change" strategies to receptive program clients. The popular thinking was, and still can be, "You can take charge of change, rather than having change take charge of you." Being the boss of change seems ideal. Who wants to be buffeted like a kayaker in unexpected whitewater?

Over the years, I have come to appreciate that storms rain down, whether I anticipate them or not. These days, my preferred approach to change is to go with the flow rather than believe I can anticipate and manage the torrents. The adage "If life gives you lemons, make lemonade" works for me.

We do not have the right to force others to see the truth in our way.
—Mohandas Gandhi

My son Nick has taught me many lessons. When Nick was little and didn't do things the way he thought he should, he would shrug his shoulders, throw up his hands, and say, "Silly me." When his experiment didn't go the way he anticipated, Nick again would say, "Silly me." I have always loved Nick's self-accepting phrase. This chapter evolved from years and years of "silly me" experiences, times when I thought I knew how to manage change. Pul-leez! Now I am content to partner with change.

Choosing to partner with, rather than manage, change allows us to see unanticipated opportunities as they emerge. I can be sure of this: *Only I can choose my attitude.*

Keeping perspective on change

Patterns emerge even in the most unpredictable of times. Margaret Wheatley (2006) reminds leaders to look beneath the surface. Wheatley's deeper view offers a refreshing perspective, and her work reveals one "fractal" after another. A fractal is a never-ending pattern moving ever inward, smaller and smaller, or outward, larger and larger. Consider a snowflake. Every discrete section of the ice crystal repeats infinitely the same elemental structure, ever tinier. Fractals are everywhere.

▶ EXERCISE YOUR EQ   ■   Take a look around you. See if you can identify a fractal, or repetitive pattern, like a honeycomb or the spiral of a snail shell.

Soothing perspective comes from finding patterns in the midst of change. Resistance, the human response to change, is predictable. Reluctant acceptance follows. Buy-in eventually occurs, and the change becomes the new norm. A pattern seems to emerge. Understanding this pattern helps us name where we are and what our options are. Keeping perspective is the first step to partnering with change.

An example of an emotional fractal is this: Every change brings about a loss. For sure, a change may lead to new gains. But something must be left behind for the new idea to replace it. When we close the door on something familiar to us, we often feel a loss. In her classic book *On Death and Dying,* Elisabeth Kübler-Ross (1969) describes the grieving process (denial, anger, bargaining, depression, acceptance) when we experiences a loss, specifically, the death of a loved one.

Sometimes we can "love" institutions and familiar ideas, much as we love a person in our lives. When that institution changes, or an idea becomes outdated, we feel loss. The "partnering with change" model described in the next section incorporates a number of Kübler-Ross's five stages of grieving.

As Kübler-Ross writes about grief, so William Bridges (1991) writes about transitions, offering another fractal of change. Writing specifically about the courage we need in order to change, Bridges observes that humans prefer to hold on to something known, even at the expense of finding something better. The "known," even if troubling or inadequate, is often preferred over the unknown. But an unknown, healthier, more pleasant, and more fulfilling option cannot be discovered without courage.

Bridges likens resistance to change to the challenge of a trapeze artist. To "fly through the air with the greatest of ease" to the other side of the circus tent, the trapeze artist must release the trapeze he is holding on to and catch another trapeze. Only with courage can he let go in order to grasp the approaching new trapeze. Paralyzed by fear of the risk he is taking, he will hang on to the trapeze he has, swinging endlessly back and forth, with white knuckles and aching arms.

Like the trapeze artist, many of us hold tight to what we know, sometimes at great expense. Bridges (1991) calls the space between the old and the new the "neutral zone." To shorten the amount of time spent in the neutral zone, Bridges provides practical coaching on how to take a "leap of faith":

1. **Learn to describe the change** and why it must happen **in 1 minute or less.**

2. **Understand who has to let go of what;** what is ending for staff members and what is beginning.

3. Take steps to **help staff respectfully let go of the past.**

> You see things; and you say, "Why?" But I dream things that never were; and I say "Why not?"
>
> —George Bernard Shaw

4. Name the skills and attitudes staff need in order to make the change, and **provide training and resources to help staff develop new skills and attitudes.**

Partnering with change can free you from staying stuck with white knuckles, aching arms, and weary souls.

The change process

▶ EXERCISE YOUR EQ   ▦   Take a moment to identify a change that you need to make but may have avoided. What are you thinking, how are you feeling, and what, if anything, do you want to do? Look at the model (**Predictable Responses to Change**) to find where you are in the change process.

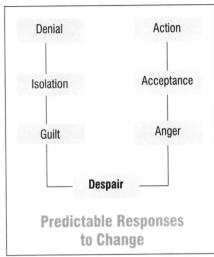

Predictable Responses to Change

To "partner" with change, the first step is to acknowledge where we are. Once we have named our stage in the change process, we can more readily make choices about where we want to go. The perspective that comes from using this model can free us to take constructive action more quickly, with confidence and a relieving sense of humor. Informed by Kübler-Ross, Bridges, and my own observations, here's what I mean.

My "back burner" gets very crowded. Does yours? Fires can start that way. Here's an approach that gives me energy to move back-burner items to the front burner so I can "get cooking."

Let's say my back-burner item is discomfort with my boss's management style. Specifically, every time my boss loses her temper and yells, I get agitated inside. Here is the pattern, often predictable, that many of us follow when a challenge arises, such as when a yelling boss knocks on our door. Using myself as the example:

1. **Denial**: Avoiding the issue, imagining everything is fine when it is not, hoping the problem will disappear if I do not dwell on it. Denial is similar to taking a snooze. For the moment, I escape what I know I need to face. I pretend to myself that my boss is just having one bad hair day.

2. **Isolation:** Cutting myself off from others, not telling anyone about the problem. In the isolation stage, I may appear at ease to others. However, I know I am keeping a secret: I am afraid of my boss's temper. This secret separates me and leads to loneliness.

3. **Guilt:** Berating myself over action I have not taken or inappropriate action I have taken. Guilt pops up when I violate my core values. Honesty is a core value. I am being honest neither with myself nor with my boss about my concerns. Guilt can also involve *blaming* another person so I can avoid changing.

4. **Despair:** Hitting the bottom and feeling helpless and hopeless. When a problem is avoided, the problem only grows. As the problem grows, my self-esteem goes down the drain. Most of us cannot tolerate despair for long. We become sick and tired of being sick and tired.

5. **Anger:** Outrage about not having faced the problem. Anger leads to clarity about who is responsible for what task. I am responsible for talking with my boss about my boundaries. My boss is responsible for dealing with emotions productively.

6. **Acceptance:** Acknowledgement of the problem (the opposite of denial), willingness to face the issue. Acceptance brings a sense of calm and resolution. I accept responsibility for allowing behavior that I do not appreciate. I decide what I need to do.

7. **Action:** Addressing and resolving the issue, moving out of inaction into productive behavior. I ask my boss if we can discuss our different styles so we can work together as productively as possible. At our meeting, I tell her I am uncomfortable and my productivity decreases when she raises her voice; that identifying and addressing problems before they become crises works better for me.

Notice how long I took before I acted. Can you picture the time I wasted by avoiding, fearing, and isolating? None of us has to travel this tortuous, long road. Consider this: Each stage (denial, isolation, guilt, despair, anger) offers a direct pathway to acceptance and action. Leaders can leap across that chasm, rather than fall into the valley of despair.

These are the tools directors can use:

1. **Acknowledgement** overcomes *denial:* Facing facts, admitting that I have a problem, owning that I am denying something that bothers me. As I acknowledge my upset feelings about working with my boss, I accept the feelings. This prepares me to take action.

2. **Connecting** replaces *isolation:* Reaching out, asking for help. Resourceful colleagues are in the wings, waiting for me to ask them for assistance. As I reach out to another person, I gain energy to take action.

3. **Accepting responsibility** overcomes *guilt.* Wallowing in guilt does not change anything for the better. As I accept my responsibility to take action, I move from stalemate to action.

4. **Trust** relieves *despair.* Have you ever felt "sick and tired of being sick and tired"? Few of us can tolerate being flat on our face for long. Any action feels better than being debilitated or overwhelmed. Trust, or faith that things have to improve, lifts us out of the pit. Each of us has access to our own source for trust, faith, or both.

5. **Clarity** is the gift of *anger.* Have you ever felt grateful that you could finally get angry? The adrenaline flow of anger sweeps us toward clarity about the action that needs to be taken. Our brain's orbitofrontal cortex empowers us to step to the side of the adrenaline rush of anger in order to gain that clarity.

6. **Acceptance** leads to a peaceful heart. I worked with a woman in Ohio who described herself as "an absolute nervous wreck" about surgery she was facing. Nothing seemed to comfort her. She was scared to death. The day she went to the hospital, peace surrounded her like a warm fleece blanket. She had accepted the necessity of the surgery. Studies show that patients who lessen their pre-operative tension hasten their own recovery.

7. **Action** frees us. When we carry the weight of an unresolved problem on our shoulders, we become bent over. When we release that weight, as a Head Start director in New Hampshire sighed, "I stand tall."

▶ EXERCISE YOUR EQ   ▦   Describe a change you are facing or an issue you know you need to address in order to "stand tall." Review the stages of the change process. In which stage are you now? Are you in denial about the issue? Are you feeling guilty about it? At any stage, you can leap across the chasm into action by using one of the seven tools just discussed. Select the tool that would be most helpful for you now.

What steps do you need to take to partner with change? Like the trapeze artist, your leap of faith will carry you to the other side and save you from hanging back forever or crashing to the bottom.

In spite of illness, in spite of the archenemy sorrow, one can remain alive long past the usual date of disintegration if one is unafraid of change, insatiable in intellectual curiosity, interested in big things, and happy in small ways.

—Edith Wharton

Notice the loss. To leap, leaders must let go of the known, the predictable. To leap, leaders need courage. Fear of loss can hold us back. I can tell myself that loss is part of life, but the pain of loss still tears at me. If I have moved on too quickly and not grieved my losses in the past, I may build up a fear of facing another loss in the future. In this way, partnering with change involves accepting the feelings of sadness, anger, fear, loneliness, and despair.

No one wants to feel those emotions. Emotional intelligence—knowing our strengths and our limitations—helps. By acknowledging how we feel about change and loss, we know better where we need to grow. This is the first step toward finding the help we need.

For example, if I am skilled at isolating myself, I know I need to take one step toward reaching out to another person for help. If denial is my middle name, I need to face facts. By having a support system, directors can ease their process of partnering with change.

When a relationship with a boss needs to change

"Managing up," or attempting to change a relationship with a supervisor, requires a lot of social EQ. We walk a tightrope between overstepping our boundaries and forging a more effective relationship with our boss. To the boss, we may be perceived as insubordinate, refreshingly honest, or anything in between. Early childhood professionals frequently tell me they face this dilemma. They ask: "What can I do if my boss gossips and I am disciplining staff for gossiping?" and "What do I do if my supervisor reverses decisions I have made because employees complain to him about what I have decided?"

> **Bam!radio**
> "Leading the Leader: Three Rules for Managing Your Boss"
> Interview with Jack Gabarro
> *Heart to Heart Conversations on Leadership*
> http://bamradionetwork.com

When you feel your relationship with your supervisor is a problem, use these EQ tips for managing up:

1. Devote energy to forging as honest a relationship with your boss as possible.

2. Ask your boss how he or she prefers you to present a new approach.

3. Check in with your boss about the best time and way to share your concern.

4. State the change you hope to make.

5. Identify the pros and cons the change will bring.

6. Remain as objective as possible to be able to hear your boss's perspective.

7. If your boss sees no reason to make changes, decide if you can be effective in your job without the support you want from above.

8. Be ready to let go and move on if you feel you are not making headway.

Not every supervisor is open to a change in the supervisor–supervisee relationship when the supervisee initiates the change. In that case, present the change in such a way that your boss can feel the change is in her best interest. Your boss may need to feel that the change is her idea, not yours.

Are you wise to go over your boss's head to her supervisor? Some leaders have taken the risk of telling their boss's boss about their difficulties. Do this "only if the stars are in perfect alignment," cautions John J. Gabarro. Otherwise, you step into a strong likelihood of being fired.

Leading organizational change

Gabarro says bluntly, "The all-purpose general manager who can parachute into any situation and succeed is a myth" (2007, 116). In many ways, Gabarro's research is relevant to early childhood, even though his research sample was 17 male business executives. As described in the chart **Five Developmental Stages of Being a Manager**, new managers experience predictable stages as they attempt to make changes:

1. Taking hold
2. Immersion
3. Reshaping
4. Consolidation
5. Refinement

The directives to "remain open to new developments" and "deal with underlying causes of residual problems" are tall orders. Openness and courage are required.

In picking your battles, ask yourself, "How important is it?" Your answer to that question will help you in almost every leadership challenge. Kathleen Reardon (2007) asks, "Does the situation call for immediate, high-profile action or something more nuanced and less risky? Courage is not about squandering political capital on low-priority issues" (61). An example of using your "political capital" is calling on someone you know for a favor. That person may in turn expect you to do her a favor.

Resilience

What a magical attribute resilience is! It is the ability to bounce back, maintain hope, see the bright side, never lose trust, and maintain spirit. Resilience is an essential EQ ability for a director. How do directors become resilient? How can they remain resilient in the midst of challenges?

Research on resilience is uplifting. A Harvard University study revealed that the unconditional loving support of one other adult can restore resilience to a person who has experienced an abusive or neglectful upbringing. Similarly, one adult giving unconditional loving kindness to a child exposed to the destructive effects of the stress hormone cortisol in utero (before birth) can help heal the child's nerve endings. That child can grow and develop in a healthy way. Her EQ and IQ will develop due, in large part, to the care of a loving adult.

Optimism's role in resilience

I was happy to discover that children's optimism about themselves is a greater predictor of their first-semester college grades than are their SAT scores. My sweet daughter, Lily JinHee, is an excellent student. Gifted as she is (isn't every child gifted in his or her own way?), Lily does not score well on standardized tests. Fortunately, her grades were strong enough to win her admission to the university of her choice. In her first semester in college, Lily aced her advanced placement chemistry and calculus courses, as part of an overall excellent first-semester average. I was not surprised when I found this research finding come true.

Optimism is a powerful force in every stage of our life. Studies show optimistic people are able to see more options, recall more, and think more flexibly than pessimists can. Optimists also share the gift of humor. Humor, after all, provides perspective and allows us to step to the side to see things anew.

Take rest; a field that has rested gives a bountiful crop.

—Ovid

If you can keep your head when all about you are losing theirs and blaming you, you're a better man than I am.

—Rudyard Kipling

A good laugh is sunshine in a house.

—William Makepeace Thackeray

Success is not the key to happiness. Happiness is the key to success.

If you love what you are doing, you will be successful.

—Albert Schweitzer

Five Developmental Stages of Being a Manager	
Taking Hold Orientation and evaluation Corrective actions	**Tasks** • Develop an understanding of the new situation • Take corrective actions • Develop initial set of priorities and "map" of the situation • Develop initial set of expectations with key subordinates • Establish the basis for effective working relationships **Dilemma** • How quickly to act on apparent problems? *Act too quickly—risks:* • Make a poor decision because of lack of adequate information or knowledge • Take actions that constrain subsequent decisions that cannot be anticipated yet *Act too slowly—risks:* • Lose advantages of the "honeymoon period" • Lose credibility because of apparent indecisiveness • Lose valuable time
Immersion Fine-grained, explor- atory learning and managing the business	**Tasks** • Develop a deeper, finer-grained understanding of the new situation and the people • Assess consequences of taking-hold period actions • Reassess priorities • Settle questions and problems concerning key personnel • Reconfigure "map" of the situation; fill out or revise the concept • Prepare for reshaping actions
Reshaping Acting on the revised concept	**Tasks** • Reconfigure organization based on finer-grained understanding • Deal with underlying causes of residual problems • Be open to unanticipated problems that emerge as a result of second-wave changes
Consolidation Evaluative learning, follow-through, and corrective action	**Tasks** • Follow through on reshaping actions • Deal with unanticipated problems that emerge as a result of reshaping stage • Remain open to new developments
Refinement Refining operations, looking for new opportunities	**Tasks** • Focus on fine-tuning operations • Look for new opportunities, such as staff development, curriculum innovation, technology integration

Adapted from John J. Gabarro, chart titled Taking Charge: Tasks and Dilemmas, in "When a New Manager Takes Charge"
(2007, 114).

Optimists live longer and suffer fewer illnesses, and if they get sick, they heal faster than pessimists. If you see the glass as half full rather than half empty, you will be a more resilient leader.

A 15-year study of 545 Dutch men revealed optimistic men had a 50 percent lower risk of dying from cardiovascular disease than the least optimistic men.

—*Archives of Internal Medicine*

Researchers note that optimistic people ask for help, cope better with difficulties, and stick with their medical treatment plans. Optimists spend more time happily reminiscing about the past, suggesting that by devoting 20 minutes each day to recalling happy memories, we can become more cheerful and upbeat.

Moods are contagious. All who are in your presence will feel your optimism. A person up to five feet away can sense our heartbeat. That heartbeat conveys optimism or pessimism, welcome or rebuff. The optimistic leader who looks for the bright side in every challenge models resiliency for her team.

Can optimism be learned? Have you ever been able to turn your pessimistic viewpoint into an optimistic one? Chances are, if you were able to do this, you allowed yourself to grow through that uncomfortable "neutral zone" of change. Transitioning from negativity to being upbeat is, in large part, through choice. As the saying goes, "When we change the way we look at things, the things we look at will change." This is not to shortchange the difficulty of letting go of beliefs and attitudes. Letting go is rarely an easy path.

Superdirector? Not.

Directors who believe they should be all things to all people often neglect to take care of themselves. As Sue Baldwin says, "Because managing a child care program is filled with interpersonal relationships all day, finding time to be alone in your personal life is important. Just as we all need people in our lives, we also need time to ourselves—time to reflect on our personal values and goals—and time to just vegetate" (1996, 5).

Have you noticed how flight attendants advise fliers to use oxygen masks: "Place the mask over your own face first," they remind us. Many of us in early childhood would help the person next to us before we took care of ourselves. This is a downside of emotional intelligence—those who are exquisitely attuned to reading other people's needs may too easily forget to take stock of their own. Sound familiar?

A support system makes self-care easier and more fun. Support system members show up in different places—in our community, professional organizations, among our family and friends, as well as at our job. The chart **Support System for Change** identifies needs that have to be met for a director to maintain resilience.

Support System for Change			
	Personal	**Professional**	**Community**
Unconditional Support			
Pushes You to Get Out of Denial			
Celebrates You			

▶ EXERCISE YOUR EQ   ▓   I invite you to fill in the boxes in the **Support System for Change** chart with names of people you count on for support. Who is your cheerleader? Who keeps you honest and encourages you to face what you prefer to deny? Who celebrates you with a card, an e-mail, or a party?

Across the top are the places you can find these people: in your personal life, professional relationships, and your neighborhood or community. The column on the left lists needs we must have met to stay resilient. Directors need unconditional acceptance, tough love, or a push to get out of denial, and a trustworthy sounding board to whom we can turn to work through challenges.

Are you ready? Name your current support system members.

The people whose names you filled in on the chart form your support system today. Do you see areas where you might need to reach out? Are you, like I once was, relying on one person to meet all your needs? I nearly wore out my best friend! Today my support system is more expansive, thanks in part to connective technologies like e-mail and listservs.

I invite you not to judge yourself. Consider your answers as data, information for you to ponder as you prepare yourself to partner with change.

Promoting resilience for others

Early childhood author Jim Greenman reminded us that every person touched by change brings a different perspective. Each perspective needs to be solicited and heard. As long as the director hears each perspective, "a participatory process in planning, design, and implementation does not have to mean an endless, egalitarian process, culminating in a compromised end product that serves no one well" (Greenman 2005, 334–35). Informal conversations with staff prior to staff meetings can reduce meeting time.

As employees feel acknowledged, heard, and appreciated, their resilience grows. If employees feel left out, unacknowledged, and underappreciated, they withdraw.

To promote staff buy-in to change:

1. **State your vision:** Be clear, strong, and articulate about your vision for change.
2. **Identify the benefits:** Name the benefits the change will bring to staff and the program.
3. **Use due process:** Involve staff at every stage of the change process. Ask their opinion, problems they anticipate, adaptations they recommend.
4. **Mobilize opinion influencers:** Employ staff who are enthusiastic about the change to engage in dialogue with others who resist change.
5. **Demonstrate willingness to adapt:** Show that you have heard your staff by altering the innovation to align with their helpful input.
6. **Take baby steps:** Gwen Morgan, with whom I teach, reminds me that staff accept change more readily if the innovation is broken down into bite-size pieces.

Effective leaders use EQ in each of these steps. They pay close attention not only to what is verbalized, but also to the energy, demeanor, and other nonverbal cues their staff exhibit.

Taking care of you

Stress goes with the territory of early childhood administration and leadership. Work-days 10 to 12 hours long leave little time for rest and relaxation. Even with all this hard work, none of us can control the future, hard as we may try. We can, however, put support systems in place, lay groundwork for improvements, and take steps toward making things better. As we promote constructive change, we need to take time to take care of ourselves to keep our energy high. Each of us finds our own ways to refresh and rejuvenate.

Picture an actual physical setting, if possible: Strolling down a beach at sunset, soaking in a bubble bath surrounded by candles, sitting by the fireside with a good book, or singing a lullaby to a child all qualify. I picture myself hugging my yellow Labrador retriever Toby, whose whole body wags when he sees me.

Replacing stress with reassurance

Directors need to get physical to take care of themselves. We all hear about the value of good nutrition, getting enough rest, and exercising regularly. Did you know that we have the potential to lower our blood pressure in 30 seconds? *Harvard Women's Health Newsletter* offers an exercise that we can do anywhere. Before doing this exercise, outlined in the steps below, check how you feel. Check in with yourself again once you have completed the exercise. Chances are good that you will feel calmer and more grounded. Feeling reassured of our well-being defuses the stress frenzy.

 EXERCISE YOUR EQ

1. Go to a place where you are free or protected from interruption.
2. Acknowledge that distracting thoughts, although likely, do not have to rob you of your quiet time.
3. Picture yourself in that place where you can relax, feel at home, comfortable, and welcomed. If you feel safe, close your eyes.
4. Recall the scents, the texture of the surroundings, the quality of the light, anything specific that will help you travel to that welcoming place.
5. Breathe in and breathe out, while placing your right hand over your heart. Feel your heart beating as you breathe.
6. If/when distracting thoughts interrupt your quiet, just say, "Thanks, but no thanks. This is my time to relax."
7. As you feel your spirit and heart calm, rest in that place of quiet as long as you can before saying goodbye and returning to your present surroundings and responsibilities.
8. Open your eyes and give yourself credit for taking care of yourself in the moment.

Nobel Peace Prize nominee Thich Nhat Hanh, Zen master, poet, and peace and human rights activist, suggests we accompany our breathing with these words: "Breathing in, I calm my mind and body. Breathing out, I smile. Dwelling in the present moment, I know this is a wonderful moment!" (1991, 10).

There is a vitality, a life-force, and energy, a quickening that is translated through you into action, and because there is only one of you in all of time, this expression is unique. And if you block it, it will never exist through any other medium and be lost.

—**Martha Graham**
Dancer, teacher, choreographer

Remember, you cannot take care of anyone else unless you take care of yourself. This can be hard for directors to remember in the moment. Transitioning from taking care of others to taking care of *you* requires taking one step at a time. Just like any change, we may feel uncomfortable at the beginning. Know that as you practice self-care, you model pathways to resilience for your staff.

Fired up or burning out?

Burnout, or losing one's energy, passion, and optimism, is a danger in service professions. One psychologist has established a website to offer tips on "caregiver's syndrome." His major tip, of course, is to take care of *you* first. Authenticity, or acting in ways consistent with our true selves, helps us stay fired up. Being authentic is the beginning of self-care.

Using authenticity to convey our hopes for change is vital. A program's staff can read how important the change is to a director. According to the authors of *Crucial Conversations: Tools for Talking When Stakes Are High* (Patterson et al. 2002), managers need to:

- Start from the heart with a caring, hopeful motive.
- Stay on track, and turn away from temptations to enter into power struggles.
- Ask yourself: "What do I really want for myself, for others, and for our program?"
- Reflect: "How would I behave if I truly believe in my dream?"

So much depends on our attitude toward change and our courage to lead on purpose.

Recognizing staff who make successful changes is essential for fostering a learning community where change for the better is valued. Ellen Clippinger, interviewed in *School-Age Notes* (September 2006), describes her approach for burnout prevention. Recognizing that very few staff members can advance by becoming their program's director, Clippinger created a five-step ladder for staff professional growth. A program review panel listens as employees report on accomplishments, workshops and courses attended, and projects completed by children in their classrooms. When a staff member moves up the ladder, that employee is acknowledged and rewarded.

Paula Jorde Bloom, an early childhood author on leadership, advises leaders, "Peeling away the layers of our motivations is not always a comfortable process, but it is a necessary step if our goal is to become an authentic leader known for integrity. Central to this process is gaining clarity about what we perceive our purpose in life to be and how we define success" (2007, 2).

When we burn out, our work loses its meaning. In the early childhood profession we are surrounded by real-life opportunities to change things for the better. If we get to the point we cannot see those abundant opportunities, we have come to a time when we need to nurture our own spirit.

*   *   *

Who is the boss of change? I hope that as a result of reading this chapter, you feel even more equipped and, perhaps, inspired to make changes to uplift children, families, and yourself. You are the one to do it.

Reflection questions

1. Is there an issue you need to address but have been avoiding or putting off? Now, review the **Predictable Responses to Change** model on p. 103. What stage are you in now? Denial? Guilt? Anger? Look next at what you need to do to break out of that "stuck" place into acceptance and action (p. 104). Write an analysis of how you might utilize the partnering with change model to help with (a) the issue you identified and (b) future issues you might face.

2. Would you describe yourself as an optimistic, "glass half full" person? Or do you, in a "glass half empty" manner, more quickly visualize problems that a change will bring? How has your attitude affected your desire to take risks to change things for the better? What are the strengths and challenges of each stance, both optimism and

---

Your heart's desires be with you!
—**William Shakespeare**

In dealing with those who are undergoing great suffering, if you feel "burn out" setting in, it is best for the sake of everyone to withdraw and restore yourself. The point is to have a long-range perspective.
—**The Dalai Lama**

pessimism? Research at least two studies on optimism. Write a reflection paper on what role optimism plays in your decision making.

3. What can you change? Can you give an example of a time you were successful in changing another adult's behavior? In terms of child development, do you think adults change children? Write a reflection paper on the serenity prayer as it applies to a particular situation you have faced with both an adult and a child whose behavior has troubled you.

Team projects

1. Self-care is invaluable to everyday leadership. Make a list of those things you currently do to maintain and restore your energy. On a scale of 1–10, rate yourself (1=*don't take care of myself*; 10=*take excellent care of myself*). Discuss your feelings and thoughts about self-care and self-mentoring. Average the scores of your team. With your team members, develop and present: (a) a list of reasons we resist taking care of ourselves, (b) daily self-care steps we can take, and (c) strategies for incorporating self-care and self-mentoring into our lives on a long-term basis, especially during hectic and stressful times.

2. Identify and share situations in which someone you know, including yourself, has attempted to make a change for the better. What was the change? How was it presented? Describe how people responded to the proposed change. As a team, review Neila Connors's statement (p. 99) on responses to change. Do her figures surprise you, or do they confirm what you have observed? Reread the pointers on how to successfully promote change for the better (p. 104). Looking back at the situations you each identified and looking forward to situations you face or may face, how might you promote a more positive response to change?

3. Elisabeth Kübler-Ross named stages of the grieving process. William Bridges likened taking risks to the moment a trapeze artist lets go of one trapeze to catch hold of the next. Both of these authors wrote in the twentieth century. Research more fully what each had to say. Which of their insights holds true today? How might advancing technology affect our grieving or risk-taking processes? Do you believe that any philosophies or values are timeless? Engage in a discussion of these issues as you present the work of Kübler-Ross and Bridges.

Bibliography

Baldwin, S. 1996. *Lifesavers: Tips for success and sanity for early childhood managers.* Stillwater, MN: Insights Training & Consulting.

Bloom, P.J. 2007. *From the inside out: The power of reflection and self-awareness.* Lake Forest, IL: New Horizons.

Bridges, W. 1991. *Managing transitions: Making the most of change.* Reading, MA: Addison-Wesley.

Bridges, W. 2004. *Transitions: Making sense of life changes.* Rev. ed. Cambridge, MA: Da Capo.

Bridges, W., & S.M. Bridges. 2000. Leading transition: A new model for change. *Leader to Leader* 16: 30–36.

Bruno, H.E. 1999. Superdirector: All things to all people but one. *Leadership Quest* 8.

Bruno, H.E. 2010. Creating relational sanctuaries for children who suffer from abuse. *Exchange: The Early Childhood Leaders' Magazine.* Jan/Feb: 64–68.

Bruno, H.E., & M.L. Copeland. 1999. Professionalism in challenging times: A new child care change management model. *Leadership Quest* (Fall).

Center for the Study of Social Policy. 2007. *Strengthening families: A guidebook for early childhood programs.* 2d ed. Washington, D.C.: Author.

Clippinger, E. 2006. Staff "lifers" in after-school and summer programs. *School-Age Notes* September.

Co-Dependents Anonymous. 1995. *Co-Dependents Anonymous.* Phoenix, AZ: Author.

Connors, N. 2000. *If you don't feed the teachers, they eat the students: Guide to success for administrators and teachers.* Nashville, TN: Incentive Publications.

Frankl, V.E. 1959. *Man's search for meaning.* Boston, MA: Beacon Press.

Gabarro, J.J. 2007. When a new manager takes charge. HBR Classic. *Harvard Business Review* 85 (1): 104–17.

Gabarro, J.J., & J.P. Kotter. 2008. *Managing your boss.* Boston, MA: Harvard Business School Press.

Greenman, J. 2005. *Caring spaces, learning places: Children's environments that work.* Redmond, WA: Exchange Press.

Kellerman, B. 2010. *Leadership: Essential selections on power, authority, and influence.* New York: McGraw-Hill.

Kübler-Ross, E. 1969. *On death and dying.* New York: Macmillan.

Moyer, D. 2007. The final test. *Harvard Business Review* 85 (1): 128.

Patterson, K., J. Grenny, R. McMillan, & A. Switzer. 2002. *Crucial conversations: Tools for talking when the stakes are high.* New York: McGraw-Hill.

Reardon, K.K. 2007. Courage as a skill. *Harvard Business Review* 85 (1): 58–64.

Rogers, F. 2005. *Life's journeys according to Mister Rogers: Things to remember along the way.* New York: Hyperion.

Sanders, H.B. 2005. *The subconscious diet: It's not what you put in your mouth; it is what you put in your mind!* Azusa, CA: Liberation Press.

Tavris, C., & E. Aronson. 2007. *Mistakes were made (But not by me): Why we justify foolish beliefs, bad decisions, and hurtful acts.* New York: Harcourt.

Thich Nhat Hanh. 1991. *Peace is every step: The path of mindfulness in everyday life.* London: Bantam Press.

Wheatley, M.J. 2006. *Leadership and the new science: Discovering order in a chaotic world.* 3d ed. San Francisco, CA: Berrett-Koehler.

Web resources

A Checklist for Managing Your Boss
   www.themorsegroup.net/newsletters/11Jan09-85JarvisBoss.pdf

Emotional Resilience: Optimism
   www.mentalhelp.net/poc/view_doc.php?type=doc&id=5789&cn=298

Getting Employees to Not Only Embrace Change but Ask for It!
   www.zeromillion.com/business/managing-change.html

The Kübler-Ross Grief Cycle
   http://changingminds.org/disciplines/change_management/kubler_ross/kubler_ross.htm

Leading Organizational Change
   www.rickmaurer.com/wp/resources/articles-and-white-papers

Navigating the Transitions of Change
   www.strategies-for-managing-change.com/william-bridges.html

Radical Self-Care for Women's Stress Reduction and Inner Peace
   http://ezinearticles.com/?Stress-Management- - -Radical-Self-Care-for-Womens-Stress-Reduction-and-Inner-Peace&id=918056

My personal introduction to the Dalai Lama was by way of television—in a hotel room. I was in Washington, D.C., preparing for a conference on children and the media and was looking for a certain news program when I happened on His Holiness saying, "Someone else's action should not determine your response." I was so intrigued. I wrote down those words, turned off the television and thought about nothing else the whole evening. . . . It sounds so simple, doesn't it? And yet what if someone else's action should be shouting angry words at us or hitting us with a rotten tomato? That doesn't affect what we do in response? Not if our compassion is genuine. Not if our love is the kind the Dalai Lama advocates.

—Fred Rogers, *Life's Journeys According to Mister Rogers*

7 Preventing Legal Issues: Policies and Procedures

Case Study—Lupe

Lupe Hernandez-Jones listed only her brother and sister on the authorized list for pickup when she enrolled her daughters, Rosa and Yvette. The girls are eager to please, obedient, and seem fearful of changes. Lupe faithfully picks up the girls each day; her brother and sister have never appeared.

At the end of their first year with you, Lupe comes to your office anxiously requesting a confidential meeting. She tearfully tells you that she and the girls escaped from the girls' abusive dad, Buster, in Tampa, Florida. At enrollment, Lupe did not mention the children's father. The director, at that time, did not ask Lupe for information about him. Lupe begs you to prevent Buster from seeing the girls. Before you can respond, a respectful Buster, baseball cap in hand, appears at your door requesting to take his daughters out for ice cream. What do you do?

Directors of early childhood programs can

take steps to prevent problems from exploding into mushroom-cloud disasters. The more preventive measures they take, the more confident and effective they become as leaders. Directors can protect their programs and the children and families in their care by planning in advance. Some problems, of course, cannot be prevented. Even for such crises, directors can prepare by having in place and practicing model crisis procedures, You might begin by planning and practicing procedures for the crises listed in **Six Common Issues Directors Face**.

This chapter provides guideposts, sample forms, and background information on the law to assist you in creating model policies and courses of action for the future. Please note that nothing in this chapter (or the book as a whole) serves as legal advice. For legal information, consult with an attorney directly.

Six Common Issues Directors Face

1. Inappropriate use of the Internet by employees and/or families.
2. Giving references for former employees.
3. Teachers babysitting for children in the program.
4. Knowing when the ADA might affect staff disciplinary action.
5. Asking appropriate job interview questions.
6. End-of-the-day disruptions.

By instituting preventive measures, administrators can nip potential problems in the bud. Each problem, if not handled preventively, could mushroom into a lawsuit. When planned for in advance, the problem loses its power to alarm, even overwhelm the director and the program.

Lawsuits wield power

Just one lawsuit has potential to put a child care center out of business. One accusation of wrongdoing, even a false one, can prompt parents to withdraw their children. An accusation of sexual abuse will inevitably and understandably trigger a fierce parental reaction. Outstanding early childhood programs, carefully co-created with families and staff over the years, can be destroyed by a lawsuit even before the suit is adjudicated in a court of law.

The court of public opinion

Our legal system guarantees the presumption of innocence until guilt is proven. Public opinion, however, is often quick to assign guilt before all the evidence is in. Directors in the field report that their fear of lawsuits detracts from their confidence as leaders.

A New England director mourned, "My worst fear has come true," when one of her teachers was accused of child molestation. Everyone, especially the director and the accused teacher, wanted proof that the abuse had not taken place. Everyone, from children to teachers, parents, and administrators, felt anxious about the potential lawsuit. In the end, the charges were dropped. Nonetheless, the center lost families as soon as the accusation was uttered. But the center survived and still thrives by continuously offering open forums for parents and staff to discuss their concerns.

Common sense principles

Common sense principles help prevent legal crises. A review of the *case law* (decisions made by courts) relevant to early childhood employment reveals underlying common sense principles. Leaders who practice these principles, both in establishing policies and in making decisions, can feel more confident that they are on the right track. The principles reflect emotional and social-emotional intelligence in practice:

- **Be consistent.** Hold all employees to the same standards. Favoritism is suspect. Courts want to make sure every employee has equal opportunities.

- **Stay objective** and act reasonably. Use the step-to-the-side process to prevent your brain's amygdala from hijacking your professional perspective. Make decisions keeping "your eyes on the prize," with the long view in mind. Wait until the adrenaline surge has subsided before acting, when possible.

- **Document** and report facts. Remember the Head Start saying: "If it isn't documented, it didn't happen." Document concrete and essential facts. Writing a novel or short story is not required. Just the facts will suffice.

- **Follow written policies** and procedures. Your employee and parent handbooks should document program standards and practices. These are "living" documents to be added to and changed as needed.

- **Honor civil rights.** Ensure that everyone is welcomed, respected, and treated without bias, especially with regard to ethnicity, religion, cultural, and age differences. [See the box **Honor Civil Rights**.]

- **Exercise "due process."** Give notice or information to all those affected before making a change. Give staff a chance to share their responses to the change by providing a "right to a hearing."

> ### Honor Civil Rights
>
> Check your state's and municipality's definitions of whose rights are protected. New Jersey, for example, has broader employment and public accommodation antidiscrimination laws than federal law mandates. New Jersey's protected categories against discrimination include: race, creed, color, national origin, nationality, ancestry, age, sex (including pregnancy and sexual harassment), marital status, domestic partnership status, affectional or sexual orientation, atypical hereditary cellular or blood trait, genetic information, liability for military service, and mental or physical disability, including AIDS and HIV-related illnesses.

The emotionally intelligent leader maintains perspective in the midst of threatening situations. Rather than being devastated by a crisis, the leader with EQ can make choices. Fortified by these principles, a leader can act more confidently. Effective leaders not only react intelligently during threatening situations, but also have preventive policies and practices in place to minimize the occurrence of such situations.

Preventive policies and practices

The question to ask, before getting paralyzed by fear of a lawsuit, is, "What choices do I have, above and beyond my immediate reaction?" Stepping back from a potentially overwhelming threat frees leaders to use their emotional intelligence. You have options, so exercise restraint rather than doing or saying something in the moment that you may later regret. Let's look at some policies you as a leader can institute that will afford you choices and a longer-range perspective.

> ## Case study—Mallorie and Macey
>
> Teacher's aides Mallorie and Macey, at your center, post a derogatory video online that goes viral on YouTube. The video portrays the teachers at your center as inept and you as a tyrant. Parents are outraged. When you call Mallorie and Macey to your office, they toss their hair and say, "We did this in the privacy of our apartment, on our own time, and it's our First Amendment right to be creative!"

Employees' inappropriate Internet use

Here's what Mallorie and Macey claim: Their video is private, protected as free speech, and not created at work. Each of these claims displays faulty reasoning.

Posting something on social networks is not private. What could be more public than the Internet? Attorney Robert Peck, expert in employment law and online behavior, says, "There's no privacy. If we put something out there online, it's public." Informa-

> **Bam!radio**
>
> "Privacy in the Cyber-Space Era: Have We All Become Public Figures?"
>
> Interview with Robert Peck
>
> *Heart to Heart Conversations on Leadership*
>
> http://bamradionetwork.com

Bam!radio

"Can You Stop Teachers from 'Dissing' Families, Children, Peers, or Your School Online?"

Interview with Tom Copeland, Deb Kimble, and Justin Baeder

Heart to Heart Conversations on Leadership

http://bamradionetwork.com

tion posted on Facebook, YouTube, LinkedIn, or any other social network is immediately no longer private.

Is the video "protected speech"? Staff can have and express their opinions, of course. However, when employees state inappropriate opinions online, it reflects negatively on your program. As a leader, you have the right to promote professionalism and regulate unprofessional behavior. Last, no matter where the statements were made (or the video created), whether at home or at work, once those statements go online, they become public.

What can leaders do to prevent inappropriate public behavior? Attorney Tom Copeland recommends:

• Promote positive use of social networking sites by discussing with staff how to get the word out about the quality of the program.

• Protect the privacy and confidentiality of children and families.

• Institute a professionalism policy that prohibits inappropriate public behavior, including Internet usage.

Does your program have a professionalism policy? If not, consider a policy such as this:

> Employees of [program name] *will conduct themselves in a manner that reflects positively on our program and on the teaching profession. Professional behavior is required in public, online, and in any other circumstance where an employee's behavior may reasonably reflect on the program and/or the profession.*

By discussing these policies and practices in advance with staff, you either prevent derogatory use of social media such as Mallorie and Macey's YouTube video, or you have good cause for disciplinary action afterward. At the same time, you can invite all staff, especially those with Internet savvy, to represent the program positively on social networking sites.

Providing references for former employees

▶ EXERCISE YOUR EQ   ▓   Consider what you would do in the situation that follows. Next, think of policies you could put in place that might prevent problems like this from arising.

Evangeline, a director across town, calls you with this request: "Jenna, who says she worked for you, is applying to be my new lead toddler teacher. Jenna says you will give her a wonderful reference. What did you think of Jenna's performance?" What would you say to Evangeline in the following four scenarios?

1. You were grateful Jenna quit because you were about to fire her for repeatedly arriving late.

2. Jenna's classroom skills were adequate; however, her gossiping and negativity troubled other teachers.

3. Jenna was one of your best toddler teachers. You believe Jenna is ready to become a lead teacher; however, you didn't have a position available.

4. Something bothered you about Jenna that you couldn't quite identify. Frankly, you were relieved when she left.

Directors often wish they could tell the whole truth about their experience with a past employee. Employees who perform well deserve glowing references. Directors want to warn prospective employers against hiring poor performers. A leader's sense of fairness tells her she should be able to share accurate, documented information. After all, if Jenna presents a danger to children, aren't we obligated to warn future employers? Unfortunately, sometimes the law and common sense do not align in life.

Likely, the answer to Evangeline's question would be the same, regardless of which scenario were true, because most center directors are instructed by their attorneys to write and abide by a policy like the one in **Policy on Requests for References**. Such a policy precludes your sharing any information on Jenna's performance—which means that Jenna's potential employer, Evangeline, has learned little to help her make an important hiring decision. On the other hand, Jenna has been protected. You have released no negative information about her, beyond the fact that you would not rehire her.

How does such a policy serve the interests of children and families? What additional policy would allow directors to share accurate information when called for a reference? Consider the sample **Reference Consent Form**, intended to be signed by new and current employees.

By signing this statement, Jenna would have consented to your sharing accurate information about her performance. This could free you to more fully answer Evangeline's questions, such as: "Do you have any reservations about Jenna's performance?" or "What skills did you observe in Jenna that would indicate her ability to be lead toddler teacher?" Depending on which boxes Jenna initialed, she would have authorized you to say more: "In my professional opinion, Jenna was not consistently punctual" or "In my professional opinion, Jenna was skilled at building partnerships with families."

Administrators are bound to convey information in an accurate, unbiased manner that honors the employee's desire for confidentiality. Using the **Reference Consent Form** allows you to align your ethical standards with the legal standards. As long as a director shares her professional opinion as based on accurate information, she will not be committing slander. A legal term, *slander* is saying something false that would cause the person's reputation in the community to be damaged. A director who shares false information about a former employee, and is sued, could be convicted and forced to pay damages. Telling the truth is the best defense against a charge of slander.

Instituting the **Reference Consent Form** with staff will ward off the problem of not being able to share your professional opinion about a former employee. By taking this preventive step, directors asked later to give references can better ensure that potential employers have accurate information.

Policy on Requests for References

Our program's policy on responding to requests for references on current or former employees is to provide only the following information:

1. Confirm or deny the individual's employment. For example: "Yes, Ms. Jenna Wrightson worked for our program" or "No, our program has not employed Ms. Wrightson."
2. State the dates of the individual's employment. For example: "Ms. Wrightson was employed by our program from March 15, 2009, to January 10, 2010."

Asked whether we would rehire a former employee, a response is optional. For example: "Yes [or No], we would [or would not] rehire Ms. Wrightson."

Reference Consent Form

I, [*name of employee*], an employee of [*name of program*], agree to hold harmless [*name of program*] for the reference that the organization may give me on my employment with the organization.

(Employee, your initials below authorize us to discuss your performance in those areas. We will not comment on areas you do not check.)

☐ Punctuality
☐ Preparation
☐ Classroom management
☐ Teaching
☐ Usage of DAP (developmentally appropriate practices)
☐ Building partnerships with families
☐ Embracing diversity
☐ Professionalism
☐ Team membership skills

Hold-Harmless Consent for Babysitting Policy

We, [*names of parents*], parents of [*names of child/ren*], hold [*program name*] harmless for any injury that may occur when we hire [*teacher's name*] to babysit.

We understand this consent takes exception to the program's no-babysitting policy.

(Parents' signatures)	(Printed names)	(Date)
(Director's signature)	(Printed name)	(Date)
(Teacher's signature)	(Printed name)	(Date)

Developing a no-babysitting policy

Toddler teacher Wanda babysits for the Palermo twins, Pasqualina and Marco, both of whom are in her classroom. One night, while the Palermos are out, Wanda trips. Pasqualina and Marco, both injured, require emergency room treatment for contusions and broken bones. The distraught parents sue Wanda and the child care center where she works. Is babysitting by staff a smart idea? Who is liable?

Staff often work second or even third jobs. Should one of those jobs be babysitting after hours for children in your program? The program may be liable if children are harmed while your teacher is babysitting for them. Parents can rightfully say to you, "We hired Wanda because her working for you means she is qualified and responsible." To protect your program, consider implementing a no-babysitting policy like this one:

> *No-Babysitting Policy—Staff members are not allowed to babysit for families with children enrolled in the program.*

What if parents insist on hiring the teacher to babysit? You could say they may do so if they agree to sign a **Hold-Harmless Consent for Babysitting Policy** agreement, which might cover you in case anything happens to the children. But think hard before deciding to allow this option, because the agreement may not always be upheld by the courts. Hold-harmless agreements can be suspect, because it can appear parents were forced into signing them. This imbalance of power is called *unconscionability*. Some programs that use the agreement require parents to sign the form each time they hire a teacher to babysit. Other centers consider the signed form adequate for a month or more.

Ensuring compliance with the ADA, as amended

Passed in 1990, the federal Americans with Disabilities Act (ADA) states that people with disabilities have a right to an equal opportunity to apply for jobs, be hired, and enjoy the benefits of employment. This does not mean that a person should be hired or retained *because of* his or her disability. It does mean, however, that a person with a disability needs to be given an opportunity equal to that of any applicant or employee without a disability. To make sure that happens, employers may need to make "reasonable accommodations" to enable that person to meet the job requirements.

Bam!radio

"Sweeping New Definitions of Disabilities, What You Need to Know"

Interview with Linda Carter Batiste

Heart to Heart Conversations on Leadership

http://bamradionetwork.com

Under the law, a *disability* is an impairment that substantially limits one or more "major life activities." On January 1, 2009, amendments to the ADA took effect. While the spirit of the original law remains the same, according to U.S. Department of Labor attorney Linda Carter Batiste, ADA, as amended, expands the definition of *major life activities* to include these major physical functions:

- immune system
- normal cell growth
- digestive, bowel, and bladder
- neurological
- brain
- respiratory
- circulatory
- endocrine
- reproductive

Employed in the department's Job Accommodation Network (JAN), Batiste predicts that disabling conditions such as cancer and seizure disorders, and intellectual disabilities such as autism (including Asperger's syndrome) and learning disabilities, are all likely to be covered. Take a look at the following dilemma.

Gertrude is your hardest worker and is dedicated to the children. Her pungent body odor, however, interferes with her work. Children don't want to be near her, and parents speak only with Gertrude's team teacher, who is becoming resentful. Other staff gossip about Gertrude.

How would you address this dilemma if you were the director? Is Gertrude covered by the ADA, as amended? What are your responsibilities, and what steps do you take?

Gertrude's body odor may simply require a change in her hygiene routine. However, given the expanded ADA, the cause of the odor may be a disability. By law, employers cannot require an applicant or employee to reveal any disability. Once an applicant or employee volunteers that information, however, employers need to offer ADA assistance. To understand what is causing Gertrude's odor, you might ask, "Gertrude, you have a pungent body odor that distances people from you. Is there anything you can share with me about the odor?" If Gertrude responds that the odor is a result of surgery and wearing a colostomy bag, she reveals a possible disability (digestive, bowel, or bladder disorder).

Once an employee has informed you of a disability, your next step is to work with her to identify and provide "reasonable accommodations" so she can meet her job requirements. Ask the employee to provide a doctor's description of the disability and recommendations for reasonable accommodations. Keep this information confidential while working with the teacher, so she can perform the functions of her job. In Gertrude's case, that may be as simple as covering her class while she takes more timely bathroom breaks.

ADA exceptions to making reasonable accommodations

The ADA envisions a workplace where every qualified person, regardless of disability, is given equal opportunity to find employment and to continue that employment productively. In some cases, however, the accommodations required for a potential employee with a disability are an *undue hardship* on the program, meaning they are too costly for the program to bear. The ADA does not require an organization to endure an undue hardship for the sake of one employee.

Administrators often worry about whether their budgets will cover the cost of making accommodations. Interestingly, federal statistics show that the average cost per reasonable accommodation is approximately $240 annually, and more than half of accommodations are $500 or less.

In other cases, an applicant, even with accommodations, might still pose a *direct threat* to herself or others. An employee with chronic progressive multiple sclerosis, who cannot hold a child without the strong possibility of dropping him, poses a direct threat to her own and others' safety.

If either of these exceptions is present—undue hardship or direct threat—the ADA, as amended, does not require employers to hire or retain the person with the disability. In those cases, the well-being of the program outweighs the individual applicant's or employee's needs.

Asking appropriate interview questions

Equal Employment Law requires directors to treat fairly each applicant for a position, regardless of the person's race, religion, age, gender, or (in most cases) national origin. When interviewing applicants, directors are required to give each person an equal opportunity to respond to the same questions. If an applicant is asked, "Can you describe a time when you faced a discipline challenge in the classroom and how you handled that challenge?" all other applicants for that position must be given the opportunity to answer the same question. If an interviewer were to use different questions for different applicants, she could be accused of favoring one applicant over another. This is why many directors choose to have a written set of interview questions and scenarios that are consistent across applicants. Consider what you would do in this situation:

Jerome's written application for preschool teacher indicates he can perform the job functions. His associate's degree in early childhood education is from a nearby community college. In his cover letter, Jerome notes that his military service in the Middle East strengthened his desire to work with young children. When Jerome arrives for the interview, he shrugs off his coat with a smile. Jerome's right arm appears to have been amputated. The interviewing team becomes anxious about what they can ask Jerome about this.

What could you have done in advance to help all parties to the interview feel welcome and prepared?

Essential functions of the job

When directors interview applicants to fill a position, they seek to hire the person who is best qualified from those who can perform the essential functions of the job. The Child Care Law Center's booklet "Employing People with Disabilities" defines "essential functions" this way: "The tasks and duties that describe the job, but only those that are essential to the performance of the job"(1996, 20).

For example, an infant teacher must be able to diaper a child. And in the event of a fire or similar crisis, a teacher must be able to assist in evacuating the building or otherwise assist in immediately responding to the emergency situation. Infants must be taken to a designated safe place. Both diapering a child and assisting in an emergency situation are essential functions of the job of infant teacher.

Whatever the job, its essential functions should be stated at the interview and in the job description in terms of the tasks the employee will complete, not as physical attributes the employee must possess. This allows applicants like Jerome to demonstrate in their own way that they can accomplish the required tasks. Having only one arm, Jerome may diaper or carry an infant in a different way from anyone else. What counts is whether he can perform those essential functions of the job. The Child Care Law Center advises:

> Physical and mental attributes, and skills based on them (like lifting, driving, and reading), should be avoided to the greatest extent possible in the list of essential functions of the job. If a physical attribute seems unavoidable to perform the job, accompany that attribute with a description of the task or goal intended to be accomplished. (1996, 21)

For example, diapering a 20-pound baby properly is an essential function of the job of infant teacher. This skill is different from the physical attribute of being able to lift 20 pounds. In the job description, "must be able to diaper a child" can replace "must be able to lift 20 pounds." An alternate approach is to link the physical attribute directly to the task to be accomplished: "Must be able to lift at least 20 pounds to be able to diaper a child." In making this subtle shift in emphasis from physical attribute to skill, leaders can open the door wider to potentially qualified candidates. If Jerome shows he can safely and properly diaper a baby as well as meet other functional requirements of the job, Jerome should be considered along with other applicants who have the same abilities.

Also invite the other applicants to demonstrate how they would accomplish those essential tasks. Consistency is important. If everyone interviewed is asked to demonstrate diapering a child, Jerome will not have been singled out. Jerome may well demonstrate his own way to safely and properly diaper a child. If so, everyone has benefited from the interviewing process, interviewer as well as interviewee.

If Jerome voluntarily names the accommodations he requires to be able to perform this task, then the interviewers may explore in greater detail what those accommodations might involve. However, if Jerome does not request accommodations, the interviewers may not ask about them.

By revising job descriptions to focus on tasks rather than attributes, administrators can prevent difficult moments at job interviews. Interviews can be restructured from question-and-answer format to a format that includes scenarios and demonstrations. In this way, applicants can share their own ways of meeting the essential functions of the job.

Planning for the unplanned: Crisis prevention

Directors can't always prevent crises. They can, however, use their emotional intelligence to deal as effectively as possible with each crisis that arises. It is deeply empowering just knowing—as Fred Rogers learned from the Dalai Lama (in the opening quotation)—that no matter how frightening or threatening, what happens around us does not have to determine our response.

Margaret Leitch Copeland's (1996) "Code Blue! Establishing a Child Care Emergency Plan" walks us through a step-by-step process of preparing for the unforeseen. She advises:

1. Brainstorm with staff all the possible crises that can occur.

2. Utilize the assistance of local crisis management experts when developing plans.

3. Post crisis plans and regularly practice carrying them out.

4. Establish a system of how to inform and communicate with parents.

5. Name a spokesperson for the organization, preferably not the director.

6. Anticipate and prepare information the media may need, and make sure the spokesperson has that information in writing.

7. Inform all others to refer questions to the spokesperson.

> What do we live for, if not to make life less difficult for each other?
>
> —George Eliot

Rehearsing these seven steps with staff on a regular basis helps prevent fear and anxiety from overwhelming individuals when a crisis erupts. State licensing standards mandate procedures for dealing with natural disasters. Sometimes the "unnatural" disasters can be just as unsettling. What if a snake slithers onto the playground, a hazardous waste truck tips over on the front lawn, or Uncle Murphy threatens a teacher? Preparing in advance for all possibilities is the best preventive medicine.

Preventing custody disputes when parents pick up children

Some divorce decrees are clear as March mud puddles. Courts may grant joint custody, but without clarifying the details. What happens if both parents arrive to pick up their baby on the same day, and an argument ensues? When parents are not married, who has the right to create the authorized list for pickup? Can one parent leave the other parent off the list? What if a mother changes her mind frequently about whether the father can pick up their child? The last thing anyone in child care wants at departure time is a disruption that leaves children feeling unsafe and unsettled.

Right of Both Parents to Pick Up Their Child
Under the laws of the state of _____, both parents may have the right to pick up their child, unless a court document restricts that right. The enrolling parent who chooses not to include the other parent's name on the authorized list for pickup must file an official court document (e.g., current restraining order, sole custody decree, divorce decree stating sole custody, judgment of adoption). Absent that document, the center may release the child to either parent, provided that parent documents the biological or adoptive parenthood of that child.

To prevent a program and the children from getting caught in the middle, directors can take preventive measures. A director's job is not to decide who has the right to the child; the court has done that already. The director's task, instead, is to support the child, which means obtaining complete information *at enrollment* in order to prevent power struggles from occurring. **Right of Both Parents to Pick Up Their Child** shows a policy on both parents' right to pick up their child. Add it to the parent handbook to prevent custody ruptures later on. The policy can be enforced at enrollment so that parents provide the pertinent court documents from the beginning. With documentation on file, leaders and staff will be prepared for end-of-day custody issues. The parent who has the right to name people on the authorized list for picking up the child will also be established. (It's the parent with custody.)

Consider how having this clear pickup policy could have changed the outcomes in the chapter case study. If at enrollment Lupe had supplied an up-to-date restraining order against Buster, you would have been better prepared to do your job. Then if Buster appeared, you could advise him that the girls could not be released to him because of the restraining order against him. Without appropriate documentation demonstrating Lupe's legal custody of the girls, Buster could claim that Lupe had kidnapped them. Or perhaps Lupe and Buster share custody of their children, but their anger at each other makes it difficult for them to plan who will pick up the girls. Worse than that, the girls might be exposed to a loud disagreement between Lupe and Buster at the entrance of the center.

To keep all children safe from harm, the **Shared-Custody Parental Agreement** policy can be included in the parent handbook as an option for parents who share custody.

By requiring parents to complete such forms at enrollment, the director prevents headaches and heartaches for everyone, especially the children. Lupe and Buster will become responsible for following their own written agreement. If one parent wants to change the agreement, he or she will have to communicate directly with the other parent before any changes can be made. This approach allows directors and staff to focus on their responsibilities, rather than get stuck in the middle of an upsetting custody battle.

> **Shared-Custody Parental Agreement**
>
> We, [*name of parent*] ("Parent 1") and [*name of parent*] ("Parent 2"), parents of [*name of child/ren*], agree that Parent 1 will pick up [*name of child/ren*] on [*day/s of week*], and Parent 2 will pick up [*name of child/ren*] on [*day/s of week*].
>
> If one parent attempts to pick up [*name of child/ren*] on the other parent's day, that parent must document the consent of the other parent to the change in schedule.
>
> Should changes occur continuously, both parents will file a revised agreement with the program promptly.

Preventing an intoxicated parent from driving a child home

Sometimes parents who appear to be under the influence of drugs or alcohol arrive to pick up their children. How can a director help her program prepare in advance for this possible scenario? What would you do in the following situation?

Divorced parents Claire McClure and Phil McClure share custody of 3-year-old Cole. Cole used to be a bubbly, curious, playful boy. Lately, Cole's withdrawn, timid manner concerns you. Both parents try to win you over to their side by telling stories about the other parent's wrongdoings and shortcomings. You feel like you are witnessing a soap opera. You try to stay neutral and be understanding.

It's Friday afternoon, just before the December holidays, when Phil McClure careens into your program to pick up Cole. You think you smell alcohol on his breath. He yells "Ho ho ho!" at everyone he encounters. Cole hides behind his teacher.

Remember that agreements made with parents *at enrollment* serve as preventive medicine. Directors can consider adding the policy on consent to safe departure to their parent handbook:

> ***Consent to Safe Departure of Children from Our Program****—If we have concern for a child's safety, regarding that child's departing with you, we will call another person on the authorized list to pick up the child.*

If the McClures signed this agreement, they agreed to a process that helps keep all parties safe. Talking with parents about this policy at enrollment and enlisting their sign-off on the policy puts into place a calming practice. Families can be reminded of the policy and their agreement to it, as well as having discussed it at enrollment. By affording families due process, a leader prevents wrenching disruptions.

Writing a model departure-time crisis procedure

A model departure-time crisis procedure carefully guides staff through a possible end-of-the-day crisis. This procedure can be added to a staff handbook and practiced at staff meetings. Employees can be invited to brainstorm any possible disruption that might occur when family members arrive to pick up their children.

Should such a crisis arise at the end of the day, directors can take these steps for everyone's well-being:

- Do not immediately release the child. Discuss your concerns with the person picking up the child.

- Engage the child in an activity with another staff member. Make sure all children are safe and removed from the crisis.

- Contact the other parent or another responsible adult on the authorized list. Enlist that person in solving the problem.

- Offer alternatives. Offer to call another person on the authorized list to pick up the child.

- Release the child with reservations. As a *mandated reporter*, call the appropriate state and/or municipal agency to report your concern. For example, ask police to shadow the car of a parent who may be driving under the influence of alcohol or another controlled substance.

- Call the authorities. When someone's well-being or safety is in jeopardy, notify the police, the Department of Social Services, and your licensor, along with any other appropriate authority.

Mandated reporters are professionals who are responsible for children's well-being and safety. State law requires mandated reporters to contact authorities if a child appears to be exposed to or in danger of abuse or neglect. Driving while intoxicated could be considered a neglectful or abusive action toward a child.

*   *   *

The adage "An ounce of prevention is worth a pound of action" holds true in child care administration. Directors aim to maintain professional perspective. They can take many steps to prevent crisis situations. Written policies and procedures in staff and parent handbooks help ward off disruptions. Safeguards can be instituted to guide programs through crises that cannot be prevented.

Whether the worry is a potential lawsuit or an emotional disruption at pickup, directors who plan ahead will have tools to use that respect everyone's rights and ensure children's well-being.

Reflection questions

1. Recall a work-related problem you have faced. Describe that problem and how you handled it at the time. Can you think of policies, procedures, or steps you might have had in place that would have either prevented the problem or made the problem less disruptive? Describe that policy or procedure.

2. Make a list of 10 questions you would like to ask a person who is applying for a position in your program. Review and rewrite those questions to make them welcoming and unbiased toward persons with disabilities. How can you make sure the questions focus more on the tasks of the job than on personal attributes? Having created these questions, would you recommend ways to rewrite the job description to be in compliance with ADA requirements?

3. Imagine that a single dad, Thomas, wants to enroll his twin sons, Ryan and Rocco, in your program. Thomas completes the authorized list for who can pick up Ryan and Rocco, but he does not include the twins' mom. Describe the steps you would take to balance the rights of both parents, while keeping the best interests of the twins in mind.

Team projects

1. Discuss professional experiences you have had where you feel you reacted too quickly to someone else. Consider what Fred Rogers learned from the Dalai Lama: "Someone else's action does not have to predict my response." Brainstorm with one another the options you have instead of reacting immediately; use websites or other sources about stress management. Develop a list of five tools you can use to remind yourself in the moment to step back rather than to overreact. Prepare and present a video or other demonstration about keeping cool under pressure.

2. Read aloud the case study about the McClures. Role-play how to apply the model departure-time crisis procedure with Mr. McClure. Now think of how you could prevent that crisis from taking place. How many indications of potential problems can you find in the case? Name the steps you could take in advance with family members to prevent the incident that occurred. Brainstorm together other potential crises that could occur when families pick up children. Select one of the most powerful crises and discuss how the crisis procedure might help.

3. Research your program's policy on giving references for current or former employees. What, if anything, would you change about that policy? Imagine that your cell phone rings: Evangeline is calling to ask you to give a reference for Jenna. What would you say, according to your current policy on references? If Jenna had signed a hold-harmless agreement allowing you to speak freely, how would you respond to each of the hypothetical situations listed about Jenna?

Bibliography

Americans with Disabilities Act of 1990, as Amended, 42 U.S.C. 12101 et seq (2008).

Bloomfield, D. 2012. *American Public Education Law*. 2nd ed. New York: Peter Lang.

Bruno, H.E. 2005. At the end of the day: Policies, procedures, and practices to ensure a smooth transition. *Child Care Information Exchange* (September–October): 66–69.

Bruno, H.E. 2010. 'Hold harmless' option for staff babysitting and employee references. *Exchange, the Early Childhood Leaders' Magazine* (May–June): 68–72.

Child Care Law Center. 1996. *Employing people with disabilities: The Americans with Disabilities Act and child care*. San Francisco, CA: Author.

Copeland, M.L. 1996. Code blue! Establishing a child care emergency plan. *Child Care Information Exchange* (January–February): 23–26.

Copeland, T. 2006. *Family child care contracts and policies: How to be businesslike in a caring profession*. 3rd ed. St. Paul, MN: Redleaf Press.

Copeland, T., & M. Millard. 2004. *Family child care legal and insurance guide: How to reduce the risks of running your business*. St. Paul, MN: Redleaf Press.

Podell, R. 1993. *Contagious emotions: Staying well when your loved one is depressed*. New York: Pocket Books.

Schimmel, D., S. Eckes, & M. Militello, 2010. *Principals teaching the law: Ten legal lessons your teachers must know*. Thousand Oaks, CA: Corwin Press.

Web resources

Americans with Disabilities Act home page
   www.ada.gov
Ethical Learning and Development Resources
   www.businessballs.com
Practical Information on Crisis Planning
   www.ed.gov/admins/lead/safety/crisisplanning.html
U.S. Department of Labor's Job Accommodation Network
   http://askjan.org
U.S. Equal Employment Opportunity Commission
   www.eeoc.gov

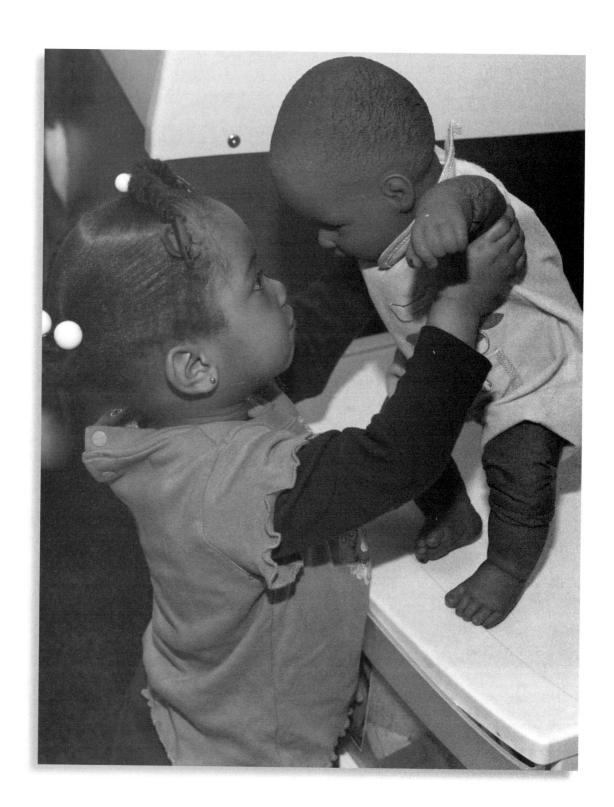

The person who says it cannot be done should not interrupt the person doing it.

—Chinese proverb

When I was young and would see scary things on the
news, my mother would say to me: "Look for the help-
ers. There are always people who are helping."

—Fred Rogers

8 Creating a Community of Problem Solvers: Winners, Not Whiners

Case Study—Gabriella and Maude

Gabriella is a free spirit. Children jump up and down in anticipation when she enters the classroom. Gabriella lives and breathes the "emergent curriculum" approach. When Javier finds a "hop toad" on the playground, for example, Gabriella spontaneously invites the children to imagine Mr. Hop Toad's world. Raina and Esther scrunch down to hop like Mr. Toad. Xavier wants to feed Hoppy a snack. Gabriella must leave at 3:00 p.m. for her second job, so she quickly passes out finger paints and paper. "Let's imagine how Mr. Hop Toad sees the world!" Gabriella says. Gabriella asks the children to spread their wet creations around the edge of the classroom floor to dry. "Tomorrow," she smiles, "We will tell each other all about Mr. Hop Toad's day." She breezes out of the classroom, waving to teacher's aide Tiara and ignoring Maude.

Maude thrives on order and organization. She believes children learn best in a structured environment with sequential lesson plans. Children pay attention to Maude because she brings engaging, hands-on, planned activities to class. Maude works hard to gather and organize materials for each lesson. When she sees the wet papers scattered on the classroom floor, she grows alarmed: "Someone will slip and fall!" Quickly, before families arrive to pick up their children, Maude collects the slippery "mess" and puts the papers into a large garbage bag. Maude thinks to herself, "Another lawsuit avoided!"

Maude's and Gabriella's very different teaching styles and approaches are a source of friction. They complain and gossip about each other to other teachers. Gabriella calls

Maude a "prissy control freak." Maude tells everyone how she is stuck working with "slobby Gabrielly." Even the children can feel the friction between their teachers.

The next morning, Gabriella, stunned, glares at Maude and demands, "What did you do with the children's finger paintings?" When you walk into the classroom, the tension is palpable. What would you do?

Directors often say, "I just want everyone

to be happy." In the best of worlds, everyone would appreciate everyone else. Differences would fascinate us. We would want to learn more about what we do not know. When we stumble and bump into each other, we would stop to talk directly about how to honor each other's space. We would value everyone's right to see the world in his or her own way. We would model for children how to solve problems respectfully. In *Slaughterhouse-Five,* author Kurt Vonnegut reminisced about such an ideal world: "Everything was beautiful and nothing hurt."

In this chapter, we will explore ways to create a community of problem solvers and transform whiners into winners.

Open communication, welcoming community

Envisioning early childhood programs as open, caring, lively, multicultural learning communities is ideal. To get there, many of us will address challenges that may be uncomfortable. Confrontation is a scary concept for many early childhood professionals. Can we become a welcoming community if we cannot openly identify, discuss, and resolve our inevitable differences? Perhaps these practices can help:

- We can agree to disagree.
- I don't have to love everyone, as long as I respect everyone.
- Facing my blind spots is difficult but also liberating.
- "My way or the highway" is the fast track to isolation.
- I have the right not to be right.

Shall we get to work on how to create a community of problem solvers? Imagine—a place where everyone is respected for who she or he is!

Supervising employees with very different temperaments, heritages, values, and backgrounds can be like herding cats. Everyone thinks she's right and heads off in her own direction. Confronting each other directly can be perceived as rude, aggressive, and distasteful. Teachers may form cliques, gossip about each other, whine to the director, and complain to parents.

Children imitate everything we do. Their mirror neurons are already hard at work, imitating adult role models. Imagine preschooler Raina whispering to her playmate Esther, "I'm not going to play with Xavier for a hundred years, are you?" Esther knows the only acceptable response is agreement. Children quickly learn the unwritten rule: "If you gossip to me, you will gossip about me."

▶ EXERCISE YOUR EQ   ▪ Check in with yourself: Do you believe our programs can be free of gossip, negativity, backbiting, and whining? Or do you believe we have to, at best, work around them?

I invite you to consider the strategies that follow. By using these tools, directors have successfully overcome gossip to create communities of problem solvers: winners, not whiners. Help is on the way. Both the NAEYC Code of Ethical Conduct (2011) and the National Association of Child Care Professionals [NACCP] Code of Ethics contain language against gossip. If it were possible to summarize the essence of both codes in one word, that word would be *respect*.

Gossip

What is gossip?

Gossip is an outmoded way to gain and maintain power at the expense of community: "Some women cannot bear to experience themselves as lesser lights; in order to shine more brightly, they must rid the stage of greater lights" (Chesler 2009, 465). Complaining about coworkers separates peer from peer. Cliques replace teams. Isolated fiefdoms crop up, intent on protecting their territory. Power struggles replace problem solving. Children learn how not to problem solve, even as we advise them to "use your words."

Why gossip?

Like bullies, gossipers wield power. Colleagues fear the consequences of standing up to a gossiper. Anyone who courageously resists Maude's gossiping is likely to be isolated, shunned, or mocked by Maude's followers. Gabriella has her own clique of supporters. Who is thinking about the children?

Gossipers establish power bases by promoting their own spin on reality. Unlike men, women tend to avoid direct confrontation, choosing instead to seek support from other women (Tannen 1990).

What about different ethnic groups and gossip? Teresa Bernandez studied three groups of women—Anglos, Latinas, and African Americans. What is your hunch about who gossips most? Bernandez found that European American women, who are most often taught that "if you can't say something nice, don't say it at all," gossip the most. Latinas also gossip. Bernandez notes religion may factor into this. Of the three groups, African American women gossip the least. Beverly

---

National Association of Child Care Professionals [NACCP] Code of Ethics

The National Association of Child Care Professionals is an association of people who are leaders in the field of early care and education. As an association, we believe that child care is a profession and that it is our responsibility as professional women and men to lead our centers in an ethical manner. Recognizing that the association is a vital link in this process, we determine to govern our individual centers as follows:

1. To maintain the ethical standards of the National Association of Child Care Professionals to more effectively serve our children, their parents, and the field.
2. To continually remember that ours is a service industry. We are committed to providing quality child care to our children and their families, and we place this service above personal gain.
3. To conduct our business in a way that will both maintain goodwill within the field and build the confidence of parents, the community, and fellow professionals. …
8. To avoid sowing discontent among the employees of competitors with the purpose of embarrassing or hindering their business.
9. To avoid possible damage to a competitor's image by purposefully misleading parents, members of the community, or fellow professionals. …
11. To conduct ourselves at all times in a way that will bring credit to our association and the child care field.

What Is Gossip?

Gossip is:

    Communicating about another person . . .

    Who is not present . . .

    With the intention of harming that person's reputation.

    Listening to gossip.

Gossip is not:

    Sharing accurate, necessary, appropriate information.

    Holding an opinion about another person.

Bam!radio

"Dealing with the Unspoken Challenges Women Educators Face"

Interview with Phyllis Chesler

Heart to Heart Conversations on Leadership

http://bamradionetwork.com

Green, in commenting on her research, observes: "Because they have been exposed to both racism and sexism, [African American] women have learned to be direct."

Feeney and Freeman (2005), in speaking about the use of the NAEYC Code of Ethical Conduct, note: "Ethical behavior requires thought and reflection, pride and humility, a willingness to change, and the courage to stay steadfast" (73). Instead of working toward being a community of problem solvers, cliques sow seeds of dissention.

Creating gossip-free zones

To borrow a line from the astronauts in the movie *Apollo 13*, "Early childhood professionals, we have a problem." Too often, staff and directors avoid conflict and "resolve" their problems indirectly through gossip, negativity, sabotage, and backbiting. Our organizational culture needs a makeover.

Are you ready to consider changing the way we do business? Here are practical, everyday approaches to transforming pettiness into professionalism:

- **Update employee job descriptions.** Add and enforce this statement as a functional requirement of the job: "Maintain a gossip-free work environment."

- **Be vocal and clear about your stand against gossip.** Picture a director who posts this sign in her office: "Is this good for children and families?" That director can place every instance of gossip in its proper perspective. "Gabriella, when you spoke to Xavier's mom about your team teacher, how was that helpful to Xavier or his mom?"

- **Apply the five steps and principles of directive supervision to gossipers.** (See Chapter 9 for the full discussion of directive supervision.) "Maude, referring to your team teacher as 'slobby Gabrielly' is out of line. This program has zero tolerance for gossip. What will you do to change your behavior?"

- **Prominently display your organization's mission statement.** Motown legend Aretha Franklin got it right: *Respect* is crucial. Early childhood mission and philosophy statements hold respect for others and ourselves as essential. Respect is demonstrated through effective communication and by placing organizational goals above personal gain.

- **At staff meetings, problem solve using NAEYC's Code of Ethical Conduct or NACCP's Code of Ethics.** Devote staff development sessions to skill building in how to create gossip-free zones. Ask staff to practice applying the ethical codes to case studies. (Examples are included in this chapter.)

- **Provide peers with empowering statements and practices to stop gossip.** Gossip-stopping statements like "I need to focus on the children right now" or "I am not comfortable talking about someone who is not present" halt gossip in its tracks. (More gossip stoppers follow in the next section.)

- **Educate and guide employees in effective problem-solving techniques.** Three techniques for resolving conflicts are highlighted later in the chapter.

- **Select and train a team of peer coaches.** Recognize employees who demonstrate problem-solving expertise by designating, training, and honoring them as peer coaches.

- **Contract for a gossip-free program.** Following sessions in effective problem solving, invite employees to read, discuss, and sign a **Problem-Solving Agreement**. Add this policy to your staff handbook, and place their signed commitment statements in employees' files.

Principle 3A–2:

When we have concerns about the professional behavior of a co-worker, we shall first let that person know of our concern in a way that shows respect for personal dignity and for the diversity to be found among staff members, and then attempt to resolve the matter collegially and in a confidential manner.

—NAEYC Code of Ethical Conduct

Ideal 2.5:

To create and maintain a climate of trust and candor that fosters two-way communication and enables parents/guardians to speak and act in the best interest of their children.

—NAEYC Code of Ethical Conduct: Supplement for Early Childhood Administrators

- **Update your staff handbook.** Add a **Problem-Solving Commitment** statement to your policies:

Our program has zero tolerance for gossip. [Alternatively, This program is a gossip-free work environment.] We are committed to respectful, problem-solving communication. As professionals, we do not have time for gossip.

Using directive supervision to weed out gossip and negativity

When ethical standards are not enforced, gossip spreads like the flu. Trish, a Bright Horizons director in Massachusetts, was "sick and tired of being sick and tired" of the debilitating effects of gossip on her program. Trish and her assistant director called a staff meeting dedicated to creating a gossip-free work environment. After much discussion, staff were asked to sign a **Problem Solving Agreement**.

The next day, when gossip resumed, Trish called each gossiper into her office and for each she applied the supervisor's five principles of *directive supervision* (see Chapter 9 for the principles). Trish reminded each gossiper her behavior was being documented; the next steps were probation and termination. Within a month, one staff member resigned and another was fired. Staff morale rose, uplifting children and families.

Peer power to stop gossip

For sure, employees feel supported in doing their part when they observe supervisors enforcing a gossip-free zone policy. What power does each staff member have to stop gossip? Consider the chapter case study. Maude may decide she will not gossip from this day forward. She may vow not to talk about Gabriella to others. Maude also resolves not to say anything when a gossiper complains to her. Maude, with her director's prodding, has decided to change her behavior in important ways.

Will these strategies be enough to stop gossip? Remember, by definition "listening to gossip" is itself gossiping. By listening to gossip, we enable the gossiper to continue spreading negativity without interruption. The gossiper may even boast that others who merely listen *agree* with her!

Instead of tacitly accepting gossip by listening to it, teachers need effective statements to stop gossip from spreading. At the same time, some peers may not yet feel confident enough to directly confront the gossiper. Teachers may fear becoming targets for gossip if they challenge the gossiper.

The next time someone you know gossips to you, try responding with one of the gossip stoppers that follow. By using one of these statements, you practice taking responsibility for your own behavior, without becoming the next bull's-eye for a gossiper. Gossip decreases and the gossiper may even have to question her motivation. As director, you can offer staff these gossip stoppers:

- "I am not comfortable talking about a person who is not present."

- "I need to focus on the children now."

Problem-Solving Agreement

I, [*employee's name*], an employee of [*program's name*], agree to promptly and directly raise any issue I have with another staff member. I agree to work with my colleague to find a mutually agreeable solution, building on both of our strengths. If, after a good-faith effort, the conflict remains unresolved, I will request a meeting with my director (or designee) and my colleague. I agree to take to that meeting at least two possible solutions that will honor the organization's and both person's needs. I agree neither to gossip about, nor hold back from resolving, an issue that affects the quality of care and education. I will participate fully in staff development sessions on problem-solving techniques.

Signature   Date

Bam!radio

"Curtailing High Turnover Among Early Childhood Educators"

Interview with Holly Elissa Bruno by Mark Ginsberg and Rae Pica

NAEYC Radio Channel

Heart to Heart Conversations on Leadership

http://bamradionetwotk.com

- "Would you be willing to talk with [name] about your concern with her?"
- "I'll go with you so you can share your concern with [name]."
- "I promised not to gossip."
- "Let's not go there."
- "Since I can't help you with that problem, please don't raise it with me again."
- "Diana Ross says: Stop, in the name of love, before you break my heart! Think it over."
- "Remember, we signed an agreement not to gossip."
- "Our mission statement on the wall says we respect differences."
- "When we earned NAEYC Accreditation, we agreed to do no harm to children. Do you want the children to learn to gossip?"

Each of these statements is respectful and effective at stopping the spread of gossip and negativity. As a leader, you can help staff say no to gossipers by including these statements in a handbook or discussing them during a meeting.

Can teachers overcome their fears and take a stand against gossip? Preschool lead teacher Danielle Donati Gulden recalls:

> I found the hardest part of working with women was gossip. I used to crave it like a drug, but have since recovered. I let my co-teachers know that I had my fill of gossip and to leave me out of the mix. Whenever I would hear gossip, I would say to myself, "Walk away, walk away." Eventually they just stopped including me in the gossip. It never felt so good to be left out. (pers. comm)

Consider **Case Study—LaVonda**. Imagine you are LaVonda's team teacher. What could you do as a peer to stop the damaging behavior? Alternatively, as director, what could you do to help prevent or resolve the conflicts involving this new hire?

Case Study—LaVonda

LaVonda was hired to replace Betty, who stole from the petty cash. Teachers resent that Betty was fired. No one wants to work with LaVonda. They avoid LaVonda, make up stories about her, and leave her out of conversations. This afternoon, Yvette and Trixie invite you to go shopping after work. LaVonda is standing beside you. They look right through her.

What do you do?

Think about responding this way: "That was rude. LaVonda is a teacher here, too. Show her respect." Taking this direct approach stops gossip in its tracks, but not every teacher feels ready to be so direct. Administrators need to help staff develop courage and skills to effectively face situations like this one. Directors can invite staff to create case studies to role-play at team meetings. With practice, each employee will hone her own style at stopping gossip.

Eliminating whining in the workplace

Just as gossip can harm workplaces, so can whining. The whiner sighs and unloads her burdens, expecting your rapt attention. If you offer solutions to her problem, the whiner is not interested. Authors Rick Brinkman and Rick Kirschner explain, "Whiners feel helpless and overwhelmed by an unfair world. Their standard is perfectionism, and no one and nothing measures up to it. But misery loves company, so they bring their problems to you. Offering solutions makes you bad company, so their whining escalates" (2002, 11).

Whiners demand control. Not only do they require your complete attention, they must control the topic, who speaks, who listens, and what the outcome will be—more whining. Whiners expect their listeners to sympathize and confirm how terrible things are. Whiners are victims. The world has done them wrong. Nothing and no one can help. The whiner sees it as your job to soothe and confirm how very difficult her troubles must be.

Why do we listen to whiners? We see ourselves as nurturers and soothers. The majority of us fear conflict. To use tough love with a whiner—that is, to coach her to take action and move on—is counterintuitive. So we sit. We listen. We console. We grow weary.

Two types of whiners

As a leader, you need to know there are two types of whiners—the situational whiner and the chronic whiner (Bruno 2011):

- **Situational whiners** struggle with a specific dilemma they can't resolve alone. Partner with them to resolve the dilemma. With solutions spelled out and action taken, their burden lifts and whining stops. In other words, once you help the lion remove the thorn from his paw, he heals and returns to his daily path.

- **Chronic whiners** are trapped in their world of no solutions. They "suffer from a severe inability to see what could and should be, but compensate with the ability to see only what's wrong with what was and what is" (Brinkman & Kirschner 2002, 169). The thorn in this lion's paw becomes a thorn in your side.

Supervising the situational whiner

Once a situational whiner gets help with her conflict, she no longer whines. With the situational whiner, ask:

- What is causing so much pain? Can you give me an example to help me understand?

- Let's imagine the problem can be resolved. What help do you need from me?

- What is one step, however small, you can take to work your way out of this dilemma?

Maintain boundaries about what you will and won't do to help. With this focused assistance, most situational whiners can work through the issue and regain their optimism. If this approach does not work, this is a circumstance in which a peer might say, "Since I can't help you with that problem, please don't bring it to me again." This phrase works like a charm. I know this from personal experience:

> When my peer Leigh Ann first complained to me about her boss, I said, "Leigh Ann, let's go talk with him and work this out." She refused. The next day, she complained again. I went through the steps above, asking her to help me understand the real issue, how I might help, and to identify at least one thing she could do to ameliorate the problem. Again, she refused. When she returned the third time with the same complaints, I said, "Leigh Ann, since I can't help you with that problem, please don't bring

Bam!radio

"Dealing with People You Can't Stand"
Interview with Rick Kirschner
Heart to Heart Conversations on Leadership.
http://bamradionetwork.com/

"Silencing the Whiners on Your Staff"
Interview with Holly Elissa Bruno
National Head Start Association radio
www.jackstreet.com/jackstreet/WNHSA.Bruno.cfm

it to me again." For the next few days, I watched her approach me, stop herself, and go elsewhere. What a relief!

Unfortunately, Leigh Ann's negativity eventually cost her her job.

Supervising the chronic whiner

For chronic whiners, feeling victimized is a way of life. Directors, as supervisors, may need to take yet another step with a chronically whining employee. Brinkman and Kirschner advise: "If you are the manager of the [chronic] whiner, it is important to take control and draw the line firmly on complaining, since this behavior, more than any other . . . can undermine and destroy morale and team spirit" (2002, 173).

For sure, a whiner's dreariness affects the mirror neurons and thus the mood of everyone he or she encounters. Have you seen the domino effect of one teacher's complaining: "We tried that before. It didn't work then and it won't work now"? A "can't do" attitude flattens everyone's spirit.

Are chronic whiners protected by the ADA, as amended?

Depression afflicts about one in 10 people in the United States (Centers for Disease Control and Prevention 2011). Chronic whiners may actually be suffering from depression. Depression robs us of our energy, optimism, and hope; whining can be a symptomatic consequence.

Linda Carter Batiste tells us that clinical depression is a disability under the Americans with Disabilities Act, as amended (podcast). However, supervisors cannot legally ask a seemingly despondent employee, "Do you have a disability like depression, perhaps?" But a supervisor can ask, "Is there anything you want to share with me about why you have been so discouraged and overwhelmed recently?"

Once the whiner tells you she is clinically depressed, however, she opens the door for ADA assistance. Thank her for confiding in you with this important information. Tell her you would like to talk through reasonable accommodations to help her do her work with the energy and enthusiasm the children need. Ask her to provide you with her doctor's description of the disability (diagnosis) and recommendations for reasonable accommodations. The remedy might be as simple as providing a safe, private place at work for her to store her medication and/or changing her schedule to ensure she takes the medication on time. Successfully treated, the whiner soon enough will become "herself" again, appreciated for her work rather than avoided for her negativity.

What do you do if a chronic whiner says nothing about disability . . . or does not have a disability and is simply an expert naysayer? For Brinkman and Kirschner (2002), the answer is confrontation: "If you don't want to talk solutions, that's your decision. But I don't want to hear any more complaining and I don't want you distracting the people around you by whining about your problems to them. When you're ready to talk solutions, I'll be here" (173).

You may need to initiate the progressive discipline process (see Chapter 9) with the chronic whiner. Your message is this: "Stop the unprofessional behavior or leave the organization." Sound too rigorous? Shore up your resolve by imagining your program without the constant whining. Oodles of time and energy will be freed up to devote to children and families!

Bam!radio
"Sweeping New Definitions of Disabilities: What You Need to Know"
Interview with Linda Carter Batiste

"How to Click with People in Relationships"
Interview with Rick Kirschner
Heart to Heart Conversations on Leadership
http://bamradionetwork.com

Principle 3.1:
We shall provide staff members with safe and supportive working conditions that respect human dignity, honor confidences and permit them to carry out their responsibilities through performance evaluation, written grievance procedures, constructive feedback, and opportunities for continuing professional development and advancement.
—NAEYC Code of Ethical Conduct: Supplement for Early Childhood Program Administrators

Problem-solving practices

Modeling problem solving for children

It is valuable to remember that children learn how to resolve their conflicts by observing adults work through their disagreements. Recalling this encourages us to keep our problems in perspective. Although difficult at times, detaching from a heated "my way or the highway" stance rewards us with cooling perspective. The key question is: *How can we resolve this issue in a way that models problem solving for the children? If children were observing us resolving our problems, what would we want them to notice?* By remaining focused on helping the children as we help ourselves, we might feel a stronger motivation for respectful conflict resolution.

Adults ask children to work through problems by saying, "Use your words." When children learn to use words instead of shoving, hitting, or snatching away a toy, children learn an approach to resolving their difficulties. Unless we use our words effectively, we cannot demonstrate to children mature, cooperative behavior.

Finding the words to use is especially difficult when a child or an adult feels angry, hurt, resentful, fearful, or helpless. For this reason, step-by-(empowering-) step practices work best.

Does venting help or hurt?

Some employees need to vent, or express their upset feelings, before they can calm down to problem solve with the other person. Some directors and supervisors encourage staff to "blow off steam" and get upset feelings out in the open before problem solving. Can we expect employees to problem solve effectively when they are still feeling wounded or "hot under the collar" about the other person?

Venting is like taking the top off a boiling pot. Releasing the steam eases the intensity. Recall from Chapter 2 the amygdala hijack concept. Goleman (2010) warns us about the temporary power of the amygdala to "hijack" our EQ and our IQ. When we feel threatened, our amygdala triggers the flow of adrenaline or cortisol through our system. If you have ever felt like running away from or yelling at another person, you may know what an amygdala hijack feels like. We enter the "fight or flight" mode. Professionalism temporarily flies out the window until we can step to the side to calm down.

Although it may feel good at the time to let loose with a verbal barrage, venting does not solve the problem. For venting to be a productive first step in problem solving, it needs to be:

- Limited in time (i.e., no more than five minutes)
- Shared with a supervisor (not with peers) and in private
- Followed up with a commitment and action plan to resolve the underlying problem

Not only does venting not solve the problem, venting itself can be construed as gossiping. However, when it adheres to the three constraints above, venting can be useful to those of us with an amygdala prone to hijacking.

By prohibiting gossip and whining, are we infringing on our employees' rights? Views differ. One attorney may argue that anti-gossip policies, procedures, and practices are violations of labor laws and that employees need to be able to express themselves freely in the workplace. One director related that in a prior profession, while working in a hospital, she was disciplined for gossiping about her supervisor while working. But, this professional says, thanks to the efforts of a labor law attorney, she was given a financial settlement to compensate for the infringement of her free speech rights.

Other attorneys, including me, maintain that organizations can set standards for employee conduct that exceed minimum licensing standards. In educational settings, teachers serve as role models for children. The organizational climate affects children and their families the minute they arrive on our doorstep. We owe children and one another a positive, uplifting environment where everyone feels free to learn and grow. Gossip and negativity harm children, their families, and our peers. For this reason, higher standards set by anti-gossip and professionalism policies are warranted.

You may wish to check with an attorney if you have concerns about labor laws or related policies and their possible applicability to no-gossiping or no-whining policies and practices.

Strategies for resolving conflict

The Z method

One effective problem-solving method, which has been adapted from a Myers-Briggs model, follows the contour of the letter *Z* (see Kroeger & Thuesen 1992, 163). At the starting point of the *Z*, the ending point, and each joint in the letter, we ask a different question. As "opponents" share answers, each person is invited to listen to how the other person perceives the situation. In the process, each may discover the value in letting go of the belief that he or she can control another person.

Let's walk with Gabriella and Maude through the *Z* method's four turning points:

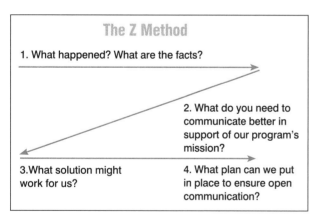

The Z Method

1. What happened? What are the facts?

2. What do you need to communicate better in support of our program's mission?

3. What solution might work for us?

4. What plan can we put in place to ensure open communication?

1. **Determine what happened; what are the facts?** Focus on your own observations: no blaming, shaming, or inflaming the other person. Judgmental accusations about the other person seriously impede mutual problem solving. Keep the focus on yourself and what you experienced. A leader can keep the discussion on track by asking questions such as:

Gabriella, could you describe what activity you did with the children on the playground yesterday afternoon?

Maude, please describe, as factually as possible, what you observed and what action you took shortly after Gabriella left for work yesterday.

When each person has described her actions and observations, we may see a shift in one or both people. Often, we are reminded we are both looking at the same glass, even though one sees it as half full and the other sees it as half empty. Facts are concrete and nonjudgmental. This first step invites each person to be more open to listening to the other.

2. **Determine what Gabriella and Maude need in order to communicate better for the sake of the children.** Once we have elicited the facts, the leader can ask:

Gabriella, what do you need to feel the classroom is open to spontaneous learning, while also affording children the predictability they need?

Maude, what do you need to feel the classroom is safe and structured and at the same time to allow for emergent curriculum?

In this step, one or both teachers may still feel the need to attack the other. Gabriella may call Maude uptight and inflexible. Remind her to keep the focus on finding solutions. Maude may repeatedly glance at her watch and imply that the discussion is pointless. Ask them both: "How can you work together to resolve this problem in a way that models problem solving for children?"

3. **Brainstorm solutions that work for the program and build on each person's strengths.** The leader might ask them:

> *Gabriella, what do you respect about Maude's teaching?*
>
> *Maude, can you name at least one solution that honors both Gabriella's and your teaching styles?*

Help each person name something she honestly values about the other. As each person hears something positive about herself from her "opponent," that opponent no longer looks like "the enemy." Ask each employee to identify the strengths the other person brings to the workplace. Invite them to brainstorm ways in which they better serve children by sharing their strengths and meeting each other's needs.

4. **Create together a plan that ensures ongoing, open communication.** The leader would ask:

> *Gabriella, what will you do in the future to work effectively with Maude?*
>
> *Maude, what steps will you take to work more effectively with Gabriella?*

I have observed that 98 percent of peer conflicts are the result of miscommunication. When a teacher feels misunderstood and unappreciated, she "turns off" the other teacher. Employees need systems for continuous communication.

Maude and Gabriella's problem is solved temporarily by putting up a drying rack. Invite them to find and agree on ongoing ways they can continuously communicate. Planning meetings every Friday afternoon? Using a shared notebook to write notes to each other? Gabriella can create an artistic cover, and Maude can organize the inside of it!

Peer coaching method

A *peer coach* is an on-call, trusted, resident "expert" who helps colleagues work through conflict. Directors can call on skillful problem solvers to serve as peer coaches.

Transitioning from indirect to direct behavior can be awkward for all of us. Some team members will be quicker than others to master problem-solving skills. Beginner problem solvers may require a director's special time and assistance to help them hone their skills. Peer coaches support the director's efforts by reinforcing problem-solving practices.

In addition to using the *Z* method, peer coaches can draw from the following five-step coaching process, made popular by professional coaches:

1. What is your **vision** of how you could work together effectively?

2. What are the **barriers** to working together?

3. Name **three steps** you can take to improve the situation.

4. **Take one step at a time.**

5. **Meet again** to discuss, "What is our vision/hope now?"

The peer coach asks the "opponents" about their hopes, barriers that get in the way, and steps they can take to make their program and classrooms highly functional

> You won't always make just the right decision about the most effective way to communicate, and that's where reflection can help. After something happens, you can rethink it and learn from it.
>
> —Janet Gonzalez-Mena

learning environments. This collaborative process invites coworkers to share responsibility for resolving their problems. Coaches remind each person to focus on what is best for children and families.

▶ EXERCISE YOUR EQ ■ Apply the five steps of the peer coaching process to Gabriella and Maude. What would you ask? What might they respond? How can you keep them on track?

Getting to Yes and Difficult Conversations methods

The strategies called Getting to Yes and Difficult Conversations emerged from work by the Harvard Negotiation Project on peaceful resolution of conflict. They share three powerful concepts:

1. Rather than waste time arguing over who should win, devote energy to understanding and accepting that each of us sees the world through different eyes.

2. Compromise often results in "unfinished business" and resentment. Aim instead for a deeper solution that honors each person's values.

3. If we look deep enough, we will find a point of agreement between the opposing parties.

As described in **Case Study—President Jimmy Carter**, President Jimmy Carter used such a strategy in 1978 as he negotiated a peace agreement with leaders of warring rivals Israel and Egypt. Notice how President Carter helped both leaders find the *yes* upon which they could agree. Consider how you might use the Getting to Yes strategy as you apply the *Z* and/or peer coaching methods of conflict resolution. What, for example, is the deeper value Gabriella and Maude share that can offset the sting of their biases?

Case Study—President Jimmy Carter

President Jimmy Carter invited Egyptian President Anwar Sadat and Israeli Prime Minister Menachem Begin to meet at Camp David. President Carter's goal was to negotiate a peace accord between the leaders, whose differences were deep, long-lasting, and painful. Neither man was willing to budge. President Sadat was about to walk out of the sessions.

At that point, President Carter asked Prime Minister Begin, "Do you have grandchildren?" Begin softened and responded that he did. Carter then asked, "Can you show us their pictures?" The proud grandfather spread photos of his energetic grandchildren on the table. "Tell us about each of these delightful children," Carter encouraged. As Begin lovingly told a story about each child, Sadat began to edge closer to see and hear who these children were.

Carter next turned to Sadat and asked the same questions: "Do you have grandchildren? Could you show us their pictures? What is each one of these glorious children like?" As Sadat beamed with pride, Begin inched closer to see and to hear.

At the end of the day, the two men agreed they wanted a better future for their grandchildren. They signed the peace agreement that brought freedom from fear to both of their countries. They agreed wholeheartedly that all grandchildren deserve a promising future, free of fear and warfare.

The Difficult Conversations method answers the question "Can I change another person?" with a resounding *no!* When we try to persuade another person that we are right and he or she is wrong, we cannot win. If we focus instead on listening to "where the other person is coming from," and he or she in turn listens to our view of reality, together we are more able to find a solution. Have you ever been able to change another person?

Apply these practices to the chapter case study scenario: When Gabriella hears that Maude feared for the children's safety, Gabriella has the opportunity to see the situation through Maude's eyes. As Maude hears how important the children's creative artwork is to Gabriella, Maude is invited to pay attention to what matters to Gabriella. With practice, team members will begin to expect differences rather than attempting to deny or destroy differences.

The Difficult Conversations strategy focuses problem solvers on three questions (Stone, Patton, & Heen 2010):

1. What happened?

2. What feelings were triggered, both expressed and unexpressed?

3. What matters to you most?

As President Carter knew, and leaders Begin and Sadat came to see, creating a better world for our grandchildren matters most. In early childhood education, what matters most? When we agree on that, we agree to resolve our interpersonal conflicts for the sake of the children. To do this, we need to detach ourselves from the desire to prevail over another person. As we look more deeply at what we all want, we can find our way back to why we are in this profession after all.

Multicultural problem-solving approaches

Case Study—Kioko

Kioko relocated with her parents from Japan when she was in high school. Now, as a bright, creative, sensitive teacher, Kioko is viewed with great respect and caring by her peers. Kioko's cultural heritage encourages her to help everyone "save face." She takes care to make sure conflicts do not come out in the open. Kioko is more comfortable listening to people complain and gossip than she is to saying anything to stop or divert them. The program has just agreed to become a "gossip-free zone." One sentence of the new policy in particular troubles Kioko: "If you listen to gossip, you are gossiping."

As her director, how can you honor Kioko's culture while upholding official program policy?

Given the richness of cultures represented in our programs, diverse approaches to conflict are to be welcomed and expected. Some cultures encourage directness. People in these cultures need little physical distance from each other as they communicate. Israeli culture might be described this way. Other cultures encourage reserve and reticence. To stand too close to a person in the Japanese culture, for example, could be offensive. How can we honor cultural differences while upholding program problem-solving policies?

The first question to ask is: Does the policy respectfully embrace cultural differences? When introducing a policy, such as the **Problem-Solving Agreement** (p. 133), invite employees to discuss the change at a staff meeting and to individually comment on the change. If you know a policy may conflict with a staff member's culture, invite that person to share her thoughts and observations with you first.

From there, a leader has at least two options—revise the policy to make it more culturally sensitive, or find ways to institute the policy while allowing each staff member to bring his or her own heritage to the practice of the policy. Look also to the spirit of the policy. In spirit, the **Problem-Solving Agreement** aims at requiring adults to take responsibility and resolve their problems together. Regarding the case study involving Kioko, you could ask her what processes work in her culture when people have unresolved conflicts. Then, you could incorporate as many of those practices as possible. Alternatively, you could work with Kioko on what she is comfortable doing and saying to promote the spirit of the policy. In the end, you may discover some approaches you never envisioned.

Debra Ren-Etta Sullivan, who wrote an account of the successful multicultural Pacific Oaks Northwest learning community she co-created with colleagues in Seattle, Washington, knows the work is never done. Nonetheless, in an online interview with Redleaf Press, Sullivan (2005) optimistically reminds us:

> When I see those who educate and care for young children advocating for the rights of all children to have a strong, healthy start in life, that makes me smile because we are growing leaders and their leadership may make all the difference in the world to the one young child who needs it most.

A multicultural community of problem solvers leads to a strong, healthy start in life.

> Never let your sense of morals get in the way of doing what's right.
>
> —Isaac Asimov

Community

Without the capacity to resolve our inevitable differences, we cannot live in a community. *Community* means living and working together in support of one another's and the community's well-being. The African adage "It takes a village to raise a child" fits early childhood programs like a beloved pair of blue jeans.

I asked colleagues across the country: "To fully participate in a multicultural community, what three ground rules would you most need that community to follow?" Here are three responses to my question from three corners of the country.

Donna Rafanello, California

1. All contributions are welcomed and valued.

2. Participants need to commit to the process and be willing to actively engage in change and to be changed by it.

3. Enter into the conversation with awareness that others' ways of doing things and thinking may be as good, or better, than your own.

Cathy Jones, South Carolina

We will:

1. Hold at the core of our community *respect* for the right to be different.

2. Have the freedom to express our differing opinions without fear of retribution.

3. Work through issues with love and respect and never walk away until consensus or resolution is reached.

Arthur LaFrance, Oregon

Our community must:

1. Have a purpose/function beyond itself.

2. Agree upon a process for inclusion, action, and dissolution before commencement.

3. Have leadership that is time limited.

4. Recognize me as leader for life, and anyone who doesn't like that should get out now!

> My thanks to fellow attorney Art for being direct (and tongue in cheek)!

▶ EXERCISE YOUR EQ   ▨   What are at least three ground rules you would establish to promote a multicultural community of problem solvers?

Reflecting on all the ideas and approaches in this chapter, what strikes you as most important? What does it take to build a community of problem solvers?

*   *   *

I have come to see that my sense of humor is one of my most valuable emotional intelligence capacities. I know, too, that when I am able to detach, step onto the balcony, and get perspective on a heated issue, I am more able to see what matters to everyone, not just to me. Humor and perspective: I don't leave home without them! At least that is what I remind myself when my old friend "my way or the highway" comes calling.

What are your most valued EQ capacities?

Reflection questions

1. What phrases and principles can you find in NACCP's Code of Ethics to support a director's efforts to end gossip, negativity, and other unproductive behavior? Apply these principles to one of the cases in the chapter.

2. Reflect on your own experience of working, studying, or living with women. What strengths and difficulties predictably emerge? Are your experiences different when you work with men and when you work with both men and women together? Do you attribute these differences to nature, nurture, or both? Find at least one research study to support your theory and one that differs from your theory.

> "Nature or nurture?" is a phrase used to acknowledge that some traits are genetic or inborn (nature), whereras others are learned and/or result from our environment (nurture).

3. Take a look at your own cultural background. Begin by reflecting on each of your names (first name, surname, middle name, and/or confirmation name). Why was each of these names chosen? Were you named after someone? What heritage does your name carry? What is your family's history in this country? Was the family name changed or lost at any point? Write a reflection paper on how your cultural background contributes to your view of family, work and success, and conflict resolution.

Team projects

1. Read the following case study about Betty. Discuss the questions. Develop a plan to (a) prevent Betty from disrupting the program and (b) hold Betty accountable for changing her behavior. What tactics does Betty use to gain power? In what ways might Betty's behavior affect team members and program morale? Have you known and/or dealt with a person who behaved like Betty? Look at the approaches described in this chapter: What action do you think you might take, both as a peer and as Betty's supervisor?

Case Study—Betty

If Alice has offended Betty, Betty will tell Carolyn and Diane about it—but in such a way as to enlist Carolyn and Diane against Alice by persuading them that Alice has, indeed, not only unfairly offended Betty but offended Carolyn and Diane as well. Of course, Alice might have done no such thing. Betty will carefully manage how she presents "past events." She will do so in order to gain the support of a clique imbued with "righteous indignation," which will then assist Betty in any future confrontation with Alice or in a decision to shun Alice. Betty must accomplish this without appearing to intend to. (Adapted from Chesler 2009, 111.)

2. Research additional problem-solving approaches, other than the ones described in this chapter. Select two approaches that appeal most to you. Prepare a presentation on each of them. Apply the approaches to Gabriella and Maude.

3. Investigate and discuss how conflict is viewed and dealt with by at least three cultures other than your own. How do you feel about these other approaches? What can you learn about conflict resolution from other cultures? As a leader of a program, what actual steps could you take to ensure that cultural differences are respected when conflicts arise?

Bibliography

Brinkman, R., & R. Kirschner. 2002. *Dealing with people you can't stand: How to bring out the best in people at their worst.* 2nd ed. New York: McGraw-Hill.

Bruno, H.E. 2007. Gossip-free zones: Problem solving to prevent power struggles. *Young Children* 62 (5): 26–27, 29–33.

Bruno, H.E. 2011. Eliminate whining in the workplace: Moving beyond "grin and bear it." *Exchange: The Early Childhood Leaders' Magazine* (July–August): 93–96.

Bruno, H.E., & M.L. Copeland. 1999. If the director isn't direct, can the team have direction? *Leadership Quest* (Winter).

Cahill, L., M. Uncapher, L. Kilpatrick, M.T. Alkire, & J. Turner. 2004. Sex-related hemispheric lateralization of amygdala function in emotionally influenced memory: An fMRI investigation. *Learning & Memory* 11: 261–66.

Centers for Disease Control and Prevention. 2011. An estimated 1 in 10 U.S. adults report depression. www.cdc.gov/features/dsdepression.

Chesler, P. 2009. *Woman's inhumanity to woman.* Rev. ed. Chicago: Lawrence Hill Books.

Copeland, M.L., & H.E. Bruno. 2001. Countering center gossip: Guidelines for implementing an anti-gossip policy. *Child Care Exchange* March/April: 22–25.

Feeney, S., & N.K. Freeman. 2005. *Ethics and the early childhood educator: Using the NAEYC Code.* Rev. ed. Washington, DC: NAEYC.

Fisher, R., W. Ury, & B. Patton. 2011. *Getting to yes: Negotiating agreement without giving in.* Rev. ed. New York: Penguin Books.

Goleman, D. 2003. *Destructive emotions: How can we overcome them? A scientific dialogue with the Dalai Lama.* New York, NY: Bantam Dell.

Goleman, D. 2010. *Emotional intelligence: Why it can matter more than IQ.* London: Bloomsbury.

Gonzalez-Mena, J. 2007. *Diversity in early care and education: Honoring differences.* 5th ed. New York: McGraw-Hill.

Jordan, J.V., ed. 1997. *Women's growth in diversity: More writings from the Stone Center.* New York: Guilford Press.

Kirschner, R. 2011. *How to click with people: The secret to better relationships in business and in life.* New York: Hyperion.

Kroeger, O., J.M. Thuesen, & H. Rutledge. 1992. *Type talk at work: How the 16 personality types determine your success on the job.* Rev. ed. New York: Delta.

Kyle, A. 2007. *The god of animals: A novel.* New York: Scribner.

National Association of Child Care Professionals code of ethics. Nd. www.naccp.org/displaycommon.cfm?an=1&subarticlenbr=287.

NAEYC. 2011. *Code of Ethical Conduct and statement of commitment.* Position Statement. Reaffirmation of 2005 rev. ed. Washington, DC: Author. www.naeyc.org/positionstatement/ethics_conduct.

Stone, D., B. Patton, & S. Heen. 2010. *Difficult conversations: How to discuss what matters most.* Updated ed. New York: Penguin Group.

Sullivan, D.R. 2009. *Learning to lead: Effective leadership skills for teachers of young children.* 2nd ed. St. Paul, MN: Redleaf Press.

Sullivan, D.R. 2005. *Interview with Redleaf Press.* www.redleafpress.org/client/archives/features/rl_Aug2005_feature.cfm.

Tanenbaum, L. 2002. *Catfight: Women and competition.* New York: Seven Stories Press.

Tannen, D. 1990. *You just don't understand: Women and men in conversation.* New York: Ballantine Books.

Woolsey, L.K., & L.-L. McBain. 1987. Issues of power and powerlessness in all-woman groups. *Women's Studies International Forum* 10 (6): 579–88.

Web resources

Are Your Workers Whiners or Winners?
www.humannatureatwork.com/Workers_Whiners_Winners.html

Articles on Conflict Resolution and Negotiation
www.abetterworkplace.com/conflicts.html

Managing in a Multicultural Workplace
www.enewsbuilder.net/theayersgroup/e_article000935108.cfm?x=b11,0,w - a935108

NAEYC Code of Ethical Conduct and Statement of Commitment
http://www.naeyc.org/files/naeyc/file/positions/Ethics%20Position%20Statement2011.pdf

Problem-Solving Techniques
www.mindtools.com/pages/main/newMN_TMC.htm

Stop the Gossip, Save Your Career
http://career-advice.monster.com/in-the-office/workplace-issues/stop-the-gossip-save-your-career-hot-jobs/article.aspx

Norming

Establishing Management Systems

> We'd all like to feel self-reliant and capable of coping with whatever adversity comes our way, but that's not how most human beings are made. It's my belief that the capacity to accept help is inseparable from the capacity to give help when our turn comes to be strong.
> —Fred Rogers, *You are Special*

> If your actions inspire others to dream more, learn more, do more, and become more, you are a leader.
> —John Quincy Adams

9 Supervision and Staff Development: Social EQ in Action

Case Study—Francia and Jasmine

Francia, an outstanding toddler teacher, is a dedicated mom to her four young children. Her husband expects a homemade meal on the table every evening, a clean house, and time with the wife he loves. Francia is highly motivated to earn her early childhood degrees. With English as her second language, no money to spare, and fears about feeling inadequate in a college classroom, Francia asks you, her director, for guidance.

Jasmine, Francia's team teacher, is due to arrive by 6:30 a.m. daily. On Monday, Jasmine arrived at 6:45. On Tuesday, she walked through the door at 7:05. Today, Jasmine showed up at 6:50 without apology. The parents of Thelonius, a toddler, wanted to speak with Jasmine. At 6:45 they told Francia they couldn't wait any longer and stormed out. Jasmine's behavior stresses Francia.

To maintain required teacher-to-child ratios in the toddler room, the director increasingly reschedules early morning meetings and phone calls to cover for Jasmine. Once Jasmine settles into the classroom, she is a creative and loving teacher.

If you were Francia and Jasmine's director and supervisor, how would you assess the situation? What steps would you take?

Supervision is helping employees perform

at their best, in service to their organization's mission. Supervision fosters professionalism in every employee and team. By working to build forthright, caring, and respectful relationships with each teacher and team, supervisors create communities of problem solvers. Supervision both invites and requires conscientious, creative, and dedicated performance.

A leader's vision sets the standard for how she supervises. In this way, supervision is a "super" way to implement a leader's "vision." Supervision, like emotional intelligence, is common sense but not necessarily common practice. When a director leads on purpose, her supervisory practice hums.

This chapter will help you successfully tailor your supervision to fit the needs of each staff member. You will learn how to discern when a teacher needs to be told what to do (directive supervision) and when she can be invited to innovate (reflective supervision). Much depends on the maturity level of each staff member and each team. You will also study how to establish a system of supervision with useful policies, procedures, and forms. Because supervision practice aligns with legal requirements, you will track the close and necessary relationship between the law and a director's actions.

While supervision is hard work, it is also a joy and an honor. Skilled supervisors, in exercising social EQ, mentor our next generation of leaders. Helping a teacher develop and soar can be just as fulfilling as helping a child discover her world.

Supervision components

Social EQ capacities

I've been doing supervision for 40 years and I'm just beginning to get the hang of it.

—Jeree Pawl

Managing people who care for and educate children requires more than an annual evaluation meeting. Supervision is the day-to-day, often moment-to-moment, responsibility to support each employee's professional growth and to ensure that the program runs smoothly.

Supervisory EQ entails the mindful, heartfelt work of continuously assessing and building upon:

1. What inspires and motivates employees

2. Staff strengths, blind spots, and developmental needs

In supervision, staff members are invited to take responsibility for their own actions, attitudes, and relationships. As the adage states, "Give a man a fish, and you feed him for a day; teach a man to fish, and you feed him for a lifetime." Supervisors help employees learn to fish.

As courageous nurturers, supervisors take stands for quality. Acting quickly to discipline a nonperforming staff member requires courage. Because children learn by observing adults, children benefit from their teachers' professionalism. Confronting employees promptly for inappropriate behavior, difficult as that is for many administrators, is an essential supervisory practice.

Insight and empathy are just as useful to a supervisor as courage. Reading our staff accurately lets us see talent and gifts they might not yet see. Supporting each employee to claim and build on her strengths, while working through her weaknesses, requires all three virtues: courage, insight, and empathy.

Staff developmental stages

If you are new to supervision, take heart. Consider all you have learned about "developmentally appropriate practice" for children. Draw upon that knowledge when working with adults. Adults, like children, grow through stages of development. Each stage predicts the type of supervision we use.

The type of supervision a director chooses depends in large part on the maturity level of the employee. Just as teachers use developmentally appropriate practices (DAP) with children, directors gear supervision to the developmental stages of staff.

In the section **Types of Supervision: Directive and Reflective** (p. 152) the adult developmental levels identified help leaders determine what supervision practice will fit. Less mature staff members are likely to need to be *told* what is expected. More seasoned employees, who already take responsibility for themselves, can be *asked* to take charge of new ventures and come up with creative possibilities. Age is not the determinant of an adult's developmental stage. Maturity and accountability are better predictors. A 53-year-old teacher can be 14 on the inside. A 20-year-old can have the maturity of an elder.

Consider how we apply principles of developmentally appropriate practice when working with children and with adults. For example, we might respectfully guide toddlers through the process of redirection. We might guide teenagers by balancing firmness with their need for autonomy. We might mentor a gifted classroom teacher to help her confidently present a workshop at an early childhood conference. Jasmine's supervisor in the chapter case study is likely to enforce the boundary for punctuality and consideration for others.

Respect the person, address the behavior

Regardless of her developmental level, each staff member, like each child, deserves unconditional positive regard. Although a person's behavior may be inappropriate, she is still worthy of respect. The person's behavior, not the person's worthiness, is the issue. Jasmine's lateness for work does not make her a bad person. Jasmine's behavior, however, is unacceptable. Toddler Israel's biting is not acceptable; however, regardless of his having hurt another child, Israel is still worthy of love and respect, as is the child Israel hurt. No one wants or deserves to be put in a box and labeled a bad or unworthy human being. If an employee senses she has been labeled an inadequate person, she will resist her supervisor's efforts, however well intentioned.

No question about it, as a supervisor, you will call upon all your social EQ skills and develop new ones along the way. Knowing what you stand for will put you in good stead as a supervisor.

The "vision" in supervision

▶ EXERCISE YOUR EQ   ▨   Ask yourself: "What do I stand for?" Then complete this sentence: I stand for _____. Do you stand for quality, equality, fairness, kindness, doing the right thing, holding people accountable?

Be assured, whatever you stand for, your purpose predicts how you will supervise others. Should you lose sight of your purpose in the midst of a particularly heated situation, step aside emotionally to regain perspective (see Chapter 2); recall your core values and why you do the work you do. Getting perspective will reenergize you to face what you need to face.

At a minimum, supervisors ensure that staff comply with licensing and accreditation standards and with personnel policies. On their busiest days, administrators may feel they merely act as watchdogs, overseeing staff to ensure that they perform essential functions of their jobs. Just as border collies patrol tirelessly to keep the flock within boundaries, supervisors can practice hypervigilance as their core function. But trust is not instilled by watchdog supervision, and watchdogs grow weary after long days of being on alert.

Supervision entails far more. Supervision with vision and social EQ can be an elegant, dynamic and creative, individualized and systematized, rewarding endeavor. In *supervision*, the Latin prefix *super* means having sight that goes "above, over, beyond." Emotionally intelligent supervision keeps leaders' eyes on quality care as they encourage each staff member to perform at her best. A leader's unique vision for quality informs and inspires every interaction with her staff. Each of us leads best by being true to our "super" vision.

Discernment, a core competency for supervisors

Directors make choices. Discerning what action to take is what leadership is all about. Whether we use thin-slicing, letter of the law, or spirit of the law to make decisions, our decisions will be measured by their effectiveness. In supervising, directors employ case-by-case methods to tailor their approach to each individual. In creating and implementing a supervision system, directors use letter of the law discernment. Any way you "slice" it, supervision is a continuous judgment call.

How can a director find time to effectively discern what's right for each employee, given all the director's other management and administrative responsibilities? Leaders are responsible for creating a community of problem solvers, an environment where adults and children alike can bloom. Child care staff report that to bloom, they need more feedback and more interaction with and attention from their directors (Kilbourne 2007). Because a director's time is limited, supervision needs to be quality time.

▶ EXERCISE YOUR EQ   ▪ Consider staff members Francia and Jasmine from the chapter opening case study. Francia and Jasmine represent two of the most common challenges for supervisors:

1. The willing employee who needs significant support to develop professionally

2. The unwilling employee, who does not take responsibility for her actions

Which staff member would you prefer to supervise and why? What are your concerns about dealing with the staff member you did not select?

Professional development may be the last thing on Jasmine's mind. Jasmine's director must supervise Jasmine to help her become more consciously professional or to find another career better suited to her style. Discerning when to "counsel staff out the door" is a useful supervisory competency.

The early childhood education field is trending toward increasingly higher standards for professional credentialing. As you discern the course you would take with Francia and Jasmine, keep in mind that supervision occurs in the context of evolving professional standards and expectations (see Chapter 15). The NAEYC Accreditation Criteria for standard 10, Leadership and Management (NAEYC 2005b), for example, require accredited programs to have a plan in place for staff professional development. Francia's personal goal to earn a degree fits into her director's goal of ensuring 75 percent of her staff members have a child development credential, associate degree, baccalaureate, or advanced degree by 2013.

Supervision is many things: a vision, commitment, style, system, and relationship. You can count on supervision to provide you with every opportunity for growth as you discern each course you will take.

Types of supervision: Directive and reflective

Directive supervision is a process for holding employees accountable for their professional performance when they do not demonstrate the ability, capacity, and/or intentionality to take responsibility for their own actions.

Reflective supervision is a process that invites and empowers staff to examine their performance and grow professionally within a nurturing, honest relationship.

▶ EXERCISE YOUR EQ   Which type of supervision would you use for Francia? For Jasmine? Which type would work better for you if you were being supervised?

Later in this chapter, as we explore directive and reflective supervision in detail, we will look back at the choices you made initially about these teachers.

The first question to ask is, "What does each staff member need to do her best work?"

Supervision systems incorporate both directive and reflective procedures. Placing these two practices in the context of a broader supervision system helps directors formulate and create a plan for supervision. A supervision system will include:

• Regular, ongoing assessment and evaluation practices

• Spontaneous interventions

Reflective supervision is instrumental in a director's ongoing evaluation, mentoring, and assessment system. Directive supervision requires spontaneous corrective intervention, backed up by a system of progressive discipline procedures. With a standard system of supervision in place, employees will know what they can expect from the director and what the director expects of them. [See **Discerning Who Needs What and When.**]

Assessing what staff need

To supervise successfully, managers need a method to assess what each staff member needs to help him develop. In effective supervision, "one size fits all" does not apply. Each employee's stage of development indicates the type of supervision that should be used. What steps will ensure that teachers arrive on time? What supervision style will help them build partnerships with families?

Paula Jorde Bloom (2005) gives us a clear method for measurement. Her stages of staff development (see diagram) identify employees' needs at different times in their career. Let's examine what each of these stages entails and how that stage of adult development predicts the style of supervision to be used. Let's study these stages from the bottom up. More staff members are likely to be at the bottom or beginning stages of staff development than at the mature professional stage at the top.

> **Discerning Who Needs What and When**
>
> In directive supervision, we *tell*; in reflective supervision, we *ask*.
>
> Directive supervision holds employees accountable when their performance does not meet expectations.
>
> Reflective supervision invites employee and supervisor to grow together in the context of a supportive, introspective relationship.

Survivor

Survivors just make it through the day. Everything feels new to survivors, who have little experience or expertise to rely on. Remember how you felt in your first job or on the first day of school? You may have gone home exhausted, wondering how you would survive until the weekend. Classroom teachers at the survival stage of staff development feel overwhelmed by the demands of the job—parents' needs, classroom management issues, required documentation, lack of planning time, children who require one-on-one care. Survivors, caught up in getting through the day, do not yet see beyond their own needs. Survivors rarely have or take time to step aside to see the program from a larger perspective.

Even seasoned professionals can return to the survivor stage. Each time a person takes on a new challenge or position, he may feel he has to start at the bottom. A teacher who suddenly finds himself in the director's position can feel overwhelmed, as if in the survivor stage. An "A" student can feel like a survivor the first day of each new course she

Stages of Staff Development
Source: Paula Jorde Bloom (2005)

takes. Fortunately, we do not have to remain at the survival level. As we develop and grow professionally, we move up to the next stage of staff development, consolidator.

Consolidator

Once a professional has "survived" the beginning stage, she is ready to "consolidate" her successful experiences and growing knowledge base. For the consolidator, not everything is new. She can build on past successes.

If her lesson plans on weather changes fascinated preschoolers this year, the consolidator can supplement that curriculum with additional teaching strategies the following year. A consolidator may have gleaned useful tips from an *Exchange* article on classroom activities or participated in a workshop that equipped her with tools on classroom management. Her lead teacher may have modeled how to partner with families whose children have ADHD. Her supervisor may have offered alternative teaching strategies.

Consolidators begin to pull these diverse strands of knowledge and competency together. Their confidence develops as their skills grow. Unlike survivors, teachers at the consolidator stage enjoy a higher comfort level with their work. Like survivors, consolidators, still early in their development, focus more on themselves than the program as a whole. Consolidators continue to require supervision that provides clear expectations and boundaries.

Young professional (the renewal stage)

Having survived and consolidated their knowledge, staff—through appropriate supervision—move up to the young professional stage. At the young professional, or renewal, stage of staff development, an employee becomes more enthusiastic and able to "direct" himself. He might feel confident with parents, curriculum, and children.

The "young professional" can be 50 years old. Age is not the determinant. Skills and competencies are. The young professional has grown to be a self-starter, initiator, and creator. He is more likely now to see the bigger picture. He acknowledges that, as a team member, his work is an integral part of the program's success. A young professional thinks first about what's best for *everyone*—not "it's all about *me*."

At the young professional stage, employees may need renewal. This is why renewal is another way to describe the young professional stage. Ideally, a person at this stage knows enough to know what he does not know. He is ready to reflect on how he needs and wants to grow and contribute, with his supervisor's support and mentoring.

To supervise employees at the renewal stage, the supervisor shifts from authority to guiding partner, from directive supervision to reflective supervision. We supervise young professionals through a collaborative relationship that invites them to reflect on their performance and goals. We also continue to offer them direction when needed.

Not every young professional is ready to transition to reflective supervision, however. Have you worked with a person who does the same thing over and over, year after year? He may feel that "if it ain't broke, don't fix it." He is likely to resist new ideas: "Why should I have to change the way I teach just to meet some new accreditation standard?" An employee with this attitude, focusing more on himself than on the big picture, may still need directive supervision.

Mature professional

Elders in Native American tribes are respected for their wisdom. Their opinions carry weight in their community. Many early childhood programs are fortunate to have "elders," that is, mature professionals, on their teams. Early childhood elders take responsibility for themselves, while encouraging and inspiring professionalism in others. Seasoned staff members "walk the walk" of quality.

My colleague Susan, with over 35 years in the field, continuously delights me with new insights and enthusiasm about being a director. Two years ago, Susan traveled to Italy to study Reggio Emilia early childhood teaching methods. Last year, Susan joined a directors' discussion group focused on enhancing infant programs. This year, Susan is taking a drawing class to sharpen her observation skills. Susan, like most of us, has her uninspired times too. On balance, however, she uses her lifelong learning skills to take risks for personal and professional growth.

Elders benefit from collegiality, appreciation, acknowledgment, and opportunities for continuous improvement. Like Susan, they need to stay inspired and avoid burnout by discovering fresh ways to find meaning in their work. Perhaps Gladys is ready to write an article for *Young Children.* Gladys may have a desire to mentor others. She may ask you to help her apply for a directorship at another center. Because you have come to know Gladys well, you can hold heart-to-heart conversations with her about her hopes and goals. You also have learned more about yourself because you accompanied Gladys on her journey.

Maslow's stages of adult development

As you have probably noticed, early childhood leaders can draw from many fields to better understand "what it's all about." We can learn, for example, from psychologists like Abraham Maslow, who studied adult development. Maslow's "hierarchy of needs" (1943) offers perspective on stages of staff members' development. Notice the parallels between Maslow's model (see Maslow's Hierarchy of Needs) and the Jorde Bloom Stages of Staff Development model.

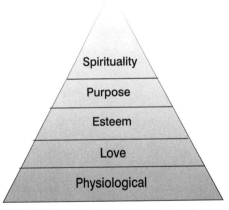

Maslow's Hierarchy of Needs
Source: Abraham Maslow (1943), 370–96.

Again, we start at the bottom and work our way up. Maslow calls the survivor stage the "physiological stage." This beginning stage of adult development is when we put a roof over our head, food on the table, and clothing on our back. We need to feel safe and secure before we feel confident to take risks to grow. Maslow's physiological stage closely aligns with the survivor stage of staff development.

With our physiological needs met, we are freer to interact more meaningfully with others. At this point, we grow upward through levels of love and esteem. At these levels, we view the world from a less self-centered perspective and begin to see ourselves as connected to others in meaningful ways. These are the consolidation and young professional stages in Bloom's model.

As we more fully mature, we are able to claim and to live out our purpose. Then, at the pinnacle of adult development, we seek deepest fulfillment. This is the stage Maslow calls "spirituality." Spirituality is the quest for a life of deeper meaning. Being religious is one of many pathways to spirituality. A mature employee may decide to work with young children who are homeless as part of her spiritual practice of "paying it forward," or giving back to others.

Using either the Maslow or the Bloom model, a supervisor can determine an employee's stage of development. To "manage through relationships," we need to ask and assess what each person needs both in the moment and in the long run. Each accurate assessment we make empowers us to discern better what type of supervision to use.

▶ EXERCISE YOUR EQ   ▨   Remember Francia and Jasmine? What do their behaviors and words tell you about their developmental stages? Are Jasmine and Francia at different stages, or the same one?

Once you determine an individual's stage of development, you know better how to match the type of supervision to that person's needs. Let's look at how that assessment process works. Fortunately, for each stage of staff development, one particular mode of supervision works better. A manager's challenge is to:

1. Assess the staff member's stage of development.

2. Apply the supervision style best suited to that person at that stage.

Supervising different generations: Millennials to boomers

A growing body of literature on identifying characteristics and needs of different generations has direct applicability to a supervisor's discernment process. As a supervisor, you may find this information helpful as you hire and work with staff in different age groups. You may also enjoy looking at yourself to ascertain if the data on your generation fits you.

Here is a breakdown, starting with the most recent generation to enter the workforce and concluding with the seniors in the workforce (Lancaster & Stillman 2002):

> **Bam!radio**
> "Manage Millennials to Get Their Best Work"
> Interview with Jeanne C. Meister
> *Heart to Heart Conversations on Leadership*
> http:/bamradionetwork.com

• Millennials (born 1981–1999) respond to brief pointers sent as text messages, anonymous mentoring, and accelerated pathways to advancement. (For more information, listen to the Bam!radio podcast with Jeanne Meister.)

• Generation-Xers (born 1965–1980), dubbed the "me" generation, expect considerable personal attention and supervision tailored to meet their career goals.

• Baby Boomers (born 1946–1964), who believe they can have it all and want to change the world, respond to supervision focused on their personal growth and supportive of their optimistic values.

• Traditionalists (born 1900–1945) expect supervisors to be authorities with high standards for employee performance and are most willing to follow the rules.

What makes the difference between the generations? Exposure to technological advances has a powerful effect on an employee's expectations about supervision. As would be expected, Boomers and Traditionalists expect direct interpersonal contact with their supervisors. More recent generations, like Gen-Xers and Millennials, who grew up having more contact with a computer screen, want more independence and less direct contact with supervisors.

As a result, Millennials may prefer an approach called "anonymous supervision." To arrange for anonymous supervision, a director needs to set up a confidential system with trusted directors and/or mentors from other organizations. Each Millennial employee is assigned one of these supervisors, who remains anonymous, from the other organization. The Millennial employee can more freely convey her issues and concerns and accept pointers online. Bulleted responses work well (Meister & Willyerd 2010). Depending on your generation, this anonymous approach may make sense, seem outlandish, or anywhere in between.

▶ EXERCISE YOUR EQ   ▨   Do your expectations of supervisors reflect your generation? Do you believe that supervising employees from different age groups in different ways is valuable? What have you done in supervising an employee of another generation that was effective, or not so effective? Do you see any way in which this generational lens might be of use?

Meister and Willyerd (2010, 4) say, "Improving your company's ability to give employees honest, timely, and useful coaching won't benefit just your 20-something workers…. All employees want to feel valued, empowered, and engaged at work. This is a fundamental need, not a generational issue."

To tell or to ask: When should each mode of supervision be used?

Use directive supervision at the early stages of staff development (survivor, consolidator, and, at times, young professional). At these stages, staff are better served when supervisors set boundaries, establish professional expectations, and make clear what the consequences of their behavior are.

For sure, Jasmine requires directive supervision to help her take responsibility for getting to work on time. Jasmine's focus, like any survivor, seems to be self-centered. She does not appear to be thinking about how her lateness affects children, parents, other staff, and program quality. In directive supervision, the leader directly and clearly *tells* the employee what's expected.

Use reflective supervision with employees at a stage of maturity, either mature or young professional, whose performance indicates their ability to observe, assess, and change to meet the needs of the program. Unlike Jasmine, Francia's desire to improve herself professionally may indicate she has the bigger picture of program quality in mind. Francia's willingness to look at herself and her openness to establish a career pathway indicates her supervisor can use reflective supervision. With reflective supervision, a leader *asks* her employee to reflect on what she values and needs.

▶ EXERCISE YOUR EQ   ▨   Identify a coworker, staff member, or peer whose behavior offends you. Perhaps this person is perpetually late, like Jasmine, or dispirits others with her negativity. Maybe she always presents herself as a victim and fails to take responsibility for herself. In her mind, someone else is always to blame. List three facts that capture this person's problematic behavior. Be specific and concrete. "Jasmine arrived at 7:05 today, although her 'start time' is 6:30," is a concrete fact. Avoid generalities like "Jasmine is always late."

Once you have written three facts, find a crayon or marker and a blank piece of paper. Picture yourself as supervisor of the person whose behavior is offensive. Imagine you have decided to call this person in for a directive supervision session. Your task is to help her take responsibility for changing her inappropriate behavior.

Picture how you would feel in the moment before you confront this person about her behavior. You do not need artistic talent to do this next task. Take your marker or crayon and draw what you would feel like and/or what your mental state would be just before you sit down with this person.

Blessed is the influence of one true, loving human soul on another.
—George Eliot

Adversity is the first path to truth.
—Lord Byron

Bam!radio
"Dealing with Problem Employees."
Podcast: Interview with Holly Elissa Bruno
www.jackstreet.com/jackstreet/KSECA.
Bruno.cfm

Now, set your list of facts and your drawing to the side for a moment. We'll come back to them after we look at some helpful research.

For 80 percent of early childhood leaders, supervision that requires confronting staff for inappropriate behavior is so daunting that they avoid it (Bruno & Copeland 1999). Directors around the country report unpleasant physical symptoms like shortness of breath, sweaty palms, stomach butterflies, and stress headaches when asked to picture direct confrontation. Seventy percent of women and 44 percent of men tend to take things personally, seek to keep the peace, and avoid conflict. For the majority of early childhood leaders, reflective supervision's nurturing process flows naturally. Affirming comes more easily than confronting.

▶ EXERCISE YOUR EQ   ▪   Where would you place yourself in these statistics? Would you be part of the 80 percent who fear conflict, the 20 percent who face conflict, or in between?

Using directive supervision

Being able to tell employees directly that their behavior needs to change is part of leadership. For the majority of early childhood professionals who are conflict avoidant, consciously learning the skills of direct supervision is liberating. At the early stages of

Principles of Directive Supervision	
Principle 1 Focus on the person's behavior, not the person.	The employee's behavior is at issue, not her worthiness as a person.
Principle 2 Be factual, concrete, and accurate when identifying the behavior.	Tell the facts about what she or he did, accurately and in sufficient detail, without shaming or blaming the employee or "sugar coating." *Res ipse loquitur,* a Latin saying, translates: "Let the facts speak for themselves."
Principle 3 Don't get "hooked" by taking what is said personally; use a "Q-Tip."	Because employees can become defensive, focus the conversation on "What will you do to make sure you do what's expected?" Do not get ensnared in a power struggle. Step to the side. Use your OFC (see Chapter 2) if you feel your amygdala may be hijacked. Put a Q-tip in your pocket. Squeeze it to remind yourself: Quit Taking It Personally.
Principle 4 Expect employees to take responsibility for their behavior.	Focus the employee on problem solving by asking: "What will you do to change your behavior?" Do not rob the employee of his chance to take responsibility by stepping in to "fix" it for him. Find a solution that is right for everyone, especially for children and families.
Principle 5 Come to a "meeting of the minds" and enforce it with a follow-up plan.	Tie a bow on this supervision meeting by making sure the employee understands what she will do differently, when you will meet to follow up, and what the consequence of her failure to change would be.

development, employees learn best when told directly what is expected of them. This means stating the "1, 2, 3" steps of the task and spelling out in detail what needs to be done. Many supervisors prefer to imagine staff will catch on by imitating model behavior. Avoidance makes the problem grow larger.

▶ EXERCISE YOUR EQ   ▨   Take a look at your drawing. Do you find signs of comfort or discomfort, confidence or fear? The majority of people who have completed this exercise draw people who look like they have put their finger in a light socket. Frowning faces, fearful faces, or butterflies in their stomachs are common. Some draw thunderbolts or turbulent weather like rain clouds. Only a few have drawn smiling faces. When asked to describe how they feel about confronting another person, they say, "Anxious, afraid, upset, angry." Is it any wonder so many early childhood professionals are not comfortable with directive supervision? Let's take directive supervision one principle and one step at a time.

Five principles and steps

Directive supervision is based on five principles. It can be challenging for directors to use directive supervision when an employee doesn't want to take responsibility for her own actions. The table **Principles of Directive Supervision** provides tips for how to apply each principle and remain objective and focused on finding a positive solution.

Let's revisit the chapter case study and put these principles to the test. Jasmine behaves like a survivor, and she needs to take responsibility for the impact of her behavior on others. Her performance will improve only if she learns to take responsibility for her actions through directive supervision.

Imagine calling Jasmine in for a supervision session about her behavior:

Director: Jasmine, when you arrived this Monday at 6:45 a.m., Tuesday at 7:05, and today at 6:50, that was inappropriate. You need to be in your classroom, ready to begin by 6:30 a.m.

Jasmine: Why are you picking on me? Melanie is late half the time.

Director: Jasmine we're talking about your behavior, not anyone else's. The actions I take with staff members are confidential.

Jasmine: I work really hard and give my heart and soul to these children. Why isn't that enough for you?!

Director: The children need you in the classroom on time. What will you do to make sure you arrive on time each day?

Jasmine: Change my start time to 7:30. You let Taylor come at 7:30!

Director: We need you for the early morning slot. Tell me what you can change to make sure you are in the classroom, prepared and ready to start, by 6:30.

Jasmine (crying or yelling): You don't appreciate anything I do! I'm a better teacher than half the staff you have here!

Director: Yes, Jasmine, when you are with the children, you are an excellent and caring teacher. That's not the issue. You need to get here on time. Here's a Kleenex. Take a five-minute break. Come back ready to share what you will do to be here on time each day.

Jasmine: All right, I suppose I could take the earlier bus, the #79 that leaves half an hour earlier. Would that make you happy?!

Director: Sounds like a plan. So, Jasmine, are you agreeing to take the earlier bus?

Jasmine: If I have to, I guess.

Director: We'll meet one week from today at this time. Taylor will cover your class. I'll also stop by each morning to check in with you. The children, their parents, and Francia will all feel better when they can count on you to be on time. If you do not arrive on time, however, the next step is probation. Please sign this Corrective Action form to indicate you agree to this plan.

Jasmine: This is hard for me. I have never been an on-time person.

Director: I understand, and I support your making the effort.

Directive supervision is respectful and not mean-spirited. Holding the line with Jasmine will help her learn how to become a professional.

Having examined the five principles for holding staff accountable, let's develop a "script" for putting the principles into practice. The chart **Putting the Five Steps of Directive Supervision into Words** shows the five steps and what Jasmine's director could say when applying them.

▶ EXERCISE YOUR EQ ▨ How do you feel about the directness of direct supervision? Take stock of your emotions. Let them give you information about your response to this process, which is counter-intuitive (feels unnatural) and as if we are acting in our shadow preferences (see Chapter 4).

For 80 percent of us, directive supervision's straightforward, no-nonsense, "thinking" approach can be problematic (see Chapter 3). Being direct and being respectful are not mutually exclusive. In fact, this process respectfully informs the employee what is expected of her and encourages her taking a mature approach. In 12-Step (AA or Al-Anon) parlance, directive supervision is "tough love."

Bam!radio
"Teacher negativity: Turning naysayers into hooraysayers"
Interview with Neila Connors
Heart to Heart Conversations on Leadership
http:/bamradionetwork.com

Putting the Five Steps of Directive Supervision into Words	
Five steps	**Sample approach**
1. State the inappropriate behavior.	"Jasmine, when you arrived Monday at 6:45, Tuesday at 7:05, and this morning at 6:50 a.m., that was inappropriate."
2. Name the expected behavior.	"You need to be here ready to start by 6:30 a.m. each day."
3. Ask what changes the employee will make to meet expectations.	"Jasmine, what will you do to get here, ready to start in the classroom, by 6:30 a.m. daily?"
4. Persist until the employee takes responsibility for identifying and taking ownership of a workable solution.	"Changing your start time is not an option, Jasmine. Your idea of taking the earlier bus will work well."
5. Make a plan for follow-through that includes notification of the legal consequences of failure to make agreed upon changes.	"Please tell me what you agree to do differently. We'll meet one week from today at 1 p.m. nap time in my office. Millicent will cover for you. I'll check in with you daily to see how things are going. This is your written notice, Jasmine. If you do not get to work on time, you will be put on probation. Thank you for coming up with a solution that will help children, families, and your team members."

Directive supervision's compliance with legal requirements

Courts require supervisors to make a "conscientious rescue effort" to help employees, like Jasmine, learn skills and attitudes to effectively perform their jobs. Conscientious rescue efforts include "enhanced supervision," such as meeting with Jasmine, being clear with her on what is expected, developing a plan for how she can improve her performance, and documenting the process.

The good news is that the five steps and principles of directive supervision align with the conscientious rescue effort courts require of employers. Most of us work in "at will" states where an employee can resign "at will" and an employer can terminate an employee's work "without cause." An employer can say "It's just not working out." Why aren't more employees simply told "It's just not working out"?

Progressive discipline

Most organizations afford employees opportunities to improve their performance. This policy is called "progressive discipline." Progressive discipline is just what it sounds like: You get three strikes before you are out. The three steps of progressive discipline are synchronized with the five steps of directive supervision. They are:

1. Written notice. The employee is called in, inappropriate behavior is identified, and a plan is developed for corrective action with a timetable for improvement.

2. Probation. If the employee's behavior does not change for the better, she is informed in a meeting and in writing that her employment will be terminated if she fails to meet expectations one more time. A second written plan is put into place for enhanced supervision.

3. Termination. The employee is fired for not meeting program standards and expectations. Document the behavior that led to the termination and the meeting at which the employee was terminated.

The informal alert precedes the three steps. An employee is informally alerted when a supervisor notices a behavior that needs to change and reminds the employee what is expected. However, many directors stay at the informal alert stage, fearful of moving on to progressive discipline steps.

If employee policies name the steps of progressive discipline, supervisors need to follow those steps. There are two exceptions. First, during the probation period—usually the first 90 days that the employee works in your program—managers have the right to let the person go "without cause" as long as the employer is not discriminating against the person in any way. The second exception is if an employee commits what courts term a "major offense." Major offenses include stealing, abuse, violence, and drinking or abusing other substance at work.

Use the **Employee Improvement Plan of Action** form (next page) for documenting the steps you have taken, pursuant to both directive supervision principles and the progressive discipline process.

▶ EXERCISE YOUR EQ   ▉   Return now to the offensive situation you identified with your own coworker, staff member, or peer. Apply the five principles and steps to your situation. Although directive supervision is designed for employee-employer problems, do you think the principles may work in other situations?

"Weeble Wobble"—help from an old fashioned children's toy:
Picture a Weeble Wobble punching bag, the inflatable plastic children's toy with a weight at the bottom. No matter how many punches the Weeble Wobble takes, it bounces back to standing tall. Directive supervision steps help you come back to your center, much like a Weeble Wobble. When you lead on purpose, nothing can take you off center for long.

"Management by walking around" (MBWA) is the management process of greeting, interacting with, and connecting informally with each employee early and often. Staff welcome this attention. Supervisors see indications earlier of problems and successes in their walkabouts. MBWA was first described by Tom Peters.

If we did the things we are capable of, we would astound ourselves.
—Thomas Edison

Employee Improvement Plan of Action: Corrective Meeting with Supervisor

Employee's name: Date & Time:

Present at meeting: (Names and job titles)

Director's concern (Briefly and factually, identify incident and/or observation):

Expected behavior (Attach/refer to center policy, job description, program mission, licensing/accreditation standard, code of ethical behavior, etc):

Plan for correcting problem:

Follow up meeting set for _____ (date and time).

Employee will:

Director/supervisor will:

Consequence if problem behavior is not corrected:

Signatures of those present:

_____
Employer

_____
Employee

_____
Witness (name and title)

Employee's comments (optional):

When reflective supervision is appropriate

Reflective supervision is what it appears to be: holding a mirror up for staff to see their own behavior in a supportive, ongoing, relational way. Reflective supervision invites staff to acknowledge and affirm strengths, grow, take risks, and overcome obstacles, all in the context of a supportive relationship. In reflective supervision, strengths are built upon while problems are worked through in partnership. "You never have to make a decision alone" is a reflective supervision principle.

Principles of reflective supervision

Self-assessment, collaboration, and frequency are hallmarks of reflective supervision. "Collaboration means the teacher and the supervisor share responsibility for figuring out together how the teacher can increase his or her ability to carry out the program's mission effectively and to facilitate change amid growth," notes Tammy Mann about her early Head Start experience. Reflective supervisors and supervisees together build relationships that:

- Foster safety and trust.
- Support and honor differences.
- Invite growth, risk taking, and humor.
- Acknowledge and build upon strengths.
- Become aware of blind spots.
- Partner on vulnerabilities.

- Slow down the process.

Reflective supervision is social EQ in action.

For reflective supervision to work, the employee must have the capacity to look objectively at herself, to identify her strengths and her weaknesses. Survivors and consolidators are rarely ready for this type of supervision. Young professionals, possessing the ability to be self-critical and aware of strengths and limitations, are candidates for reflective supervision. They are eager to make changes to become even more effective.

Reflective supervision in practice

Practical steps to take with an employee in reflective supervision practice have been articulated by the Michigan Association for Infant Mental Health (2002, 3):

- Agree on a regular time and place to meet.
- Arrive on time and remain open, curious, and emotionally available.
- Protect against interruptions (e.g., turn off the phone, close the door).
- Respect each supervisee's pace/readiness to learn.
- Invite the sharing of details about a particular situation, infant, toddler, parent, competencies, behaviors, interactions, strengths, concerns.
- Observe and listen carefully.
- Strengthen each supervisee's observation and listening skills.
- Ally with the supervisee's strengths, offering reassurance and praise as appropriate.
- Listen for the emotional experience that the supervisee is describing when discussing the case or response to the work (e.g. anger, impatience, sorrow, confusion, etc.).
- Respond with appropriate empathy.
- Invite the supervisee to have and talk about feelings awakened in the presence of an infant or very young child and parent(s).
- Wonder about, name, and respond to those feelings with appropriate empathy.
- Encourage exploration of thoughts and feelings that the supervisee has about the work, as well as about one's responses to the work, as the supervisee appears ready or able.
- Remain available throughout the week if there is a crisis or concern that needs immediate attention.
- Suspend harsh or critical judgment.

As the teacher grows, the supervisor grows

The mirror that supervisors hold up to employees reflects the supervisor's image as well. Reflective supervision invites the supervisor to examine and stretch along with the supervisee. Often supervisors see areas of their own that need improvement. A supervisor might find she needs to assess herself:

- Am I patient?
- Can I delegate?
- Am I jealous of this employee in any way?
- Was that my own "blind spot" I just bumped into?

If you are irritated by every rub, how will your mirror be polished?

—Djalal ad-Din Rumi

What we see depends mainly on what we look for.

—John Lubbock

Treat people as if they were what they ought to be and you help them to become what they are capable of being.

—Johann Wolfgang von Goethe

Self-assessment can be as simple as asking:

Name three of your accomplishments in your classroom so far this year.

What are the challenges you face?

What strengths of yours are most helpful to children and families?

- Can I accept honest feedback from my employees without getting defensive?
- Am I willing to change, as I expect my employees to change?

As seasoned supervisor Emily Fenichel observes (2002, 14): "Supervisors and mentors need to resolve their own conflicts about exercising priority before they can establish clear expectations of their students or employees." Reflective supervision opens a manager's eyes to her own strengths and challenges, as well as to those of the person being supervised. Reflective supervision is a gift to everyone.

Bloom's *Blueprint for Action* (2005) provides helpful written tools, such as **Self-Assessment Tool #1** to support our reflection with employees like Mary Catherine, in the case study below. Remember, the purpose of reflective supervision is to help each employee reach her full professional potential while furthering program vision and mission.

Case Study—Mary Catherine

Mary Catherine is gifted one-on-one with children. She has shown patience, understanding, and encouragement with Solomon, a 3-year-old with developmental delays. Mary Catherine painstakingly built trusting relationships with Solomon's divorced parents. Her gentle persistence and clear documentation were instrumental in the parents' agreement for Solomon to be evaluated by early intervention specialists.

Before Solomon was in Mary Catherine's room, his parents blamed the center for Solomon's difficulties. Mary Catherine turned all of that around. However, her classroom management skills are lacking. Her classroom grows out of control while she focuses on one child at a time.

As her supervisor, what are your options?

▶ EXERCISE YOUR EQ   Complete **Self- Assessment Tool #1** and **Self-Assessment Questionnaire** (p.165). Replace "teacher" with the term that describes your work, if necessary.

Reflective supervision practices, as evidenced by Bloom's form, include:

- Self-assessment accompanied with supervisor's assessment.
- Sharing these assessments.
- Identifying strengths and challenges.
- Affirming strengths and partnering on challenges.
- Selecting three goals.
- Developing a plan for change including objectives, steps, and a timetable.

What additional skills would you like to gain?

Through reflective conversations with Mary Catherine, we support her in gaining the skills that she needs to improve. Should Mary Catherine not master those skills, we may, through reflective supervision, help her find a position or a workplace that can use her one-on-one skill. Or, we may rely upon directive supervision to hold her accountable for not developing classroom management skills.

Reflective supervision promotes quality by calling upon the director's insightful, nurturing skills. Directive supervision requires the director to take a stand for quality, no matter how intimidating the situation may be. Both directive and reflective supervisory skills are essential for program quality.

The practice of reflective supervision carries over to the whole organization. Just as individuals are encouraged to grow, so is the community. To promote "slowing down the process" (see p. 166), leaders can include these items in staff meeting agendas:

- Affirmations: Each staff member, one at a time, shares with the person to her left one thing she appreciates about that person. This continues until everyone has spoken.

- Good news: Go around the circle, inviting each staff member to state something he has done at work that he feels good about.

- Team problem solving. Encourage staff to raise something about the program that needs improvement or that an individual requests help on. Devote time to problem solving together.

- Rumor mill grinds to a halt here. Use humor to let staff know they can bring rumors they have heard to the meeting for clarification and answers. Facts will win out over the rumors.

- Treasure hunts. Send small teams on a treasure hunt, handing them checklists to inspect for quality. Reward the teams when they report.

Employees feel respected when a supervisor reserves time for mutual problem solving at staff meetings and dedicates one-on-one time to reflecting over a cup of tea with employees about their dreams and challenges.

Self-Assessment Tool #1: Goals Blueprint

Teacher's name_____ Date_____

Strengths as a teacher:

1.
2.
3.

Areas in need of improvement:

1.
2.
3.

Goal: _____

Objectives:

1.
2.
3.

Source: Reprinted, with permission, from Paula Jorde Bloom, *Blueprint for Action: Achieving Center-Based Change through Staff Development,* 2nd ed. (Lewisville, NC: Gryphon House, 2005).

Self-Assessment Questionnaire

What are:

1. Three successes you have had in your classroom?

2. Your strengths that are most helpful to children and families?

3. Additional skills that you would like to gain?

Creating your system for supervision

Skilled supervisors use both directive and reflective supervision as part of their overall systemic plan for supervising staff. Let's look now at how the two approaches can be embedded into a system that continuously encourages staff to do their best work for the program.

A supervision system must meet these four functions:

1. Creation and enforcement of policies and procedures, such as evaluation tools, as well as ongoing posting of new information.

2. Continuous assessment and recognition of each staff member's developmental needs, accomplishments, and "stretch" goals.

3. Intervention early, especially when change is required.

4. Maintenance of individual supervision within a system that upholds the organization's vision.

Annual Employee Evaluation Instrument

Employee name_____ Date_____

Employment period reviewed_____

Employee accomplishments:

Progress toward annual goals:

Goal 1:

Goal 2:

Goal 3:

Areas for improvement:

Goals for next year:

Goal 1:

Goal2:

Goal 3:

Overall rating: Average_____ Good_____

Outstanding_____ Other_____

Employee comments:

Signatures: _____Date: _____

Slowing Down the Process

Slowing down the process is a reflective supervision practice that entails taking time with employees individually and at staff meetings to ask:

- How was your week?
- What is going well?
- Do you have anything that is bothering you?
- What do we need to think about?
- Has anyone heard a rumor you want to check out?

This practice surfaces issues early and lets employees know you are open to hearing about them.

To regularize these processes, directors rely on standard forms, such as the corrective action (**Employee Improvement Plan of Action**, p. 162) and teacher self-assessment forms. Policies, procedures, and evaluation tools, all placed in the employee handbook, create and communicate the system for supervision. Directors can create, share, and/or purchase standardized forms for ongoing employee evaluations.

Sources of online supervision forms and checklists include:

SUPERvision Series

ncchildcare.dhhs.state.nc.us/providers/pv_supervision.asp

Teacher Self-Evaluation Form

www.eced-resources.com/index.php/2005/11/11/teacher-self-evaluation-form

Child Care Lounge: Printable Forms

www.childcarelounge.com/printables/printable-forms.php

Completed forms must be signed or initialed before copies of these are placed in the employee's personnel file. Annual staff evaluation forms also require a standardized form. Employees come to count on being treated fairly in the usage of these forms. Standardized forms for the employee's annual review are essential.

At the annual review, employee and supervisor share their assessments of the employee's work record and progress toward goals in the past year. Stretch goals are mutually agreed on for the year ahead. The **Annual Employee Evaluation Instrument** is completed by both supervisor and staff member.

Evaluation time

360-degree evaluations

Some supervisors choose to include a "360-degree" evaluation tool. This evaluation invites everyone who is part of the circle (360 degrees) to evaluate one another. The employee evaluates the supervisor. Employees evaluate each another. The supervisor evaluates herself and each employee. An excellent example of a 360-degree instrument is offered in *A Great Place to Work* (Bloom, Hentschel, & Bella 2010). In that resource, you will find evaluation instruments and scoring templates.

Garbage-can dynamic

The first time a supervisor asks staff to evaluate him or the program, he is likely to experience the phenomenon known as the "garbage-can dynamic" (Cohen, March, &

Olsen 1972). Staff often "dump their garbage" all over a 360-degree program evaluation form the first time they are asked complete it. Any stored up issues, unspoken hurts, snippets of anger, or resentment get dumped.

Supervisors need to step to the side emotionally, remind themselves not to take the results personally, and examine information objectively. By the second or third 360-degree evaluation, employees will have dumped their stored-up issues and are likely to express more timely and constructive views.

Avoiding annual evaluation pitfalls

First, schedule annual employee evaluations to take place at each employee's anniversary date (of hire). Programs that conduct everyone's annual review at the same time each year can find that productivity takes a tumble. Fear is contagious and can affect even the most seasoned and professional staff member. Anxiety spreads like the measles. To prevent collective annual review jitters, space out the evaluations by individualizing them to fall on each employee's start date.

Second, make sure that annual evaluations are not the only time you and your employees sit down together to assess their performance. Understandably, employees fear annual evaluation meetings if they have not received steady feedback throughout the year.

By using the five steps of directive supervision and continuously encouraging staff via reflective supervision, managers prevent unwelcome surprises and employees know where they stand. More important, employees have benefited throughout the year from a supervisor's ongoing interest in them and their improved performance.

Third, give employees notice of personnel policy changes that affect them and the opportunity to discuss their feelings and thoughts about these changes. This goes a long way in meeting the requirement of providing staff with notice about what affects them. Tack up any new policy that comes across your desk, and post any changes made to policies and procedures. By dating each posting, you can periodically check to make sure all postings are timely and up-to-date.

Bring these policies to everyone's attention at staff meetings. When appropriate, make one copy for each employee, ask each person to initial it as evidence that she or he has read and understood the policy, and place that initialed statement in each employee's file. This meets the supervision function of "ongoing posting of new information."

Supervision as an evolving process

Consider a system of supervision as both a noun and a verb. Nouns, like an apple or a post office, are solid and stable. Verbs, like *to throw* or *to stir fry*, are more active. As a noun, supervision is a protective, well-maintained system shored up with written standards and procedures; ongoing, shared information; evaluation processes; staff meetings that inform as well as slow down the process; individual reflective sessions; and daily management by walking around. In this way, a supervisor establishes and maintains an overarching system to meet each employee's needs in the context of the organization's mission.

As a verb, systemic supervision works like emergent curriculum in the classroom. Managers employ the most effective supervisory style required in the moment. "Teachable moments," or mutual learning opportunities, pop up at any time. Supervision is a richly challenging daily opportunity to model for employees the way we want them to interact with children. Today, Jasmine may learn best from directive supervision; tomorrow she may be more prepared to reflect on how she can help Clarence's family.

Supervision and staff development plans

In 2005, NAEYC updated its books about NAEYC Accreditation standard 6, *Teachers*, and standard 10, *Leadership and Management* (NAEYC 2005a & b). NAEYC's standards require accredited programs to comply with these criteria, among others:

- Program Standard 10—Leadership and Management, Criterion 10.E.10: An individual professional development plan is generated from the staff evaluation process and is updated at least annually and ongoing as needed.

- Program Standard 6—Teachers: The program employs and supports a teaching staff that has the educational qualifications, knowledge, and professional commitment necessary to promote children's learning and development and to support families' diverse needs and interests.

Directors are expected to create and implement a plan that places each employee's professional development goals in a comprehensive program. This plan must ensure that teachers meet academic course requirements within a certain number of years. Annual stretch goals for employees must include pathways for staff members to further their education and complete degrees. By meeting these goals, programs can meet NAEYC professional standards for a well-educated staff. A supervisor who does her job well will be on her way to meeting and exceeding these standards.

Supervision, like any other EQ practice, is both an art and a science. The more open we are to learning and practicing, the more proficient we become.

Reflection questions

1. Think back over the supervisors and/or teachers you have experienced so far. Who was your favorite? What competencies did this person demonstrate with you? How would you describe the person's supervision and/or teaching style? What in particular about that style endeared the person to you? In retrospect, was this person using directive, reflective, or both practices with you? Now reflect on a supervisor or teacher whose style did not work for you. Can you identify what in that person's style was mismatched with your learning style? What does this tell you about supervision practice? Write a summary about the kind of supervisor or teacher you need to perform at your best.

2. Cathy Jones, with over 30 years' experience in early childhood education, makes the following observation on challenging employees: "Difficult employees often just want to be heard. To get attention, like difficult children, they engage in annoying and nonproductive behaviors. Providing a mechanism for them to have a voice is often helpful. They also need to be guided to find solutions. . . . When given a way to shine for doing the right/good/productive thing, the focus can change. Sometime folks in child care are negative because the field is not an appropriate choice for them. Sometimes the best we can do is counsel them into another line of work. Allowing negative employees to continue disrupting and stirring up things is so disrespectful to the children and those employees who are trying their best. Turning a deaf ear has to be strategic and seldom used. When good employees consistently complain about a negative employee, that should be an immediate red flag!" Do you agree? What have you learned about dealing with difficult people? How do their needs differ from your

own? How are their needs the same? Write a reflection on your experience with difficult colleagues.

3. Complete Exercise Your EQ on page 164. Based on your responses, assess your potential strengths and challenges as a supervisor. What steps might you take to expand your competencies as a supervisor?

Team Projects

1. Reread together Mary Catherine's case on page 164. Identify and discuss the supervision challenges, as well as the approaches you might take if you were her supervisor. Do the same with Francia and Jasmine's case (p. 149). Present a report on the important points in your discussion.

2. Investigate what makes an effective supervisor by interviewing people who supervise employees. Meet first with the group to develop interview questions for the supervisors you plan to interview. Create questions that will help you track down answers that will be useful to you. Possible questions include: "What has been your greatest challenge as a supervisor?" "What part of supervising do you most enjoy?" and "Do you have forms you can share on how you document supervision?" Once you agree on the questions, each of you will interview three supervisors. Regroup to develop a PowerPoint report on your findings for the class.

3. As a group, create at least two factual cases of employees like Jasmine, with problematic behavior. Make a video that captures the difficult behaviors in your case studies. Practice together how to apply the five principles and steps of directive supervision to each situation. Show your video to your class and facilitate small group discussions on applying directive supervision to the cases.

Bibliography

Bloom, P.J. 2005. *Blueprint for action: Achieving center-based change through staff development.* 2nd ed. Lewisville, NC: Gryphon House.

Bloom, P.J., A. Hentschel, & J. Bella. 2010. *A great place to work: Creating a healthy organizational climate.* Lake Forest, IL: New Horizons.

Bruno, H.E., & M.L. Copeland. 1999. If the director isn't direct, can the team have direction? *Leadership Quest.*

Cohen, M.D., J.G. March, & J.P. Olsen. 1972. A garbage can model of organizational choice. *Administrative Science Quarterly* 17 (1): 1–25.

Fenichel, E.S. 2002. *Learning through supervision and mentorship.* Washington, DC: Zero to Three.

Katz, L. 1972. Developmental stages of preschool teachers. *Elementary School Journal* 73 (1): 50–54.

Kilbourne, S. 2007. Performance appraisals: One step in a comprehensive staff supervision model. *Exchange, the Magazine for Early Childhood Leaders* 174: 34–37.

Kloosterman, V. 2003. A partnership approach for supervisors and teachers. *Young Children* 58 (6): 72–76.

Lancaster, L.C., & D. Stillman. 2002. *When generations collide.* New York: HarperCollins.

Maslow, A.H. 1943. A theory of human motivation. *Psychological Review* 50: 370–96.

Meister, J.C., & K. Willyerd. 2010. Mentoring Millennials. *Harvard Business Review* May: 1-4.

MI-AIMH (Michigan Association for Infant Mental Health). 2002. *Best Practice Guidelines for reflective supervision and consultation.* Southgate, MI: Author. www.mi-aimh.org/documents/20100204_bpgrsc.pdfRecommendedReferencesforPreparingforEndorsement/09-GuidelinesforReflectiveSupervisionandConsultation.pdf.

NAEYC (National Association for the Education of Young Children). 2005a. *Teachers: A guide to the NAEYC Early Childhood Program Standard and Related Accreditation Criteria.* Washington, DC: Author.

NAEYC. 2005b. *Leadership and management: A guide to the NAEYC Early Childhood Program Standard and Related Accreditation Criteria.* Washington, DC: Author.

Neugebauer, B., & R. Neugebauer. 2005. *Staff challenges: Practical ideas for recruiting, training, and supervising early childhood employees.* Redmond, WA: Exchange Press.

Norman-Murch, T., & G. Ward. 1999. First steps in establishing reflective practice and supervision: Organizational issues and strategies. *Zero to Three* 20 (1): 10–14.

Parlakian, R. 2001. *Look, listen, and learn: Reflective supervision and relationship-based work.* Washington, DC: Zero to Three.

Pawl, J., & M. St. John. 1998. How you are is as important as what you do. In *Making a positive difference for infants, toddlers, and their families.* Washington, DC: Zero to Three.

Peters, T.J., & R.H. Waterman, Jr. 2004. *In search of excellence: Lessons from America's best run companies.* New York: HarperCollins.

Web resources

Directive Supervision

www.paperboat.com/index.php?option=com_content&view=category&id=8&layout=blog&Itemid=10

Early Childhood and Specialized Personnel Development

http://cdd.unm.edu/Ec/index.htm

How to Implement Progressive Discipline

http://ced.blr.com/b/discrimination-harassment-discipline/archive/2011/08/11/how-to-implement-progressive-discipline.asp

Progressive Discipline

www.indiana.edu/~uhrs/training/ca/progressive.html

Self-Assessment for Directors and Administrators of Child Care Programs

http://ncicdp.org/compensation/community-workbook/admin

Supporting Teachers, Strengthening Families

www.naeyc.org/ecp/trainings/stsf

> Often, problems are knots with many strands, and looking at those strands can make a problem seem different.
>
> —Fred Rogers, *You Are Special*

> I am always doing that which I cannot do, in order that I may learn how to do it.
>
> —Pablo Picasso

10 Financial Management: Holding the Purse Strings

Case Study—Adrienne

Adrienne, a seasoned and talented lead toddler teacher, was recently named director of her program, Heaven on Earth. Founding director Rosalia followed her dream by returning to Honduras with funding to establish a Montessori preschool. Adrienne told the board in her interviews how inadequate and inexperienced she was with budgets. "Don't worry, we'll help," board members assured her.

Working overtime to reinvent relationships with her staff and deal with power struggles among board members, Adrienne delays learning about financial management. When a freak tornado devastates the playground, Adrienne forces herself to look at the budget. Numbers swim like sharks before her eyes. "I don't have a clue!" she cries frantically.

You are the first person Adrienne calls to ask for help. What kind of assistance can you offer her?

If social intelligence is crucial for managing

interpersonal challenges, which intelligence is essential for money management? Depending on people skills for cash flow reports, computing depreciation, and FICA allocations sounds like putting lipstick on a pig (as my friend Marylou says). "Reading" people may not be helpful when what we need to read is the budget book. Have we come to the end of the usefulness of EQ?

In this chapter, we will discuss best practices and tools for setting up and managing budgets for early childhood centers. Through the experiences of Adrienne in this chapter, we will see ways in which she uses her IQ and EQ to achieve financial management success. (Please note that financial terms appear in bold and are defined in the **Glossary of Budget Terms** at the end of the chapter.)

Money: Loaded in more ways than one

Olivia Mellan and Karina Piskaldo (1999, 47) explain why money is a loaded topic.

> For most people, money is never just money, a tool to accomplish some of life's goals. It is love, power, happiness, security, control, dependency, independence, freedom, and more. Money is so loaded a symbol that to unload it—and I believe it must be unloaded to live in a fully rational and balanced relationship to money—reaches deep into the human psyche. Usually, when the button of money is pressed, deeper issues emerge that have long been neglected. As a result, money matters are a perfect vehicle for awareness and growth.

We often relate to money as if money were a person. Sometimes we are indirect and fearful. Other times we are forthright and confident. Our relationship with money is complex and deeply emotional. Adrienne's early learning about managing money is likely to hold clues to her approach today.

Recalling early messages about money that we "caught" when we were children is informative. Low confidence as a money manager usually has historical roots. Mellan and Piskaldo continue, "We grow up in families where nobody talks about money. Most people will immediately protest: 'Not true. My family talked about money all the time.' When I ask, 'How did you talk?' they reply, 'My father worried about not having enough, and he yelled at my mother for spending too much'" (1999, 150).

Studies show that men and women view money differently. Jennifer Harper (2006) notes in a *Washington Times* article, "They may have money in their purses and a decent salary, but many women fear they'll lose their income and end up a bag lady, forgotten and destitute."

Harper goes on to quote MSN money columnist Jay MacDonald: "'Bag lady syndrome is a fear many women share that their financial security could disappear in a heartbeat, leaving them homeless, penniless, and destitute. . . . Lily Tomlin, Gloria Steinem, Shirley MacLaine, and Katie Couric all admit to having a bag lady in their anxiety closet.'"

This "great depression" about money may derive, in part, from the Great Depression of the late 1920s and early 1930s. Children grew up with out-of-work parents and empty plates, and felt lucky to have a roof over their heads. My mother dropped out of high school in tenth grade to support her family of seven siblings and a single mom.

Slogans like "A penny saved is a penny earned" or "Waste not, want not" conveyed Great Depression coping strategies. My mother taught me how to darn socks, grow my own vegetables, and hunt like a lioness for bargains. My family dressed in hand-me-downs even when we could afford new clothing.

Children learn about money through their parents' attitudes and actions, the media, and other people in their environment. For early childhood programs, decisions about how money is spent communicate messages to children, families, and staff. Program directors play a key role in allocating money in a balanced way. The following sections show how Adrienne, the director in the chapter case study, works hard to keep a balanced budget and adapt to unexpected expenses.

Folks with plenty of plenty, got a lock on the door. 'Fraid somebody's gonna rob 'em, while they're out making more. What for? I got no lock on the door. That's OK with me. They can steal the rug from the floor, that's OK with me, cause the things that I prize like the stars in the skies are all free.
—**"I Got Plenty of Nothing"** from George and Ira Gershwin's *Porgy and Bess*

When a man keeps hollering, "It's the principle of the thing," he's talking about the money.
—**Kin Hubbard**

When I dare to be powerful—to use my strength in the service of my vision—then it becomes less and less important whether I am afraid.
—**Audre Lorde**

Coming clean is not the same as money laundering

Managers like me often feel less confident about managing finances than they do about managing relationships or day-to-day program operations. When it comes to budgets, new directors may feel they are bumping around like a toddler in a high-tech, grown-up world. They often feel behind on the learning curve and fear they will mess things up.

Liz, who directed programs in New Jersey for years, offers this advice:

> Hire someone who does nothing but budget, contracts, money issues, etc. Running an early childhood program is a business, but the humanization of the business is what is critical. The person hired needs to be able to communicate with parents in a warm and welcoming way. You don't want a budget person or financial secretary to be nasty to those parents who might be late with tuition, or to be rude to a vendor. Her or his actions reflect on how the children are treated in the center.

When I was a new manager, I struggled to handle numbers by myself. Asking for help felt like admitting I was the great imposter. I was in awe of leaders with Donald Trump-like confidence. Tell me you love "number crunching" and you have my attention. Trust me; I know this is one of my blind spots.

I sympathize with Adrienne, the new director in the case study. Yet somehow, my business runs smoothly and at a profit. I keep fastidious records. Bills are paid on time, vendors (salespeople) are content, and the checkbook balances. My profit and loss statements (**P&L**) are more comforting than worrisome.

I have learned to work through my fears to deal with budgets, financial planning, bookkeeping, and balance sheets. How? First, I hire competent, trustworthy professionals. My wise accountant, Tony, breaks chunky problems down into pieces I can grasp. My bookkeeper, Denise, continuously updates me on the status of budget items, flagging anything that needs my attention. One click on Denise's software program puts everything into instantaneous perspective. My financial planner, Gerry, devotes hours to explaining financial planning concepts to me, with ample real-world examples and generous time for my plodding questions.

Second, I give up feeling like an imposter. Assuring myself, as I assure others, that we all have different strengths, I ask for help. "Break it down for me like I'm in second grade" is my straightforward and useful request. My uncle, Arthur Bruno, says in his Sicilian dialect: "Sometimes we have to walk into the mouth of the wolf." Hello, Wolf! Slowly, I am coming to understand the basics of managing the purse strings. Every step of the way, I call upon emotional intelligence to grow and ask for help.

▶ EXERCISE YOUR EQ   ▦   That's my story and I'm sticking to it! What is your story? What childhood messages did you receive about the meaning of money and how to manage it? How do you think these messages impact your confidence and money management skills today?

Budget as both policy and map

Keeping our "eyes on the prize" in financial management is especially helpful (see **Top 10 Financial Management Pointers**, p. 178). A budget follows our dream and turns it into reality. Details make better sense in a larger context. If a director sets staff development as her priority, scheduling and financing a staff retreat will bring that priority to life.

In this way, the budget is the policy statement for a program. What a director targets for the greatest expenditures is what she values and needs most. In early

Top 10 Financial Management Pointers

1. Remember the big picture. Your program needs to be able to pay its bills on time.
2. The amount of money you take in needs to at least equal the amount you pay out, plus allow for enough "wiggle room" (**liquidity** or **cash flow**) to pay your bills on time.
3. Employee compensation is the largest expense in early childhood program budgets.
4. Tuition is the primary source of revenue.
5. Last year's budget is usually the best resource you can use in preparing next year's budget.
6. Each month, make sure your income is at least equal to your expenditures.
7. Regularly provide up-to-date budget reports to people who need to know.
8. Ask for help any time you need it. Outside auditors give perspective.
9. Hire competent people to work with you on the budget.
10. Do a cash flow analysis and maintain a reserve fund to have money when you need it.

Ask, "Are we bringing in enough money to operate a quality program while covering our expenses?" That simple question keeps everything else in perspective.

childhood programs, staff salaries are the greatest expenditure. This suggests that the well-being of our employees is a high priority. The purpose and goals of a program take shape through dollars dedicated to make them real.

Like a map, a budget predicts and guides. The budget is a center's financial framework. It predicts what a director will spend and shows whether spending aligns with that prediction. In practical terms, according to colleague Cathy Jones, a budget:

1. Predicts the cost of running the center.
2. Keeps track of actual costs.
3. Flags changes to make when the prediction and the reality are at odds.

Expenses, like an unexpected tornado, can hit a program out of the blue. Energy costs for heating can skyrocket. Gasoline prices can prevent staff from making a long commute. The original budget must be brought up to date to account for what really happens (**actual expense budget**). The good news is that, with each passing year, a director will be able to use the current year's actual expense budget for making the next year's projected budget.

Adrienne's Revenues

Revenues	January	February	March
Tuition:			
Parent Fees	$14,429	$14,438	$13,224
Subsidy	15,773	14,498	16,112
Food Program	4,900	5,087	5,243
Other:			
Accreditation Grant	2,000		
Total Revenues	$37,102	$34,023	$34,579

▶ EXERCISE YOUR EQ   Recall the chapter case study and walk through Adrienne's budget (see **Adrienne's Revenues** and **Adrienne's Expenses**) to get a sense of her program's **viability** (financial health). For an indication, let's start by looking at the first three months of last year's budget. Use your EQ to assess how you feel about delving into budgets and numbers. If fear arises, not to worry; we will walk through this one step at a time.

Look at the left-hand column in **Adrienne's Revenues** to locate funding sources. Tuition brings in the largest amount of money. Subsidy (tuition paid by the state for some children) is a second form of income. Tuition and subsidy add up to the money flowing into Adrienne's program. Other income in the left-hand column also contributes to the inflow.

Like most programs, Adrienne's center receives funding for food. States provide monies to make sure children receive nutritious meals and snacks. The last item in the revenue column is a $2,000 grant from a local agency to help Heaven on Earth prepare for reaccreditation. The sum of the items in each column shows Adrienne's **revenue** for that month.

Now examine **Adrienne's Expenses** to determine how much money was spent each month. Compare the income to the expenses to assess whether Heaven on Earth made money, lost money, or broke even.

The **Reconciliation Budget** shows remaining money after bills were paid. Good news for Adrienne! For each of those three months, her program earned money, or **net income.**

Adrienne's Expenses

Expenses	January	February	March
Payroll:	$21,249	$20,877	$20,854
Workers' Comp	614	599	599
Payroll Deductions (incl. FICA/Social Security)	2,100	2,064	2,067
Insurance	579	623	612
Retirement @.02	425	418	418
Supplies	200	76	183
Telephone	98	98	98
Utilities:	843	765	824
Electricity			
Water			
Garbage Fee			
Rent	1,270	1,270	1,270
Food	2,986	2,077	2,664
Liability Insurance (due quarterly)			533
Advertising	212		
Accreditation Fee Step 1	350		
Custodial Services	1,000	1,000	1,000
Loan Repayment	1,000	1,000	1,000
Total Expenses	$32,926	$30,867	$32,122

Reconciliation Budget

Reconciliation Budget	January	February	March
Revenue	$37,102	$34,023	$34,579
Expenses	32,926	30,867	32,122
Net Income	$4,176	$3,156	$2,457

Given that the program was **in the black** (made more money than it spent) during this time period last year, Adrienne feels more confident about looking back over the remaining nine months of last year's budget. She is keeping her fingers crossed that she has enough of a budget surplus to accomplish her goals for the upcoming year, which include:

✓ Hire an infant teacher to replace Lonni, who retired at a salary of $23,000.

✓ Purchase new playground equipment and surfacing. Bids have come in between $12,000 and $18,000.

✓ Resurface the playground: $2,000 for wood mulch, $8,000 for rubber mulch.

✓ Fund a staff team-building retreat, off-site, for $500.

✓ Bring in a consultant for $700 to help teachers build classroom portfolios or investigate to see if your resource and referral agency has a trainer at no cost.

▶ EXERCISE YOUR EQ   ▨   For Adrienne's program to afford these changes, how much will she need to cover the additional expenses?

The budget seesaw

Budgets are all about money coming in and money going out. Money coming in is **revenue** or **income**; money going out is **expenditure** or **expense**.

Picture this scene on Adrienne's new playground: Brady, 25 pounds, sits on one side of the seesaw while his friend Marshall, 40 pounds, climbs on the other. Clunk! Brady yells, "No fair!" Teacher Tamjin captures the teachable moment and helps the boys analyze what happened. Tamjin pushes down on Brady's side. Balance is achieved.

This common sense principle applies to budgets. Buying playground equipment must be balanced by spending less on something else, or by raising additional funds. Figuring out the options can be a treasure hunt. Fortunately, early childhood management has evolved to a place where many budgeting tools are available to help. Finding the software package that fits your program's needs can be the beginning of that treasure hunt.

Help in Finding Financial Management Software That Meets Your Needs

• Ask other directors what software works for them.
• Meet with a director to learn more about the software he or she uses and how student, family, and program data is used.
• Tell vendors you would like to try out the system before you purchase.
• Attend conferences with exhibit halls. Most of the software vendors there will be glad to help.
• You may have a trusted family member who is a capable accountant. Ask him or her to design a financial management plan to meet your specific needs. This will ensure that your software investment pays off and aligns with your needs and expectations.

Source: Cathy Jones, assistant professor, early childhood education, Spadoni College of Education, Coastal Carolina University.

Software for early childhood financial management

More good news: Directors can choose and use budgeting software, such as *EZ-Care2, Childcare Manager,* and *Procare Software* (see **Help in Finding Financial Management Software That Meets Your Needs**). Child care financial management software provides a framework that can be continuously updated. In the click of a key, directors can use software to enter and sort data to show:

• Percentage of children enrolled compared to a program's licensed capacity
• Actual cost per child
• Attendance records
• Payroll from a particular week
• How to develop a new annual budget, step by step
• The reconciliation budget: predicted expenses versus actual expenses

- Eligibility for and reimbursement amounts for the food program
- How to plan menus
- Children and family records, like inoculations and medications
- How to post reminders to families on the system
- Employment records
- Professional development hours and staff scheduling

Each year, updates to early childhood management software include new bells and whistles. For the latest information, go to http://childcareexchange.com.

Line items and consistency

Adrienne thinks she can find additional money for playground expenses by saving money on Lonni's replacement, Regina, since she has fewer years of experience. Regina will start at a salary of $17,500, and Adrienne wants to know if she can use that savings toward equipment.

Her predecessor's annual budget predicted "business as usual." The budget did not include plans for playground equipment replacement costs, nor did it include funds for an off-site staff retreat. Adrienne needs to fund both of these while operating within the projected budget for this **fiscal year.** A fiscal year begins and ends the same time annually, typically July 1 through June 30. Some programs start their fiscal year on January 1.

▶ EXERCISE YOUR EQ ▮   Adrienne says that she hopes to replace Lonni (who earns $23,000 annually) with Regina (whose salary will be $17,500). Project the difference in Regina's salary from Lonni's salary, beginning October 1, for the rest of the fiscal year.

Use your EQ to help Adrienne brainstorm low- or no-cost ways to replace playground equipment and surfacing (donations from local businesses, workdays by parents, etc.). Ask Adrienne to investigate off-site retreat locations that might be free or low-cost (local foundations, nature centers, someone's home).

Adrienne worries that the money she saves on Lonni's replacement is in a different line item (Salary) than the playground equipment line item (Equipment). Each **line item** lists one type of expense, such as salaries or rent. Adrienne does not know if she can mix these apples and oranges. She wants to know, "Will I be robbing Peter to pay Paul?" (See **Money Management Advice for New Directors** for more on this topic.)

In the short term, income from one line item can be moved to cover an expense in a different line item. Replacing playground equipment is a one-time expense (paid in full in one payment). Adrienne may be able to transfer salary savings to cover the **one-time expense** of replacing playground equipment. Money from the "Salary" line item can be moved to the "Equipment" line item.

In the long term, however, Adrienne needs enough money to attract and keep excellent staff. If Adrienne wants to promote quality, will paying new staff a lower salary achieve that goal? Saving money in this way may bolster the bottom line (keeping your program in the black), but a short-term increase to the bottom line may lead to a long-term decrease in quality.

Money Management Advice for New Directors

1. Don't sell yourself or your staff short. If you wear yourself out, you wear out your human capital. Capital is an asset of your program. In the end, you will just be worn out and will not save anything.

2. Do your homework before you start. A quality program does much more than "just loving the kids."

3. Don't underestimate your real costs. Otherwise, you may end up paying for quality out of your personal budget.

Source: Cathy Jones, assistant professor, early childhood education, Spadoni College of Education, Coastal Carolina University.

Playground expenses may be covered financially, but what will be the expense to the program's quality? By funding playground expenses from salary savings, Adrienne can make a short-term fix (immediate solution). Eventually, Adrienne hopes to increase salaries and provide incentives to keep quality staff. She will need a plan to meet this goal.

Ongoing expenses, like salaries, are a predictable budget line item. Ongoing expenses demand ongoing revenue. Rent or mortgage payments are ongoing expenses. To pay monthly rent, Adrienne needs a steady influx of money ($1,270 each month). Short-term gains cannot be relied on for ongoing expenses.

Depreciation

Depreciation shows how much value equipment loses each year after purchase. Heaven on Earth's playground equipment, currently eight years old, is not likely to last more than another two years. The original purchase price for the equipment was $15,000. To report her loss to the insurance company, how does Adrienne compute the actual value of the equipment?

Here is a simple, easy method for computing depreciation:

1. List the purchase cost of the product.
2. Find the number of years the product was guaranteed to last.
3. Divide the purchase price by the number of years of the warranty.

Adrienne's first task is to find out how long the equipment was guaranteed to last. The playground equipment vendor's guarantee was for 10 years. If each year the equipment drops in value by 10 percent, by the end of eight years, the equipment has lost 80 percent of its value, or $12,000. Subtract this amount from the purchase price, and you can see how products quickly depreciate:

$$8 \text{ years} \times 10\% \text{ or } \$1,500/\text{year} = \$12,000.$$

As Adrienne subtracts the depreciated amount ($12,000) from the purchase price ($15,000), she discovers the equipment's value has decreased to $3,000. This information is helpful for Adrienne as she budgets for replacement of large items. (See **Depreciation of Adrienne's Playground Equipment** for a calculation of the equipment's depreciation for each year.)

▶ EXERCISE YOUR EQ   ▨   Try computing the depreciation value of classroom furniture, your computer, or some other item. You can even go online to look up the "Blue Book" value of your car. To what degree have your items depreciated? Now you will be able to confidently compute the depreciation of items in your early childhood center!

Depreciation of Adrienne's Playground Equipment

Purchase price—first year	$15,000
Second year	13,500
Third year	12,000
Fourth year	10,500
Fifth year	9,000
Sixth year	7,500
Seventh year	6,000
Eighth year	4,500
Ninth year	3,000
Tenth year	1,500
Eleventh year +	0

Help from Your Board

Board members can bring professional expertise, such as accounting, financial planning, legal, and marketing savvy.

Boards of early childhood programs often do the bulk of their work in subcommittees:

- Finance and Fundraising
- Personnel and Policy
- Planning
- Executive

The Executive Committee is composed of board officers: president, vice president, secretary, and treasurer (or secretary-treasurer), plus chairs of each of the three other subcommittees. Working closely with your board's Executive Committee is wise.

An accountant will have to help you calculate the depreciation of your large equipment and real estate items. The breakdown provided in Depreciation of Adrienne's Playground Equipment is for budgeting purposes only and is not to be used for audits or financial reports.

Budget reports

Adrienne wants to work with her board to be sure everyone is apprised of important budget information (see **Help from Your Board** for more on this topic). Adrienne invites the board's Finance Committee to work with her on funding the playground and staff retreat. She already has worked with the Personnel Committee for her new hire, Regina.

In the chapter case study, Adrienne "inherits" a power struggle among board members. Roderick, a lawyer and chair of the Finance Committee, competes with financial planner Placido, chair of the Planning Committee. In an effort to "bring Placido down to earth," Roderick insists on a **cash flow analysis**.

Roderick argues the program may look good on paper but could put itself out of business next month due to cash flow problems. As Gwen Morgan and Bess Emanuel (2009) note in *The Bottom Line for Children's Programs,* far too many well-intentioned programs have failed for lack of cash flow. Tuition was owed, but not enough was paid on time to meet the payroll. Roderick also requests information on fixed and variable costs.

In cooperation with her Finance Committee, Adrienne uses her software to prepare and present a cash flow analysis as well as cash reserve reports.

Cash flow analysis

A cash flow analysis is a record of how money flows into and out of a center. This analysis shows how much money was received and spent during a given period of time. A budget may predict an income of $37,000 in January. If the food program or tuition subsidies are late that month, the actual amount a center takes in will be less. Paying staff salaries may be difficult. Just getting by every month does not allow the center to generate enough revenue for unexpected costs or periods of low enrollment.

For this reason, maintaining a **cash reserve** is wise. A cash reserve, like a savings account, holds funds a director may need to use for unexpected reasons. Adrienne may have been able to use funds from the cash reserve to cover the cost of the playground equipment. She adds cash reserve reports to the list to give to her board on a regular basis.

Knowing monthly revenues and expenditures is rarely enough. A safer approach is to generate a cash flow analysis. This analysis shows whether there is money "in hand" to pay bills on time. Take a look at the information Adrienne can generate for her board by using the **Cash Flow Analysis** table (p. 182).

Remember Adrienne's budget? For the first three months there was a positive cash flow, meaning every month the center took in more revenue than was expended. A storm in April caused unforeseen roofing damage that was not covered by her insurance. How did that affect her cash flow?

Notice that the budget loss of $3,544 in April is indicated by parentheses. In a cash flow analysis report, amounts that appear in parentheses are **in the red** (not enough money to cover expenses).

Cash Flow Analysis

Cash Flow	January	February	March	April	May
Revenue	$37,102	$34,023	$34,579	$35,221	$37,000
Expenses	32,926	30,867	32,122	38,765	32,763
Net Income	4,176	3,156	2,457	(3,544)	4,237
Cumulative	$4,176	$4,176+	$7,332+	$9,789–	$6,245+
Cash Flow		3,156=$7,332	2,457=$9,789	3,544=$6,245	4,237=$10,482

Collecting money owed

Adrienne uses her EQ to stay on top of situations where tuition is **in arrears,** or has a history of being unpaid. To keep cash flowing, directors can use these strategies recommended by experienced peers (Neugebauer & Neugebauer 2007, 86–89):

✓ Spell out policies at enrollment.

✓ Keep in close touch with families.

✓ Be alert for freeloaders.

✓ Make it easy to pay.

✓ Collect fees in advance.

✓ Collect a deposit.

✓ Enforce late payment policies.

✓ Offer to deal with problems in advance.

✓ Act quickly on delinquencies.

✓ Offer repayment options.

✓ Have parents sign a promissory note.

✓ Sue in small claims court.

✓ Stop providing care.

Telling a family they can no longer enroll their child can be painful, for the child and everyone who cares for the child. Effective directors are proactive and tell parents immediately that money is due. Directors also can collect a deposit in advance of at least two weeks' tuition. By using "letter of the law" skills, you will be able to hold everyone to the same standard. Otherwise, within just a few weeks, a single family can owe a substantial portion of a center's projected monthly revenue.

A promissory note, signed by one or both parents, commits the family to pay the full amount owed plus a set interest. Promissory notes help when significant tuition payment sums are in arrears. Should legal action be taken, a promissory note supports the center's case and documents the parents' acknowledgement of responsibility. Promissory note forms are available online or at office supply stores.

To keep a child enrolled in a program, the family needs to pay both current tuition and past-due payments on time. **Garnishing** the parents' wages or suing for past-due tuition requires a lawyer's action. When wages are garnished, an amount is taken off the top of the earnings and sent directly to the center. Going to court costs time and resources; having effective financial management practices in place will help prevent costly situations from arising.

Budgeting for part-time children and teachers

Imagine that an automobile manufacturer in Adrienne's community lays off employees, several of whom have children in her center. Due to their new financial hardships, many of these parents request part-time child care slots. Can toddler Tarak come Mondays, Wednesdays, and Fridays? Marta's mom finds a job from noon to 5 p.m. and wants to bring Marta for afternoons only.

To assess Adrienne's ability to provide part-time care, use this checklist:

____ Program has a waiting list of children who need care at different times.

____ Parents' needs match up with another family's needs.

____ Teacher and family needs match.

____ Families are charged for part-time slots, whether the child attends or not (just as with full-time enrollees).

Similarly, teachers may want to **job share** (together do the work of one full-time teacher). Bertie wants to work Monday through Wednesdays; Jamie prefers Thursdays and Fridays. Together they make up one full-time equivalent (FTE) teacher. Regina wants to work only afternoons. She has not found another teacher to job share. To schedule part-time teaching, Adrienne must ask:

❑ Can children's need for quality care be met with this arrangement?

❑ Will this new staffing pattern align with enrollment? For example, if afternoon enrollment is higher than morning enrollment, Regina is needed more in the afternoon.

❑ Is another staff member willing to job share, effectively creating an FTE with Regina?

❑ How will this change affect other staff?

Adrienne wants to help her families and staff. Can she schedule for part-time teachers and children and still come out with a balanced budget? As long as Adrienne can ensure that all the children will receive the best possible care, she is willing to be flexible.

Part-time options require careful tracking and bookkeeping. Often directors offer part-time slots only when children from different families attend, as if they were one full-time child. This allows two children the opportunity to attend without financial risk for the center. Similarly, job sharing allows two part-time teachers to share the work of one full-time teacher. Each part-time employee is paid according to the percentage of full-time work he or she does.

Utilities, personnel, and rent costs continue to accrue even when no children are attending. Adrienne must plan enrollment, schedule teachers, and charge tuition in a way that keeps her program operating smoothly. Adrienne offers this schedule to accommodate two families needing part-time child care:

	Monday	Tuesday	Wednesday	Thursday	Friday
A.M.	Tarak	Marta	Tarak	Marta	Tarak
P.M.	Tarak	Marta	Tarak	Marta	Tarak

Similarly, Adrienne develops this schedule for two teachers requesting a job share arrangement:

	Monday	Tuesday	Wednesday	Thursday	Friday
A.M.	Bertie	Bertie	Bertie	Jamie	Jamie
P.M.	Bertie	Bertie	Bertie	Jamie	Jamie

Offering parents part-time slots is a family-friendly, but not always business-friendly, practice.

In both cases, each slot is filled each day. Programs can charge a daily fee that is a little higher than the weekly fee for part-time slots. Directors can refuse a request for a part-time teaching position if that change will affect children and the program negatively.

For Adrienne to budget for part-time children and teachers, she needs to think in terms of full-time equivalents (FTEs). Adrienne computes percentages of a full-time enrollee or a full-time teacher. She asks, what percentage of an FTE is Tarak? Marta? What about Bertie and Jamie? What percentage of an FTE is each teacher?

▶ EXERCISE YOUR EQ   ▨   Help Adrienne by computing Bertie and Jamie's FTE percentages.

Benefits for one full-time teacher can add approximately 28 percent to the cost of employing that teacher.

Allowing staff to work part time can be both a family-friendly and program-friendly policy. Job sharing can be beneficial to the budget's bottom line if less is paid to each teacher in terms of benefits. Benefits include health and dental insurance, 401(k) contributions, life insurance, disability insurance, and a discount on child care.

Both Bertie and Jamie assure Adrienne that their spouse or partner's benefits cover them. Because neither is full time, neither qualifies for benefits. Job sharing for Regina is not an option until another teacher joins her to make one FTE.

Fixed and variable costs

Roderick, the Finance Committee chair, e-mails a reminder to Adrienne to report on fixed versus variable costs as soon as possible. Adrienne uses her common sense to understand the difference between a fixed cost and a variable cost. Although few things are permanent, Adrienne expects monthly rent to be a fixed cost. The landlord has promised not to raise the rent for two years. Repaying a loan at the same amount each month is another fixed cost.

Variable costs are less predictable. If Tarak's family moves to Arizona, for example, that family's tuition payment ends. If Heaven on Earth implements a **sliding scale** (which allows families of different economic means to pay what they can afford), tuition is variable, not fixed. Variable revenues can change suddenly. Adrienne's budget must account for the variation in income.

Adrienne assumes correctly that fixed costs are best met by predictable sources of income. With this in mind, Adrienne can better estimate how many variable expenses, such as new equipment and a staff retreat, she can take on. She e-mails her report to Roderick.

Wage and hour considerations

All this work on FTEs and benefits packages raises another issue for Adrienne: How does Heaven on Earth comply with federal wage and hour laws? Adrienne heard a nearby center was penalized for not paying staff properly under these laws.

The bottom line of wage and hour laws is that "staff must be paid for the hours they work" (Morgan & Emanuel 2009, 35). That required three-credit hour course, the weekend "spruce up" of school grounds, and attendance at the annual statewide early childhood conference are all work time for which a teacher must be compensated. Morgan and Emanuel (2009) provide this summary of wage and hour law considerations:

- Staff must be paid for the hours they work. No employee can work 40 hours or more per week unless she is compensated. Hours in excess of 40 must be compensated at a time-and-a-half rate. If the Department of Labor determines that you have violated these rights of employees, you will have to make substantial back payments.

- The concept of "compensatory time" does not apply to any employee covered by wage and hour laws, unless it is used within the same work week and is less than 40 hours.

- If the employer requires the employee to do anything, the employee must be paid for the time spent doing it. This includes training, conferences, and parent meetings. For example, if the center requires an assistant teacher to take a course in order to do her job better, the center director must pay for the course, and for the hours spent taking it. However, if the employee is taking the course because the employee aspires to become a lead teacher (or achieve any role advancement), then the center director is not required to pay for the time or the course. In that case, the employee is not required by the employer to take it, and the benefit is to the employee rather than to the center.

- Audits may be routinely conducted by government or can be initiated in response to complaints by disgruntled employees. Wage and hour officials do not reveal to you whether there was a complaint.

Starting from scratch: Your first budget

Now that Adrienne feels more confident managing a budget, she is freer to dream of founding her own center. Like Adrienne, most new directors step into leadership of an already established program, with a budget in place. With her dream of going out on her own tucked tightly under her heart, Adrienne looks for help to develop her business plan and start-up budget.

Fortunately, Adrienne can turn to many helpful resources, including:

- Small Business Administration (SBA)
- Resource and referral agency (R&R) for local early childhood programs
- State regulatory agencies, especially licensing
- Legislators, such as members of Congress
- Utility companies for cost estimates and package plans
- Online websites for cost comparisons of equipment and supplies
- Information on salaries in the field and, if available, in a particular locale
- State and local professional organizations
- Workshops on finances at early childhood conferences
- A local directors' support group
- Software programs for early childhood financial management

A business plan, including the proposed start-up budget, needs to be thorough, detailed, and clear before potential lenders or partners can be approached.

New directors can easily underestimate start-up costs. The local Small Business Administration (SBA) will help aspiring business owners think through unforeseen expenses. Some SBAs can provide links to small business "incubators," which specialize in setting up first-time entrepreneurs for success.

▶ EXERCISE YOUR EQ   ▪   List all the costs a new program will have. Next, list all the sources of income. When you finish each list, go back to see if you can add even more possibilities.

What's the secret to financial management?
There are no secrets. The key is in being detailed, comprehensive, and staying up-to-date. Thinking, "I'll get to the budget tomorrow" just doesn't work.

—**Cathy Jones**
Assistant professor

Directors starting up a new program can be tempted to choose lesser quality items for the sake of saving up front. Think long-term when it comes to quality. Less expensive, lower quality equipment and furnishings help today but harm tomorrow. Cheaper items can wear out before the budget can afford to replace them. Every purchase, from toys to tables, needs to stand up to the daily wear and tear they will receive. Vendors of toys and classroom and playground equipment often set up display booths at state and national conferences. Online schedules for conferences list participating vendors.

Consider these tips for designing a start-up budget:

- After space is secured and furnished, personnel will be your greatest ongoing cost. Remember Adrienne's operating budget? Personnel costs ran between 57 and 62 percent.

- The costs of furnishing a room can range from $5,000 to $35,000, depending on room size and children's ages.

- Build in a cushion (financial safety net) to carry your center while enrollment builds. Initially you will not need as many staff as you need at full operation.

- Are you comfortable with your staffing plan? Have you considered how many staff you will need when you open?

- Plan for advertising costs. Sometimes a local newspaper will feature your new center. Continued advertising costs money. Have you developed a Web site? Posted jobs or advertisements on Craigslist (*www.craigslist.org*) or Monster (*www.monster.com*)? Listed in the yellow pages? Joined the chamber of commerce, Facebook, or LinkedIn to spread the word?

- Basic office equipment will be required, such as computers, office supplies, a copier, and a desk and chair. Used and donated office equipment can lower expenses.

- Adrienne plans to use all the assistance she can find to help her get started. She wants to be confident and prepared when she takes her business plan (and her dream) to the bank for funding.

Start-up budget

Adrienne's start-up budget will include the items in the **Start-Up Budget** chart, along with their estimated cost. The column on the right will be filled in as soon as Adrienne makes the purchases. Being able to compare actual costs with estimated costs will be useful information.

EQ plus IQ in managing money

"I have a legal problem," directors often tell me. To listen, I shift into my "lawyer brain." Approximately 80 percent of these problems turn out to be personnel problems not requiring legal skills. Interpersonal problems can feel beyond our understanding, so much so that we imagine them to be legal problems. How refreshing to know that a manager's EQ can help her resolve these dilemmas. Imagine the relief on a director's face when she remembers that human problems, like budget problems, can become manageable when we use our EQ.

As Roger and Bonnie Neugebauer (2007, 7) remind us, "Directors of child care centers must be as effective at managing money as they are at caring for children." (See **A Voice from the Field on Overcoming Budget Problems** for more advice on this issue.) We have helped Adrienne use her EQ to guide her IQ in managing her program's finances. Could it be that we know more than we think we do about finances?

Start-Up Budget		
Before Opening	Estimated Cost	Actual Cost
First month's rent/mortgage plus any deposits		
Utilities:		
Water		
Electricity		
Garbage		
Other		
Remodeling costs		
Furniture for classrooms		
Kitchen equipment		
Office equipment		
Toys and manipulatives for children		
Consumable supplies, such as toilet paper, napkins, drawing papers, art materials, etc.		
Licensing fees		
Taxes		
Liability insurance		
Director salary for one to two months		
One week's personnel salary for training		
Advertising for the center		
Advertising for staff		

A Voice from the Field on Overcoming Budget Problems

1. A center, in operation for over 15 years, lost a hefty source of funding. The director thought the center would have to close. She called her staff together and met with them and, after that, with the families.

   Throughout both meetings, she invited each group to brainstorm solutions to this problem. In the end, they were able to come up with enough good ideas to save the center. Additionally, they felt they had a stake in the solutions. That "buy in" was the best part.

   The director's attitude was positive in public even though, in private moments, she cried many tears. I don't think the families and staff ever knew her agony. They saw instead her hope and her love for the children.

2. I served on an advisory board that worked with a program having financial problems. No one had ever worked with this center to uncover the "real costs" involved in its operation. The director's budget showed no reconciling between the projected budget and the actual costs.

   Our board helped the director identify and tabulate the actual costs. Once the figures were out in the open and decided upon, we were able to support the director in making necessary changes. She began to make better use of staff time. She changed policies on part-time slots for children. A new after-school program brought in more funding. Parent fees were raised a little.

   Often, just getting help to see your program through new eyes makes all the difference.

Source: Cathy Jones, assistant professor, early childhood education, Spadoni College of Education, Coastal Carolina University.

▶ EXERCISE YOUR EQ   ▨   How do you think Adrienne can handle the power struggle between her two board members? Attorney Roderick was competing with financial planner Placido to be seen as the board's expert on budgeting. What would you recommend? Use your social EQ.

Reflection questions

1. Our values about money, as well as our confidence about managing money, can have a lot to do with the way we were raised. Make a list of five to ten messages you got in your early years about money and its management. What memories stand out more than others when it comes to learning about money? Write about whether or not the "bag lady/bag man" fear applies to you. Note what you can do or have done to gain confidence and expertise in managing money.

2. Balancing your personal checkbook and figuring out your own budget both serve as starting points in learning about program budgets. List your own fixed costs and revenues. From those figures, create your personal start-up budget for the rest of the year, beginning tomorrow. Look through your checkbook to identify variable expenses and unexpected income. With these figures, create a budget of income and revenue for the remainder of the year. Can you create a balanced budget for yourself in advance?

3. Shopping has become an American pastime. My mother taught me to be a huntress for the best bargains. If you are a shopping machine, how can you be sure your "shop 'til you drop" approach does not torpedo your budget? List 10 realistic strategies to help you keep within budget, regardless of the allure of buying "just one more thing." Teachers often spend their own money to create hands-on classroom activities and to decorate anew each season or month. Can you think of alternate resources and ways for teachers to access ample creative supplies without using their own funds? Again, list at least 10 alternative resources and/or approaches.

4. Research early childhood financial management software options. Write a comparison with recommendations for beginning directors.

Team projects

1. Imagine being a director who must raise some "hot button" budget issues with teachers. The most pressing issue is whether to continue to offer reduced child care tuition for employees as a benefit. Your generous policy has attracted excellent teachers. Loss of income has become a serious drawback. The second hot button issue is how to design and fund a family-friendly space and atmosphere where families drop off and pick up their children. Finding room for easy chairs and a "muffin and coffee" service is your goal. Later on, you hope to provide teachers with a lounge of their own. Create a budget for each project with estimated costs. Make a chart listing the pros and cons of both major items to be discussed. Strategize how to present and discuss these issues effectively with the teachers. Present this to your group, as if they were your staff members. If possible, create a PowerPoint presentation to help visual learners.

2. Go on a well-planned "treasure hunt" to investigate resources available to help a new director get started. Decide first what specific area or topic each person will investigate. **Top 10 Financial Management Pointers** on page 176 will help. When done investigating, prepare together a "Financial Resources Notebook" for new directors.

Include the names of organizations and individuals, contact information, Web addresses, fact sheets, regulatory standards, and other useful information. Present this to your group.

3. Interview up to three early childhood administrators each about their "learning curve" in mastering all the facets of financial management. Create a list of interview questions including: (a) What stages did you pass through in gaining expertise? (b) What helped and hindered you along the way? (c) What advice would you give new directors? Create a list of tips for your group based on the interviews. As a team, create a "director's map to financial management expertise" to show the stages a director passes through on the way to becoming a confident fiscal manager.

Glossary of budget terms

Actual expense budget: A running tab of what you pay out and take in each month, as compared to what you predicted in the projected budget.

Cash flow analysis: A process you can use to find out how much money you have on hand.

Cash reserve: A fund you can use on "rainy days," especially when your cash flow is weak.

Depreciation: The anticipated loss of an asset's value over time.

Expenses: What you pay out (e.g., salaries, insurance, supplies, fees, consultant and trainer costs).

Fees: Additional costs for parents, including registration, co-pay, special supplies, and special event fees.

Fiscal year: The year as measured by your program's budget, usually July 1–June 30.

Garnishing: Taking a percentage "off the top" of someone's income to pay unpaid bills directly to the program.

In arrears: Past-due amounts; unpaid bills.

In the black: The program is making enough money to pay all its bills.

In the red: The program does not have enough income to meet its expenditures.

Job sharing: Two teachers work at complementary times to do the work of one teacher.

Line item: The term for each item that needs consideration in the budget, such as "personnel," "utilities," and "supplies."

Liquidity: Like cash flow, being "liquid" means you have monies on hand to use when you need them.

Medicaid: Employer's required payments into employees' funds for future medical care.

Net income: The total earned after expenditures are taken out.

One-time expense: Like paying the fee for a marriage certificate, you hope you only have to pay this once.

P&L: Acronym for profit and loss statement.

Payroll: The actual costs of salaries, including your own.

Projected budget: Your prediction about upcoming costs over a period of time.

Reconciliation: The process of checking your prediction of what would be earned and spent against what was actually earned and spent. Reconciling is making adjustments in incoming and outgoing resources.

Revenue: Incoming money, usually from parent fees, child care subsidies, and grants.

Sliding scale: Adjustments in the amount you charge, based on a family's income or based on the number of children the family and/or teacher enrolls.

Social security: Employers contribute to each staff member's social security fund, maintained by the federal government.

Spending down: A phrase used to describe the process of paying out the monthly/regular expenses in a timely way. A board member may ask about your "spend down" this month.

Taxes: The percentage of income federal, state, and local governments charge to provide their services.

Viable: Operating "in the black," as opposed to in debt.

Workers' compensation: A system regulated in state law that issues payments and provides medical care to employees who are injured or disabled during the course of their employment, regardless of fault (www.legal-explanations.com/definitions/workers-compensation.htm).

Bibliography

Copeland, T. 2008. *Getting started in the business of family child care.* St. Paul, MN: Resources for Child Caring.

Copeland, T. 2010. *Family child care record-keeping guide.* 8th ed. St Paul, MN: Redleaf Press.

Copeland, T. 2011. *Family child care 2010 tax workbook and organizer.* St. Paul, MN: Redleaf Press.

Gross, M.J., J.H. McCarthy, & N.E. Shelmon. 2010. *Financial and accounting guide for not-for-profit organizations.* 7th ed. New York: Wiley.

Harper, J. 2006. Nearly half of women fear life as a bag lady. *The Washington Times.* Aug. 23.

Jack, G.H. 2005. *The business of child care: Management and financial strategies.* Clifton Park, NY: Delmar Learning.

Mellan, O., & K. Piskaldo. 1999. Men, women, and money. *Psychology Today* Jan/Feb: 36.

Morgan, G.G., & B.R. Emanuel. 2009. *The bottom line for children's programs: What you need to know to manage the money.* 5th ed. Waltham, MA: Steam Press.

Neugebauer, R., & B. Neugebauer, eds. 2007. *Managing money: A center director's guidebook.* Redmond, WA: Exchange Press.

Web resources

ChildCare.net
   http://childcare.net
Child Care Exchange
   http://childcareexchange.com
National Association of Child Care Resource and Referral Agencies
   www.naccrra.org
U.S. Small Business Administration
   www.sba.gov

The roots of a child's ability to cope and thrive, regardless of circumstance, lie in that child's having had at least a small, safe place (an apartment? a room? a lap?) in which, in the companionship of a loving person, that child could discover that he or she was lovable and capable of loving in return.

—Fred Rogers, *You Are Special*

The path of learning and development is more like that of a butterfly than that of a bullet. Our job is to provide a setting where a group of energetic, idiosyncratic seekers go about this task and where all—adults and children—thrive amidst the daily rigors of group living.

—Jim Greenman, *Caring Spaces, Learning Places*

11 Do No Harm:
Building Safe, Sustainable, Healthy Learning Environments

Case Study—Beatrice and Aurora

Beatrice and her cousin Aurora have taught preschool and kindergarten for years. The cousins promised themselves that one day they would start their own program. Aurora yearns for the pine trees and clear streams of her childhood. Beatrice, raised in the city, prefers cozy window seats to getting her feet muddy. Their grandmother names Beatrice and Aurora as beneficiaries in her will. "Aurora! We can do it! Nonna has made it possible for us to build our own center!" Beatrice cries. The cousins hug and cry in joy, but neither one's vision of the perfect center looks anything like the other's.

What building and grounds design do you think could integrate the visions of both Beatrice and Aurora?

Ernest Hemingway's short story "A Clean,

Well-Lighted Place" is set in a European café protected from the troubles and dangers of the world around it. In reality, as Hemingway wrote about the warm golden light of the café, the darkness of the Spanish Civil War chilled the hearts of villagers around him with fear.

In ways both literal and metaphorical, our children and families live on the edge of danger. Safety is not guaranteed. Good health is more a gift than a given. Many children are left behind when it comes to being assured of clean, well-lighted, happy environments.

Early childhood leaders have the honor and challenge of creating environments for children where no harm can befall them. To learn, a child first needs to feel safe. Danger or fear of danger impedes a child's learning ability. Studies show children who do not feel safe in their environments will focus on self-protection, rather than being relaxed enough to explore and learn in their environment (Goleman 1997; Hannaford 2002). Our job is to remove danger, prevent harm, and provide welcoming, inspiring, healthy environments, all of which evaporate fear from a child's psyche. As early childhood leaders, we have the power to create "relational sanctuaries" where all children, including those struggling with post-traumatic stress disorder (PTSD) can learn to trust and thrive (Bruno 2010).

In this chapter, we will focus on standards for safety and health. These standards are the cornerstone for early child care building designs, policies, and practices. The principle "Do no harm" underlies every system that leaders build and manage, from playground safety to food service, from classroom equipment to emergency procedures. When adults take responsibility for healthy and safe environments, children are free to discover their world without barriers to impede them.

Doing no harm also includes protecting the natural world for all future generations. The "greening" of early childhood programs helps ensure children will always have trees to climb, streams to cross, and dragonflies to ponder.

Guiding principles

Guiding principles are touchstones to return to in our commitment to create safe spaces, policies, and practices for children to learn. Just as a person or program has core values (see Chapter 4), administrators need guiding principles to make sure each step they take furthers those values. If a leader's core value is "Do no harm," she will ask herself the following questions to be true to her core value. Guiding principles for health and safety are embodied in these questions.

Is every structure, piece of equipment, policy, and practice designed to:

- Comply with established standards for health and safety?
- Anticipate possible harm, and prevent that harm as much as possible?
- Utilize "universal precautions"?
- Attend to special needs: Do we meet and exceed the Americans with Disabilities Act, as amended (ADA), requirements?
- Welcome children's and families' ethnic and cultural differences?
- Promote the well-being of our natural environment?

Whether an administrator is drafting a policy for safety procedures or designing a building, playground, classroom environment, or entryway, she will benefit from asking these questions each time.

Building from the bottom up:
Resources, experts, advisors, support

As a leader, your vision, core values, and principles will become the guiding light that brightens every meeting, debate, and ground breaking. You will not have to be an expert on how to renovate or build from the ground up. Nor will you have to be an expert on equipment, playground design, or medical procedures. You will, however, need the willingness to:

- Learn the essentials (concepts, terminology, alternative approaches).
- Explore resources (people, websites, places to visit).

- Ask for help (experts, practitioners, government agencies).
- Involve your communities (families, staff, business communities).
- Engage your board and/or other advisors.
- Manage your budget wisely (see Chapter 10).
- Keep your eyes on the prize: Does every step further our goal?
- Ask: Is this safe? Is this healthy? Are we preventing hazards? Are we protecting the environment?

Architects and builders are ready to help early childhood administrators create safe, healthy, and happy environments. Leaders can ask around to find architects who are available, reasonable, and compatible. They also can use the Internet to investigate clients' ratings of architects or call other local programs to ask about their experiences with architects. Resource and referral agencies may be able to provide names of architects other programs have used.

A growing number of architectural firms offer "green" or environmentally sound designs. Recycled flooring, solar panels, and other energy-efficient building materials may be available. You can request that these be included in your options. Architects may also propose creative ways to utilize remnants of older buildings in the community. Just by asking, you may discover that you can respect the environment and build cost-effectively at the same time.

Administrators may find—once they share their vision, lists, pictures, or sketches with an architect—that not everything they had in mind is possible. Although a leader won't always get exactly what he wants, he will be given realistic alternatives. The architect's job is to know what is feasible, what is reasonable, and what meets standards. As an administrator, you will be able to ask the architect for designs of the building or renovation or for a computerized virtual tour of the designs. As with a doctor's visit, you, as a client, have the right to ask for a "second opinion" from another architect.

Partnering with a board of advisors

If a board of directors or advisors is in place, administrators will benefit from partnering with that board. Invite them to help. Chances are good that someone on the board is, has worked with, or knows of an architect. Work with board subcommittees. The Finance Committee chair can help project a budget for building or equipment costs. A Planning Committee, involved from the start, can help administrators envision how proposed changes will improve the program. Work closely with the Executive Committee, the board's leadership team, to look at the proposal from all directions.

If a board of advisors is not in place, administrators can form a design team to help during construction or renovation. Family, friends, neighbors, and business people can provide support and also "play devil's advocate." It is best to select people who are not all "yea-sayers" (rubber stamps) or "naysayers" (pessimistic or negative about change). Ground rules should be set with this team, especially on decision making. Will the design team be a group of advisors to you? If so, make that clear. If design team members will have more authority, spell that out. Otherwise, team members may build contradictory expectations. Any building erected on shifting sands instead of solid ground is likely to collapse.

Community input sounds like a mechanical process. Inviting people to share their dreams and hopes for a children's learning space, however, can be anything but mechanical. You may learn about resources you never envisioned, including construction

In early education, the mantra should be "Plant early, grow strong," and schools should do their best to lead by example in their day-to-day operations and overall culture.
—**Susan Leger-Ferraro**
Raising a Green Generation

In many centers or play areas of family child care homes, you have to look hard to find anything of beauty. Child care and aesthetics do not necessarily go together. Perhaps the lack of aesthetics is a sign of the times—a sign that other considerations take priority over beauty.
—**Janet Gonzalez-Mena**

professionals who might donate services. I have seen whole communities mobilized by wanting something better for their children.

Consider utilizing focus groups. Focus groups often sit in a circle and individually share ideas as equals, without fear of judgment. An administrator (or other individual) prepares the questions, facilitates the focus group meeting, and records responses. Everyone shares ideas. Children express what they want: "Can we milk cows? Make ice cream? Fly on an airplane in the sky?" Families discuss what they need and would love to see: overnight care, bilingual classrooms, a "one-stop shop" to drop off dry cleaning and pick up wholesome meals when they pick up their children. Community leaders may even want to publicize the early child care program free of charge to attract new businesses to the area.

As with a board of advisors or a design team, administrators must be clear on the role of focus groups from the start. An administrator who is gathering ideas is not taking orders. Brainstorming sessions for community input can lead to unrealistic expectations. Not everyone's "wish list" will come true. As a leader, set ground rules and expectations in writing and announce them verbally. Tell community members up front that although you do not guarantee you will meet everyone's needs, you value their input. This due process approach creates community interest, generates great ideas, and may elicit volunteers and contributions.

Help is all around if you ask and ask wisely.

NAEYC Program Standard 9:

The program has a safe and healthful environment that provides appropriate and well-maintained indoor and outdoor physical environments. The environment includes facilities, equipment, and materials to facilitate child and staff learning and development.

—National Association for the Education of Young Children

Fundamental building blocks for safety and health

Not everything that is beautiful is safe; not everything that is safe is beautiful. Recall Beatrice from the opening chapter case study. She sketches a tree house she remembers happily from her own childhood, high in the branches, with a retractable rope ladder. When her friends uttered the magic words, "Rapunzel, Rapunzel, let down your hair," she unfurled the rope ladder so they could climb up. Enchanting, but is the tree house safe?

Or consider Maximilian as he walks through the orderly Sunday school classrooms of his *schule*. Everything is neat—so neat, in fact, that every room looks just the same. In Max's program, families come from Ukraine, Poland, Israel, and Russia, bringing different traditions and expectations for what a space should look like. Uniformity may ensure safety, but does sameness support diversity? Can a child's imagination be sparked in the midst of such uniformity?

Do no harm: Is the structure safe?

"Do no harm," a guiding principle for early childhood leaders, can be evaluated with one simple question: In everything we do, are our families and staff free from danger?

The following health and safety standards guide the design of a physical environment to prevent injury while maximizing learning:

- State licensing requirements
- Local building and sanitary codes
- Fire and emergency codes
- Federal laws such as the Occupational Safety and Health Act (OSHA) and the ADA
- Accreditation standards
- Environmental rating scales
- Quality checklists

Lawful standards for health and safety

Whether an administrator is building a center from the ground up or renovating an existing facility, she needs to be mindful of requirements for creating safe and healthful environments. Chances are good that an administrator will be working with architects, builders, and/or other facilities professionals. These professionals can expand the knowledge you will need about federal, state, and local standards. Anyone involved in building must keep in mind the "Do no harm" principle by making sure governmental health and safety standards are met and, ideally, exceeded.

State licensing standards are the first place to investigate what "Do no harm" means in a particular state. Licensing standards set the bottom line, or baseline standard, for safe and well-run programs. Although standards can look like "legalese," they are usually broken down into common sense steps. Not to worry if standards appear overwhelming. Administrators can ask for assistance every step of the way.

You can start by going online to read your state's licensing requirements. While reading the requirements, keep a running list of questions about how your current or envisioned building can meet each standard. Call your state's early childhood licensing office and ask who might be able to work with you to design, build, or renovate your facility and develop safe practices.

Each program is assigned its own licensor, usually by region. Licensors are there to answer questions and to help programs meet the standards. Administrators will benefit greatly if they cultivate a good working relationship with licensors. To become better educated about your region's licensing requirements and procedures, consider the following guidelines:

- Contact directors of nearby programs for the names of their licensing representatives.
- Call your local resource and referral agency for information about licensors in your area.
- Use your social EQ to develop a working relationship with your assigned licensor.
- Licensors can be extremely helpful in answering a variety of questions. Ask as many as you can imagine. No question is a "stupid" question.

Having had the honor of serving as the keynote speaker at the National Licensing Seminar, the annual conference of NARA (National Association of Regulatory Administrators), I can assure you that licensors want to help. Unfortunately, licensors are often viewed like a dentist. Everyone knows going to the dentist is necessary, but who would visit a dentist more than required? As you build a relationship with your licensor, you will likely discover a fellow traveler who cares deeply about quality. The sooner you develop a working relationship with your licensor, the faster and more confidently you will be able to proceed in your projects.

Licensing standards, crafted by state legislators, can be unique to each state. Nonetheless, some standards are the same across the country. Each state sets a minimum amount of space for each child per classroom. Generally speaking, in the classroom, each child needs 35 square feet of space. On the playground, square footage per child increases to 75 feet to allow children the ability to "cut loose" and whoop with energy. Go online to find your state's standards for space per child.

Licensing requirements for safe and healthy practices for groups and individuals usually include:

- Written parental permission for program staff to administer medication to children

- Certification that all program staff are tuberculosis free
- Mandatory reporting of observed or suspected child abuse and neglect
- Permission to seek emergency care for children
- Records of medical examinations and immunizations
- CPR training for staff

Remember, licensing requirements are the bottom line. You are free to substantially exceed the bottom line to strengthen your program.

Local zoning, building, and sanitary codes

Local zoning, building, and sanitary codes vary by community. Just as the state has standards for early child care programs, so does the local government for any town, city, or county.

Zoning laws specify where child care programs can be built. Since you, as a current or future administrator, will be in charge of a business, think of zoning laws that allow for businesses rather than for residential dwellings. When possible, programs should be built in an area zoned for the business of child care. This is especially important if an individual wants to convert a residential home into a child care facility. Zoning variations (exceptions to zoning code requirements) can be formally requested. However, zoning boards can be strict about granting variations.

Building codes set standards for quality of construction and usage of space. Just as licensing standards vary by state, building codes can vary from city to city or town to town. Nonetheless, some standards are universal. Most building codes establish the first floor as the location of infant and toddler classrooms. This "Do no harm" requirement makes sure the youngest and less mobile children can be readily evacuated in an emergency. Requirements for building and grounds safety usually include provisions for:

- Minimum square footage of usable floor space for each child in activity rooms
- Exterior doors and windows
- Stairways, ventilation, and lighting
- Bathroom facilities
- Food preparation area
- Drinking water
- Minimum square footage for outdoor play area
- Outdoor play area equipment and cushioning materials, such as mats, wood chips, or sand

Building code inspectors can make visits before, during, and after construction. Inspectors make sure materials and processes meet standards. If, for example, an administrator is renovating an existing building, an inspector will most likely check for lead paint, asbestos, and radon gas. Administrators and builders will do well to develop a cordial, professional relationship with building inspectors to promote efficient, timely inspections. Social EQ is a leadership asset in virtually every undertaking.

Sanitary codes focus on keeping buildings clean. Good lighting, proper bathroom facilities, and fresh air quality all quash the spread of disease. Sanitary codes determine air circulation patterns so that each center space is guaranteed freshly replenished air. Sanitary codes set the hot water temperature, usually in line with state licensing requirements, to prevent scalding while ensuring cleanliness.

Convenient location of bathroom facilities also falls under sanitary code requirements. Are sinks and toilets close and accessible for children and staff, whether children and staff are inside the building or outside on the playground? Effective lighting contributes to keeping areas free of mildew and mold. Being able to see clearly is essential to safety at all times of the day and night. Lighting must meet sanitary code standards.

Town or city offices and the local chamber of commerce can provide zoning, building, and sanitary codes. Before administrators build or renovate, they will need to submit plans to each of these authorities for approval. Directors tell sad tales about being sent back to the drawing board for making (often costly) changes without authorization.

Administrators can ensure that health and safety standards are upheld daily by using policies like the sample **Cleanliness Policy**. When "Do no harm" becomes second nature to every staff member, cleanliness is a guaranteed practice.

Fire and emergency evacuation plans

Do you recall the last time you waited outside during a fire drill for the "all clear" signal? For years, when we evacuated buildings, we assumed fire or a fire drill was the reason. For centuries, wood was the dominant building material, and because wood ignites easily, fires were common.

After the terrorist attacks of September 11, 2001, early child care programs began developing evacuation plans for unforeseen disasters. Homeland security set new standards for safety, and communities are still updating fire codes and broadening evacuation plans for whatever danger may arise.

The variety of disaster situations that can arise in early childhood settings is remarkable. Listed below are emergencies that programs have already experienced. Some of these emergencies may be unsettling to read about. Call upon your emotional intelligence for help if this list troubles you:

- A parent arrives with a weapon.
- A wolf ambles onto the playground; children rush to pet the "doggie."
- A truck with hazardous waste overturns near the center.
- A homeless man uses the center grounds for shelter.
- A prison escapee makes a beeline for the center.
- An enraged boyfriend violently attacks a teacher on the playground.
- A drive-by shooting occurs when children are outside playing.
- A zoo animal gets loose while children are on a field trip.
- A sleeping child is left behind on the school bus.
- A van driver falls asleep while driving and crashes the van.
- A teacher has a mental breakdown in the classroom.
- A child dies during a classroom activity.

Cleanliness Policy

All staff at _____ are responsible for the cleanliness of their area of responsibility. While ongoing cleaning throughout the day is essential, programs should ensure a cleanup is conducted upon completion of projects, snacks, lunch, and during rest so that the area is clean for the next activity and contributes to the professional atmosphere of the center. Each teaching team is responsible for the care and cleaning of their class space daily, and the entire staff shares in the cleaning of the center common areas.

Minimum Cleanup Times

- Transition between morning activity and morning snack
- Transition between mid-morning activity and lunch
- At completion of lunch
- Transition between afternoon activities and afternoon snack
- At the end of the day

Please remember that tables must be sanitized before and after all snacks and meals.

Source: *Staff Handbook* (n.d.), Live & Learn Early Learning Center, Lee, NH.

OSHA 1910.1030(b): *Blood borne pathogens* means pathogenic microorganisms that are present in human blood and can cause disease in humans. These pathogens include, but are not limited to, hepatitis B virus (HBV) and human immunodeficiency virus (HIV).

• An intoxicated and belligerent family member threatens children and staff.

Of all the emergencies administrators need to plan for, fire is only the beginning. For this reason, administrators must ensure that their programs comply with fire codes, emergency evacuation, and homeland security standards. (See **Code Blue** and **Emergency Backpack Supplies** for more on this topic.)

▶ EXERCISE YOUR EQ   Make a list of possible emergency situations, and then outline sample safety procedures. Consider the list of possible emergency situations on the previous page you design emergency procedures for a variety of possible dangers.

OSHA, the federal Occupational Safety and Health Act, requires programs to take "universal precautions" for the safety and health of children, families, and staff. Universal precautions are actions taken to prevent the spread of dangerous illnesses by "blood borne pathogens" or germs. Hand washing is a universal precaution against the spread of pathogens. Disinfecting toys, classroom surfaces, and "mouth-ables" (anything acceptable for young children to put in their mouths) is another universal precaution.

These precautions are "universal" because they assume anyone might currently be infected with a contractible disease, not just one or two children. In this way, children are not singled out. Instead, with universal precautions, early childhood professionals assume that every child may be infected with an illness such as AIDS or HIV. Universal precautions apply to all programs that bring children and/or adults together, including early child care programs, hospitals, and restaurants.

The Americans with Disabilities Act (ADA), discussed in Chapter 7, was enacted into law because people with disabilities found themselves unable to enter, use, enjoy, or be employed in the same facilities as people without disabilities. Perhaps because European countries dealt with war on their own soil, those countries were ahead of the United States in making provisions for injured veterans. Seats on European buses and trains were reserved for individuals with disabilities. Ramps for people in wheelchairs were commonplace.

In 1990, the United States caught up with European countries in making spaces safe and welcoming for people with disabilities. Passage of the ADA has ensured that anyone who enters a child care center has equal access to the facilities. A child in a wheelchair can gain access to the center by means of a ramp, an ADA mandate. Similarly, the ADA requires bathroom facilities designed for the use and safety of children and adults with disabilities.

As directors build or renovate, they need to consider how every child, family, and staff member, regardless of disability, can participate in and enjoy program activities.

The ADA does not require administrators to expose their programs to "undue hardship" by spending the majority of a construction budget on ADA accommodations. Usually, a reasonable, considerate approach suffices.

Architects, builders, and licensors can work with directors on meeting ADA standards. Administrators can also go online (*www.ada.gov*) or simply call 800-514-0301 for assistance from federal government agencies. For assistance in creating and coordinating plans for children with special needs, directors can contact the American Public Health Association (APHA) and American Academy of Pediatrics (AAP) for national health and safety guidelines.

Accreditation standards

Each accrediting agency, such as NAEYC and NACCP, sets detailed standards for safety and healthfulness of physical facilities, including classroom and playground space and equipment. Accreditation agencies usually set more rigorous standards than states. Although directors may not immediately apply for accreditation, they can use the standards to guide the overall creation and subsequent operation of their programs. Later, when directors do apply for accreditation, they will be ahead of the game. Staff will be accustomed to working with the higher standard.

Environmental rating scales

Environmental rating scales are additional tools to assess your program's strengths and weaknesses in providing safe and healthy spaces for children and adults. Thelma Harms, Richard Clifford, and Debby Cryer (2005), from the University of North Carolina at Chapel Hill, are leaders in the design and implementation of these scales. Detailed rating scales can be found in Chapter 15.

An example of an NAEYC accreditation standard for physical environments is as follows:
The outdoor play area is arranged so that staff can supervise children by sight and sound.

Marcy Robertson (2005, 23) notes: "For many directors, the environmental rating scales provide a quality tool through which to view their programs, to support and involve their staff, and to measure their progress. In the United States the scales have also been attached to state licensing initiatives and other methods of ensuring quality, such as quality ratings for child care centers."

After directors design or renovate a building with these standards in mind, they must consider additional practical policies and procedures to promote health and safety once the building is completed.

Policies and practices to ensure health and safety

Meeting requirements from the start puts a program's physical environment and policies in good stead for everything that follows. Now let's look at practices and policies that continue our guarantee to "Do no harm." I have chosen key policies and practices. You may think of others of particular importance to you. Policies and practices often come about because a director sees a need to create steps that were not already in place. At the end of this chapter, I will give you some examples of current, evolving policies to think about that have not yet been fully tested.

Checklists for weekly "walks around the center"

Checklists can be formulated on a number of health and safety topics. One checklist might focus on cleanliness procedures and practices. Another checklist might address readiness for evacuation. Still another checklist can assess whether toys and equipment are well maintained and safe. Checklists can help administrators focus on all the different ways a program is safe, secure, and healthful for children, families, and staff.

Cathy Abraham (2007), in her article *Licensing Scavenger Hunt,* turns what could be a "been there, done that" job into an adventure. Abraham notes that the important task of meeting child care licensing regulations every year can be dry and repetitive. Her scavenger hunt activity adds fun to the topic through staff interaction. The first task on the hunt sends employees off with the **Licensing Scavenger Hunt** checklist and the instructions: "Physically locate the following items within the building…. No guessing!"

Other lists can focus on cleanliness measures and specifics such as square footage requirements for infants and the number of puzzles in the 4-year-olds classroom. To make these valuable exercises even more engaging, administrators can roll up lists and tie them with a ribbon like treasure maps, divide staff into heterogeneous (different classroom) teams for the hunt, and reward winning teams.

You can create your own checklists from any number of sources. Checklists based on state licensing standards like Abraham's are always useful. Not only may your licensor arrive unannounced at any time, but more important, you and the licensor will have the same goal in mind—keeping everyone safe from harm. If your program is accredited, use accreditation standards as the basis of your checklists. Inviting and engaging your staff in creating classroom checklists can increase "buy in" to complying with checklists requirements. Ready-made checklists are also available. (See the **Safety Checklist** for one example.)

Licensing Scavenger Hunt	
Item	Location
☐ Thermometer	
☐ Fire extinguisher	
☐ Parent handbook	
☐ Licensing regulations	
☐ Tissues	
☐ Fax number to program's supervising office	
☐ Extra children's clothing	
☐ Children's emergency cards	
☐ Child abuse hotline	
☐ Choking/CPR chart	
☐ Employment posters	
☐ The lost and found	

Procedure for handling and reporting accidents

Preventing accidents by keeping buildings and grounds safe is the goal. With children's high energy and quest for exploration, along with their proximity to other children, some falls and scrapes cannot be prevented. Administrators can prepare staff and families in advance to deal with and report accidents.

Keep "due process" in mind; give people the information they need and the opportunity to talk about what happened. As my retired friend, Frank, now a priest in the mountains of New Mexico, advises, "Facts have dimensions. Fear has no dimensions." Keeping accurate accident reports and sharing the information about the accident immediately with families is the best policy.

Steps directors can take (Click & Karkos 2011, 297) include:

1. Each child's file should contain a form signed by the parents authorizing emergency medical treatment.

2. Have a standard form on which pertinent accident information can be recorded. Complete it as soon as possible after the accident. (See the **Child Care Injury Report** on page 205 for a sample form.)

Safety Checklist

CLASSROOMS

Furniture is free of sharp corners.

All furniture is an appropriate size for the children using it and has been tested for safety.

Safety devices are on all electrical outlets.

Childproof locks are on cupboards containing cleaning supplies.

Hot water is set at 120 degrees Fahrenheit.

All toys less than 1½" in diameter have been removed. Staff have been trained to use the "choke tube" measuring tool.

No small objects such as pins, thumbtacks, nails, or staples are available to children.

All broken toys or parts of toys have been removed.

Art supplies are free of toxic ingredients.

There are no loose or torn carpet areas.

Vinyl flooring is not slippery.

Each classroom has a working smoke detector.

An emergency evacuation plan is posted in a visible place in each classroom.

Directions for emergency shut off of gas, electricity, and water are posted in a visible place.

The infant/toddler room has one clearly marked crib on wheels for quick evacuation of non-walking children.

OUTDOORS

All equipment has an adequate fall zone with safety-certified ground cover.

All moving parts on equipment have been checked for defects.

All equipment meets licensing requirements.

There is adequate spacing between pieces of equipment.

Platforms have sturdy guardrails.

Play equipment is sturdy and free of sharp edges or splinters.

There are no loose nuts or bolts on the equipment.

Play equipment is anchored firmly to the ground.

There are no tripping hazards, such as raised concrete on walkways or warped surfaces on climbing equipment.

Grass has been cut; walkways are free of debris.

The playground is free of broken toys, glass, or any objects that may have been thrown into the area.

All fences are at least 4 feet high and have securely latched gates.

Sandboxes are clean and are raked at least once a week.

Riding toys have a low center of gravity and are well balanced.

The riding area for wheel toys is separate from other play areas and away from traffic patterns.

The riding area for wheel toys is smooth and not slippery.

Children and staff members are aware of the rules regarding use of equipment.

Source: Phyllis Click and Kim Karkos, *Administration of Programs for Young Children*. 8th ed. (Belmont, CA: Wadsworth, Cengage Learning, 2011), 295.

3. Call paramedics or take the child to the nearest emergency room as required by the nature of the accident.

4. Telephone the parents as soon as possible. If the child is to be taken out of the school, ask that the parents go directly to the hospital.

5. If the injury seems minor and does not require emergency care, the parents should still be notified. A joint decision can be made if the child should stay at school or be taken home.

6. If the child stays at school, make sure that teachers watch for any further signs of difficulty during the day.

7. Answer any questions the other children may have as completely and honestly as possible. Reassure them that the injured child is receiving care.

Biting policy

Two-year-olds bite. Before children can adequately express themselves with words, they need to make their point. Biting another child says, "Hey, I'm angry!" or "No, you can't take my toy!" When my son Nick was 2, I encouraged Nick to "use words" instead of biting or hitting. Nick's teachers followed the same plan. Nick, like other children, outgrew his need to bite as his verbal ability grew. Of course, until Nick outgrew the biting phase, I kept my fingers crossed each day!

Biting upsets parents. Consider the following scenario in which a child bites fellow toddler Djabril. When you inform Djabril's mother that her child was bitten, she reacts strongly. Seeing the bruise on Djabril's cheek is alarming. The director shares with the parent a completed accident/incident report detailing the facts: what happened, when, and what steps were taken. It is important to note that one fact that should not be included in this report is the name of the child who did the biting. This is confidential information. Imagine how the "biter" might be shunned if the information were freely released.

One parent in West Virginia, an attorney, threatened to sue a director who would not reveal who had bitten the attorney's son. Fortunately, the director had included the **Sample Biting Policy** shown below in the parent handbook.

When the attorney parent continued to threaten a lawsuit, the director took another approach. She investigated why the biter's identity is confidential. She discovered the child who is bitten is not likely to be at risk of contracting disease. The biter, if he or she breaks the skin of another child, is the one exposed to blood borne pathogens. In the end, the father dropped his threat. More importantly, the child, like Nick, outgrew the biting stage. Staff took special precautions to work with the biter as they saw his frustration rise.

Sample Biting Policy

In the event that another child bites your child, we will make every effort to keep your child safe and prevent the biting from recurring. We will report the biting incident to you, using our Accident Report Form. We keep the identity of the child who did the biting confidential. We work with that child to help her/him learn other ways to express feelings.

Mildly-ill-child policy

Parents know children need to be home to heal from illnesses and hurts. Families, however, do not always have the luxury of staying home with a sick child. Hourly wage earners experience a particularly difficult bind if they stay home with the child. Not every employer is "family friendly" enough to support parents taking days off. Family members may fear they will lose their jobs if they stay home with their child.

Teachers frequently report children arrive without a fever, but within two hours, the child's temperature rises. Teachers

CHILD CARE INJURY REPORT

TO BE COMPLETED FOR ANY INJURIES THAT REQUIRE TREATMENT, OTHER THAN MINOR SCRAPES OR BRUISES, AND RETAINED ON FILE AT THE PROGRAM FOR 3 YEARS FROM THE DATE OF INJURY.
NOTE: FIRST AID TREATMENT MUST BE PROVIDED BY A STAFF PERSON WHO IS CERTIFIED IN FIRST AID.

NAME OF CHILD CARE PROGRAM

NAME OF INJURED CHILD   DATE OF BIRTH

DATE OF INJURY: _____   TIME OF INJURY: _____

WHERE WAS CHILD WHEN HE/SHE WAS INJURED? _____

WHAT WAS CHILD DOING AT TIME HE/SHE WAS INJURED? _____

HOW DID IT HAPPEN? _____

TYPE OF INJURY & BODY PART INJURED:

WHAT FIRST AID TREATMENT WAS GIVEN, & WHAT TIME AND DATE WAS THE FIRST AID PROVIDED?

NAME OF STAFF PERSON WHO ADMINISTERED FIRST AID

IF INJURY REQUIRED ADDITIONAL MEDICAL TREATMENT, IDENTIFY THE INDIVIDUAL OR MEDICAL FACILITY THAT PROVIDED THAT TREATMENT:

DATE, TIME & METHOD OF PARENT NOTIFICATION:

I HAVE REVIEWED THE ABOVE INJURY REPORT AND CERTIFY IT IS TRUE AND ACCURATE TO THE BEST MY KNOWLEDGE

WITNESS_____   DATE_____

                                                                                                      DATE_____
STAFF PERSON RESPONSIBLE FOR SUPERVISION OF INJURED CHILD AT TIME OF INJURY

                                                                                                      DATE: _____
CENTER DIRECTOR/ FAMILY CHILD CARE PROVIDER

I HAVE READ THE ABOVE INJURY REPORT AND HAVE EXAMINED MY CHILD'S INJURY.

COMMENTS: _____

PARENT'S SIGNATURE   DATE SIGNED

Source: Live & Learn Early Learning Center, Lee, NH.

suspect the child was given Tylenol or aspirin before school and that the fever returned once the medicine wore off. Phoning a parent at work to pick up her ailing child can be difficult for everyone involved. Some parents react with frustration, desperation, or anger. An administrator's hope of balancing individual family needs with program needs becomes mutually exclusive:

- Relocate the child to a safe, loving, and healing home environment.
- Keep staff and children safe from the spread of illness.
- Support the family in staying gainfully employed.

For a time, some programs attempted to remedy this dilemma, caring for "mildly ill" children in a separate room with specially assigned nurses. Hospital child care programs seemed best suited to take on this responsibility. However, the number of children needing this service is unpredictable, and nursing care is expensive. Costs quickly became prohibitive for most centers. Only a handful of programs for sick children are currently in operation.

How can administrators ensure health and safety while honoring family needs? Some conditions are non-negotiable. Children cannot come to or stay in child care if they exhibit:

- Ongoing diarrhea
- Temperature above 100 degrees (armpit temperature)
- Vomiting twice in one day
- "Pink eye" or conjunctivitis
- Other contagious illnesses, including measles, rubella, mumps, strep infection, head lice or scabies, impetigo, pertussis (serious coughing), Hepatitis A virus, influenza, chicken pox, and tuberculosis
- Other changed behavior that may be indicative of serious illness (e.g., crying, crankiness, listlessness, disorientation, difficulty breathing)

A director's written policies should state the action a program will take if a child becomes ill. In addition to forewarning parents, administrators can help them find resources in the community for backup care. Some family home providers will care for mildly ill children. Resource and referral agencies may also provide a list of programs or individual providers who can help.

Note that HIV/AIDS is not listed among the illnesses that would keep a child out of a program. In fact, HIV/AIDS is an ADA-protected disability for which directors must make reasonable accommodations. Universal precautions shield everyone from blood borne pathogens and ensure HIV-positive children, staff, and directors the confidentiality they deserve.

Sex offenders

People convicted of sex offenses, such as child molestation and rape, are free once they have served their sentences. The severity of the sexual offense dictates the level of each offender. Usually a higher number (level 3 or 4) indicates a more serious offense.

States and communities keep lists of registered sex offenders by residential address. Sex offenders are required to report to authorities if they relocate. Lists of sex offenders are available as a matter of public record. Contact police for a list of sex offenders in your vicinity. What can early childhood programs do with this information?

Remember I said we would take a look at safety and health challenges that have not yet been consistently resolved by policies and practices? Here is an example. I invite you to consider what you would do if you were the director in each of these not unlikely scenarios.

CORI (Criminal Offender Record Information) searches are mandated as part of the early child care hiring process. Sometimes, however, CORI checks take more time than a director has. Imagine that Rhonda's infant teacher enlists in the army without telling her. Rhonda's program is in crisis until she replaces the teacher. One applicant, Ryan, appears to meet all the requirements for infant teacher. Rhonda hires Ryan one month before Ryan's CORI reaches Rhonda. If Ryan's CORI reveals Ryan is a "level 3" sex offender, what can/should Rhonda do?

Most directors tell me they would terminate Ryan's employment. If Ryan is in the probationary period of his employment, especially in an "at will" state, Ryan can be terminated. This action aims to protect children. A director who faced this issue wanted to terminate the employee. She met with significant resistance from the employee's job counselors. Her desire to protect children and families was not the "slam dunk" she had hoped for. In such instances, I think of one director who wisely said, "When the law doesn't make sense, I make my decision based on the fact that I have to live with myself when I go home for the day."

▶ EXERCISE YOUR EQ   ▦   What would you decide to do about Ryan? Consider parents' concerns for their children. In the "spirit of the law," also assess Ryan's rights. In this country, convicted felons who have served time and "paid their debt to society" can be entitled to equal employment opportunities. Ryan's job counselors and advocates assure Rhonda that Ryan has made a turnaround in his life. If you were Rhonda, what would you do?

An equally complex dilemma arises if a parent is a registered sex offender. Assume Ryan's son and daughter are enrolled at your program. Because Ryan has custody, he has the right to drop off and pick up his children. Other parents feel they have the right to protect their children from exposure to sex offenders. How do you ensure safety while respecting parents' rights? Ryan's son and daughter, Mark and Maura, are worthy, as all children are, of respect. Mark and Maura want their dad to come to family night with them. What would you do?

One program worked through the challenge in this way. The director, after listening to everyone's point of view, spoke with local police and her licensor. The father agreed to be accompanied by a third party when he engaged in center activities. The third party could be the family social worker, a staff member assigned by the director, or another respected party known to the program and to the families, but most importantly, to the children.

Keeping medical records

A medical history for each child will be collected at enrollment, and these records will need to be updated and maintained while the child is within the care of the center. The medical data must be documented in concise, accurate, and up-to-date ways. Software packages (see Chapter 10) make the task of tracking this information easier. Each child's file should contain:

Health and medical data:

✓ Record of immunizations

✓ Doctor's examination records and findings

EPI training for staff:
EPI (epinephrine) shots restore normal breathing after a bee sting or other allergic reaction. As with other medications, parents need to complete and sign your medication administration form and provide doctor's dosage instructions. Promote health and safety by providing and requiring EPI administration training for staff. Only staff who have completed this training can administer an EPI.

✓ Medical history of conditions and/or allergies that may affect the child while in your program

✓ List of ADA accommodations agreed upon and signed by doctor and family

✓ Details of treatment plan for early intervention

Family data:

✓ Signed release to get emergency care for child

✓ Authorized list of persons who can pick up the child

✓ List of people to be contacted in an emergency if parent is not available

✓ Field trip permission form(s) completed and signed

✓ Authorization to administer medication, including specific instructions as to dosage, timing, and other instructions from the doctor

✓ Permission to use photographs of the child for educational purposes (with special consent forms for online photos)

✓ Completed application form with all relevant information

✓ Family history information relevant to the child's care

✓ Cultural preferences and preferred practices

Child's growth and development:

✓ Child's *in utero* (mother's pregnancy) relevant information

✓ Record of physical and developmental growth

✓ Comments submitted by professionals working with the child, including teachers, speech pathologists, and therapists

✓ Progress on treatment plans

Food program management and safety

Headlines scream out warnings about contaminated foods. Manufacturers recall once trusted food products. Studies on childhood obesity warn us against foods that families may serve regularly. With food preparation and service, "Do no harm" is again the nonnegotiable bottom line.

As with any other aspect of our programs, the government sets standards in health and safety in handling food. Food must be fresh, healthy, and prepared and served in a hygienic way. Meals and snacks must be age appropriate. MyPlate, which replaced the familiar food pyramid in 2011, is a federally approved guide that tells us what percentages of each food group is appropriate daily. (See the **MyPlate** section later in this chapter for more on this guide.)

Infants' and preschoolers' diets will differ accordingly. At six months, children will likely have developed enough to be able to swallow and digest solid food of the proper consistency and amount. Preschoolers can be served a fuller range of healthy food options.

Some programs employ cooks who prepare meals and snacks daily. Other programs rely on catering services to deliver prepared food. In either case, the director's job is to make sure children are given fresh, nutritious food under hygienic circumstances. An outbreak of salmonella or other food-borne illness would be disastrous.

Just as with building design and renovation, state and federal standards are in place to guide directors through the essential bottom lines of safely serving healthy food. Use your leadership EQ in hiring food service staff whose competencies include attention to health and safety.

Childhood obesity

Alarming statistics have emerged about the percentages of our children who are over-weight. In 2007–2008, an estimated 16.9 percent of children and adolescents aged 2–19 were obese (Ogden & Carroll 2010). Tracking obesity to its most dominant causes is easy: Children consume foods with hollow (non-nutritious) calories that are high in fat and sugar. Children sit and look at screens far more than they actively engage in play. According to a recent report by the Joan Ganz Cooney Center at Sesame Workshop (Gutnick et al. 2011, 16), children ages 8–10 spend about five and a half hours each day using media. Actual exposure is even higher—sometimes eight hours a day—because kids often use more than one type of media at the same time. Even children as young as 3 years old go online daily.

Thanks in part to First Lady Michelle Obama's effort to eliminate childhood obesity, healthful changes are under way. Fruits and whole grains are replacing high-fructose treats. Physical exercise is being promoted along with more nutritious eating.

In the push to eliminate childhood obesity, using your EQ about cultural differences is valuable. I listened as a mother who was a Chinese immigrant spoke with tears about a preschool teacher's "advice" about the woman's child: "Your daughter might need to lose some weight," cautioned the teacher. "She's not able to play freely on the playground." The child's doctor gave the mother the same advice. The mother, however, was raised to believe a thin child was in danger of illness or even death, whereas a stocky child would be able to combat illness better. Similarly, the term *gordito* is an affectionate compliment to a stocky Hispanic child. In that child's culture, a well-fed child is a healthy child.

Using your indoor and outdoor physical space wisely models for children that sustainability and healthy eating are one and the same. Rusty Keeler, author of *Natural Playscapes,* advocates teachers and children growing food together as a productive learning experience. In an *Exchange* article, Keeler advises, "Low planter boxes can be home to experimental garden plots. What you decide to plant is up to the children and you: is it neat rows of edible nasturtiums, a tall forest of corn or sunflowers, or a lettuce and carrot landscape?" (2009, 98). Keeler adds, "Children's gardens are an invaluable tool for teaching about science, food, time, responsibility, and life" (99). Along the way, children and teachers may experience how appealing "real" food can be. Good nutrition does not have to be boring.

Hours of operation and required meals

State licensing standards connect hours of operation with number of meals provided. Traditional half-day schools, often called "nursery schools," are required to provide a nutritious snack at mid-morning or mid-afternoon. The children are expected to have eaten a main meal before they arrive and to eat one soon after they return home.

On the other end of the care continuum, programs providing nine hours of care (or more) must provide two-thirds of a child's daily food requirements. The assumption is the child will eat at least one meal at home each day.

When it comes to infants, some general guidelines apply to ensure that each child receives proper nutrition. However, infant classrooms utilize individualized feeding plans. Each baby is on his own schedule. Children who are breastfed may not take solid

Child hunger and child obesity are really just two sides of the same coin. Both rob our children of the energy, the strength, and the stamina they need to succeed in school and in life. And that, in turn, robs our country of so much of its promise.

—First Lady Michelle Obama

The longer children are in a program's care, the greater percentage of their daily nutritional requirement directors must meet.

food. A mother may breastfeed at the center and/or leave adequately labeled bottles of breast milk for her child. Directors need to pay attention to families' cultural values in determining together what each child needs and when.

MyPlate

The food pyramid was replaced in 2011 with MyPlate, a new guide for "building a healthy plate" on a budget. The new guide changes some of the recommended food portions and physical activity priorities.

The new MyPlate graphic features a plate with balanced, healthy proportions of whole grains, protein, fruits, and vegetables. Protein can be found in non-meat sources such as fish, nuts, and legumes. For the federal government's nutrition guidelines, or to download MyPlate and other resources, go to www.choosemyplate.gov.

Food allergies

Children and adults are increasingly diagnosed with a variety of food allergies. Some of these allergies, especially peanut allergies, can result in critical and sometimes fatal reactions. Other foods causing allergic reactions include tomatoes, milk and other dairy products, and chocolate.

At enrollment, directors should ask each parent whether his or her child has any food allergies or dietary restrictions. A child's medical examination record should also state diagnosed allergies and procedures for prevention and treatment for allergic reactions. Anyone serving food to children needs to read labels closely for "hidden" ingredients. Eliminate foods or food products that cause allergic reactions for children or staff.

Religious and cultural preferences

In some religions and cultures, certain foods are not allowed. For example, Muslims do not eat pork. When Jewish families follow kosher diets, a number of dietary practices must be honored. For example, dairy products cannot be served alongside certain other products. Some Catholic Latino families follow the precept of not eating meat on certain days. Invite parents to share their cultural and/or religious food requirements. When possible, honor each family's requests.

Potluck meals . . . Out of luck?

For years, early childhood programs have invited families to "bring a dish to share" as part of a potluck meal. Families were especially encouraged to bring dishes that reflected their ethnic or cultural heritage. Potluck gatherings provided a natural way for families to enjoy and learn about one another's different traditions.

Today, holding potluck meals is under question. Might centers be liable if someone becomes ill after eating a potluck dish? Directors have attempted to prevent this problem by asking families to display a list of ingredients used in the dish. This would enable people with food allergies to make informed decisions about which dish to sample.

Another challenge with potluck dishes derives from families' different hygienic standards and traditions in food preparation. One family may be rigorous in washing all surfaces and implements. Another family might have more relaxed standards.

If a program sponsors a potluck meal and a participant becomes sick as a result, the program might be liable. This concern has led some directors to eliminate food brought from home, including children's birthday cakes.

▶ EXERCISE YOUR EQ   ■   Hearing these warnings about potluck meals, how do you feel? What has been lost, and what has been gained? If families, excited about sampling foods of many cuisines, were to say: "Let's have another potluck family night. What fun we had the last time!" what would you say?

Should smokers be allowed to work with children?

Of course, smoking in the presence of young children is not allowed. The literature on how harmful secondhand smoke is to children and adults is now well documented. Research is emerging about thirdhand smoke as well.

Thirdhand smoke is the residue that attaches to the smoker's hair, clothing, and skin. Thirdhand smoke also insinuates itself into the surfaces of the physical environment where smoking takes place. Some studies show that children are harmed by exposure to caregivers who smoke. Even if the caregiver does not smoke at work and showers before coming to work, the residue of smoke in her system can work its way into the system of a child.

Harvard University pediatrician Jonathan Winickoff and colleagues (2009) urge educators to think twice about exposing children to thirdhand smoke. In an interview (podcast), Winickoff said: "Once thirdhand smoke is absorbed into clothing, the skin, and even the smoker's breath, it can be transmitted and breathed in by children. . . . For children who may be susceptible to these tobacco toxins, such as those with asthma, I don't think it is a safe situation." In the same interview, Susan Offutt, from National Louis University's McCormick Center for Early Childhood Leadership, remarked, "Children don't get to speak up and say, 'I don't want to smell like smoke or be exposed to smoke.' . . . It's our responsibility to be that voice."

▶ EXERCISE YOUR EQ   ■   Do you think we should protect young children from thirdhand smoke? What if doing so would mean you would lose some of your best teachers?

Suzi Brodof, leader of a large child care agency, took a stand after her toddler granddaughter came down with asthma. No one in the child's family or environment smoked, with the exception of her beloved caregiver. By age 2, Suzi's granddaughter was reaching out for her breathing machine and using it independently.

Suzi and her board took action and instituted a "no smokers" policy for anyone hired into her agency to work directly with children. The policy, however, "grandparented in" employees hired before the policy took effect, allowing them to keep their jobs. What was the rationale for this? Firing employees retroactively for a new policy did not seem fair. Suzi did, however, set up resources to help current employees quit smoking.

> **Bam!radio**
> "No Smokers: Setting Up Policies Barring Smokers in Early Childhood Settings"
> Interview with Jonathan P. Winickoff
> *Heart to Heart Conversations on Leadership*
> http://bamradionetwork.com

Safe and sound

The "Do no harm" standard for early childhood programs makes sense. We want everyone to be safe. We want to offer nutritious, healthy meals. We want buildings and grounds to be free of danger. With the help of established standards, we will know how to prevent harm.

If a crisis occurs, we want procedures in place to respond quickly and fully. This "Do no harm" precept is the cornerstone for all early child care buildings and environments, from classrooms to food preparation to emergency medical procedures. Now that we have established the cornerstone for health and safety, we can step up to creating environments for children to learn, grow, and thrive. Are you ready?

Reflection questions

1. Imagine you have chosen to build a child care center "from the ground up." What is your vision for the new structure? What environment do you want to create for children and families? In what ways would your new building be beautiful? What would you do to make sure each space is safe and inviting? Investigate and list all the resources available to you to help you accomplish your goal. Write a comment next to each resource on your list, explaining the assistance that resource provides.

2. Maximilian, over coffee, asks your advice in converting the temple Sunday school into a viable and appealing early childhood center. Help Max identify the various groups of people who have expectations for the program. Advise Max on how he can use both his EQ and social EQ to work with each group and with his whole community. What questions do you feel Max needs to ask himself about his goals and how realistic they are? Where might you and Max look to find information on renovating the existing building? Write or record a summary or a dialogue between you and Max on important points in your discussion.

3. Kindergartner Philippa (Pippa) has asthmatic reactions during which her breathing becomes labored. Her doctor has prescribed an EPI device. This device enables epinephrine to be injected into Pippa's thigh. The injection works quickly. Pippa feels like her energetic self again. Pippa's mother, a nurse, says Pippa knows how to use her EPI. Her mom explains she has shown Pippa how to use the EPI at home and that she feels Pippa needs to be able to help herself more quickly than a staff member could. How would you respond to Pippa's mom? What policy might you put into place or call upon to support your decision? Present your policy and summary to the class.

4. Look into the research on thirdhand smoke, including articles that refute the research as well as those that support it. Draw your own conclusion about whether child care programs should institute "no smokers" policies. Draft a model policy and share it with colleagues. Do you think our profession is ready to take this step?

Team projects

1. Reread Beatrice and Aurora's case on the chapter opening page. What might Aurora, who loves nature and the great outdoors, want to incorporate into an early childhood building? Now imagine "city girl" Beatrice's vision for a new building. As far as Beatrice is concerned, the farther away she is from "vermin" (mosquitoes, spiders, snakes, crows, and "smelly" animals), bad weather, and sunlight, the happier she is. As a team, envision a center, indoors and out, that incorporates the best of both cousins' visions without "creating a monster." Now research just how much of the great outdoors can safely be included in an early childhood building. For example, what about animals? How "wild" can the outdoor playground environment be? Visit local early childhood programs to see how they answer these questions. Present a conceptual design that incorporates the "forever wild" elements Aurora craves, in a way that is safe enough for Beatrice.

2. Brainstorm what you imagine to be in the job description of an early childhood licensor in your locale. What might be the licensing agency's mission? What do you expect the core values and code of ethical behavior for state licensors to be? What procedures do you think the agency has in place if a program is out of compliance with standards? What else would you like to know about your state's licensing agency? Divide these questions among team members for research. Be sure to interview at least one licensor.

3. Keeping in mind that licensing standards are the basic, rather than the ultimate, standards for health and safety, compare other professional standards. Look into NAEYC's and NACCP's accreditation standards. Examine a copy of a quality rating scale, such as the ECERS-R. Check out Head Start's directives on health and safety. Research actual checklists used by directors to make sure their programs are safe and healthful. Which of these standards, or what combination of standards and practices, do you recommend and why?

4. Childhood obesity has grown to epidemic proportions in this country. The federal MyPlate initiative replaces the food pyramid and sets new standards for healthy eating. If you were director of an early childhood program, what are at least five things you could do to promote healthy nutrition and eating habits at your program? Consider the foods, cooking, and eating practices of at least three cultural groups. How can your initiative honor the practices of diverse cultures while working to eliminate childhood obesity?

Bibliography

AAP (American Academy of Pediatrics), APHA (American Public Health Association), & NRC (National Resource Center). 2002. *Caring for our children—National health and safety performance standards: Guidelines for early care and education programs.* 3d ed. Chicago, IL: Author.

AAP (American Academy of Pediatrics) & NASN (National Association of School Nurses). 2005. *Health, mental health, and safety guidelines for schools.* Chicago, IL: Author.

Abraham, C. 2007. Licensing scavenger hunt. *Exchange* 173: 80–82.

Bruno, H.E. 2010. Creating relational sanctuaries for children who suffer from abuse. *Exchange* 191: 64–68.

Carter, M. 2006. Rethinking our use of resources: Part 2—Space, attitude, and attention. *Exchange* 167: 18–20.

Click, P.M., & K.A. Karkos. 2011. *Administration of programs for young children.* 8th ed. Belmont, CA: Wadsworth, Cengage Learning.

Copeland, M.L. 1996. Code blue! Establishing a child care emergency plan. *Exchange* 107: 17–22.

Decker, C.A., J.R. Decker, N.R. Freeman, & H. Knopf. 2008. *Planning and administering early childhood programs.* 8th ed. Upper Saddle River, NJ: Prentice Hall.

Epstein, A.S. 2007. *The intentional teacher: Choosing the best strategies for young children's learning.* Washington, DC: NAEYC.

Goleman, D. 2005. *Emotional intelligence: Why it can matter more than IQ.* 10th ann. ed. New York: Bantam Dell.

Gonzalez-Mena, J. 2010. *Foundations of early childhood education: Teaching children in a diverse society.* 5th ed. New York: McGraw-Hill.

Goodenough, E., ed. 2003. *Secret spaces of childhood.* Ann Arbor, MI: University of Michigan Press.

Greenman, J. 2005. *Caring spaces, learning places: Children's environments that work.* Rev. ed. Redmond, WA: Exchange Press.

Greenman, J. 2005. *What happened to MY world? Helping children cope with natural disaster and catastrophe.* South Watertown, MA: Bright Horizons.

Gutnick, A.L., M. Robb, L. Takeuchi, & J. Kotler. 2011. *Always connected: The new digital media habits of young children.* New York: The Joan Ganz Cooney Center at Sesame Workshop.

Hannaford, C. 2002. *Awakening the child heart: Handbook for global parenting.* Captain Cook, HI: Jamilla Nurr Publishing.

Harms, T., R.M. Clifford, & D. Cryer. 2005. *Early Childhood Environmental Rating Scale.* Rev. ed. New York: Teachers College Press.

Hemingway, E. 1925. A clean, well-lighted place. In *The short stories of Ernest Hemingway.* New York: Charles Scribner's Sons.

Jonathan Diamond Associates, Inc. (Producer). 2009. When learning comes naturally [Television broadcast]. Boston, MA: American Public Television.

Keeler, R. 2008. *Natural playscapes: Creating outdoor play environments for the soul.* Redmond, WA: Exchange Press.

Keeler, R. 2009. Playscape plants. *Exchange* 189: 98–99.

Leger-Ferraro, S. 2010. Raising a 'green generation.' *Exchange* 193: 88–90.

Louv, R. 2008. *Last child in the woods: Saving our children from nature-deficit disorder.* Updated and expanded ed. Chapel Hill: Algonquin Books.

Metrocom International. (Producer). 2008. Where do the children play? [Television broadcast]. Ann Arbor, MI: Michigan Television.

Ogden, C., & M. Carroll. 2010. *Prevalence of obesity among children and adolescents: United States, trends 1963–1965 through 2007–2008.* Hyattsville, MD: National Center for Health Statistics.

Rivkin, M.S. 1995. *The great outdoors: Restoring children's right to play outside.* Washington, DC: NAEYC.

Robertson, M. 2005. Using the environment rating scales for quality improvement projects. *Exchange* 165: 23–26.

Sobel, D. 2008. *Childhood and nature: Design principles for educators.* Portland, OR: Stenhouse.

Winickoff, J.P., J. Friebely, S.E. Tanski, C. Sherrod, G.E. Matt, M.F. Hovell, & R.C. McMillen. 2009. Beliefs about the health effects of "thirdhand" smoke and home smoking bans. *Pediatrics* 123 (1): 74–79.

Web resources

Choosemyplate.gov
   www.choosemyplate.gov
National Association for the Education of Young Children (NAEYC) Early Childhood Program Standards
   www.naeyc.org/academy/primary/standardsintro
National Association of Child Care Professionals (NACCP) Accreditation Standards
   www.naccp.org/displaycommon.cfm?an=1&subarticlenbr=237
Natural Learning Initiative
   www.naturalearning.org
Nature Explore: Connecting Children with Nature
   www.arborday.org/explore
Occupational Safety & Health Administration (OSHA)
   www.osha.gov
Sample Early Child Care Forms: New York State Office of Children & Family Services
   www.ocfs.state.ny.us/main/forms/day_care

> What nourishes our imagination? Probably more than anything else, loving adults who encourage children's own choices of imaginative play.
>
> —Fred Rogers

12 Curriculum Choices: Roots and Wings

Case Study—Marisol

Marco's mom, Marisol, wants her son to "have all the breaks in life" she never had. She plans to use her hard-earned savings to send Marco to private school when he turns 5. Marisol supported your program's individualized curriculum when Marco was an infant and toddler. "That was then," she insists. "Now Marco needs to learn reading, writing, and math. I use flash card drills at home. Show me how you are preparing Marco to get top grades on Whitestone Preparatory School's admission test." Marco thrives on outdoor play and hates sitting still. How do you partner with Marco's mom to help Marco?

Early childhood leaders have the honor of

creating and maintaining wondrous environments for learning, for both children and adults. Early childhood teachers understand the function of emergent curriculum and the value of both play and structure in a child's development. Families and school systems may prefer traditional classroom teaching. In the chapter case study, Marco's mom uses flash card drills at home and wants her son's preschool teachers to do the same. As a leader, you are likely to engage with families in the debate over what is best for their children.

The pendulum swings left to right, right to left, whether we nudge it or not. One day, parents applaud their child's free-form finger painting. The next day, parents demand children learn the "basics"—the three Rs (reading, 'riting, and 'rithmetic). One decade, architects design windowless schools to focus children away from distractions. The next decade, architects design open classrooms that invite children's imaginations to soar indoors and out. One year, legislators fund early childhood programs. The next year, early childhood programs scrap to survive. Legislation to "leave no child behind" teeters from push back by educators tired of "teaching to the test."

Watching the pendulum swing is akin to watching a Ping-Pong match. Our necks grow weary! Where in this bouncing, back-and-forth and up-and-down movement is something steady, predictable, and enduring about how children learn?

In this chapter, we will explore spaces, places, and approaches to learning that help children develop fully, regardless of today's trend or yesterday's tradition. As Pulitzer Prize-winning journalist Hodding Carter Jr. said: "There are only two lasting bequests we can give our children: One is roots, the other is wings." Whatever else may change, our goal is always to leave our children with those two fundamentals. We will identify:

- Principles about curriculum that free children to learn.

- Learning environment concepts that invite children to wonder, play, and discover.

- Social intelligence principles active in learning organizations for children and adults.

- Curricular approaches that bring structure and grounding to the learning process.

We stand on their shoulders: Roots of early childhood learning theory

Before early childhood administrators and teachers can design curriculum or spaces, they need to understand how children learn. To reach an informed conclusion about this, let's look at innovators in early childhood education theory and practice.

Froebel, Dewey, Montessori, Piaget, Erikson, Vygotsky, Pikler, Gerber, Gardner, and Rogers spun varied threads of child development theory that catch our eye today. You have probably studied these theorists. Building on your knowledge, I aim to capture each educational seer's gift to us. In particular, we will examine how each theorist connects human relationships with learning.

Friedrich Froebel

Play is the highest level of child development. . . . It gives . . . joy, freedom, contentment, inner and outer rest, peace with the world. . . . The plays of childhood are the germinal leaves of all later life.

—Friedrich Froebel

Friedrich Froebel (1782–1852) was born in Oberweissbach, Germany. Froebel created kindergarten, or "children's garden," out of his vision of school as a garden for "growing" children who learn as they play. Froebel said, "Let us learn from our children. Let us attend to the knowledge which their lives gently urge upon us and listen to the quiet demands of their hearts." Teachers tend the garden, nourishing and supporting seeds as they grow into saplings. Children, like flowers, grow strong with sunlight, fresh air, and ample nourishment, surrounded by loving support. Froebel's gift to us is this: Children blossom through play and being well cared for by adults.

John Dewey

The child's own instinct and powers furnish the material and give the starting point for all education.

—John Dewey

John Dewey (1859–1952) was born in Burlington, Vermont. Dewey's message, above all, was to respect the child. A child's education must be alive, active, and interactive. "Education," he said, "is a process of living and not a preparation for future living" (1897). Dewey believed education for children involves and integrates the child's community and social world. Curriculum should grow organically from a child's world—her home, her backyard, her friendships, her skipping and tumbling. A teacher's work is to help the child make sense of her world. Dewey's gift to us is this: Create child-centered or "integrated" curriculum.

Maria Montessori

Maria Montessori (1870–1952) was born in Chiaravalle, Italy. Montessori, the story goes, was admitted to medical school when only men were permitted to study medicine by writing her name on her application as "M. Montessori." Montessori observed children with new eyes to develop theories on how children learn. To Montessori, children are passionate treasures full of unfolding fascination and competency. Environments for learning must honor children. For example, chairs cannot leave children's legs dangling, and saws and knives must be sharp enough to use.

Children, Montessori observed, are innately capable. The teacher's job is to:

- Observe and listen for the child's natural curiosity.
- Support the child as he fulfills his quest to learn.
- Step to the side, ready to observe the child's next burst of curiosity.

Montessori favored "cheerful" environments full of sensory tools to help children discover, where teachers "teach little and observe much." Montessori's gift to us is this: Support the child's learning by trusting and supporting the child's innate curiosity and ability with appropriate tools.

Erik Erikson

Erik Erikson (1902–1994) was born near Frankfurt, Germany, and he identified stages of children's emotional and social development. At every stage, children need the loving support of adults. From the beginning (birth to age 1), children learn to trust through a caregiver's warmth and fulfillment of needs. With trust, a child is free to explore and grow. Toddlers (ages 2–3) learn autonomy if they are not condescended to or shamed. Between ages 4 and 5, a child gains a sense of purpose, as we support her initiative instead of "guilting" her.

In some ways, Erikson foresaw the future of neuroscientific studies by paying attention to the importance of relationships at every stage of a child's development. Without relational kindness, children grow into struggling adults who ask, "Can I trust? Am I confident enough to dream and to follow my dream? Will self-doubt and distrust nip at my heels all the days of my life?"

Although Erikson's rather lockstep views on child development have been criticized, his gift to us is this: Children's emotional well-being is closely linked with their ability to learn.

Jean Piaget

Jean Piaget (1896–1980) was born in Neuchâtel, Switzerland. As an epistemologist, Piaget studied knowledge, its origin, and its definitions. Educators, he observed, need to understand how a child's mind works. In particular, how does a child gain knowledge? Piaget's answer to this question is that children learn by living.

The educator's job is to encourage inquiry and support the child's natural quest for knowledge. Piaget believed that "construction is superior to instruction." Children are not empty vessels waiting to be filled with information. Some of Piaget's research is now questioned because of his research methods, such as using a small, homogeneous sampling. Piaget nonetheless left us with this gift: Children are born to find answers with our support.

It is necessary for the teacher to guide the child without letting him feel her presence too much, so that she may always be ready to supply the desired help, but may never be the obstacle between the child and his experience.

—Maria Montessori

The greatest sign of success for a teacher is to be able to say, "The children are now working as if I did not exist."

—Maria Montessori

There is in every child at every stage a new miracle of vigorous unfolding, which constitutes a new hope and a new responsibility for all.

—Erik Erikson

The principle goal of education in the schools should be creating men and women who are capable of doing new things, not simply repeating what other generations have done.

—Jean Piaget

Lev Vygotsky

Lev Vygotsky (1896–1934) was born in Orsha, Russia (Belorussia). Early on, Vygotsky saw the inadequacy of intelligence tests in identifying a child's gifts and recognized the importance of social relationships and cultural contributions within a person's development. With proper "scaffolding," or support within constructive relationships, children learn, grow, and develop their gifts. In addition to scaffolding, Vygotsky developed the concept of a person's "zone of proximal development" (ZPD). In the ZPD, teachers observe, anticipate, and stand ready to support a child as he stretches to learn the next important life lesson. Vygotsky's gift to us is this: Relationships are crucial to a child's learning.

Howard Gardner

Howard Gardner (b. 1943) was born in Scranton, Pennsylvania, and is noted for his concept of "multiple intelligences." Like Vygotsky, Gardner was disenchanted with the idea that one test—the IQ test—could define intelligence. After observing young children's differing talents, interests, and capabilities, Gardner named at least nine intelligences. Along with kinesthetic, musical, and spatial intelligence, Gardner identified social and emotional intelligences.

Gardner's gift to us is this: Both children and adults have differing intelligences and are diversely able and talented.

Fred Rogers

Fred Rogers (1928–2003) was born in Latrobe, Pennsylvania. Neither researcher nor scientist, Rogers was a creator and a communicator. After more than 25 years working with public television, "Mr. Rogers" left a visual and written compendium of emotional and social EQ insights. Children need to feel safe, valued, listened to, and encouraged to express their feelings. "Children are not merely vessels into which facts are poured one week and then when it comes time for exams, they turn themselves upside down and let the facts run out," Rogers said. "Children bring all of themselves, their feelings, and their experiences to the learning" (1994, 87).

Rogers taught through relationships. He looked through the television camera lens into the eyes of each child watching. For Rogers, the relationship is the message. This understanding, that relationships are at the heart of learning, is only one of his many gifts to us.

Emmi Pikler and Magda Gerber

Emmi Pikler (1902–1984) was born in Vienna, Austria. In 1946, the Hungarian government invited her, a pediatrician, to establish residential programs for children who were orphaned or whose families were unable to care for them after the war. Pikler accepted the challenge. Impersonal orphanages, which institutionalized children, were far from what Pikler envisioned. Instead, she created nurseries wherein:

1. Caregivers were specially prepared to build a trusting, respectful relationship with each child.

2. Children (babies and toddlers, in particular) were supported as they initiated their own learning.

Children raised in Pikler programs grow confident while being trusted to know what and when to learn. Pikler observed, "As a matter of principle, we refrain from teaching skills and activities which, under suitable conditions, will evolve through the child's own initiative and independent activity" (Pickler 1971, 91). Janet Gonzalez-Mena observes that with few manufactured toys and unencumbered settings, "Pikler children have far fewer accidents than children not raised in Pikler environments" (pers. comm.).

The focus is on what children can do, not on what we expect they will do according to our preconceived notions of ages and stages. Pikler left us with this gift: Respect the child to "know" when she is ready to transition in her development.

Magda Gerber (died 2007), born in Hungary, continued the work of Emmi Pikler and leaves us with this gift: "In time, not on time." Pikler and Gerber believed children are motivated to learn when they need to learn. Children do not develop on someone else's timetable. In response to Janet Gonzalez-Mena's question, "What is one piece of advice you have for those of us who work with infants and toddlers?" Gerber responded, "Slow down."

Rooting curriculum in the wisdom of many cultures

You may have noticed the innovators discussed in the previous section are of the European tradition. The early childhood field does not yet fully study or incorporate the wisdom of Asian, African, South and Central American, Middle Eastern, American tribal, or island cultures. When it does, we are sure to find emotional and social intelligence theories and practices enlightening for everyone.

Leaders of the National Black Child Development Institute (NBCDI) have created a helpful guide titled *School Readiness and Social-Emotional Development: Perspectives in Cultural Diversity* (2006). Edited by Barbara Bowman and Evelyn K. Moore, this book is full of information on helping young children be successful from the start. Bowman tells us that risk to African American and Latino children can be alleviated if early child care administrators and teachers:

1. Understand cultural differences. Classroom teachers need to know about the culture of the children in their classrooms and how to bridge between what the children know and what they want them to learn.

2. Identify and treat children who have special needs. Children who are highly stressed, have a disabling condition, or whose development is atypical need a working system for diagnosis and treatment.

3. Recognize the importance of relationships.

To read more on Latino insights into early childhood development, see *Connections and Commitments: Reflecting Latino Values in Early Childhood Programs,* by Constanza Eggers-Pierola (2005). Close, loving, family-like relationships are seen as key to a child's development.

Brain development research and learning theory

Looking back on the message of each of these early childhood innovators, I see two principles emerging. First, respectful, loving relationships are essential to learning. Second, each child innately (spontaneously from within) seeks to know his world. The early childhood leader's job is to scaffold the child's learning with supportive teaching strategies and curriculum that can adapt and evolve to meet children's needs. How do these principles and concepts line up with neuroscientific research on children's learning?

From Neurons to Neighborhoods: The Science of Early Childhood Development (Shonkoff & Phillips 2000) became the seminal book on the science of children's brain

By observing different cultures, we see that there are many ways to go about caring for and educating children. There's no one right way.
—Janet Gonzalez-Mena

Help teachers understand that teaching is not just about the transmission of academic knowledge and skills but also about motivation and dispositions, which stem from satisfying adult-child relationships. This means teachers understand and relate to culturally diverse children, their families, and communities in positive ways.
—Barbara Bowman and Evelyn K. Moore

The amount and quality of love a child receives have long-lasting neural consequences . . . An emotional void often proves fatal to babies. Neglect produces children whose head circumferences are measurably smaller, whose brains on magnetic resonance scanning evidence shrinkage from the loss of billions of cells . . . Twenty years of longitudinal data have proven that responsive parenting confers apparently permanent personality strengths.
—Thomas Lewis, Fari Amini, and Richard Lannon
A General Theory of Love

development. Brain development research findings have been spilling out like lava since the early 1990s. Most recently, Ellen Galinsky's *Mind in the Making* further confirms the invaluable interplay of educational opportunities in the active brains of young children. Galinsky (2010) says that learning is fostered through trustworthy and caring relationships with adults who keep children safe, help them feel secure, and give them structure.

Findings to date include these principles:

1. Brain pathways, established in early childhood, (most often) remain with us the rest of our lives.

2. We learn though relationships, by our interconnectedness with others.

3. The more respectfully loving the relationship, the healthier the child.

4. Our cells imitate (mirror neurons in particular) the neurons of our closest caregivers early in our life (from birth to age 3).

5. Experiences destructive to healthy brain development can be countered or reversed through loving relationships that a child experiences in her early years.

6. Our brains have "plasticity"—flexibility to adapt, change, and learn throughout our lifetime.

Healthy and respectful relationships are essential for children to learn. The early childhood professional's job is to facilitate the child's unfolding, not to dump in facts and figures while extinguishing the child's desire to learn. Brain research and early childhood learning theorists agree at heart. Rooted in the secure arms of trusting relationships, a child can spread her wings to soar into the world of curiosity and wonder.

Relationships are at the heart of learning

With these gifts from early childhood theorists, how does a director go about creating environments where children can learn? Keep in mind these five keys when contemplating curriculum and space design for children:

1. The child is the curriculum.

2. Environment is the teacher.

3. Teachers facilitate learning by supporting a child's natural curiosity.

4. Relationships provide a secure base for and much of the substance of a child's early education.

5. Boundaries, alternative teaching strategies, and structure scaffold a child's learning.

In respectful, supportive relationships, children naturally explore their environment, ready to grow and learn. *The relationship itself is a teacher.* Let's examine these keys one at a time.

Child as curriculum

Imagine seasoned director, Chris, has a mission statement that announces: "The child is the curriculum." Chris's challenge is to help teachers hone observation skills and expand their horizon of emergent learning experiences for children. Does Chris use a written curriculum? "Yes," she responds, "but as a resource, not a determinant."

What if the planned curriculum focuses on families, but instead the children are curious about why and how shells wash up on the seashore? Chris's teachers can antici-

The Italian schools of Reggio Emilia are acclaimed for the stunning environments their educators have created, and they provoke us to recognize the instructive power of an environment. This is not a new concept, but in their schools we see vibrant examples of learning environments that dazzle our senses, invite curiosity and discovery, and most importantly, foster strong, respectful relationships. Reggio educators seem to have a different notion about the role of the environment in educating children, for unlike the typical U.S. early childhood classroom, their walls aren't covered with alphabet letters, calendars, and job charts. Nor do you find commercially produced bulletin board displays, labels on every shelf and surface, and rules posted. What could they be thinking?

—Margie Carter,
*Making Your Environment
"the Third Teacher"*

Creating an engaging, inspiring environment is not just interior decorating.

—Margie Carter

pate ways children can find answers to their questions. With Chris's support, teachers can set up a center with hands-on activities about ocean currents and seashells. Teachers can incorporate the children's interests into the planned curriculum by discussing "families in the sea."

A teacher's artistry is demonstrated through his ability to fan the curiosity of all his students. He will use a variety of creative teaching tools to connect with each student and different groups of students with different needs. A field trip to the beach may not have been planned, but the teacher will find ways to engage all the students in preparing enthusiastically for the visit.

According to Judith Pack, possibilities for spontaneous learning abound if teachers are committed to "watch the children at play in order to better understand how they view the world" (2011, 40). To Pack, each day with children is a curricular adventure as long as the teacher:

- Stops what she's doing to investigate with the children.
- Is comfortable and in tune with "interruptions."
- Follows an interest, request, or delight of the children.
- "Gives time over" to the spontaneous event, or what David Hawkins calls the "insuppressible impulse" (2002, 23).

Giving over time may feel like surrendering control of the classroom unless the teacher is fully grounded in the theories of how children learn.

▶ EXERCISE YOUR EQ   ▦   When you recall the list of early childhood learning theorists, which pioneer(s) does Chris's approach illustrate best?

Environment as teacher: Creating learning spaces indoors and out

"Same old, same old" classrooms put children, and many adults, to sleep. Instead, inviting places inspire children to wonder, wander, and explore. Children need safe spaces with quiet places for calm and reflection. Children equally need, as Bev Bos and Jenny Chapman (2005) have modeled, adventuresome areas to let out energy, refine gross motor skills, and make their way in the world. Children learn in environments rich in resources to connect them to information. For these reasons, the environment becomes the curriculum.

From birth, and most likely before, babies are intensely aware of their environments. They watch and taste, touch and rattle, roll and toss, squirm and wiggle their way to learning. Children learn about life primarily through relationships with others. Children also learn by observing and interacting with their environments. Early childhood leaders can create spaces and places that honor and engage children's quest to learn by interacting with their surroundings.

Margie Carter (2007) refers to the Reggio Emilia concept of seeing the environment as "the third teacher." Carter encourages us to ask what values and messages our environments communicate to children and their families.

My understanding on learning environments is this: Use your imagination and skill to help children grow their imaginations and skills. In this way, each learning space will be fresh and inviting, rather than "fungible" (like malls or pinto beans—just the same).

In Chapter 11, we examined the hefty list of requirements for safe and healthy environments. Compliance with these requirements is necessary for everyone's well-being. However, compliance can have an unintended and sometimes unfortunate side effect.

In many centers or play areas of family child care homes, you have to look hard to find anything of beauty. Child care and aesthetics do not necessarily go together. Perhaps the lack of aesthetics is a sign of the times—a sign that other considerations take priority over beauty.

—Janet Gonzalez-Mena

Early childhood spaces can often look alike. Equipped with safety-tested furniture and toys from well-known companies, and arranged in acceptable room and playground configurations, our programs are safe but not unique.

Of late, practitioners have been breaking out of the sameness mold. As you read about four diverse approaches to learning, consider how a director might call upon her staff and her own unique values and vision to create wondrous and one-of-a-kind learning spaces.

1. **Nature Action Collaborative for Children**, an international organization, unites landscape architects, health care professionals, early childhood educators, and environment groups, such as Jane Goodall's organization, Roots and Shoots (*www.rootsandshoots.org*). You can join at no cost and go online at to share and gain information and ideas on new ways to reconnect children with nature.

2. **Music and movement in the outdoor classroom.** "Because an outdoor classroom can usually offer more space for large-motor movements than an indoor classroom, children are able to freely experiment with multiple locomotor and non-locomotor activities. And, because sounds are absorbed in the outdoors in a way that's impossible inside, children can create their own music without disturbing other children" (VanGilder, Wike, & Murphy 2007, 53). The authors note that making music outdoors can offer children with special needs more ease in making neurological connections. Ideas include:

   • Act like a tree to make its leaves "dance."

   • Move like creatures you see (squirrels, robins, inchworms).

   • Sing songs about what you notice.

   • Be free to play "big" outdoors in ways you cannot indoors.

3. **Living willow huts.** Can you imagine creating an outdoor hut for children that bursts into life in the spring? Rusty Keeler (2008) provides us with step-by-step instructions and drawings about how teachers and children can plant willow rods or shoots to make living willow huts. The plants sprout into tunnels, fences, huts, or anything else a child and teacher can envision.

4. **Consider the walls.** "I am . . . encouraging teachers to step back and critically examine the quality and quantity of commercial materials on their walls to determine whether they actually contribute to children's learning or whether they ultimately silence children" (Tarr 2004, 92). Tarr suggests that as children create both design and content of classroom displays, they learn more than they would from looking at a poster or commercially made decorations.

Teachers facilitate learning by supporting curiosity

Vygotsky gave us the term *scaffolding* to describe the teacher's purpose in a child's education. The teacher scaffolds the child's environment with layer upon layer of inviting learning opportunities. As Fred Rogers reminds us, a teacher does not download information and, with a click, impart that information to a child's waiting brain. He uses his passion, creativity, and authenticity in dancing with each child's curiosity. Teaching is an art we develop over a lifetime.

Carol Copple and Sue Bredekamp (2006) say that effective teachers:

• Get to know each child's personality, abilities, and ways of learning.

• Make sure that all children get the support they need to develop relationships with others and feel part of the group.

Characteristics of effective early childhood teachers:

Passion

Perseverance

Willingness to take risks

Pragmatism

Patience

Flexibility

Respect

Creativity

Authenticity

Love of learning

High energy

Sense of humor

—**Laura J. Colker**, "Twelve Characteristics of Early Childhood Teachers"

- Work to build a strong sense of group identity among the children—to develop what is called "the circle of we."
- Create an environment that is organized, orderly, and comfortable for children.
- Plan ways for children to work and play together collaboratively.
- Bring each child's home culture and language into the shared culture of the class.
- Discourage tattling, teasing, scapegoating, and other practices that undermine a sense of community and make some children feel like outsiders.

Seasoned teachers are continuously learning new ways to touch children's lives and spark their curiosity. These teachers are the mature professionals (see Chapter 9) that are a director's delight. Mature professional teachers inspire other teachers to keep learning and growing along with the children. Each director's job is to help teachers share their gifts while continuously learning new approaches to teaching.

Relationships are everything

Fish need water. Humans need air. Children need love. Things don't get much simpler than that.

Studies on "failure to thrive" babies sadly demonstrate the lifetime pain and suffering of unloved children. Loved children learn with confidence. Relationship is everything. "Infants just a few days old can distinguish between emotional expressions," note Lewis, Amini, and Lannon (2000, 61). "Mothers use the universal signals of emotion to teach their babies about the world. . . . Emotionality gives the two of them a common language years before the infant will acquire speech."

The work of an early childhood leader is, above all, to facilitate the sharing of unconditional human regard, or love. With love at the core, everything else flows. Author Frances Carlson (2006) documents the lasting benefits of the respectful, loving physical touch teachers give children. Even children with PTSD (post-traumatic stress disorder) can be loved out of terror into hope and confidence. The pathways (ganglia) of their neurons, stunted by trauma, stretch out and grow into healing connections. The same is true of adults. In accepting, loving relationships, adults who were abused as children learn to trust and thrive. Make no mistake, leading on purpose is leading with a wise and loving heart.

Boundaries, alternative teaching strategies, and structure scaffold a child's learning

NAEYC Accreditation standards and many state licensing regulations require programs to use a written curriculum. Leaders can choose from a number of prepared curriculum packages that meet these requirements. *The Creative Curriculum*® *for Infants, Toddlers, and Twos* and *The Creative Curriculum*® *for Preschool,* from Teaching Strategies, are well-known, purchasable curricula. Written curriculum guides with topical units, lesson plans, and a variety of teaching strategies provide structure and boundaries to a teacher's approach to learning. Any prepared curriculum, however, does not dictate a teacher's actions. Instead, the curriculum provides teachers with options within its framework.

Instructional strategies teachers can use to support children's learning include:

- Encouraging.
- Modeling.

What I have heard from creative people over the years is that their early urges toward unique self-expression were respected and supported by some loving adult in their young lives—someone who would even let them paint a tree blue if that's what they felt like doing. When a friend of mine was a little boy, he liked to draw and paint a lot. One time he drew a tree and colored it blue, and some grownup said to him, "Why did you color a tree blue? Trees aren't blue!" My friend didn't draw a tree again for years . . . not until one of his teachers told him that artists can make things any shape and any color they want.

—Fred Rogers
You Are Special

- Demonstrating.
- Acknowledging.
- Creating or adding challenge.
- Providing information.
- Offering cues or hints to help a child step up to her next level of competency (Bowman, Donovan, & Burns 2000, as related by Copple & Bredekamp 2006, 32–33).

Children respond to a wide range of teaching strategies like these. Facilitation, the strategy that has been the primary focus of this book, is one of a number of strategies on Copple and Bredekamp's continuum. A significant part of a director's supervisory time with her teachers focuses on helping teachers become artists in the classroom, adding more and more vibrant colors to their palettes.

"Intentional teaching," according to Ann Epstein (2007), involves being both aware of and selective about alternative teaching strategies to meet children's differing needs. The intentional teacher is focused on her goals for the children and is well versed in developmentally appropriate practice (DAP). Teachers guide children's learning by intentionally choosing approaches that will work best for the child and the age group. A teacher can encourage children to work in pairs, small teams, or as a whole group, depending on children's learning needs and developmental levels.

Teachers in many ways are magicians, prepared to pull out their hat of strategies to reach each class and child. Written curricula provide a context for teaching creativity to occur. A written curriculum, however, does not tie a teacher's hands or dictate that she walk a narrow path. Teachers are invited to create within the curriculum, adapting to children's curiosity and the changing events in their lives.

Play is the child's pathway to learning. Play is the work of the child. Through play, the child learns lifelong skills of inquiry, exploration, and understanding. The child also learns to negotiate, share, and cooperate. Gross motor skills are developed, and physical challenges present opportunities to enhance a child's self-esteem and determination. Through relationships formed during play, children develop social and emotional intelligence that will put them in good stead for the rest of their lives. When families fear their children will not do well on academic tests, families can become less willing to support their children's learning through play.

Science has discovered emotionality's deeper purpose: the timeworn mechanisms of emotion allow two human beings to receive the contents of each other's minds. Emotion is the messenger of love; it is the vehicle that carries every signal from one brimming heart to another. For human beings, feeling deeply is synonymous with being alive.

—Thomas Lewis,
Fari Amini, and
Richard Lannon
A General Theory of Love

Unrest and the best of "Teaching to the Test"

▶ EXERCISE YOUR EQ   ▇ Consider Marco and his mom in the chapter case study. Marco appears to have thrived and learned through play and exploration. Marco's mom now has a different goal. She wants Marco to perform well on traditional pencil-and-paper testing. She is no longer satisfied with what she perceives to be a play-every-day approach to learning. If you were Marco's teacher, how would you explore this issue with his mom? What assumptions are being made about what is "good" for Marco, both by his mom and by you?

Marco's story is a familiar one. Parents insist that their children be able to readily display knowledge of letters, words, numbers, colors, and facts. Social-emotional development takes a back seat when traditional teaching methods are valued. When curriculum becomes an either/or topic—either "sit still and memorize" or "learn through play"—the child stands to lose. Lilian Katz (2008) reminds us when curriculum is viewed as either "spontaneous play or formal academic instruction," the emphasis may be off the mark. Katz explains:

I suggest that when young children engage in projects in which they conduct investigations of significant objects and events around them and for which they have developed the research questions to find out things like how things work, what things are made of, what people around them do to contribute to their well-being, and so forth, their minds are fully engaged. Furthermore, the usefulness and importance of being able to read, write, measure, and count gradually becomes self-evident (56).

Emphasis on "school performance" and "teaching to the test" has led to disheartening consequences in the public schools. In 2011, the Atlanta school system was rocked by cheating scandals. Sadly, the cheating was not only by students but by teachers as well. When teachers' jobs depend on students' performance on standardized tests, some teachers at wit's end have sacrificed ethics for survival. Any teacher knows that each group of students, like every individual child, learns differently. Are we setting up teachers and children for failure by expecting every child to demonstrate her knowledge the same way, on written tests? I hope that by the time you are reading this page, you have seen more of a resolution on this dilemma.

> **Bam!radio**
>
> "Leading with Integrity in a Dysfunctional Education System"
> Interview with Dr. Andres Alonso.
> *Heart to Heart Conversations on Leadership*
> http://bamradionetwork.com

Effective assessment of young children

Leaders will be challenged with finding a balance that is best for children and their families. Measurable learning outcomes for young children are becoming commonplace. This trend has now reached early childhood programs, with most states as well as Head Start programs articulating specific learning outcomes for children to achieve by the end of preschool. The following are just a few examples:

In language and literacy

- Predicts what will happen next in a story (Colorado).
- Identifies words that rhyme (Ohio).

In mathematics

- Determines "how many" in sets of five or fewer objects (South Carolina).
- Matches and sorts shapes (Washington state).

In social-emotional development

- Shows increasing abilities to use compromise and discussion in working, playing, and resolving conflicts with peers (Head Start).

Measurable learning outcomes and developmentally appropriate practices are also connected with cultural beliefs and practices. Depending on a culture's values, standardized outcomes may or may not be appropriate. For example, in an Asian culture where overt conflict is to be avoided, requiring a child to use discussion when resolving conflicts may not be considered respectful. In collective cultures where being part of a group is valued over individual accomplishment, children may shy away from "standing out" within the group context.

> Close early relationships instill a permanent resilience to the degenerative influence of stress, while neglect sensitizes children to those effects.
>
> —Thomas Lewis, Fari Amini, and Richard Iannon
> *A General Theory of Love*

▶ EXERCISE YOUR EQ   ▦   Early childhood leaders often find themselves, both by individual preference and according to prevailing curriculum standards, balancing two curricular goals—establishing loving relationships and achieving measurable outcome testing.

"Take a sounding" (a nautical term for determining the depth of the water) on your preferred approach to curriculum. Do you focus more on the interpersonal relationship between teacher and child? Do you favor being able to measure a child's skills and competencies? Have you already found ways to balance interpersonal and objective measures?

Experts generally agree that the assessment of young children serves three purposes:

- Making sound decisions about teaching and learning.
- Identifying significant concerns that may require focused intervention for individual children.
- Helping programs improve their educational and developmental interventions.

Indicators of effective assessment include:

- Ethical principles guide assessment practices.
- Assessment instruments are used for their intended purposes.
- Assessments are appropriate for ages and other characteristics of children being assessed.
- Assessment instruments are in compliance with professional criteria for quality.
- What is assessed is developmentally and educationally significant.
- Assessment evidence is used to understand and improve learning.
- Assessment evidence is gathered from realistic settings and situations that reflect children's actual performance.
- Assessments use multiple sources of evidence gathered over time.
- Screening is always linked to follow-up.
- Use of individually administered, norm-referenced tests is limited.
- Staff and families are knowledgeable about assessment (NAEYC & NAECS/SDE 2003, 3).

When considering assessments for young children, realize that assessment is already occurring every day. Examples of appropriate assessment for young children include work samples, teacher observations, checklists and inventories, and parent conferences (SECA 2000). Collected over time, a child's work samples reveal a natural progression of interests and skills. Ongoing written notes about a child's behavior become an informal assessment. Assessment for young children is active, ongoing, and dynamic.

You will have ongoing opportunities during your early childhood career to work toward balancing interpersonal and objective measures. Your knowledge as a leader of early childhood growth and development and the curricula that support that growth will continue to be invaluable.

Learning organizations

When I walk into lively child care programs bustling with enthusiastic children and adults, I join right in on the happiness. When I walk into an early childhood center bogged down with unhappy adults, I fear for the children. We know moods, like colds, are catching. How can negative adults uplift children? In Chapter 8, we looked at many ways in which a leader can promote group well-being and optimism.

Now we will, in the words of chef Emeril Lagasse, "Kick it up a notch!" Massachusetts Institute of Technology professor Peter Senge (2006) writes about "learning organizations" in his book *The Fifth Discipline*. In a learning organization or community, everyone grows. No one stops learning just because of status or title. Learning organizations welcome and promote experimentation and innovation.

In the early childhood field, administrators and teachers often think of maximizing children's opportunities for growth and development. What if administrators viewed adult growth and development as equally important? We know children learn more by observing and interacting with their teachers and environments than they can from any lesson plan, no matter how brilliantly conceived that plan might be. Similarly, adults need challenging opportunities and support to grow.

Emotional and social EQ support and maximize everyone's opportunity to learn. How about parents, brothers and sisters, aunts, uncles, and grandparents who accompany their children along the path of growth and development? Might the cooks, maintenance staff, vendors, and board members in early childhood programs want to grow?

This is all possible, according to Senge, in "organizations where people continually expand their capacity to create the results they truly desire, where new and expansive patterns of thinking are nurtured, where collective aspiration is set free, and where people are continually learning how to learn together" (2006, 3). Learning organizations help us "discover how to tap people's commitment and capacity to learn at *all* levels" (4, emphasis added).

How can you as a leader co-create a learning organization? To co-create you involve all members of your organization, both internal and external customers (see Chapter 15). These five "disciplines" that set learning organizations apart provide pathways:

1. Systems thinking
2. Personal mastery
3. Mental models
4. Building shared vision
5. Team learning

Each discipline is "concerned with a shift of mind from seeing parts to seeing wholes, from seeing people as helpless reactors to seeing them as active participants in shaping their reality, from reacting to the present to creating the future" (Senge 2006, 69). I have yet to see a bored child in the presence of actively inquisitive adults.

Director as environment and curriculum

What an idea! Picture this: As directors and staff learn and grow, so does the program. When leaders make it OK to make mistakes, everyone gets permission to take risks. When administrators scaffold the growth of every child, family, and staff member, they support their own learning. Talk about modeling! Leaders of early childhood programs continuously create curricula and strategies for both adult and child development.

Let the pendulum swing as it may. Some things are timeless. Building relational environments that celebrate growth and learning will never go out of style.

When you ask people about what it is like being part of a great team, what is most striking is the meaningfulness of the experience. People talk about being part of something larger than themselves, of being connected, of being generative. It becomes quite clear that, for many, their experiences as part of truly great teams stand out as singular periods of life lived to the fullest. Some spend the rest of their lives looking for ways to recapture that spirit.

—**Peter Senge**
The Fifth Discipline

Reflection questions

1. Reread the case study about Marco and his mom. This case raises the challenge of honoring a parent's desires ("teaching to the test") while still being true to early childhood theory (supporting a child's natural curiosity). Reflect on the parent's position: What are all the reasons Marco's mom wants Marco to "pass the tests"? Now reflect on Marco's learning through play and his love of the outdoors. Write a dialogue between Marco's mom and the program director or lead teacher on this topic.

2. Reflect on your favorite places and spaces when you were little. What were those places like for you? How did they enchant or enrich you? Did you feel safe there? In what way did those places contribute to your learning? Design a Model and/or describe an early childhood program space (indoors or out) that re-creates the best of those environments you experienced as a child.

3. Take a look at the list of innovators in early childhood theory (pp. 218–21). Choose the person whose theories most appeal to you. Investigate more about this person, about his or her life and teachings. See if you can learn more about the culture and times in which this innovator lived. Choose three to five aspects of this person's life, times, and theories that fascinate you most. Write a brief profile (description).

Team projects

1. Re-read director Jamilah's case study in Chapter 4. Discuss and identify the barriers Jamilah faces as well how she might achieve her vision. Using your emotional and social EQ, develop strategies for Jamilah to use with each of the barriers she faces. Present these strategies to others.

2. Go on a treasure hunt of early childhood programs in your locale to discover classroom and/or playground designs that are imaginative, unique, and inspire children to wonder, grow, and learn. With permission, take photographs and interview staff about how children and teachers use the space. Identify the underlying reasons why these designs work for children. Prepare and present a visual report on the treasures you discovered.

3. Many curriculum packages, such as the *Creative Curriculum®,* are available for programs to purchase, adopt, and use. Explore at least three of these options. What is available and how do users feel about the curriculum? Present samples of different curricula and lead a discussion about the pros and cons of curriculum packages.

Bibliography

Bos, B., & J. Chapman. 2005. *Tumbling over the edge: A rant for children's play.* Roseville, CA: Turn the Page.

Bowman, B.T., M.S. Donovan, & M.S. Burns, eds. 2000. *Eager to learn: Educating our preschoolers.* Washington, DC: National Academies Press. www.nap.edu.

Bowman, B., & E.K. Moore, eds. 2006. *School readiness and social-emotional development: Perspectives in cultural diversity.* Washington, DC: National Black Child Development Institute.

Carlson, F.M. 2006. *Essential touch: Meeting the needs of young children.* Washington, DC: NAEYC.

Carter, M. 2007. Making your environment "the third teacher." *Exchange* 176: 22–26.

Ceppi, G., & M. Zini, eds. 1998. *Children, spaces, relations: Metaproject for an environment for young children.* Reggio Emilia, Italy: Reggio Children.

Copple, C., & S. Bredekamp. 2006. *Basics of developmentally appropriate practice: An introduction for teachers of children 3 to 6.* Washington, DC: NAEYC.

Curtis, D., & M. Carter. 2003. *Designs for living and learning: Transforming early childhood environments.* St Paul, MN: Redleaf.

Day, M., & R. Parlakian. 2004. *How culture shapes social-emotional development: Implications for practice in infant-family programs.* Washington, DC: Zero to Three.

Dewey, J. 1897. *My pedagogic creed.* New York: E.L. Kellogg.

Eggers-Pierola, C. 2005. *Connections and commitments: Reflecting Latino values in early childhood programs.* Portsmouth, NH: Heinemann.

Elliott, S., ed. 2008. *The outdoor playspace naturally: For children birth to five years.* Sydney, Australia: Pademelon Press.

Epstein, A. 2007. *The intentional teacher: Choosing the best strategies for young children's learning.* Washington, DC: NAEYC.

Galinsky, E. 2010. *Mind in the making: The seven essential life skills every child needs.* New York: HarperCollins.

Gonzalez-Mena, J. 2011. *Foundations of early childhood education: Teaching children in a diverse society.* 5th ed. New York: McGraw-Hill.

Greenman, J. 2005. *Caring places, learning spaces: Children's environments that work.* Redmond, WA: Exchange Press.

Hawkins, D. 2002. *The informed vision: Essays on learning and human nature.* New York: Algora Publishing.

Katz, L. 2008. Another look at what young children should be learning. *Exchange* 180: 53–56.

Keeler, R. 2008. Living willow huts—Part 2: Constructing a living willow hut. *Exchange* 179: 78–80.

Lewis, T., F. Amini, & R. Lannon. 2000. *A general theory of love.* New York: Vintage.

Lilley, I.M. 1967. *Friedrich Froebel: A selection from his writings.* Cambridge Texts and Studies in Education series. Cambridge, UK: Cambridge University Press.

Mooney, C.G. 2000. *Theories of childhood: An introduction to Dewey, Montessori, Erikson, Piaget, and Vygotsky.* St. Paul, MN: Redleaf.

NAEYC & NAECS/SDE (National Association of Early Childhood Specialists in State Departments of Education). 2003. *Early childhood curriculum, assessment, and program evaluation: Building an effective, accountable system in programs for children birth through age 8.* Position Statement. Washington, DC: Author. www.naeyc.org/files/naeyc/file/positions/pscape.pdf.

Pack, J. 2011. Spontaneity and the pursuit of beautiful opportunities. *Exchange* 201: 40–43.

Pikler, E. 1971. Learning of motor skills on the basis of self-induced movements. In *Exceptional infant*, vol. 2, ed. J. Hellmuth, 54–89. New York: Bruner/Mazel.

Rafanello, D. 2005. Tending the garden: What gardening can tell us about running our centers. *Exchange* 162: 12–13.

Rogers, F. 1994. *You are special: Words of wisdom from America's most beloved neighbor.* New York: Viking Adult.

SECA (Southern Early Childhood Association). 2000. *Assessing development and learning in young children.* Position Statement. Little Rock, AR: Author. Online: www.southernearlychildhood.org/upload/pdf/Assessing_Development.pdf.

Senge, P. 2006. *The fifth discipline: The art and practice of the learning organization.* Rev. ed. New York: Doubleday.

Shonkoff, J.P., & D.A, Phillips, eds. 2000. *From neurons to neighborhoods: The science of early childhood development.* A report of the National Research Council. Washington, DC: National Academies Press. www.nap.edu/books/0309069882/html/.

Stoecklin, V.L. 2005. Creating outdoor spaces kids love. *Professional Connections* 8 (42): 1–5.

Tarr, P. 2004. Consider the walls. *Young Children* 59 (3): 88–92.

Thomas, J. 2007. Early connections with nature support children's development of science understanding. *Exchange* 178: 57–60.

VanGilder, P., A. Wike, & S. Murphy. 2007. Early foundations: Music and movement in the outdoor classroom. *Exchange* 178: 53–56.

Web resources

About Learning: 12 Theories of Education
www.funderstanding.com/content/about-learning

Creative Play Makes for Kids in Control
www.npr.org/templates/story/story.php?storyId=76838288

National Program for Playground Safety
www.playgroundsafety.org

NAEYC: "Yeah, But's" That Keep Teachers from Embracing an Active Curriculum (PDF)
http://journal.naeyc.org/btj/200507/03Geist.pdf

Reggio Emilia Approach: Environment as Teacher
www.brainy-child.com/article/reggioemilia.html

If I was looking for a child-care provider, I'd start with a short tryout. Then I'd listen to what he or she could tell me about my child. Does the account of their time together suggest alertness, interest, and those all-important three Cs: caring, confidence, and common sense?
—Fred Rogers, *You Are Special*

Even the highest towers begin from the ground.
—Chinese proverb

13 Marketing and Development: If You Build It, They Will Come

Case Study—Milagros

Milagros has just been named director of a Head Start program, which is housed in an old brick mill building where shoes were once made. Her program is one of 10 social service agencies in the building. The building itself sorely needs a makeover. Cold as a fortress, the old mill looks harsh and impersonal. Milagros wants to welcome and honor the diverse families who come to her center.

What steps can she take to change the dour impression people get when they see the old mill?

Have you said to yourself, "That will never

happen" or "That person will never change" or "Over my dead body!"? I have.

When I was younger, I boarded an underground train from West Berlin to East Berlin, beneath the foreboding barrier of the Berlin Wall. I eyed somber Soviet soldiers standing guard with scary weapons at abandoned subway stops along the way, as my palms sweated and my heart leapt into my throat. The customs inspectors, also underground, took what felt like a day and a night to allow us entry.

When at last I climbed into the East Berlin daylight, my vision was darkened again by destruction in every street block. Bullet and mortar holes pockmarked buildings. Piles of rock and rubble crowded alleyways. Soldiers' heels clicked sharply on cobblestone streets. Only during a quiet respite in the one café open to visitors could I shake the weight of the wall. On that day, I could not imagine that the Berlin Wall could fall.

Years later, the unimaginable happened. Piece by piece, the wall fell, peacefully. As I watched televised scenes of long-separated family members from both sides embracing, I promised myself I would expect miracles. If that wall could fall, others can too.

Examples of falling walls abound all around us. Walt Disney's larger-than-life dream became a reality because of his deep beliefs. "If you can dream it, you can do it," Disney said. "Always remember that this whole thing was started with a dream and a mouse." Kevin Costner's character dreamed of transforming his cornfield into a baseball diamond in the movie *Field of Dreams*. Against considerable odds, he built the field. Players came, fulfilling the movie's premise: "If you build it, they will come."

In this chapter, we will confront "stuck" beliefs in our field and figure out creative ways to help obstacles crumble and dreams come true.

Getting "unstuck"

My great concern is not whether you have failed, but whether you are content with your failure.

—Abraham Lincoln

"Stuck" beliefs are myths, with a shard of truth, that hold us back. Here are some examples:

- We don't have money to improve our buildings and grounds.
- We should never "blow our own horn" and brag about our program's strengths.
- We've tried, but we can't attract diverse staff or families.
- Retaining staff is impossible. We'll lose our best staff to public schools.
- We don't have time for fund-raising and need to hire a professional fund-raiser.

Not every director believes these myths. However, on "bad hair days" (those "shadow" times Carl Jung indentified [see Chapter 4]), worries can pester even the most positive director. Rather than let debilitating myths sneak up on a down day, directors can call out these myths in advance. Every myth contains just enough truth to be convincing. For example, bragging offends many people. However, sharing good news differs from bragging, especially when that news applauds families and staff.

The power of optimism plays out neurologically and spiritually. Studies show optimists possess better memory, envision more possibilities, are more competent at problem solving, and live longer, happier lives than pessimists (*American Psychologist* 2000; Mayo Clinic 2008). Optimists, willing to take risks for the better, forge new connections between brain cells. A sense of humor and perspective about failure are an optimistic leader's tools.

When we shut down possibilities, we squash hope. The only way to see what's on the horizon is to look up. The saying "One door closes so another can open" is a useful management mantra. Are you ready to discover possibilities, build new brain pathways, and knock down moldy brick walls?

Myth #1: We don't have enough money to improve our grounds

First impressions count. Our ever vigilant mirror neurons react to new people and environments in a snap. Mirror neurons register a "take" or "sense" of people and places long before our conscious brain can assess situations. There is barely enough time for our professional perspective to kick in.

The moment a family first spies the outside of an early care and education program, adults and children form a judgment for better or worse about what they will find inside. The program's curb appeal, or sensory first impression the program exudes, inspires potential clients to drive in or drive by. A director and her team can choose ways to showcase a program as beautiful on both the outside and the inside.

▶ EXERCISE YOUR EQ ▦ Picture the outside of the building you are in now. What do you recall about the building? What impression did the building give you? Did you feel welcomed or put off even before you entered the building? What would you change about the outside of the building to make it more welcoming? If you need to, step outside the building for a second look.

Directors have told me, "We don't have money to invest in unnecessary items like landscaping or a new sign out front when we are dedicating our funds to quality care within our walls." Other directors have said, "We don't own our building. We have to accept what the landlord dictates." Let's explode these myths.

The curb appeal of a program, in addition to its impact on someone's first impression, communicates more about what goes on inside the program than you might think. For that reason, paying attention to how the program is presented, even before a person enters the building, is important. Anyone who crosses the threshold should do so with pride.

When you think about improving the outside of a child care center, imagine:

- Working with children to plant flowers such as marigolds, sunflowers, morning glories, or snapdragons at the base of the program's sign. All of these flowers grow easily from inexpensive packs of seeds.

- Inviting a local landscaping company to donate its time and skill to make over the front yard. Agree to post a sign thanking them for their expertise and generosity.

- Sponsoring a grounds "beautification day" with cleanup activities and prizes for families.

- Enlisting discount stores that sell outdoor plants to contribute new plants each season.

- Holding a competition among staff and/or families for creative and inexpensive makeover ideas. Choose, use, and reward the best.

- Erecting a Plexiglas-covered standing bulletin board to display children's artwork for passersby to admire.

- Tying brightly colored balloons to the outdoor sign to welcome new families or celebrate children's birthdays.

Imagine all the ways in which you could "make over" the front of an early childhood building with less than $100.

▶ EXERCISE YOUR EQ ▦ Add more creative and inexpensive ideas to the list. Notice the "bang for the buck." Little money but big hearts make for great innovations.

Myth #2: "Blowing your own horn" is unnecessary in early childhood education

Many of us were taught that drawing attention to ourselves is inappropriate. Have you ever felt uncomfortable when someone picked you out of a crowd, presented you with an award, or asked you to be the center of attention? If so, you are not alone. Introverts, 51 percent of us (see Chapter 4), aren't the only ones who avoid being put on the spot. Often, I proudly watch early childhood professionals receive awards. They run like gazelles off the stage, saying, "I didn't do anything special" or "The team deserves this, not me."

Whatever your personal beliefs are about modesty and "not blowing your own horn," ask yourself, "How can we communicate our program's specialness to others?" Your community (families, children, staff, neighborhood, town, or city) benefits from the message "Our program is a great place for children." I invite you to let go of the myth that promoting programs is unnecessary and immodest. Consider the importance of marketing. Do not think of it as blowing your own horn, but as a functional business strategy for the vitality of a program.

Marketing is a creative opportunity to invoke one's emotional and social intelligence. By paying attention to the needs of the people being served, directors can distinguish their program in the marketplace. Marketing is presenting a program to families in an inviting, welcoming manner that indicates how they will be treated. Effective marketing also shows that families can entrust their children to a program. Curb appeal is part of a program's marketing strategy. Even before they walk through the door, families want to anticipate good things.

Marketing in early childhood education is not a glitzy, cosmetic, or shallow affair. Marketing communicates, with and without words, a program's uniqueness. The marketing adage "Distinguish yourself in the marketplace" urges directors to share their program's special strengths with the world. Even if a program has a waiting list from here to the Galapagos Islands, the program still needs marketing. Sharing the good news about a program uplifts everyone. Everyone can point with pride to the grounds, the building, and what lies within.

▶ EXERCISE YOUR EQ   ▪   Write about three ways in which you want your program to be special. Think of what you might offer that not every other program offers.

> Most executives cannot articulate the objective, scope, and advantage of their business in a simple statement. If they can't, neither can anyone else.
>
> —David J. Collins and Michael G. Rukstad

> Clarity about what makes the firm distinctive is what most helps employees understand how they can contribute.
>
> —David J. Collins and Michael G. Rukstad

> Marketing creates a targeted message to a particular audience who wants to hear that message.
>
> —Larry Thorner
> Early childhood program director

Marketing 101: It's a plan

"Marketing strategy" is formulating a plan to present a program's uniqueness and strengths to others. "Distinguishing ourselves" is setting a program apart by communicating our special vision, core values, purpose, and offerings. Distinguishing ourselves tells others what unique qualities, programs, clientele, and/or staffing make the program "one of a kind." All early childhood programs offer care and education to young children. In what original ways will your program provide quality care? Communicating this message can make or break a program's financial security.

Harrington and Tjan (2008) offer these three components for formulating an effective marketing plan:

1. Map out your real market.

2. Understand your customers' objectives and work flow.

3. Develop products that provide what users value most.

Here's how this business terminology translates to the business of early childhood.

Map out your real market

To map out a program's real market, directors must take an objective look at the families they serve and envision those they might serve in the future. Directors can start by studying the families already enrolled. The goal is to discover who currently finds the program attractive. Software applications, such as Microsoft Word or Excel, offer useful tools for this kind of study.

Consider current family demographics. Demographics include income level, employment, location in the community, community involvements, ethnicity, size of family, and modes of transportation. Directors can make it easy to tally this data by creating a chart or a spreadsheet (a page broad enough to pick out important data easily) with several categories, such as those listed in the **Family Demographics** chart. Next, directors will fill in the chart with information about each family.

As directors tally this information, they will notice commonalities. For example, are most wage earners employed by the same or similar businesses? Are only certain neighborhoods represented? What percentage of families uses their own vehicles instead of public transportation? From this data, a program's "typical family" will emerge.

A similar market analysis of a program's employees, particularly the teaching staff, produces valuable information. This time, directors will create a second spreadsheet and tally data about employees by using the questions in the **Staff Demographics** chart.

Data about the "typical staff member" will emerge from this spreadsheet. This is the employee who chose the program, perhaps over other centers. This profile of current employees can alert leaders to "markets" they tapped into for hiring that may still not be fully utilized. Look for trends (indications of possible directions you can go with this information).

Now that the director has valuable marketing information about future families and employees, he needs to locate people who fit the description of the typical family and employee. Employees are often a program's best recruiters. As a director, you may want to offer incentives to current employees who refer new hires who stay with you for six months or more. Word of mouth is a highly effective mode of advertising. Sharing with families and staff that you expect to have openings and would like their recommendations can be an effective marketing tool.

Note that leaders are not "stuck" with only one group of families or one source of staff members. In addition to identifying your current market, marketing surveys point the way to new markets. You will have options. Who else could you reach out to, and who else might add depth and variety to the program?

Understand your customers' objectives and work flow

Stepping back to see the big picture is valuable. In the business of early childhood, "understand your customers' objectives and work flow" translates to "understand your families' needs and the demands placed on them." Marketing information, when tallied, may surprise directors. Or directors may know the program's families and employees well, and so the data reinforces their expectations. Completing this marketing survey exercise with board members enlarges the circle of information and involvement.

Imagine you are a director who has gathered valuable marketing information from your surveys. You have identified your current "real market"—those people who have selected you and your services. Knowing the profiles of your "typical" family and employee tells you your current market niche. That niche is the segment of families and staff members to whom your program appeals. With this information, you can target similar families and potential employees and determine how best to serve them.

Effective program leaders monitor how well they are meeting the needs of current families. They routinely ask, "How are we do-

Family Demographics

✓ Where do our families live in our community?
✓ How far do they travel to our program?
✓ What transportation do they use? What transportation options are available to them?
✓ What is their income level?
✓ How many children are in each family, and what is the likelihood of each family having additional children?
✓ Where do the wage earners work?
✓ What jobs do the wage earners perform?
✓ How did the families hear about our program?
✓ In what other community organizations are families involved (religious, civic, etc.)?

Staff Demographics

✓ What neighborhoods do these staff members represent?
✓ What transportation do they use?
✓ In what other community organizations are they active members?
✓ How many children do staff have, and how many are they likely to have?
✓ How did they hear about our program?
✓ What factors led them to accept employment with us?
✓ Who composes their family?
✓ What is the income level of the family overall?
✓ What ethnicities and/or cultures are represented in your staff?

Set marketing goals:
• Emphasize the quality of our program.
• Share with parents the wonderful things we do each day for children.
• Share with parents the education of the staff members and the materials and equipment we provide for the children.
• Emphasize that we do everything possible to offer good pay and benefits to staff to lower turnover.

—Larry Thorner
Program director

ing?" They hold exit interviews with families who age out of the program or otherwise choose to leave. Directors ask clients how they feel about the services, what worked best, and what they would change or add. Highly valuable marketing information is gained from exit interviews.

Leaders don't need to wait for an exit interview, however, to gather this important information. They can survey families often—both formally by written questionnaires and informally as families are greeted each day. They can also provide a suggestion box, check it daily, and make every effort to respond within a day to each person who made a suggestion. If you do this, word will get out that you take suggestions seriously.

Develop products that provide what users value most

Continuously asking current customers (both families and staff) to give feedback helps directors understand what customers value most. Administrators can ask, "What do you like best about our program?" and "What else might we offer that would matter to you?" In Chapter 14, we will look at "family-friendly practices." Family-friendly practices include efforts to make life easier for families, such as parents' date nights; sleepovers for children; nutritious, affordable meals available to go; hair cutting services; and connections to "sick child" family care providers.

When a leader asks families what they need, she needs to be clear that she is open to suggestions. By the same token, she does not want to give the impression that she takes orders like a waitress. Effective directors let people know they plan to improve services whenever feasible, but due to financial or staffing reasons, or because an idea discriminates against certain groups, not every suggestion can be implemented. Setting realistic expectations pays off later.

Directors can also anticipate the customers' needs, which is a total quality management (TQM) principle (read more in Chapter 15). Anticipating the customers' needs is thinking of something helpful to the customer even before the customer thinks of it. For example, imagine a director who provides one pickup time a month when the program's cook demonstrates how to make yummy, nutritious snacks for children. Families will welcome this instruction, especially when the cook offers samples to taste and take home. Leaders know immediately if an innovation meets parents' needs; contented sighs will echo down the hallways.

While it is important to address the needs of your current market niche, it is also important to prepare to diversify your market. Let's consider what to do if your marketing strategy targets diversifying your staff and your clients but you are scratching your head about how to do that.

Developing your staff and clients

Myth #3: We'll never be able to diversify our staff or our families

A director can do a great deal to foster a multicultural environment that attracts new staff and families.

Creating a welcoming environment for diverse cultures

The first step is to tell the truth: "Houston, we have a problem." If marketing assessments show that staff and families are homogeneous, this issue can be addressed with the board, staff, and, as appropriate, families. Everyone benefits from a richly diverse environment. Children especially, who will inhabit a world far more ethnically diverse

Regularly ask families:
- How do you feel about our current services?
- What else do you need?

Different groups have different needs, and people of color have a strong need for connection and empowerment. What you see in the cafeterias are affinity groups: separate "spaces" that facilitate positive identity exploration, where people can pose questions and process issues.

—Beverly Daniel Tatum

Percentage of Prekindergarten Children Ages 3–5 Who Were Enrolled in Center-Based Early Childhood Care and Education Programs, by Child and Family Characteristics: Selected Years, 1991–2005

Characteristic	1991	1993	1995	1996	1999	2001	2005
Total	53	53	55	55	60	56	57
Poverty status							
Poor	44	43	45	44	51	47	47
Non-poor	56	56	59	59	62	59	60
Race/ethnicity							
White	54	54	57	57	60	59	59
Black	58	57	60	65	73	64	66
Hispanic	39	43	37	39	44	40	43
Mother's education							
Less than high school	32	33	35	37	40	38	35
High school diploma or equivalent	46	43	48	49	52	47	49
Some college, including vocational/technical	60	60	57	58	63	62	56
Bachelor's degree or higher	72	73	75	73	74	70	73

U.S. Department of Education, National Center for Education Statistics. 2007. *The Condition of Education 2007* (NCES 2007-064), *Indicator 2*.

than even the most diverse parts of the United States today, need to get to know their neighbors, regardless of whether they live across town in the *barrio,* the penthouse, or "the hood."

The second step is to work together to investigate ways to diversify programs in far more than a cosmetic way. Leaders can devote some staff meeting time to brainstorming possibilities. They can bring in professional advisors or community experts to share ideas. Each staff member can be asked to take responsibility for finding at least one effective way to bring more diversity to the program. A director's passion for multiculturalism makes a significant impact on program diversity.

Debra Sullivan (2010), author of *Learning to Lead,* walks the talk. When she and her management team decided to learn Spanish to serve families better, she arranged lunchtime Spanish language classes. Whenever employees felt their cultural practices weren't fully heard or valued, Sullivan made sure everyone's approaches were honored. For example, when Asian staff members viewed direct problem-solving methods as uncomfortably aggressive, she took time to work through subtler, less confrontational approaches. When men grew tired of women's need to "over-process and debrief everything," Sullivan, with humor, amended her ways. She is clear that we model our vision. Her program was and is richly diverse. The message got out: Working here is a great place for everyone of every culture.

The director's ethnicity and cultural mores can establish her program's climate. Beverly Daniel Tatum (2003) reminds us that in powerful ways, stated and unstated, we communicate which culture is dominant (*"Why Are All the Black Kids Sitting Together*

We all have misinformation about people different and like ourselves, and we're all exposed to stereotypes. Prejudice is like smog: No one says, "I'm a smog-breather," but if you live in a smoggy place, it's hard to avoid breathing it. When I hear someone say, "There's not a prejudiced bone in my body," I say, look again. Because there are bones in there that you may not want, but they're there.

—Beverly Daniel Tatum

in the Cafeteria?"). Just as moods are contagious in organizations, so too are messages about how to act and what to value.

The ethnicity or culture powerful enough to set the standard for behavior in the organization is the "dominant" one (podcast). For example, many black early childhood professionals indicate respect by using the titles Ms. and Mr. when addressing other adults. I learned while working with early childhood professionals of the Muscogee and Cherokee tribes that the term "Indian" can be preferable to "Native American." In a predominantly Anglo organization, staff members may be expected to send thank-you notes for any gift they receive. In Mexican American early childhood organizations, looking directly into another person's eyes may indicate disrespect. Paying attention to indicators of respect makes a difference, especially if the dominant organizational ways differ from your own.

The problem with a dominant organizational culture is that people of other heritages and practices can feel invisible, underappreciated, or rejected. Homogeneous organizations in which everyone looks the same are the result. This leads some directors to throw up their hands and say, "How can I attract staff of other cultures if they don't see anyone who looks like them here?"

Recall how Sullivan and her staff learned Spanish to meet the needs of their program's children. Her team made the commitment *together* to become Spanish speakers. Imagine the difference this makes to families for whom Spanish is their mother tongue.

▶ EXERCISE YOUR EQ   With classmates or colleagues, make a plan for diversifying a program. What steps will you need to take? Leaders often go through this same process with their boards and family advisory teams. If, in the end, only one effective change is made, a program has still begun to change in a meaningful way.

Learning to address and respond to cultural conflict

The third step directors can take to grow a multicultural organization is to prepare for and address potential conflicts. For example, leaders need to do everything they can to "run interference" (deal with bias in advance) before a new team member arrives. Being the only one of a particular ethnicity in an organization can be overwhelming. Each new employee can be assigned a "buddy," someone who is open-minded, empathetic, and demonstrates ample EQ and social EQ. Directors can prepare staff in advance by educating them on essentials about the new staff member's culture. Leaders co-create an environment of trustful risk taking wherein staff are encouraged to share their fears and hopes while working together to create a welcoming environment.

We know early childhood professionals are uncomfortable with conflict. Tatum (2003) takes on this issue as it pertains to race by saying:

> Some people say there is too much talk about race and racism in the United States. I say that there is not enough. . . . We need to continually break the silence about racism whenever we can. We need to talk about it at home, at school, in our houses of worship, in our workplaces, in our community groups. . . . It means meaningful, productive dialogue to raise consciousness and lead to effective action and social change. (193)

If teachers can have these important conversations with children, adults in our programs can have these conversations with one another.

Over the years, I have learned not to expect people who differ from me to come to me. I must go to them, and go willingly, to learn and grow in ways that are not always comfortable. I listen, and when I "get it wrong" I immediately apologize, ready to listen more deeply. At first, I may well hear anger and rage. Anyone who feels as if she has not been heard—or worse, as if her voice is not welcomed—has every right to her feelings.

Remember now the majority of individuals take things personally? As I listen, I remind myself of the Q-TIP principle, "Quit taking it personally," and listen from the heart. For me, this is a spiritual process wherein I rely upon the support of a power greater than myself to keep the faith. As Maureen Walker said (2001):

> The path to relational healing leads us on a journey fraught with risk and imbued with promise. It is a journey of courage and faith: the courage to be mindful and to grieve, to risk letting go of old relational images that function to *contain* our anxieties, in hopes of discovering and enlarging our capacity for richer authenticity. The path to relational healing invites us to enter into conflict with faith in our human possibilities and with desire for the emergence of something new (8).

Along the way, by listening and asking honest questions, I hear about the individual's experience while learning about her cultural experience. For me, this is a lifelong passion and process. The moral of my story is this: Step outside your comfort zone. Go on a treasure hunt.

As a director, your first effort to diversify may be the hardest. With each subsequent effort, however, you will build upon your experience. If your team pulls together in support of growth, your new staff members will put the word out that your program is a haven for teachers and families. In the end, you and your staff have walked the talk right down the path toward understanding.

Practical ways to grow a multicultural staff

Many national groups offer tips for diversifying your staff. For example, the National Education Association (NEA) (Center for Teaching Quality 2009) recommends:

1. **Recruit teachers from support staff.** Research has found that programs that help paraeducators become teachers offer a tremendous opportunity to increase the supply of ethnic minority teachers. This pool of school employees (teaching assistants, clerks, and others with or without a bachelor's degree) are largely minorities. They are generally committed to education and tend to stay for long periods in the profession. Many are more mature individuals with extensive classroom experience who have roots in their communities and are accustomed to working with challenging students.

2. **Look to high school students.** Early recruiting—getting high school students interested in teaching—is another suggestion. The NEA recommends identifying students through career surveys, counseling, motivational workshops, summer college preparatory courses, and the promise of financial aid.

3. **Use programs offering support** on increasing staff diversity. EducationWorld suggests, for example:

   - the Hispanic Association of Colleges and Universities, representing 275 colleges and universities with high Hispanic enrollments, which offers advice to school districts interested in recruiting Hispanic graduates.

   - the National Alliance of Black School Educators and HBCU (Historically Black Colleges and Universities) Connect, which do the same for the African American community (Chaika 2004).

4. **Work with what you have,** especially if your staff is homogeneous (all from the same background or culture). Derman-Sparks, an advocate for multicultural and

The classroom—not the trench—is the frontier of freedom, now and forevermore.

—Lyndon B. Johnson

According to the U.S. Department of Education's National Center for Education Statistics, the children in early childhood programs are already more representative of future ethnic diversity than our employees.

anti-bias education in early childhood, has recently taken on the challenge of working with all-white groups. She and Patricia Ramsey (2005) suggest this practical tip to help children and adults in homogeneous settings:

> Invite individuals from various racial/ethnic groups in your community to interact with children on a regular basis. Ongoing face-to-face contact is the best way to break down barriers, recognize similarities, and see differences as enriching rather than as uncomfortable or strange (20).

Myth #4: Staff retention is impossible

Staff retention not only is essential, it is also a pleasure. We yearn to be part of a loving community. Early childhood programs can be the most loving of learning communities. If each staff member knows how important she is to the team, she feels valued. Employees who help create the program's mission are personally dedicated to making that mission come true. As a leader, exercise every bit of your EQ and social EQ to learn about your staff, anticipate their needs, support their growth, and build a lasting team.

Remember the research about staff motivation (Chapter 1)? Money isn't the answer. Working "on purpose" is. If a teacher is passionate about what his center stands for, he will stay for years. If a teacher feels the director's respect, support, and appreciation, she will not leave. If a teacher can fulfill her own professional purpose while furthering the program's mission, she will stay. She will also inspire others to join the team.

The relationship that directors build with each staff member can significantly affect a staff member's longevity. The dedication a leader invests into building a team can significantly affect the loyalty of the team. Coming back on an Amtrak train after working near New York City, I engaged in a spirited conversation with two men in my compartment, one a health care executive and the other a well-known New England businessman and television personality. I asked them, "What's the secret to keeping your best employees?" The men responded in a heartbeat, "Trust your people, respect them, and be loyal to them. They, in turn, will be loyal to you."

Established practices of staff retention include:

1. Staff who have a strong personal commitment to children and families are more likely to stay in a program.

2. A distinct, well-defined program philosophy and goals encourage professional commitment, especially when joint staff effort is involved in their development.

3. Opportunities to share ideas and support each other personally and professionally—formally through mentor teams and staff meetings and informally through social events and places to gather/relax—strengthen staff relationships.

4. Effective communication among staff and between staff, management, and families is critical.

5. Meaningful involvement in decision making improves staff morale, job satisfaction, and commitment.

6. Where staff regularly feel respected and appreciated and experience communication of both, healthy climates thrive. (Klinkner, Riley, & Roach 2005, 95)

Let me tell you about Marge from Connecticut. Marge was hired from her community. An active community member, she volunteered in soup kitchens, built Habitat for Humanity homes, and taught Sunday school. Everyone liked Marge and her preschool. She hired parents as teachers' aides and supported them as they completed their early childhood degrees. Marge held an annual staff retreat where community members volunteered services like massages and pedicures and center families contributed meals. People sang, laughed, shared stories, and looked forward to having fun together. Over the years, "graduates" from Marge's program, long since grown up, asked if they could come back and work there. Marge never had much money. She had enough EQ and social EQ to stretch from here to the North Pole. Marge's program is a model for staff retention.

It's not the big things that kill us; it's the little things. Little things we do every day make all the difference. Directors can be endlessly creative about ways to recognize and thank teachers (see **Little Gifts for Teachers** for a few ideas). Surprises like placing "gotcha" notes (caught you doing something great) in a teacher's box, providing creamy lotions and quality soaps in the staff bathrooms, and handing out donated gift certificates at staff meetings all cheer a teacher's day. Surprises work best. Directors do well to remember that a true surprise can't be repeated. A director in Virginia called me, frantic that her staff expected a bigger and bigger holiday banquet each year: What could she do this year to top last year?! Keep your surprises fresh to avoid building unrealistic expectations of entitlement.

▶ EXERCISE YOUR EQ   ■   Think of three inexpensive or free surprises a classroom teacher would like to receive from her director.

Make no mistake about it, being an advocate for excellent salary and benefits packages for early childhood professionals is also important. Director Lucinda e-mailed me about the "fantastic" benefits package she negotiated for her staff after getting the staff's input. The staff didn't get everything on their wish list, but knowing that Lucinda was going to bat for them made a difference.

Staff retention, in a word, is social EQ. Relationships are golden. Keeping each relationship revitalized and dynamic is the greatest predictor of staff retention. As a leader, strive for the long view, step onto the balcony for perspective, pick your battles, and maintain an "attitude of gratitude." Leaders exercise courage when they hold staff accountable for unprofessional behavior. They use EQ when they say goodbye to non-productive team members. Your team will notice each battle you fight for quality, both outside and inside of yourself.

Myth #5: We need to hire a professional fund-raiser

Roger Neugebauer, founding editor of *Exchange* magazine, surveyed more than 100 early childhood programs to find out what makes fund-raising efforts successful or unsuccessful. When the surveys were assessed, Neugebauer compiled "Keys to Success

Little Gifts for Teachers

For more ways to reward teachers and other team members, consider these inexpensive, personal ideas:
- A night at the movies: A bookstore gift certificate, microwave popcorn, bottle of lemonade or favorite soft drinks, wrapped in the film section of the newspaper.
- Pasta dinner: A basket of specially shaped pasta, pasta sauce, fresh Italian bread, and a small chunk of Parmesan cheese with a simple grater.
- Homemade mix: All the ingredients for the teacher's favorite cookies (sprinkles, chocolate chips, icing) or pancakes (dry mix and small bottle of syrup), along with a pretty mixing bowl and spoon from a local discount store.
- Gift basket for the classroom pet (if the teacher is using her own money for pet supplies), including food, treats, toys, and shavings.
- Make note cards using rubber stamps. Attach a special pen.
- Gift certificates to craft stores and other shops the teacher frequents for special supplies.
- Disposable camera with a frame for the pictures.
- Afternoon off certificate when you or a floater will cover the classroom.
- Aprons or smocks to wear for messy activities, with teacher's name stenciled on.
- Flower bulbs (narcissus, amaryllis, hyacinth), glass "stones," and a pretty pot in which to grow the bulbs.
- A floater for the classroom at pickup time to allow teachers to have more in-depth conversation time with families.

Ideas from "Preschool Teacher Gift Ideas," 2001, The Dollar Stretcher.com. www.stretcher.com/stories/03/03dec01a.cfm.

in Raising Funds" (2007, 104–06):

1. **Define your purpose.** Be clear on your intention for the fund-raising event. Let that intention motivate volunteers.

2. **Set a goal.** A specific dollar amount sets a measurable standard that people can rally around.

3. **Know the audience.** Are you likely to have individual donors, or will you need to approach organizations and businesses? Or both? Know the financial means of your audience, and their history of giving.

4. **Make it fun.** Choose an activity that people will look forward to and get excited about, something that will take them out of their ordinary day and bring some laughter and good times.

5. **Build on strengths.** Capitalize on the skills and talents of your staff and volunteers.

6. **Look for repeaters.** When a project has been successful the first time, repeat it and you won't have to worry about "reinventing the wheel" each time.

7. **Be cost-effective.** The return on time invested (R) equals expense incurred (E) subtracted from total income (I) divided by the total number of hours spent by staff and volunteers on the project.

8. **Publicize aggressively.** Start with being clear on what your "product" is (what you are selling/offering), whether it is a chance to win something or outright support for your program. Get the "right message to the right people."

9. **Maximize publicity.** Use the fund-raiser to inform people about your program and how special it is. Include bulleted information on your program in the publicity.

10. **Thank contributors.** Contact everyone who helped. Let them know how much you raised and how their contribution will make a difference. Written notices on stationery unique to your program work best.

In addition to these steps, Kathy Hines (2007) recommends that directors ask donors to say why they decided to contribute. Identifying what motivates each donor is valuable. Is he particularly invested in helping children who have special needs? Does the donor want to improve business in the area by ensuring quality child care? By paying attention and showing sensitivity to the donor's motivation, you honor the donor and build an ongoing relationship.

Say no way to "no way"

If these five common myths in our profession can be faced down, how many other myths are we ready to challenge? Perhaps you have heard that "We can't find enough qualified staff" or "We're in a hiring crisis." Remember that in every myth is a shard of reality. Hiring and retaining qualified teachers is a challenge for directors. The director who says "I'll never find enough qualified staff" will find that her prediction comes true.

> The most productive form of director feedback to staff is immediate acknowledgment of a job well done.
> —Joan M. Klinkner, Dave Riley, and Mary A. Roach

> Failure? I never encountered it. All I encountered were temporary setbacks.
> —Dottie Walters

Case Study—Sheila

Sheila is discouraged about ever finding enough qualified staff. She fears her best teachers will accept offers with better pay from the public schools. Sheila admits she is behind the times when it comes to advertising online to fill teaching positions. How would you use your EQ to help Sheila work on her attitude and her competencies?

Self-fulfilling prophecies like this show that our future takes the shape we expect it to take. Self-fulfilling prophecies in neuroscience terms add up to brain pathways that are stuck in place. If I expect the worst, I will get the worst. If I am willing to take on the myth, I have a fighting chance of getting different results. Every director I know who believes she can find and retain qualified staff hires and keeps her staff.

You will have scads of opportunities to either accept or challenge negative beliefs. I invite you to challenge any negative you are told. Someone believed the Berlin Wall could fall. You can be that someone in our field.

Reflection questions

1. Can you remember a time you accomplished something you never thought you could? Can you recall a belief of yours that you no longer hold dear? Have you observed changes in the world that make your life different than when you were little? Choose the most powerful of your recollections or observations about the "Berlin Walls" that have fallen in your lifetime. Record an oral reflection on a video/DVD (or write one) about the way that situation was, the way it is now, and what brought about the change.

2. Imagine you are placed in charge of raising money for a child care program. Where would you start? What resources can you find to help? What are some of your options for raising money? Investigate examples of successful early childhood fundraising activities. Call programs in your area and select your favorite fund-raising idea. Put together a plan with your goal, measurable objectives, and publicity activities. Check your plan against Roger Neugebauer's suggestions on page 243.

3. How much experience and exposure do you have to people of cultures and ethnicities other than your own? Would you like to change this experience and exposure in any way? Review the steps Debra Sullivan took and the recommendation by Derman-Sparks and Ramsey. Describe how you would like to expand or alter your exposure to other cultures. Research what is available in your community and online. List at least five steps you will take to broaden your horizons in diversity.

Team projects

1. Recognizing and honoring teachers for their accomplishments and their EQ and social EQ competencies can take many shapes. Brainstorm as a team all the ideas you can on teacher or staff recognition. From this list, each of you will select an approach or idea you find especially inspiring. Research the idea to "round it out" with concrete examples and, if possible, real-life examples of how this idea has been used in early childhood programs. As a team, compile a list of recommendations for teacher recognition.

2. With rapid changes to technology, marketing strategies must change too. Share with your team all the ways in which word can get out to potential new teachers and directors. Go online to find the best examples of how technology can further our recruiting processes. Discuss how you might use technology to reach out to potential hires in emotionally and socially intelligent ways. Write a brief guide to using technology when recruiting staff members.

3. Curb appeal can influence a potential customer to "drive in or drive by." Together, make a checklist of customer-friendly characteristics you would like to see on the outside of early childhood centers. Tour early childhood programs in your area to assess their curb appeal. Take your cameras with you. Prepare a PowerPoint presentation on the best and worst curb appeal practices.

Bibliography

Center for Teaching Quality. 2009. *Strengthening and Diversifying the Teacher Recruitment Pipeline.* Washington DC: National Education Association.

Chaika. G. (2004, October 12) Recruiting and retaining minority teachers: Programs that work! EducationWorld School Administrators Articles. www.educationworld.com/a_admin/admin/admin213.shtml.

Collins, D.J., & M.G. Rukstad. 2008. Can you say what your strategy is? *Harvard Business Review* (April): 82–90.

Derman-Sparks, L., & P. Ramsey. 2006. *What if all the children in my class are white? Engaging white children and their families in anti-bias multicultural education.* New York: Teachers College Press.

Derman-Sparks, L., & P. Ramsey. 2005. What if all the children in my class are white? Anti-bias/multicultural education with white children. *Young Children* 60 (6): 20–27.

Finegan-Stoll, C. 1999. The goal of diversity training: To 'teach tolerance' or model acceptance? *Leadership Quest* (Spring): 10–12.

Goffin, S.G., & V. Washington. 2007. *Ready or not: Leadership choices in early care and education.* New York: Teachers College Press.

Gonzalez-Mena, J. 2007. *Diversity in early care and education programs: Honoring differences.* 5th ed. New York: McGraw-Hill.

Harrington, R.J., & A.K. Tjan. 2008. Transforming strategy, one customer at a time. *Harvard Business Review* March: 62–72.

Hines, K . 2007. Circles of support. In *Managing money: A center director's guidebook,* eds. R. Neugebauer & B. Neugebauer, 109–??. Redmond, WA: Exchange Press.

Kagan, S.L., & B.T. Bowman, eds. 1997. *Leadership in early care and education.* Washington, DC: NAEYC.

Klinkner, J.M., D. Riley, & M.A. Roach. 2005. Organizational climate as a tool for child care staff retention. *Young Children* 60 (6): 90–95.

Mayo Clinic Staff. 2008. Positive thinking: Reduce stress by eliminating negative self-talk. www.mayoclinic.com/health/positive-thinking/SR00009.

Neugebauer, R. 2007. In *Managing money: A center director's guidebook,* eds. R. Neugebauer & B. Neugebauer, 104–106. Redmond, WA: Exchange Press.

Sullivan, D.R. 2010. *Learning to lead: Effective leadership skills for teachers of young children.* 2d ed. St. Paul, MN: Redleaf Press.

Tatum, B.D. 2003. *"Why are all the black kids sitting together in the cafeteria?" and other conversations about race.* 5th ed. New York: Basic Books.

Taylor, S.E., M.E. Kemeny, G.M. Reed, J.E. Bower, & T.L. Gruenewald. 2000. Pyschological resources, positive illustrations, and health. *American Psychologist* (January): 99–109.

Torres, J., J. Santos, N.L. Peck, & L. Cortes. 2004. *Minority teacher recruitment, development, and retention.* Providence, RI: Education Alliance at Brown University.

U.S. Department of Education, National Center for Education Statistics. 2007. *The condition of education* 2007 (NCES 2007-064).

Walker. M. 2001. *When racism gets personal: Toward relational healing.* Wellesley, MA: Wellesley College, Stone Center.

Web resources

Department of Education Equity Assistance Centers
www2.ed.gov/programs/equitycenters/index.html
Department of Education: What Works Clearinghouse
http://ies.ed.gov/ncee/wwc
Interview with Beverly Daniel Tatum
www.pbs.org/race/000_About/002_04-background-03-04.htm
National Center for Education Statistics
http://nces.ed.gov
Preschool Teacher Gift Ideas
www.stretcher.com/stories/03/03dec01a.cfm
Valora Washington on Social Justice
www.uuworld.org/2000/0100feat4.html

Performing

Putting Principles into Practice

> For child care to be a healthy part of children's growth, parents and child care providers have to work together closely. The most important thing is that both parents and providers work together as partners to keep the child-parent relationship as strong as it can be.
>
> —Fred Rogers, *You Are Special*

> Call it a clan, call it a network, call it a tribe, call it a family. Whatever you call it, whoever you are, you need one.
>
> —Jane Howard, Journalist and writer

14 Every Child's Family: Building Partnerships

Case Study—Mr. Khan

Mr. Khan wants to enroll his children—Amin, 4, and Roshon, 20 months—in your program. Mr. Khan has read your mission and vision statements. He is attracted to your school's emphasis on respecting cultural diversity. Mr. Khan advises you that Amin, born a prince, will grow up to assume leadership responsibilities in their home country. He expects you to treat Amin as the prince he is and will become. Roshon was betrothed at birth. Her intended husband, back home and now 22, lives with his three wives. Mr. Khan expects you to teach Roshon to become an obedient wife and mother.

What are your feelings about Mr. Khan and his requests? What assumptions do you bring to this conversation? How might you honor his wishes? Do you want to honor his wishes?

We all know what family is. We instinctively

know what family is, based on our firsthand experience as a member of a family (or not having been part of a family). Our experience often predicts what we think a family is and should be. Early experiences imprint on us a powerful sense of family. Before we had words, we had family. Before we started school, we had family. Before we made life choices, we had family. Before we knew what a family was, we had family.

That knowledge is both the good news and the problem. Feelings about family run so deep that questioning our assumptions about family can be awkward and unwelcome. In this chapter, we will explore ways to learn about, appreciate, and partner with the richly diverse families in early childhood programs.

We are family

Children believe the world is as they experience it. If Mousadi has a mom and a dad, Mousadi believes a mom, dad, and son are family. Rico's foster family is Rico's family. Wentworth and his two dads are Wentworth's family. Mandy and her mom are a family. So interwoven is our personal experience into our definition of family that we develop deep feelings about what families should be like. It's no wonder that when I ask early childhood professionals about their core values, many simply say "Family."

Our feelings about family are so preconsciously deep that stepping back to get perspective may be difficult. Institutions that "just are" can be tricky to question. Have you ever found yourself acting just like your mom when you swore you never would? This deep, unspoken family connection can be explained in a neurological way (Lewis, Amini, & Lannon 2000).

As infants, our neurons line up with the neurons of our primary caregiver like iron filings to a magnet. Through this alignment process we learn from that caregiver what love is. If we are fortunate to be raised by a loving family, we are set for life to look for other loving people. Our neurons will line up in healthy ways. If we are not so fortunate, we can end up "looking for love in all the wrong places." Like those iron filings, our neurons will home in on empty places.

In this chapter, I invite you to examine the meanings and varieties of family. I also invite you to identify those traits in families that "rub you the wrong way." Is it the "high maintenance" mom, or the family who sends the nanny for the children? Can we find a connection point on which to build a partnership for the sake of the children, especially when we don't share the same philosophy or practices?

Marveling at diversity among children can be a delight. Marveling at diversity in adults can require conscious effort. When another adult embodies values, practices, and perspectives far different from ours, we can feel out of sorts. Each family we greet offers us an opportunity to grow professionally as we examine our attitudes and biases about differences.

Children and families come to expect that their future school experiences will be like their experiences in their early childhood program. The quality of the experiences a leader and her program provide to a family can contribute to or harm the family's trust in all future educational experiences. If a teacher or director decides that a family's values or practices are not acceptable, that judgment can negate the family's desire to keep their children in the program. What precedent for all future learning do we want to set for families?

EQ and understanding families

▶ EXERCISE YOUR EQ   ▦ Consider the chapter case study: meeting with Mr. Khan calls for emotional and social intelligence. Step back. Imagine you are sitting with Mr. Khan. Check in with yourself: How do you feel about his requests? What information does your physical response offer you?

Using EQ, walk yourself through the following process:

1. **Physical response?** Acknowledge your physical and psychological responses to the situation.

2. **Feelings?** Identify the feelings associated with your responses (anger, sadness, fear, shame, guilt, joy, etc.).

If the doors of perception were cleansed, everything would appear to man as it is, infinite.
—William Blake

"Home is the place where, when you have to go there, / They have to take you in."
—Robert Frost
"The Death of the Hired Man"

3. **Assumptions?** Ask yourself what information your feelings are giving you. Reflect on the assumptions you are making. Do your assumptions and values match the family's?

4. **Professional perspective?** Use this information to act wisely in the moment. How can you respond respectfully and professionally?

A common knee-jerk response to Mr. Khan's attitude is: "Who does he think he is?" Like a Halloween cat, some of us may "get our backs up." People who make a snap judgment like this tend to answer the four EQ questions in the following way or in a similar way:

1. **Physical response?** My jaw is set. My face is heating up.

2. **Feelings?** I am offended to be asked to treat his son differently from his daughter. I am angry.

3. **Assumptions?** That man is wrong! I am ready to make Mr. Khan the "bad guy." Stepping back, I begin to see that I am affronted because my core values (gender equality, individual freedom) are challenged. I assume each child deserves choices about her future.

4. **Professional perspective?** My amygdala is hijacking my professionalism. Adrenaline has robbed me of perspective.

How might we be more curious and open to hearing about Mr. Khan's cultural heritage and beliefs?

Later in this chapter, I will tell you what I learned from the seasoned midwestern director who actually had Mr. Khan knock on her door. Family members like Mr. Khan can challenge our assumptions about what is right for families.

We are not our feelings. Emotional intelligence theory reminds us that feelings are part of us, but they need not control us. Although a teacher may feel angry about Mr. Khan's statements, the teacher is more than her anger. The teacher's biased emotional reaction to Mr. Khan does not have to dominate her relationship with him. Stepping onto the balcony of perspective allows her to use the NAEYC Code of Ethical Conduct rather than be blinded by her own bias.

Since we all have our own assumptions about the way families "should be," we might find it worth our time to find out what other people's assumptions are.

Family: It's not just what we think it is

Exploring Glasgow, Scotland, on a quest to learn more about my mother's family, I walked through the gates of the St. Mungo Museum of Religious Life and Art and was enchanted. The museum explores the world's six major religions and the cultures, ethnicities, and religions embodied by the people of Glasgow. The museum showcases how families in each group deal with life's passages, in an effort to promote greater understanding and respect.

The first room I visited focused on birth. Our entry into the world is marked in many unique ways. One group plunges an infant into a pool of water in the ritual of baptism. Another group celebrates a bris, the traditional circumcision of male babies performed by a *mohel* (pronounced "moy'l"). A third group welcomes a newborn into the clan with a naming ceremony.

In a nearby room, I discovered initiation rites. Diverse "coming of age" family practices are lavishly pictured. Jewish 13-year-olds, with deliberate concentration, read

> We don't see things as they are. We see them as we are.
> —**Anaïs Nin**

> Families are of primary importance in children's development. Because the family and the early childhood practitioner have a common interest in the child's well-being, we acknowledge a primary responsibility to bring about communication, cooperation, and collaboration between the home and early childhood program in ways that enhance the child's development.
> —*NAEYC Code of Ethical Conduct and Statement of Commitment*

from the sacred book, the *Torah,* in the original Hebrew. The bar or bat mitzvah in Judaism is pictured beside a procession of Catholic girls in frilly white dresses, hands devotedly pressed in a steeple of prayer. Every Catholic boy and girl chooses a saint's name as a confirmation name. Turkish tradition crowns 13-year-old boys while cloaking them in the robes of royalty just before group circumcision initiates the boys into adulthood. At age 15, a Latina girl celebrates *la quinceañera,* the equivalent of a "sweet sixteen" ritual. Families work for months to ensure their daughters' *la quinceañera* memories will be treasured for a lifetime.

Other rooms display rituals and passages of marriage, growing into old age, and death. The diverse rituals of each group fascinated me. The universal acknowledgment of life's passages equally fascinated me. I stood for a moment, grateful for the gift the museum had given me—a glimpse into the meaning of family in all of its embodiments. I had never seen such an intriguing portrayal of family diversity.

Defining "family"

Since my time in Glasgow, I have asked students: "How do you define family? What is the meaning of family values?"

Over the years, my students have come to define *family* as "two or more people who share similar values and goals." Does that definition cover your family? Does the definition leave anyone out? Might it be too inclusive? Are team teachers a family? Are fellow devotees of salsa dancing family? Pinning words on an ever-changing, yet constant, reality can be like catching fireflies on a July night.

Given the diversity of families, what can *family values* mean? If a politician says he or she stands for family values, whose family values does that person promote? *Family values* most often refers to the desire to return to the good old days, when dad and mom were happily married, children were obedient and loyal, and everyone was of one ethnicity. Did such a family ever exist?

The history of the American family

Stephanie Coontz (2000) probed statistics on the American family going back to the time our country began. She scoured the data on a quest to discover if there ever has been an "all-American family."

Can you imagine what Coontz discovered? At no time other than during the 1950s was the nuclear family (dad, mom, 1.5 children, and a cocker spaniel named Checkers) ever the norm. "Not only was the 1950s family a new invention, it was also a historical fluke" (Coontz 2000, 28). Like Glaswegian families, American families have always been diverse: one-parent households, older children or grandparents raising children, foster families, adoptive families, extended families, same-sex parents, and religious communities. "Our recurring search for a traditional American family model denies the diversity of family life, both past and present" (Coontz 2000, 14). When we look to the past for family values, we discover, as did Coontz, that no one type of family values prevailed. *What would politicians make of this information?*

Labeling families

Have you ever walked into the teachers' lounge, only to be barraged by complaints about certain families, often referred to as "those people"? As a bright-eyed and bushy-tailed first-year teacher, I soon learned that negativity about families could rain on my enthusiasm. After a while, I stayed away from complaints about how bad Tommy's

Definitions of family:

1. A group of individuals living under one roof and usually under one head.

2. A group of persons of common ancestry.

3. A group of individuals united by certain convictions or a common affiliation.

—**Merriam-Webster's Collegiate's Dictionary**

There are two ways of exerting one's strength; one is pushing down, the other is pulling up.

—**Booker T. Washington**

father was, or how Tommy was just as hopeless as his father. Labeling a family negatively or gossiping about that family's foibles robs the family and us of dignity. Real people become cartoon characters, easy to criticize and easily diminished. In the end, everyone's integrity is harmed.

With the knowledge that families are naturally diverse and that no one type of family is superior to another, let's consider how to partner with every family we meet.

Labeling families as being "at risk" for abuse or neglect has been common practice. If you or your family were labeled at risk, how would you feel? Stigmatizing or isolating a family often begins with a negative label. Once labeled, the family might be pitied or shunned, categorized for likely failure.

The exercise **Finding Strengths**, from the Cornell Family Development Press, illustrates another way of thinking about families.

Preventing and countering family abuse and neglect

The Center for the Study of Social Policy (CSSP) invites us to take the approach for preventing child abuse proposed in *Strengthening Families: A Guidebook for Early Childhood Programs* (2007). Reading that guide, I was heartened to learn that 70 percent of individuals who were abused as children do not abuse their own children (1–8). I was heartbroken, however, to discover that the leading cause of death in the first year of a child's life is homicide (1–8).

Isolation predicts whether a family will nurture or abuse. As noted in the CSSP study (2007), "The single factor most commonly identified in the child abuse and neglect prevention literature is development of empathy for the self and others through caring relationships with friends, intimate partners, family members, or professional therapists or counselors" (1–8). Of all the institutions studied by the CSSP, early childhood programs played the greatest role in potentially reversing abuse and neglect by strengthening family resilience.

Instead of looking only at a family's weaknesses, CSSP encourages us to seek and build on a family's "protective factors," or positive attributes. Protective factors include characteristics like creativity, initiative, humor, intelligence, and access to good health care and a support system (see **Protective Factors** list).

As professionals, we can build on these family strengths. Connecting with a parent's sense of humor or with her initiative to want more for her children honors the parent. From that starting point of respect, we begin to build a relationship that could lead to a partnership for the good of the whole family, especially the children.

Asking parents the following questions can help you provide support when strengthening protective factors with families (Bruno 2007, 22–29):

1. What is difficult for you as parents?

Finding Strengths

One helpful way that early childhood professionals can help families build on their strengths is through "peripheral vision": the ability to see a wider view of a family's strengths despite the reality of the struggles. Sometimes a family's problems seem so overwhelming that it is hard to see their strengths, and even harder to reflect them back to the family.

As an early childhood leader, you often help the most distressed and vulnerable families in a community. It can be challenging to look for strengths while you also see the reality of struggles. Families can be overwhelmed by their daily challenges as well. They may be so accustomed to seeing their deficits that they might not believe you when you reflect a strength back to them.

How has a struggle in your own life helped you ultimately find a hidden strength you didn't know you had? How can we help families look for and find the hidden strengths in their struggles? When leaders believe in a family's strengths, this becomes a powerful tool to help families believe in themselves and their ability to set and reach their goals.

Finding Strengths Exercise © Dr. Claire Forest. Used with permission from Dr. Katie Palmer House and Dr. Claire Forest, Empowerment Skills for Family Workers: Instructor Manual. To order the original publication, see www.FamilyDevelopmentCredential.org/publications.php. The National Family Development Credential Program is located at the University of Connecticut, Pediatrics Dept.

Protective Factors

- Parental resilience
- An array of social connections
- Adequate knowledge of parenting and child development
- Concrete support in times of need, including access to necessary services, such as mental health
- Healthy social and emotional development for children

Source: CSSP 2007, 1–5.

2. Can our staff help you deal with these challenges in any way?

3. Our program wants to be a welcoming place for families—where parents feel comfortable asking for help. What are some of your ideas on how we might do that?

4. We are particularly concerned when parents seem stressed, isolated, or overwhelmed. How might we reach out better to parents in times of stress?

5. We want to make it easy for families to communicate directly with each other. How can we do that?

These questions can lead to rich discussions with many parents, not just the parents who may concern you. Sometimes the families who look the best on the outside are the families who are struggling most at home. A family's economic background does not predict the family's stability. Strategies for early childhood programs to promote healthy families include:

Of the 825,000 substantiated cases of child abuse or neglect in the United States in 1999, 14 percent represented children under one year of age; 24 percent represented children from ages 2 to 5.

—**The Center for the Study of Social Policy**

- Devote time to building honest, trusting relationships with the child's family.
- Invite parents to play with and observe their children in the classroom. Together, identify the child's strengths and needs.
- Co-create a classroom parent support team and a parent advisory group.
- Offer speakers and workshops on topics requested by parents, and include parents in the planning.
- Find ways for families to communicate and share resources directly with each other, for example, through a parent bulletin board.
- Pay attention to even the subtlest of indicators that a child is under undue stress. (Bruno 2007, 29)

Nostalgia for a more placid past fosters historical amnesia.

—**Stephanie Coontz**

Building bridges and capitalizing on family strengths is a worthy goal. In cases, however, where abuse or neglect is suspected or likely, our responsibility as mandated reporters takes precedence. If we believe a child is in danger, we need to work with other professionals who can step in to prevent abuse and neglect.

Abuse and neglect are unfortunately very common. During 2010, according to statistics from the U.S. Department of Health and Human Services, over 700,000 children were victims of abuse or neglect. More than 75 percent of these children experienced neglect, 15 percent suffered physical abuse, and nearly 10 percent suffered sexual abuse (ix). These "official" reports of abusive behaviors are estimated to be far lower than actual incidents of abuse, however. According to a 1995 Gallup Poll, almost 25 percent of surveyed adults reported that they had been victims of sexual abuse as a child (English 1998).

As a survivor of abuse and neglect, I would like to believe that families, with help, could break the cycle. However, I know through experience that not every family is open to change. In those cases, protecting the children becomes our priority.

Practices for connecting with families

The "ask and listen" process

The "ask and listen" process is common sense but not common practice. At heart, this practice requires us to step aside from our assumptions and judgments, to open our hearts to learning more about each family. This process works especially well when we find that a family member like Mr. Khan "pushes our buttons."

The ask and listen process has three components:

1. Bring a curious, receptive, generous attitude to the conversation.

2. Listen without judging, as if you were on a treasure hunt.

3. Acknowledge your bias, and then place it to the side, in order to fully hear the other person.

Have you been pulled over for speeding by a police officer? If so, he probably asked, "Do you know how fast you were going?" Does that question feel open-ended to you? Most likely, it does not. The officer already knew the answer. His radar gave him all the data he needed. Rather than asking an open-ended question, the officer made an indirect statement: "I know exactly how fast you were going. You were speeding." Although he is likely right, his approach, along with the ticket, can send drivers into a tizzy.

The "open end" of an *open-ended question* is an invitation to the other person. Curious people who want to learn something new ask open-ended questions. "Can you tell me about your child?" opens the door for a parent. A *redundant question* slams the door to further sharing. "Will you ever get here on time?" sounds like "You are always late." Redundant questions are really statements with a question mark at the end. The police officer in the earlier example was not interested in the driver's response. Most drivers get the message.

Our EQ tells us that consistency between the words we use and our nonverbal behavior is an indicator of honesty. Redundant questions rarely fool the listener. A scowling face is not an openly questioning face. The redundant questioner will be perceived as not being fully honest with the listener. Simple as that may sound, according to Myers-Briggs statistics, 53 percent of us have difficulty asking open-ended questions (Myers et al. 1998, 157–58).

Most of us want to be respected and accepted for who we are. We already know our imperfections, and being reminded of them can be painful. A parent, when asked a redundant question, shuts down. He not only distances himself, but he also may feel resentful or angry. A parent who is listened to carefully is much more likely to become a partner. When leaders "ask and listen," they invite the best from themselves and others. Effective administrators put aside being "judge and jury" and wholeheartedly connect with the parent. When we listen with honest curiosity, we are on the path to learning about family diversity.

We respond with openness to an open-ended question. We feel the negative judgment in a "redundant" question. We tend to avoid people who judge us negatively.

Suspending judgment to make room for wonderment

Malcolm Gladwell (2005) confirmed that, whether we want to or not, we make judgments about others "in the blink of an eye." Recall the chapter opening case study. Even if you want to be open to Mr. Khan, you may have initial biased reactions. Our early experiences lead to expectations for behavior.

For example, I expect girls and boys to have a right to the same opportunities. When I was raised, girls were shut out of career choices and boys were not allowed to cry. Ensuring that children will have many opportunities is important to me. Mr. Khan's culture appears to afford more rights to males than females. He asks if I will treat Amin as royalty while I teach obedience to Roshon. My gut responds, "No way!" My negative judgment leaves no room for wonderment.

What if, instead, I set aside my assumptions so I can *ask* and *listen* to Amin and Roshon's dad? Perhaps I could learn about the traditions, practices, and hopes of this man who differs from me? If I listen in wonderment, might I hear how this father loves

Ask and Listen Steps

Acknowledge the assumptions you bring to the conversation.

Set the assumptions to the side. This does not require you to let go of your assumptions. However, you do need to accept that, to another person, the glass may be half empty. Accept that you view the same situation differently.

Stay focused on serving children and families. Choose to learn about another family's practices, values, beliefs, and desires.

Find common ground. Seek points of agreement, ways in which the family's uniqueness can be honored along with the program's vision.

Name the differences. Level with one another about what appears to be non-negotiable (e.g., state and federal laws and regulations).

Review together standards and requirements set by laws, regulations, accreditation, and program philosophy. Together, find ways to honor the family's differences while acting "in the spirit of the law," or help the parent find another program that better fits the family's needs.

Bam!radio

"Bridging the Disconnect between Educational Leaders and Diverse Families"

Interview with Eileen Kugler

Heart to Heart Conversations on Leadership
http://bamradionetwork.com/

---

his children? That he wants what is best for them? That he wants to prepare them for success using the standards of his religious and cultural traditions?

The poet Samuel Taylor Coleridge suggested we take a "willing suspension of disbelief" to enter a realm of possibility. The ask and listen process opens that realm to us as early childhood leaders.

Immigrant Families

Interacting with immigrant families in particular may require us to set aside our negative judgments. Each family brings its own set of values, cultural heritage, and expectations. Your own family's values, cultural heritage, and expectations may be very different from an immigrant family's. For example, a Hmong family may be wary of Western medical interventions and prefer their own spiritual practices (Fadiman 1997). A Mexican American family may refuse to share family information with you for fear their relatives will be deported. A Haitian family may not want to talk about relatives back home who suffered grave devastation from the 2010 earthquake.

"We need to change the way we determine if a family cares," advises author Eileen Kugler(podcast). "A general announcement of a family night, even if it's in that family's language, may not be seen as an invitation to that family" Staff may need to make direct contact with individual families to ensure their participation. Kugler also recommends making home visits. "There is no greater honor than asking a family if you can visit them in their home. To have someone come to their home is a great honor." Some families hold educators in such high regard that they may not feel comfortable approaching an early childhood professional with a question or concern. However, if the teacher or director makes a home visit and takes the ask and listen approach, families may begin to trust more.

If you look at the history of immigration in America, you will see that most immigrant groups faced deep discrimination upon arrival and afterward. At Ellis Island, many families lost their names to an inspector who could not understand foreign languages. Japanese Americans—U.S. citizens—were herded like animals from their homes and businesses to be interned in camps during World War II. "Unsuitable" groups were given restrictive quotas, whereas far more generous quotas were afforded to those of Northern European heritage. Take a look at the laws sweeping our country today to prevent members of certain immigrant groups, particularly people of Mexican ancestry, from becoming citizens. "Give me your tired, your poor, your huddled masses yearning to breathe free" remains an ideal, not always a reality.

Given the pervasive negativity toward immigrants, families you meet often need your considerable time and understanding before trust can develop. If you become frustrated in the process, recall the difficulties your ancestors faced when they arrived on these shores. Kugler (podcast) advises that providers maintain connections in the community to "safe" services, including social workers and health services that will not place a family at risk of deportation. Partnering with community agencies can lead to more effective partnering with immigrant families.

Third space

Janet Gonzalez-Mena (2007) likes to call the relationship that develops between people "third space." She describes third space as "moving from dualistic thinking to holistic thinking in the face of what seems to be a contradiction or a paradox." She goes on to say, "If I disagree with something you are doing with your child, it's possible I have a blind spot. My blind spot leads me to consider our differing views to be a *problem*. What do I do?" (1).

Reframing the issue—putting it in a new "picture frame"—helps us look at the same picture in a new way. For example, Gonzalez-Mena recommends we reframe this situation from "I have a *problem* with you" to "You and I have *different views*." She credits Barrera and Corso (2003) for this perspective on third space: "A third space perspective does not 'solve the problem.' Rather, it changes the arena within which that problem is addressed by increasing the probability of respectful, responsive, and reciprocal interactions. In so doing, an optimal response to the situation becomes more likely" (81).

Can I share with you now what I learned about how to welcome Mr. Khan from these theories and practices? Instead of advising Mr. Khan to find another program, the director said to him: "I would like to learn more about you and your family's culture. Could you tell me what it means to be a prince in your culture?" Mr. Khan explained that a prince was responsible, accountable, and decisive. The director said that her program encouraged all children to learn those traits.

The director next asked, "Could you tell me more about Roshon's role as an obedient wife?" Mr. Khan, appearing to hold back tears, said simply: "Things are unsafe back home. You can never tell if your car might ignite with a bomb, or if the marketplace will erupt with gunshots. The wife and mother helps us all feel safe and treasured, and that life will go on. She is the glue of the family." "What are your hopes for both of your children?" inquired the director. "Ah," Mr. Khan sighed, "I just want them to be happy."

Did the director enroll Amin and Roshon? Yes. Did the children thrive? Yes. By asking and listening, the director and Mr. Khan found the best of possibilities in each other. A family that appeared unacceptable became part of the program's family.

That director taught me a lifetime lesson.

> ### Ask and Listen: Open-Ended Questions
>
> - Tell me about your child.
> - What is important to you in raising your child?
> - What activities does your family enjoy together?
> - What soothes or comforts your child?
> - I am interested in learning more about your culture. What do you recommend?
> - Tell me one of your favorite early memories of your child.
> - Is there anything else you would like to tell me to help me understand about you and your family?

No two alike: The ever changing American family

When the dominant culture prevails

How far can the willow bend before it snaps? When does valuing family differences seem to go too far? At times, our state, federal, or professional standards require us to enforce what is right for the majority while abandoning the differences of the minority.

In the early childhood profession, standardized practices prevail over individualized approaches in many cases. For example, universal precautions such as hand washing and wearing plastic gloves when preparing food are required. Class sizes are mandated. Child abuse and neglect are criminal offenses in this country. By law, we are mandated reporters of abuse.

Consider what you would do in the following situation:

Case Study—**Jessica**

New toddler teacher Jessica tells you emphatically that Ho Sook's parents must be reported for abuse. While changing Ho Sook's diaper, Jessica noticed bruises all over the toddler's bottom and lower back. Resolutely, Jessica states she must do her duty as a mandated reporter. As Jessica's director, what do you do and say?

Would you report Ho Sook's parents for abuse?

Unless the child is in immediate danger, you could contact the parents first to find out what might have happened. If you ask her, Ho Sook's mom would tell you about "Mongolian spots," blue and black skin pigmentation common among Asian, African, and Latino children. These spots typically disappear by adolescence. Taking time to make the call and preserve a moment for wonderment can protect the child, your program, and your partnership with Ho Sook's family. Jessica might learn that "ask and listen" works.

Imagine a different scenario in which Jessica notices red streaks down young Lia's back. Now Jessica knows to ask Lia's parent before calling social services. The parent happily notes how much healthier Lia is this morning than she was over the weekend, when Lia was "coming down with a cold." Lia's mother describes the "coining" process of quickly running hot coins in a line down a person's back to expunge illness. The parent explains that she learned coining from her mother, just as her mother learned the process from her grandmother. Jessica is now able to research coining, particularly as a Hmong practice.

In the process of learning about Lia's culture, Jessica can read Anne Fadiman's *The Spirit Catches You and You Fall Down* (1997) about a Hmong child's painful history in America. The child described in Fadiman's book was lost between the dominant (American) culture's medical practices and her own culture's traditions. According to American doctors, the child's parents were negligent. According to the parents, the American doctors were harming their baby.

When dominant and nondominant cultures clash, a decision needs to be made. Sadly, our country has a history of quashing the rights of minorities. During World War II, when Japanese Americans were interned in camps, they lost their homes, businesses, and often their self-esteem. Indian tribes and African Americans have also suffered unbearably. Even today, immigrants in this country, as well as the nation's poor, often get second-class treatment. Early childhood programs can be a beacon, helping our future generations diminish cultural misunderstanding and injustice.

Jessica can thank Lia's parents for explaining coining to her. She can also affirm for them how energetic Lia is this morning. Jessica and her director need to balance the expectations of the larger society with the desire to honor the family's practices . The director may point out to Lia's parents that mandated reporters—such as early childhood professionals, doctors, and nurses—are required by law to report signs of abuse. She can explain that not every mandated reporter will ask them about the origin of the red marks on Lia's back before calling authorities. For this reason, Lia's family may need to inform others on a "need to know" basis about the nature of the well-intentioned cultural practice.

Legal status of "the family"

Traditionally, laws have given spousal rights only to couples united by marriage, meaning married couples have rights unmarried couples do not. Laws have also defined marriage as a union of a man and a woman. This definition does not extend marriage protection to unmarried couples, including same-sex partners. In 1996, Congress passed the Defense of Marriage Act to nullify states' legalization of gay marriage.

Massachusetts was the first state in America to legalize same-sex marriage, followed by Connecticut, Iowa, New York, Vermont, New Hampshire, and the District of Columbia. Other states, like New Jersey, have instituted "civil union" status. Civil unions carry some of the rights previously afforded only to married (heterosexual) couples.

Worldwide, the legal definition of marriage is evolving. The Netherlands made same-sex marriage legal in 2001. Canada allows gay couples to marry without a residency requirement. This applies to same-sex couples of all nationalities. This changing definition of marriage and family carries over to early childhood.

▶ EXERCISE YOUR EQ   ▨   Do gay and lesbian families, staff, and children feel welcomed to your center? How many books in your classrooms depict all kinds of families? Is your program welcoming to transgender and transsexual families?

Where do you stand on this as a leader? Even if a leader welcomes all families, he may find that program families do not welcome one another. In that case, the leader and all families together can examine the program's mission in line with accreditation standards. In the end, families who discriminate against other families may choose to leave for more homogeneous programs.

Families of children with special needs

Perhaps you have read the story about the family who thought they were making a trip to sunny hill towns in Italy? When they excitedly got off the airplane, they discovered they had landed in an unknown country they had not prepared to explore. The story's sweet conclusion is that the family, although stunned, found many things to love about their unexpected destination. Families of children with special needs are often given a copy of this story by well-meaning professionals.

The moral of the story often holds true: each child with special needs is a gift to her family. However, painful ongoing dynamics burden these families too. The divorce rate in general is high—approximately 50 percent for first marriages—but it is even higher for couples with children with disabilities (Marshak & Prezant 2007). Depression is common. Guilt- and shame-filled responses like "What did I do wrong?" are natural. To say "I know how you feel" rarely is a comfort.

Case Study—Laura

Laura's mom, Mrs. Petrozullio, believes her daughter is perfect. Every time Laura's teachers attempt to share information on Laura's troubling behaviors, Mrs. Petrozullio insists: "Laura never does that at home. You must be provoking her!" Last Friday, Laura bit Alonzo; Monday, she punched Josephina in the belly. Today, Laura, refusing to sit with the others at circle time, began to pull belongings out of children's cubbies. Laura often talks to herself, making no sense to others. She rarely, if ever, makes eye contact. Laura's teachers, becoming anxious, want Laura to be evaluated. They fear Mrs. Petrozullio's reaction.

As director, what would you do? Would the "ask and listen" process help?

Absolutely. There are many times when a parent of a child with special needs yearns to simply be heard by someone who also loves the child. By calling upon your EQ to listen in all ways to Mrs. Petrozullio, you will also help Laura. You might ask: "Tell me what it's like raising Laura along with your other two children, especially given how different Laura's interests are from her sisters'."

The Americans with Disabilities Act, as amended, ensures that all children and adults, including those with special needs, have opportunities to grow and learn. Our challenge in early childhood is to find ways to support parents and teachers with all the extra responsibilities that attending to children with special needs brings.

Strengthening Families (CSSP 2007, 3–11) offers early childhood professionals the following guidelines for working with families of children with special needs:

1. Connect families with parenting materials and websites, support groups and play groups, and community resources specific to their children's special needs.

2. Check regularly with parents about their challenging parenting issues.

3. [Be] sensitive to parents' frustration, protectiveness, guilt, loss, and other related feelings, and acknowledge challenges.

4. Support parents in developing appropriate developmental expectations for their special needs children.

5. Check in with parents about the impact their children's special needs are having on family dynamics and parental stress.

6. [Be] especially supportive at the time that special needs are initially identified.

7. Provide speakers and resources [for parents] on topics of interest and concern.

8. Ensure that parent-child activities are appropriate for families with children with special needs.

I offer you this additional list of recommendations for working with families of children with special needs, based on my own experiences and research:

1. Ask parents to describe their child. What delights, soothes, inspires, and engages the child?

2. Provide factual feedback daily.

3. Share the good news along with the difficult news.

4. Invite parents to the classroom to play with and observe their child.

5. Ask parents what they do at home that helps the child. Learn from their experiences. Tell parents when their advice has been useful. Give concrete examples.

6. Together, look back over the child's progress, and identify patterns of behavior that may require additional help.

7. Have resources available (DVDs, websites, articles) as well as contact information (professionals, support groups, other parents willing to share their experience).

8. Instead of saying "I know how you feel," consider saying, "I can only imagine what this is like for you. I am interested in hearing whatever you want to share so we can work together. We both love your child."

Early childhood professionals can be an invaluable source of support and comfort to families with children with special needs.

"Perfect" families

Have you known anyone who grew up in the "perfect" family? Were you so fortunate? If I asked you to describe the perfect family, what would you say? One possible answer is, "I envision a family in which children and the adults who care for them are treasured, safe, nurtured, challenged to become the best they can be, and above all, loved unconditionally."

No one grows up in a perfect family, although a family may appear to be perfect on the outside. Dark secrets of violence, abuse, and neglect can lurk inside seemingly "perfect" homes. Be aware that children from seemingly perfect families may also be in need. As a leader, you can support your staff in learning more about how to recognize indicators of possible abuse and neglect (Bruno 2007, 24):

✓ **Abnormal startle responses:** Children respond to unexpected noises or movements with an instantaneous, fearful, and magnified reaction.

✓ **Memory and concentration problems:** When asked a seemingly simple question, abused children may look like little adults, frowning in concentration, as if their lives depended on getting the answer right.

✓ **Feeling worse when reminded of the trauma:** Children who have been abused often tense up in discomfort upon seeing an adult enter the room, such as when a relative comes to pick up the children.

✓ **Avoidance:** Neglected children, who fear revealing family secrets, may avoid situations where they could "slip up" and reveal something they were told never to tell. This reluctance can show up as resistance to new things, or even to playing freely.

✓ **Hypervigilance and hyperarousal:** Children with PTSD (post-traumatic stress disorder) resulting from abuse are on the lookout for danger. They may fret and worry greatly about situations in which they have little or no control. Relaxing at nap time may not be possible for the hypervigilant young child.

For helpful information on what teachers can do to help traumatized children, go to www.ready.gov/kids/home.html and www.nmha.org/go/information/get-info/coping-with-disaster.

Something I learned as a student in an early childhood class in 1967 stuck in my mind. "Your client is not the child, but the family." The teacher of that class, Lilian Katz, University of Illinois professor and a pioneer in the field, is the one who made that statement. I have never forgotten what she said, but it has taken many years for the field as a whole to begin to understand and embrace that concept.

—Janet Gonzalez-Mena

Parents out-needing children: "High maintenance" family members

Can you name a family who is not under stress? I cannot think of one. Every family faces challenges and stressors. Stressed family members can spill over their anxieties onto us.

Do you know a family member who is "high maintenance"—who needs or demands so much of your time that you feel in danger of neglecting your other responsibilities? Such people need a great deal of attention and care, and often they need useful information. Use your emotional intelligence to listen beneath the words. Ask yourself, "What does this person really need from me?"

As you work with such family members, the following process, taken a step at a time, will help both the parent and the program:

1. Give the parent your total attention for a specific, reasonable, and limited amount of time.

2. If advisable, set up a regular time to talk with the parent.

3. Assist the parent in meeting other parents with similar questions and concerns.

4. Help the parent find and connect with community resources.

Top 10 Family-Friendly Practices

Form parent advisory groups to allow parents to share new ideas and common concerns. Parent advisories can also advise the director on questions about how the program is doing.

Invite speakers to share topics of interest to parents. Popular topics include discipline, ADHD, toileting, what to expect at different stages of development, and activities to do with children at home.

Post colorful bulletin boards for families to share information with one another.

Provide opportunities for parents to use their strengths to assist the program. Reading stories, raising money, and participating in cleanup days are all activities that contribute to program quality.

Offer "Parents' Night Out" events, in which programs stay open late on Friday evenings to allow parents time together without the children.

Feature yoga and exercise classes on site for parents and children.

Provide spa treatments, offered without cost by local massage therapists and cosmetologists, to rejuvenate parents and alleviate parental stress.

Provide a family lending library of DVDs, books, games, and resource materials.

Provide additional staffing for the end of the day to enable families and teachers to talk while the additional staff members care for the children.

Plan family recognition dinners and events with food, transportation, and child care provided to celebrate the families in the program.

5. Enlist the parent in using his strengths and skills to help in the classroom or the program.

6. If the parent's demands on you become overwhelming, help her find another program that might offer her more individual attention.

In the best-case scenario, family members who need extra attention will evolve into your program's most energetic supporters. In the worst-case scenario, such family members may benefit from your assistance in finding another program that better fits their needs.

Family-friendly practices

Being "family friendly" means placing the needs of families first by offering services to reduce stressors and enable families to enjoy quality time.

Family-friendly programs might offer haircuts for children; dry cleaning drop-off and pickup; freshly cooked, nutritious meals to go; and sleepovers for children, all to reduce family stress. When you read about quality in Chapter 15, you will see how "total quality management" principles set the standard for anticipating your clients' needs.

Gwen Morgan, early childhood leader, discovered that a defense company in the Northwest pioneered in the use of early childhood family-friendly practices during the intensity of World War II. To help its labor force (many of them women) meet urgent U.S. construction goals, this company, Kaiser Shipyards, hired the most qualified teachers from around the country to care for the children, paid them generously, and covered their moving expenses and housing. Teachers were treated as invaluable professionals, with management listening to and implementing their ideas for improvement. One poignant image sticks in my memory: the program had special bathtubs, raised to the level of the teachers, designed to reduce stress on teachers' backs when bathing children.

Kaiser Shipyards provided 24-hour child care. A special care unit staffed by a medical team served children who were ill. Children and their families received free medical and dental care on site. A family's every possible need, right down to an extra shoelace or spare button, was taken care of in advance. The funding that empowered Kaiser to be so family friendly flowed from the U.S. government's War Office. Company employees built naval warships on site. No cost was spared to serve the war effort.

Today, military funding is dedicated to other efforts. Nonetheless, Kaiser's family-friendly methods can still be practiced. Using our EQ resourcefulness, we can engage parents and meet their needs without huge additional funding. Consider the family-friendly practices outlined in **Top 10 Family-Friendly Practices**.

Family as teacher, ECE professional as learner

In the end, as at the beginning, we have choices. Today, a parent like Mr. Khan may walk through your door. Tomorrow, a 16-year-old mother may seek your services. She may want to put her friends on the list of people authorized to pick up the baby. Each person we encounter will offer an opportunity to learn more about "family" in all of its meanings. Families who feel our respect and appreciation will readily become our partners in helping each child become her or his best. Barriers we put up to keep others out become cages for ourselves. Each child and her family is a gift, if we choose to open our hearts to the possibility. We just need to ask and then listen.

Directors have the opportunity to create with their staff environments where every child's family is welcomed. Consider how you, as a leader, would build bridges with the two families described below.

> Ideal 2.4:
>
> To listen to families, acknowledge and build upon their strengths, and learn from families as we support them in their task of nurturing children.
>
> —*NAEYC Code of Ethical Conduct and Statement of Commitment*

Case Study—Baby Emmaline Rae

Baby Emmaline Rae's father Wilbur tells her teacher, Luis, that Luis cannot change Emma's diaper. "If any man sees my daughter unclothed, she will be shamed," Wilbur warns. Wilbur and his family are dedicated members of their church. The church requires modesty, especially between the sexes. Wilbur has never given his daughter a bath, changed her diaper, or seen her unclothed. He relies on his wife and female church members, all of whom are strongly supportive. Luis is your best infant teacher. You are often understaffed.

What is your feeling response to Wilbur's demand? What assumptions do you bring to the conversation? How can you apply the "ask and listen" process? What solutions might you develop together?

Case Study—Scooter

School-aged Scooter enjoys being in your summer camp and after-school programs. A theatrical child, he will try on anything from a frothy wedding dress to a Darth Vader mask. He likes to wrap long, bright scarves around his neck and pretend he is flying like the Red Baron or dancing like Isadora Duncan. Ramon, Scooter's dad, is fiercely supportive of Scooter's individuality. His other dad, Timothy, instructs you to "make Scooter fit in better and act like a boy." Timothy and Ramon, at pickup time, find their son playing dress-up with girls while most of the boys are outside playing soccer. Timothy demands that you "tell Scooter in no uncertain terms never to play dress-up again."

How do you feel about Timothy's instructions to you? Have you felt "caught in the middle" like this before? What guidance does the *NAEYC Code of Ethical Conduct* offer? What is your professional challenge with this family? What steps would you take?

Reflection questions

1. In what ways do you predict that families in the future, 100 or 500 years from now, will have evolved? What, if anything, is "timeless" or enduring about families? What is most likely to change, or even become extinct, about the family as we know it today? Consider this: In 1977, sociologist Amatai Etzioni predicted marriage would be extinct by the 1990s. Prepare a representation (collage, drawing, poem, song, paper) that conveys your prediction.

2. Investigate the evolution of the family: since the beginning of time, what has changed and what has endured? Choose a particular ethnic group or culture. Re-

search ways in which that group's family traditions, practices, values, and beliefs have evolved. Write a paper on your findings.

3. Identify at least two types of families that differ from your own family of origin or your chosen family. Consider families that differ from yours in ethnicity, culture, religion, and sexual orientation. List what you would like to learn about these families. Interview a member of each of those types of families, using the "ask and listen" process. Summarize in writing the insights you gain.

4. Brainstorm as many family-friendly practices as you can. Identify what your own program is presently doing to be family friendly. Visit other programs or interview other directors to get additional ideas. Make a list of at least ten family-friendly practices that could be put into effect today. Estimate the cost (if any) of each practice. Present these practices to your class or colleagues.

Team projects

1. As individuals, write your definition of family and list your family values. As a team, share your definitions and lists. What do you have in common with your team members, and what is different? Research definitions of family and family values (online and through journal and other articles, books, and/or interviews). Present a report on the meaning of family and family values from at least three different viewpoints.

2. Research and discuss the benefits and challenges of working with families as partners. Identify situations in which you have both enjoyed and felt challenged in your relationships with families. Prepare three case studies of challenging situations with client families. Using resources such as *Young Children* and *Exchange, the Early Childhood Leaders magazine,* find at least five pointers apiece on how to partner better with families. Lead a class discussion on your case studies. Present the pointers you found.

3. Brainstorm a list of all the possible varieties of families (e.g., foster families, same sex parents, nuclear, entire village). Research the history of at least three types of families in American history. What legal recognition has that type of family enjoyed? What discrimination has that group faced? Present your findings to the class. Invite fellow woarkshop participants to speculate on what type of family will be the typical in the future, and what type will be most protected by law.

4. Many early childhood programs are homogeneous, representing families that have a great deal in common. How diverse is your own program, and how diverse would you like it to be? Identify programs with genuinely diverse families. Interview the directors of those programs to discover the factors and/or efforts that led to that program's heterogeneity. Prepare a list of steps early childhood programs can take to promote and ensure family diversity.

Bibliography

Barrera, I., & R.M. Corso. 2003. *Skilled dialogue: Strategies for responding to cultural diversity in early childhood.* Baltimore, MD: Brookes.

Bloom, P.J., & E. Eisenberg. 2003. Reshaping early childhood programs to be more family responsive. *America's Family Support Magazine*: 36–38.

Bowman, B., & E.K. Moore, eds. 2006. *School readiness and social-emotional development: Perspectives in cultural diversity.* Washington, DC: National Black Child Development Institute.

Bruno, H.E. 2003. Hearing parents in every language: An invitation to ECE professionals. *Child Care Exchange* Sept/Oct: 58–61.

Bruno, H.E. 2007. Teachers may never know: Using emotional intelligence to prevent and counter child neglect and abuse. *Dimensions in Early Childhood* 35 (3): 22–29.

Bruno, H.E. 2010. Building relational sanctuaries for children who suffer from abuse. *Exchange, the Early Childhood Leaders' Magazine*.

Christian, L.G. 2006. Understanding families: Applying family systems theory to early childhood practice. *Young Children* 61 (1), 12–20.

Coontz, S. 1997. *The way we really are: Coming to terms with America's changing family*. New York: Basic Books.

Coontz, S. 2000. *The way we never were: The American family and the nostalgia trap*. New York: Basic Books.

Crittenden, D. 1999. *What our mothers didn't tell us: Why happiness eludes the modern woman*. New York: Simon & Schuster.

CSSP (Center for the Study of Social Policy). 2007. *Strengthening families: A guidebook for early childhood programs*. 2nd ed. Washington, DC: Author. Online: www.cssp.org/reform/strengthening-families/resources/body/SF_Guidebook_2nd_Ed.pdf.

English, D.J. 1998. The extent and consequences of child maltreatment. *The Future of Children* 8 (1): 39–53.

Fadiman, A. 1997. *The spirit catches you and you fall down: A Hmong child, her doctors, and the collision of two cultures*. New York: Farrar, Straus and Giroux.

Gladwell, M. 2005. *Blink: The power of thinking without thinking*. New York: Little, Brown.

Goleman, D. 2006. *Social intelligence: The new science of human relationships*. New York: Bantam Books.

Gonzalez-Mena, J. 2007. What is third space and how do we get there? Paper presented at the NAEYC Annual Conference, 7–10 November, Chicago, IL.

Gonzalez-Mena, J. 2008. *Child, family, and community: Family-centered early care and education*. 5th ed. Upper Saddle River, NJ: Prentice Hall.

Im, J.P., R. Parlakian, & S. Sánchez. 2007. Understanding the influence of culture on caregiving practices. *Young Children* 62 (5): 65–67.

Katz, J.N. 2007. *The invention of heterosexuality*. Chicago: University of Chicago Press.

Keyser, J. 2006. *From parents to partners: Building a family-centered early childhood program*. St. Paul, MN: Redleaf; Washington, DC: NAEYC.

Kugler, E. 2011. *Innovative voices in education: What it takes to engage diverse communities*. Lanham, MD: R&L Education.

Lewis, T., F. Amini, & R. Lannon. 2000. *A general theory of love*. New York: Vintage.

Marshak, L.E., & F.P. Prezant. 2007. *Married with special-needs children: A couples' guide to keeping connected*. Bethesda, MD: Woodbine House.

M.A. Mason, A. Skolnick, & S. Sugarman, eds. 2003. *All our families: New policies for the new century*. 2d ed. New York: Oxford University Press.

Meyerowitz, J. 1994. *Not June Cleaver: Women and gender in postwar America, 1945–1960*. Philadelphia, PA: Temple University Press.

Myers, I.B, M. McCauley, N. Quenk, & A. Hammer. 1998. *MBTI Manual: A Guide to the Development and Use of the Myers-Briggs Type Indicator Instrument*. 3rd ed. Mountain View, CA: CPP.

National Center for Victims of Crime. 2008. Child sexual abuse. Washington, DC: Author. www.ncvc.org/ncvc/main.aspx?dbName=DocumentViewer&DocumentID=32315#13.

Powell, D.R. 1998. Research in review: Reweaving parents into the fabric of early childhood programs. *Young Children* 53 (5): 60–67.

Ury, W. 1999. *Getting to peace: Transforming conflict at home, at work, and in the world*. New York: Penguin Group.

U.S. Department of Health and Human Services. 2010. *Child maltreatment 2009: Summary*. Washington, DC: Author. www.childwelfare.gov/systemwide/statistics/can/stat_sexAbuse.cfm.

Web resources

Council for Exceptional Children Publications and Products for Families
www.cec.sped.org/Content/NavigationMenu/AboutCEC/Communities/Families/CEC_Publications_and.htm

Family-Centered Practice
www.childwelfare.gov/famcentered

Harvard Family Research Project
www.hfrp.org

Partnering with Families and Communities
http://pdonline.ascd.org/pd_online/success_di/el200405_epstein.html

Recognizing Child Abuse and Neglect: Signs and Symptoms
www.childwelfare.gov/pubs/factsheets/signs.cfm

> Please think of the *children* first. If you ever have anything to do with their entertainment, their food, their toys, their custody, their child care, their health care, their education—listen to the children, learn about them, learn from them. *Think of the children first.*
>
> —Fred Rogers, *You Are Special*

> The noblest moral law is that we should unremittingly work for the good of mankind.
>
> —Mahatma Gandhi

15 Quest for Quality: Professionalism Isn't Just a 15-Letter Word

Case Study—Gracie

During her initial 12 years with your program, toddler teacher Gracie performed well. This year, however, the quality of Gracie's work has plummeted. Gracie complains she doesn't have patience or energy to complete "all those nitpicky" classroom portfolio tasks. She has started to call in "sick" most Fridays and Mondays. She brushes parents off instead of taking time to answer questions.

Melvin, Gracie's team teacher, is exhausted from attending to all the things Gracie neglects. Today, you found Gracie nodding off during the children's naptime. When you bring these issues to Gracie's attention, she sniffs, "I'm depressed, that's all. What's a few bad months compared to years of giving my heart and soul to the children?"

What action will you take with Gracie? Might Gracie have a disability covered by the ADA? What questions can you ask Gracie?

Here's the truth: I balked when first asked to

present a seminar on professionalism. My unspoken reaction was "Professionalism? Ugh. That's all about rules and codes and dried-up sounding standards." My inertia wasn't helped by the response of students and a number of practitioners when I asked them, "On a scale of 1 to 10, how interested are you in professionalism as a topic?" Their level of interest was as underwhelming as mine.

Remember that not
getting what you want is
sometimes a wonderful
stroke of luck.

—The Dalai Lama

I thought I could graciously escape the request by recommending colleagues far better versed than I on professionalism, codes of ethics, and accreditation standards. Avoidance worked for a while. I was asked again, this time by an organization that wouldn't take no for an answer.

The time had come for me to face my disinterest in a topic I had mentally labeled "rule bound" and "uninspiring." I knew I had to drop my attitude to dive deeper into what professionalism and quality are all about. I began my quest to discover whether codes of ethics and accreditation standards could inspire people and, more than that, pulse at the heart of our work.

In my quest, I discovered something compelling. Professionalism is more than just a 15-letter word; professionalism is integrity under pressure. When confronted with a wearying, seemingly unsolvable conundrum, I can listen to the quiet voice within when bolstered by the written word without. In a profession where "Do no harm" is the heart of what we do, children's well-being always comes first.

More than just a 15-letter word: The Clarence standard

I call this my "Clarence standard." Clarence was an unforgettable toddler with a teen mom who was at school all day. In Clarence's world, his teacher was his second mom. Her love for him carried him through the day and, at times, the night. As caring as his teacher was, however, she also was repetitively late.

I can still see Clarence now, pressing his face against the window glass, positioning himself so he could spot his beloved teacher the minute she got out of her car. When the teacher did not appear, heartbreaking teardrops poured from Clarence's eyes. Sure, the teacher always had an excuse for her lateness (the car broke down, the cat threw up on the rug, her boyfriend needed something). Nothing, however, could take my eyes off the prize: Do no harm to that child. Be here to welcome him to his classroom home each morning. Clarence deserved that and more.

With the Clarence standard of professionalism, decisions come easily. Professionalism is doing the right thing, especially when there's an easier way out. Quality is providing children with the best of everything we can within our resources.

When is a profession professional?

Some people still question whether early childhood education is a profession. In their view, an early childhood teacher is a "glorified babysitter." Babysitters, after all, get paid for playing with children. I trust the Clarence standard of professionalism, but how will others trust that early childhood education is a profession?

Every profession works through the process of defining what professionalism means. What "value added" does our profession offer? What behaviors ensure that customers receive our best? What reputation do we want to have? These are questions that each professional organization must answer. As times change, professional standards change along with them. However, some core values are timeless. Those values will not change and can be said to "withstand the test of time."

As we seek to define professionalism in early childhood, we need to know what will endure. Stephanie Feeney (2012) summarizes her research on what makes a field a profession:

1. Specialized body of knowledge and expertise

2. Prolonged training

3. Rigorous requirements for entry and practice

4. Standards of practice

5. Commitment to serving a significant social value

6. Recognized as the only group that can perform a task

7. Autonomy

8. Code of ethics (24)

▶ EXERCISE YOUR EQ   ▨   In your opinion, how does early childhood as a field measure up to each of these standards?

In Feeney's assessment, the early childhood field meets the definition of a profession in some ways but not all. Can you guess the results of her evaluation? Yes, early childhood stands strong in having a commitment to serving a significant social value. Furthermore, the field is in the process of meeting the professionalism criteria in the categories of specialized body of knowledge and expertise, prolonged training, and code of ethics. We require additional improvement, however, in standards of practice, recognition as the only group that can perform the task, autonomy, and rigorous requirements for entry and practice.

Here's a challenge in meeting that last external standard: Do we want to exclude practitioners who do not excel at taking courses but excel as teachers of children? Feeney points out:

> As a field, inclusiveness and diversity are among the core values that bind us philosophically. Yet, professions are by their nature delineated and exclusive. One of our greatest strengths, our democratic beliefs, is an obstacle to moving toward exclusivity. This is one of the reasons that we continue to be reluctant to stake out a strong claim for the professional recognition we would like as a field. (2012, 26)

Does that leave us at a standstill? Or do we have choices?

Definitions of "professional" that embrace emotional intelligence

How does *professionalism*, so defined by external objective standards, fit with our understanding of emotional and social intelligence? After all, EQ relies on an individual's integrity in how he conducts himself and interacts with others. Can an objective standard, which can sound dangerously close to a one-sided IQ approach (thinking unencumbered by emotion), embrace and honor EQ's holistic ways?

This question is before us now. As a leader in the early childhood profession, you will significantly affect how professionalism and quality are defined. Standards for quality and professionalism must be "living." When standards are living, they embrace the heart and mind as no longer separate.

▶ EXERCISE YOUR EQ   ▨   Consider the following standard of professionalism from Wright State University College of Education and Human Services and how it explicitly incorporates EQ. In what ways does this standard connect the heart and the mind? How might a director "measure" a staff member's competency in an area such as this?

> *Teacher candidates and candidates for professional roles are knowledgeable, competent, and sensitive in working with diverse populations and in diverse settings.* Diversity is fused with the development of emotional intelligence and professionalism to facilitate sensitive and respectful communication in all settings. (2000)

The definition of quality in our profession will continue to evolve as our knowledge base and understanding evolve.

The foundations of justice are that no one be harmed, and next that the common weal (well-being) be served.

—Cicero

To me, professionalism is doing the best I can in whatever role I hold, continuing to develop relevant and up-to-date learning, sharing that knowledge, and working together to achieve the best possible outcomes.

—Jenni
Program director

Quest for quality: Who defines quality in our profession?

For defining *quality*, most professions turn to a central authority for the answer. Lawyers turn to the American Bar Association. Doctors rely on the American Medical Association. In early childhood, naming a central authorized organization is not easy. Our authorities on quality are professional organizations such as NAEYC, NBCDI, and NACCP; state licensing authorities; federal regulators and private organizations; or some combination thereof. Each of these entities offers valuable contributions, but none has the ultimate authority to define quality for early childhood. This ambiguity contributes to the complexity of understanding quality in early childhood.

Because there is no central authority for the early childhood profession, and because of the evolving nature of the field, drafting standards for quality is not an easy task. Objective criteria for quality and professionalism can display the dry elegance of a captured butterfly pinned to a scientist's display board. Instead of a fluttering and danc- ing creature, the butterfly is stuck as an inert specimen. As opalescent and delicate as this butterfly is, it no longer flies.

The point is this: In early childhood, professionalism and quality do not hold still. They grow and change as the field evolves and changes. Given the dynamic nature of our profession, can we isolate standards for quality that are timeless and enduring? Can those standards embrace emotional and social intelligence as a complement to rational analysis?

Definitions of quality that honor cultural diversity

"Top quality," "the highest standard of quality," and "first-rate performance" all aim to describe the best of the best. How does a director know her program is a quality program? In the highly interpersonal, culturally diverse field of early childhood, can external, across-the-board standards reflect the quality of different communities? When is one's "personal best" good enough? Must we be perfect to be professional?

Defining quality is akin to choosing a political party. So much depends upon our own view of the world. Stephanie Feeney, Nancy Freeman, and Eva Moravcik, authors of *Teaching the NAEYC Code of Ethical Conduct,* note: "To a large extent, professional values and ethics are an extension of personal values and morality, so we begin with those topics" (2005, 17).

Personal values predict our definition of quality. One director may see quality as treating each person who comes through her door as a special, unique individual. An- other director may understand quality as "crossing all the t's and dotting all the i's" on accreditation checklists. Incorporating Reggio Emilia observation and documentation techniques may be another director's vision for quality.

Most professions, as noted previously, rely on external, objective standards for quality—passing a rigorous test like the bar exam or national medical boards, for example. Relying on external standards ensures consistency. Yet this approach also brings drawbacks.

For example, if a person is not good at taking tests, should he be excluded from a profession? Picture a highly competent infant teacher whose learning disabilities prevent her from wrapping her mind around university courses. Does a director further or lessen quality by letting her go? Courage, caring, and integrity are key to early child- hood professionalism and quality. No standardized test today accurately measures these qualities.

Or consider one of my colleagues, Luis Vicente Reyes, who recalls getting poor marks as an infant teacher from external evaluators. Luis maintains his more physical, "roughhousing" ways are gender-based and particularly appealing to active, energetic children in his care. He felt the external evaluators unfairly held him to a female standard for care. Early childhood education needs a quality measurement system that honors and embraces diversity of culture, gender, and ability.

What is the verdict on professionalism and quality in early childhood education?

When push comes to shove, how do we know where "true north" is? How do we know the right thing to do, especially when people can't see eye to eye and the stakes are high? Thanks to our professional codes of ethics, we have tools for resolving dilemmas at our fingertips. Some of a leader's most common professional challenges include:

- Resolving differences when both "sides" are convinced they are right.
- Helping employees measure their actions by whether they are honoring professional core values.
- Enlisting the dedication and passion of the entire staff to work toward the highest of standards, including seeking and maintaining accreditation.
- Continuously assessing our quality, weeding out our shortcomings.
- Selecting from the variety of quality assessment tools available. Which ones are the best?

Let's continue our quest for professionalism and quality by helping a colleague, Mohammed, whose "team" is ready to throw him under the bus on his first day.

Case Study—Mohammed

Mohammed, new director of Kids Come First Academy, has taken the "outside pathway" to leadership. He was selected over several internal candidates, all of whom are female. The academy's board of directors expects Mohammed to "take charge of unruly teachers and turn the school around" to meet NAEYC's accreditation standards. Board chair Reginald lets Mohammed know that the prior director, Pam, was fired for failing to persuade teachers to complete required classroom portfolios.

Mohammed was attracted to the position because the school looks like the United Nations in terms of family diversity. As Mohammed prepares for his first all-staff meeting, he questions, "How on earth can I motivate teachers, many of whom resent me already, to dedicate themselves to quality?" Over lunch, Mohammed admits to you that he has never been the only male in any of his prior leadership positions. "How can I steer resistant teachers through accreditation when they won't even look at me?" he asks.

Mohammed's dilemma is not unusual. With evolving accreditation standards, as with any change, some staff members resist: "Who has time, with our already demanding jobs, to work on all those classroom portfolio details?" "Who's going to cover my classroom while I do all that documentation and fill out all those forms?" "You're driving me to burnout!" Directors, who aim to improve program quality while hoping to make everyone happy, find themselves facing the same problem as Sisyphus, a character from Greek mythology.

Fighting an uphill battle

Sisyphus's responsibility was to push a ponderously heavy, round rock up to the top of a mountain. He fortified himself, took a deep breath, and got to work coaxing the rock up the steep incline. Each day, Sisyphus toiled and sweated. Each day, he pushed the rock a little farther up the mountain. Regardless of how hard Sisyphus pushed or how high he aimed, the heavy rock rolled right back to the bottom of the mountain at the end of the day.

Leaders, like Sisyphus, often feel alone in their push to the mountaintop of quality. To roll the rock to the top and keep it there requires a team dedicated to the same goal. Persuading teachers to take a stand for quality, especially when that stand requires additional rigorous work, calls upon every bit of EQ the leader has painstakingly developed. The goal of this chapter is to team up to help Sisyphus roll the stone to the top.

Resolving dilemmas from an ethical viewpoint

Feeney and Freeman (2011a) offer these steps for resolving dilemmas:

1. **Identify the problem and determine if it involves ethics.** At this stage, we need to know the definition of ethics without getting lost in semantics.

2. **Identify applicable core values from the NAEYC Code.** Review the core values (discussed later in the chapter).

3. **Identify the stakeholders affected by the situation.** Who will be affected by the outcome?

4. **Look for guidance in the NAEYC Code.** Find the most applicable sections.

5. **Identify the most ethically defensible course of action.**

Identify the problem and determine if it involves ethics

Take a moment to identify the problems Mohammed faces. His ultimate problem is enlisting his team to dedicate themselves to quality by working toward accreditation. Along the way, he faces the problem of working with staff who resent him because he was hired as director while they were not. Gender may present another problem; Mohammed is wary of leading a team in which he is the only male. The board's expectations are high. Mohammed's predecessor was fired for failing to move the accreditation process along—specifically for not persuading teachers to complete required classroom portfolios. He may face insubordination if teachers refuse even to look at him. At the root of all these problems is this: Who is putting the best interests of the children first?

Next we must ask, "Does this problem involve ethics?" to continue with the first step of Feeney and Freeman's dilemma-solving process. Feeney and Freeman advise: "Ask yourself whether the terms *right* and *wrong* or *fair* and *unfair* apply" (2011, 68). What do you think? Is refusing to complete classroom portfolios a matter of right or wrong? Do the teachers have a plausible claim that their work with children does not allow them time for portfolios? Are the children in the program being treated fairly as a result of this unresolved adult conflict?

Stepping back to get some essential definitions may be valuable. What are ethics? Feeney (2012) counsels us to distinguish ethics from morality.

> Morality refers to beliefs about right and wrong that guide an individual's behavior. It involves what people regard as good, right, or proper; their beliefs about their

obligations; and their ideas about how they should behave…. Personal morality is influenced by the views of family, community, culture, and religious institutions; lessons learned from these sources are powerful and lasting. But it is important for early childhood educators to remember that we live in a diverse society and that people they encounter in the workplace may have different values and a different morality from their own. (63)

Moral codes differ. Our individual sense of right and wrong evolves from our background and what matters most to us. Could the teachers believe their resistance is right, based upon their moral standards? Teacher Vivian, a fair-wage advocate, may believe teachers should be paid for taking on major new responsibilities. Teacher Courtney's moral compass tells her that families deserve respect, which she demonstrates by professionally documenting children's growth and development.

Feeney next defines ethics:

Ethics are an extension of personal values and morality that involve examining the moral dimensions of relationships and then making choices between competing values. Professional ethics involve reflection on moral beliefs and practices carried on collectively and systematically by the members of a profession. The terms ethics and morality are sometimes used interchangeably, although ethics implies a critical reflection on morality. (2012, 63)

Got it: Moral codes are personal. Ethical codes are professional. This definition brings us closer not only to what defines quality but to how to help Mohammed with his dilemma. Sounds like although our personal values can differ, as they often do, professional ethics, like a wise elder, help us resolve our differences fairly.

Now we are getting down to something that matters. Vivian's and Courtney's moral codes may differ. Yet Mohammed can help them resolve their differences. Feeney and Freeman say the next thing to do is "decide whether there is an ethical *responsibility* (with only one acceptable response) or an ethical *dilemma,* a situation with at least two possible justifiable resolutions" (2011a, 68). What do you think: Does Mohammed have an ethical responsibility to push for accreditation? Or does he face an ethical dilemma with at least two possible solutions? Between the value of taking a stand for better pay and the value of doing whatever it takes to improve the program for children, does one take precedence over the other?

Identify applicable core values from the NAEYC Code

NAEYC's core values are to:

- ✓ Appreciate childhood as a unique and valuable stage of the human life cycle.
- ✓ Base our work on knowledge of how children develop and learn.
- ✓ Appreciate and support the bond between the child and family.
- ✓ Recognize that children are best understood and supported in the context of family, culture, community, and society.
- ✓ Respect the dignity, worth, and uniqueness of each individual (child, family member, and colleague).
- ✓ Respect diversity in children, families, and colleagues.
- ✓ Recognize that children and adults achieve their full potential in the context of relationships that are based on trust and respect. (2011, 1)

In your professional opinion, does Mohammed have an ethical responsibility to lead his team through the accreditation process, or does he face an ethical dilemma?

Are taking a stand for a worthy wage and going above and beyond for the sake of children, regardless of compensation, both values that are reflected in the NAEYC Code?

Mohammed could maintain that accreditation is based on the core value that "Children and adults achieve their full potential in the context of relationships that are based on trust and respect." Certainly, programs that qualify for accreditation will tell you the process brought staff, families, and children closer to achieving their full potential. Respect was raised. Hard work together fostered trust.

Likewise, Vivian could also maintain that the core values defend a worthy wage. Take a look: "Respect the dignity, worth, and uniqueness of each individual (child, family member, and colleague)." What next steps would Mohammed take if, in his professional opinion, he faces an ethical dilemma of two competing goods—worthy wage and giving our best to children regardless of pay?

Identify the stakeholders affected by the situation

The stakeholders are people affected by the dilemma and who therefore "have some stake in the outcome" (Feeney & Freeman 2011a, 68). The leader must consider: "What do I 'owe' to each of these individuals or groups?" (68). Who are the stakeholders at Mohammed's center? Everyone is a stakeholder. Children and families, staff, the community, the leadership, and the profession are all affected by the situation.

- Children deserve quality care.
- Families warrant respect and professionalism.
- Teachers deserve supportive and compassionate work environments.
- The board needs to be honored for their funding and support of the process.
- The entire community and the early childhood profession benefit from a program's success.

The director wants to do the right thing by all his constituents.

Look for guidance in the NAEYC Code

When two competing goods must be reconciled, look for guidance in the NAEYC Code. Here is the prism through which all other parts of the Code are measured:

> Above all, we shall not harm children. We shall not participate in practices that are emotionally damaging, physically harmful, disrespectful, degrading, dangerous, exploitative, or intimidating to children. *This principle has precedence over all others in this Code.* (2011, 3)

Mohammed knows that an accredited program has earned that status because it has met the high standard of doing no harm. Furthermore, accreditation measures a program's degree of success in establishing the next principle listed in the NAEYC Code:

> We shall care for and educate children in positive emotional and social environments that are cognitively stimulating and that support each child's culture, language, ethnicity, and family structure. (3)

On the other hand, the Code also sets a high standard of care and respect for staff. Specifically:

> In a caring, cooperative workplace, human dignity is respected, professional satisfaction is promoted, and positive relationships are developed and sustained. Based upon our core values, our primary responsibility to colleagues is to establish and maintain

settings and relationships that support productive work and meet professional needs. The same ideals that apply to children also apply as we interact with adults in the workplace. (5)

The Code promotes respect for diverse points of view, cooperative workplaces, and productive work environments. Above all, however, the Code holds the early child care profession to the central standard of doing no harm to children.

Identify the most ethically defensible position

By taking these steps, leaders like Mohammed will see what they must do. Mohammed's priority is to lead a program that meets and exceeds accreditation standards. Before he can get to work on that, however, he commits to sitting down with Vivian and Courtney to help them understand each other's values in the context of professional ethics. Mohammed decides that he will develop tangible ways of ensuring that teachers get the assistance they need to complete their portfolios. With clear goals in mind, he persuades the board to supply cameras for documentation, along with training and consultant support to get the job done, so that teachers do not lose energy for their primary responsibility of teaching. By the time Mohammed meets with the whole staff, he finds Vivian and Courtney have made his pathway easy. The accreditation process begins.

Functional versus dysfunctional teams

As Mohammed takes on the challenge of pursuing accreditation, he may also want to keep in mind the characteristics of functional versus dysfunctional teams. Author Patrick Lencioni (2002) compares the traits of these workplace teams in the adjacent chart.

Mohammed's staff appears to be lacking trust, commitment, and focus on achieving the collective result of meeting accreditation standards for a quality program. Lencioni advises, "A little structure goes a long way toward helping people take action that they may not otherwise be inclined to do" (2002, 214). Good news! Accreditation processes provide more structure than the frame of a skyscraper. Charts and checklists abound.

Functional versus Dysfunctional Teams

Functional Team	Dysfunctional Team
Members trust one another.	Absence of trust
They engage in unfiltered conflict around ideas.	Fear of conflict
They commit to decisions and plans of action.	Lack of commitment
They hold one another accountable for delivering in accord with the plans.	Avoidance of accountability
They focus on the achievement of collective results.	Inattention to results

The nursing profession's quest to redefine quality

To gain perspective, let's consider another service profession's quest to define quality. During the 1980s, I served as vice president for academic affairs at a University of Maine campus. The head of the nursing faculty was one of my direct reports, and our shared goal was to provide the best possible nursing education for our students and the communities they served.

Our campus had traditionally offered an associate's degree in nursing, but change was in the air. I found myself on the bumpy road of shifting standards. For years, nurses had been educated in hospitals through hands-on experience with patients. Hospitals granted students professional titles like RN (registered nurse) and LPN (licensed practical nurse). Missing from most hospital training programs, however, were courses that broadened a nurse's understanding, such as Social Determinants of Health (offered at the University of Washington School of Nursing). While nursing students could give shots and take blood pressure, they were not consistently exposed to the research and rationale behind the processes.

Quality varied from one hospital's training program to another. As a result, nurses were paid little. The status of the nursing profession was low, despite how hard nurses worked and how valuable their services were.

Low status and inadequate pay for hard, invaluable work—do these sound familiar? The nursing profession's quest for quality provides clues for the early childhood field to examine.

> Not everything that is faced can be changed, but nothing can be changed until it is faced.
>
> —James Baldwin

Bam!radio

"Underpaid Early Childhood Professionals: Finding the Path to Better Pay."
NAEYC Radio interview with Mark Ginsberg.
http://bamradionetwork.com/

Nationwide, nursing educators devised a plan to break the profession out of the low-status and low-pay morass. Their vision was to professionalize nursing so that no one could challenge the importance of a nurse's work or the value of her education. As the professional organization set standards to require baccalaureate degrees for nurses, associate degree RN and LPN programs were targeted for extinction. A rigorous curriculum was put into place that ensured exposure to the "why's" and not just the "how to's" of nursing practices.

Consider the nursing profession today. Notice the high demand for nurses, the salary increase, and the rigorous educational requirements. These victories were hard won. In the process, however, a number of "practical" nurses who could not transition into the new educational requirements were left behind.

NAEYC's rigorous accreditation standards, which went into effect in 2006, are reminiscent of the efforts made by nursing educators to uplift the profession's standing. What was gained and what was lost in this process of standardizing quality and defining professionalism through consistent, objective, and at times, impersonal standards?

As the early childhood field increasingly values emotional and social intelligence, its professional standards must encompass this knowledge. Note the difference in these two statements:

1. Revised standards clarify how we understand quality.

2. As we clarify how we understand quality, our professional standards change.

This is the chicken or the egg dilemma of defining quality, outside in or inside out.

An evolving definition of professionalism

Should early childhood follow suit with the nursing profession? What can we learn from their experience? Understanding the value of emotional and social intelligence holds a key to the answer. Our "bedside manner" is our ability to read people and to intuit what to do with that information. Early childhood practitioners may have PhDs in life skills but only a few college courses toward an associate's degree. Can the descriptions and photos in a portfolio convey that practitioner's competencies?

▶ EXERCISE YOUR EQ   ■   The definition for early childhood professionalism must embrace nonverbal, often difficult-to-measure, but invaluable interpersonal expertise. Capturing the quality of a caregiver's smile is like pinning a butterfly to a display board.

Remember the leader's challenge of holding two opposing values, one in each hand? The medical profession is taking note of two things:

- The high value patients place on a doctor's bedside manner
- Medical students' lack of training in this area

To remedy this disparity, the medical field is increasingly including EQ in its evolving definition of quality. This quest for quality is similar to changes occurring in early childhood. The field recognizes the need for professional standards that combine core competencies and interpersonal skills. Professionalism and quality are closely knit, so understanding professionalism can clear some fog.

In *Is Profession a Noun?* (2008), Gwen Morgan takes on the challenge of defining professionalism. Morgan "tells it like it is" in saying, "We encounter turbulence and discomfort when we try to give [professionalism] a definition." After painstakingly outlining the history and evolution of professionalism, Morgan concludes, "We need to make our meaning clear, especially in our own minds. To do this, we need to develop our 'only if's.'" She then goes on to offer the following guidelines.

Professionalism (in early childhood education) is a noun, but only if:

- Our knowledge base is free of gender bias and encompasses a valuing of caring as essential.
- Our professional education can enable us to relate to other helping professions and collaborate well with a focus on families.
- The recognized knowledge base meets all the needs for those in the field, including infant/toddler teachers, teachers of children with special needs, teachers in school-age programs, directors, family child care providers.
- Our concept is one of lifelong learning at all degree levels and beyond, with opportunity to gain in status and salary for individuals in the field through more learning.
- There is no permanent social class distinction between newcomers entering the field in assisting roles; [the lack of distinction] occurs only if they will be given opportunities to move into more complex roles.
- We can define a parent/professional relationship that does not rely on a status inequity, that primarily negotiates and exchanges information rather than imposing expertise.
- Our higher education system can offer access to many more group members with low incomes and minority group members, most of whom will be employed while learning.
- Our field would attract generalists who care about working with children, families, and community and would offer supports to enhance their work, income, and self-esteem.
- We would welcome diversity of cultures, races, and lifestyles, for both men and women. We would welcome, not exclude, and emphasize cooperation, not competition.
- The content of educational opportunities is both challenging and suited to the work performed.
- Our profession would develop leaders to speak out for our principles—valuing the uniqueness of each child and creating intimate, safe, and healthy environments for small numbers of children.
- We would view parents as colleagues (rather than clients, patients, or customers) in the task of raising a generation of active, healthy, and involved citizens.

Given the evolving nature of our profession, let's now look to the business field to see if its understanding of quality might help us.

Total quality management

Total quality management (TQM), in theory and practice, provides clues to quality.

Every time you are asked to complete an evaluation form, you benefit from total quality management (TQM) standards. When you find fresh fruit at a hotel registration desk and chocolates on your turned-down bed, you benefit from TQM. When you read books such as Paula Jorde Bloom's *Blueprint for Action: Achieving Center-Based Change through Staff Development,* you find TQM principles applied to the early childhood education field. When you review NAEYC standards for classroom and program portfolios, you also see TQM in action.

TQM views quality as a start-to-finish process of creating a product or providing a service that is just what the customer needs. Total quality management practice shifted the focus from the provider's needs to the client's.

This may be hard to picture, but prior to TQM, customers' opinions were not considered important. Manufacturers virtually held consumers hostage. When Henry Ford proclaimed, "They can have any color Ford they want, as long as it is black," he spoke for his times.

Competition pushed manufacturers and service providers to scurry for ways to distinguish themselves in the marketplace. Suddenly, a black automobile was not enough. The company that provided variety was the company customers preferred.

Three flavors of ice cream—vanilla, chocolate, and strawberry—no longer attracted customers. Baskin-Robbins became a household name when it distinguished itself by offering 31 flavors of ice cream in 1953. Does anyone recall a day when automobile companies did not introduce a new model every year? Shifting the focus to customers' needs and wants changed everything. TQM drove this revolution.

Total quality management, the brainchild of W. Edwards Deming, emerged after World War II. Deming viewed TQM as meeting and exceeding the needs of the customer by providing excellence in service and product. Given Henry Ford's attitude, Deming's idea of shifting the focus from the manufacturer's needs to the customer's needs was a radical notion.

Deming's ideas on quality, so readily accepted and practiced today, were not immediately embraced in America. Sent by the United States government to assist in revitalizing the Japanese economy, Deming took his ideas with him to Japan. The rest is history. Japanese producers embraced TQM. In a short space of time, Japanese products became synonymous with quality. Sony and Mitsubishi dominated the electronics market. "Made in Japan" came to mean a better product.

American manufacturers took notice when their customers purchased a Toyota or Honda over Lincoln Town Cars and Pontiacs. Toyota not only rivaled American car companies, Toyota outpaced all-American favorites like American Motors. Henry Ford would be eating his words.

This shift to focusing on customers is significant for early childhood programs. Customers, thanks to TQM, have come to expect not only quality workmanship and products but quality service as well. As service providers, early childhood professionals function in a world of TQM expectations.

What are those TQM expectations and standards? In a nutshell, providers need to practice these principles:

1. The customer is always right.

2. Anticipate the customer's needs.

3. Not only meet but exceed the customer's expectations.

4. Serve both internal and external customers.

5. Empower employees to make appropriate decisions.

6. Benchmark, or regularly evaluate, yourself, your service, and/or your product.

7. Practice continuous improvement.

Let's take these principles of quality one at a time to see what they tell us about quality in early childhood.

The customer is always right

When Mrs. Petrozullio declares that her daughter Laura is perfect and accuses you of provoking Laura's disruptive behavior, is Mrs. Petrozullio right? When Tedy's grandmother insists she has paid her bills, but you have no record of her payments, is Tedy's grandmother right? How about toddler teacher Missy, who calls in sick every Friday and Monday only for you to discover she is cavorting at the beach over her long weekends? Is Missy right? What could Deming have meant? How can someone who is just plain wrong be "right"?

With the help of emotional intelligence, we can find a deeper answer. What is the basic need of each family and child? Respect. Each person who walks through the door is worthy of respect. In this way, the customer is always right. That is, each customer has the right to our respectful attention.

I recently asked a group of customer service professionals: "Is the customer always right?" A young man shouted, "*No way!*" He was unwavering and certain that one family he had worked with was wrong. He felt his duty was to show the family how wrong they were. The customer service provider may have won the battle, but he lost the war. Had the family felt respected, they may have been much more open to entertaining other viewpoints. Admitting a mistake to a judgmental person is next to impossible.

Mrs. Petrozullio, Tedy's grandmother, and Missy all had stories that differed greatly from their director's understanding of the situation. Nonetheless, by giving each person the benefit of the doubt, the director respectfully moved from a "gotcha" attitude to problem-solving mode. This does not mean Missy's absenteeism was acceptable, nor was delinquent bill paying. However, by using social EQ and due process (see Chapters 3 and 4), a director can identify the underlying issues and assess whether those issues can be mutually and respectfully resolved.

Anticipate the customer's needs

There is magic in this principle: Anticipate and act on the customer's needs. If an early childhood education program can provide families with something they need that they have not yet dreamt of, a director brings magic to the moment.

Director Johanna in New Hampshire provides "sleepovers" for children when the stressors in their parents' lives overwhelm them. Johanna believes her job is to "make things easier for families to enjoy being with their children."

Have you ever received a gift you adored but never knew you wanted? For my 60th birthday, I invited friends to "surprise me" in any way they wished. Throughout that year, I received phone calls, cards, and gifts I never anticipated.

My favorite gift arrived via UPS from my sunny Miami colleague, Luis Hernandez. Luis graduated from college in chilly western Massachusetts and recalled New England winters with a shiver. His gift to me was a multicolored, transparent 14-foot banner of tropical fish. You can bet that in a heartbeat I unfurled those fish to dart across my ceiling. Every time I looked up, I smiled. Luis had anticipated my need—the warmth of the tropics in the ice of Massachusetts!

Early childhood programs have opportunities daily to anticipate and meet families' needs (see Chapter 14). Here are some examples directors have shared with me:

✓ Offer steaming cups of freshly brewed coffee or herbal tea to parents, sending them on their way with a smile after they drop off their children.

✓ Bake healthy oatmeal cookies or other snacks with the children. Send a bag of these treats home with each child.

✓ Create a cozy drop-off space for families, with overstuffed chairs and couches.

✓ Surprise parents with a special photograph of their child along with a "frame" decorated by the child.

✓ Schedule family nights with fun intergenerational activities.

✓ Organize trips for families to the child's next school to meet teachers, view the facility, and begin relationships to smooth the transition from your program.

▶ EXERCISE YOUR EQ   ▨   In our service profession, respecting customers and anticipating their needs are two indicators of total quality. Consider how you may have anticipated another person's needs. Have you, like Luis, given a gift that was longed for but not requested? What additional ways can directors "surprise" families by meeting their needs and unspoken desires?

Not only meet but exceed the customer's expectations

Every family has the right to expect an early childhood program that meets state licensing requirements. Clean surfaces, safe spaces, and a beneficial teacher-child ratio are some of the expectations families have that licensing standards require.

Licensing requirements set the basic standard, not the optimal standard. States vary on what that basic standard is. As a program leader, you will have the right to go far beyond the basics. Classrooms that are colorful and intriguing for children, with spaces for different activities, meet and exceed licensing requirements. Teachers who have studied early childhood and are richly experienced in and passionate about the field meet and exceed licensing standards. Offering chair massages to overwhelmed parents is not mentioned in any licensing standard I have read.

The **Stairway to Quality** helps us picture how to not only meet but exceed customer expectations. Accrediting agencies' standards are full of examples that show how to create quality services far beyond basic licensing requirements. Go to www.naeyc.org/academy to compare NAEYC's Accreditation standards with your state's licensing requirements.

Serve both internal and external customers
External customers

To provide quality, service providers must intimately know their customers. Who are these customers? Yes, early childhood programs serve children. As Fred Rogers reminds us, "Think of the *children* first." Our contracts for service, however, are not with the children but with the family.

According to total quality management principles, "external customers" are customers who pay for services. External customers come to programs "from the outside." Your job as a leader is to serve families while they are with you, in a way that supports

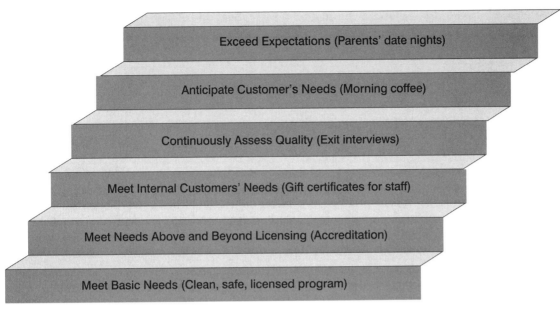

Stairway to Quality

and improves the quality of life when they are not with you. Picturing a program's external customers is not difficult. Finding customers who are not families, however, may be like a Where's Waldo? puzzle.

TQM theory expands the definition of customer. Not only do early childhood programs serve external customers, they serve internal customers as well. Who could these be? In addition to families, who else depends on a program's services? To answer these questions, picture others who need a director's attention and care.

Internal customers

As you may imagine, internal customers come "from within" an organization. Internal customers do the work of the organization. Teachers, custodians, part-time staff, cooks, administrators, consultants, board members, and other staff are internal customers. All of these individuals have needs. Internal customers may not always be clear on expressing these needs, however. Although directors are not mind readers, they may feel like they need this skill! If a director fails to anticipate, meet, and exceed her internal customers' needs, she can find herself in an unhappy organization.

Internal customers are members of an organization. Internal customers serve external customers.

The **Stairway to Quality** applies to internal customers too. Teachers' basic needs are a regular paycheck, a steady job, and a furnished classroom. They also need effective supervision, feedback on their performance, and interconnectedness with colleagues. They need recognition for their contributions and rewards for going above and beyond what is expected. Beloved directors anticipate and exceed employees' needs.

No pressure, no diamonds.
—**Mary Case**

Examples of meeting and anticipating internal customers' needs include:

✓ Hold annual staff retreats in alluring settings.

✓ Provide enjoyable team-building activities.

✓ Bring in inspirational trainers on desired topics (e.g., classroom management).

✓ Give out gift certificates to acknowledge special contributions.

✓ Pay for staff to travel and attend early childhood conferences.

✓ Mentor staff individually to help them realize their worth.

✓ Create a staff lounge, as comfy and welcoming as home.

What motivates internal customers the most?

Employees leave their jobs when one or more of the following needs are not being met: trust, hope, sense of worth, and/or competence (Branham 2005). How do directors help staff remain motivated when career choices are somewhat limited within early childhood programs?

Research from Harvard Business School (Butler & Waldroop 1999) offers guidance. Financial rewards do not sustain staff motivation. Although making a reasonable wage is crucial, being paid well is not the major motivator for most staff. Nor is being competent in a particular line of work. In other words, an employee may be competent at number crunching but not enjoy working with figures. Doing what we do well also does not necessarily motivate us.

Employees are most highly motivated when they are doing work aligned with their deeply embedded life interests (DELIs) (Bruno & Copeland 2000). DELIs include:

1. **Mentoring and counseling:** Helping others grow professionally.

2. **Managing people:** Motivating others to achieve success.

3. **Managing projects/enterprises:** Taking the lead on an endeavor.

4. **Translating technology:** Applying computer expertise to ECE settings.

5. **Theorizing:** Leadership on envisioning "big picture" innovations in the field.

6. **Number crunching:** Figuring out accurate and streamlined budgets/finances.

7. **Artistic expression:** Creating an original way to do the work.

8. **Teaching:** Delighting in contributing to growth and knowledge.

Identifying your DELIs is an important first step in being highly motivated as an administrator. Likewise, helping staff members uncover their DELIs revitalizes them (Bruno & Copeland 2000). The more closely our daily work aligns with our deeply embedded life interests, the more content we are professionally.

> The greatest good you can do for another is not just share your riches, but to reveal to him his own.
>
> —Benjamin Disraeli

Do you know a director who yearns for the classroom? His DELI may be teaching, not mentoring, managing people, or managing projects. His excellence in the classroom may have propelled him into administration. He left his passion back in the classroom with his students. Only in the classroom with the children does he feel renewed and uplifted.

Do you work with a teacher who enjoys helping new teachers develop? That teacher's DELI may be mentoring and counseling. A wise director finds ways for the teacher to mentor others.

Do you know a staff member whose clothing and jewelry are "wearable art" and whose classroom vibrates with learning experiences? Her DELI may be artistic expression. Intuitive directors will invite that staff member to beautify shared center spaces.

Honoring staff members as internal customers is a clue to staff retention as well as to quality. One director created titles to capture the DELI of each of her staff members. She dubbed one teacher "Creator of Special Moments," another "Family Comforting Specialist," and another "Bulletin Board Expert." Internal customer satisfaction directly influences external customer satisfaction.

Was anyone excluded from the internal customer list? Unless the director's needs are anticipated and met, the pivotal internal customer will be hurting. Self-care for directors, including participation in directors' support groups and leadership courses, travel to inspiring conferences, and vacation time away from the program, is invaluable for the number one internal customer: you. Quality begins with you. Add the director's name to the top of the list! For a director to lead on purpose, she needs to take care of herself, especially when demands on her are the most frantic.

Empower employees to make appropriate decisions

One morning, a janitor in a Richmond, Virginia, early childhood center welcomed a new family when no one else was available. Nothing in the janitor's job description told him to welcome visitors and put them at ease. Nevertheless, the janitor took time away from his assigned duties to greet the family and show them around the center. The janitor did what the program needed. He felt empowered to make the decision to help. Effective leaders create working environments in which employees feel empowered to put TQM into action.

An empowered employee is at ease making customer-friendly decisions in the moment. Most job descriptions include boilerplate, generalized phrases such as "Be a team player" and "Perform any additional tasks assigned by the director." Nonetheless, some employees take the stance that they will not do anything that is not literally stated in their job description. With TQM, employees know quality begins with them. TQM furthers the supervision principle to expect employees to take responsibility for their own professionalism.

Benchmark yourself, your service, and your product

The term *benchmarking* derives from the marks a worker carved onto a bench with a knife each time a product or process was successfully completed. Before calculators and computers, benchmarks served as record keepers. Henry Ford's Model T assembly line workers used benchmarks to tell the history of their productivity.

I often picture myself carving a notch in a bench when I complete a challenging task. On my office whiteboard, I marked off each chapter of this book as I completed it and again as I revised it. Seeing each tangible mark inspired me to keep going. Celebrations of accomplishments are another form of benchmarking.

My administration class visited director Nicole St. Victor at the Yawkey Center, in Dorchester, Massachusetts, on the first day NAEYC external evaluators were scheduled to review her program. Nicole wheeled out her program's portfolio in an impressive set of hanging files. Each of the 10 NAEYC standards was sectioned off in order. Within each section, Nicole had placed file after file of documentation on how the standard was met (see **NAEYC Program Standards: Nicole's Benchmarks**). Despite her in-depth, first-rate benchmarking, Nicole was still apprehensive about the evaluation. The prospect of our quality being judged as "passing" or "failing" activates sweaty palms for many of us.

NAEYC Program Standards: Nicole's Benchmarks

1. *Relationships:* Promotion of positive relationships with all children and adults.
2. *Curriculum:* Leads to social, emotional, physical, language, and cognitive development.
3. *Teaching:* Developmentally, culturally, and linguistically appropriate and effective.
4. *Assessment of Child Progress:* Ongoing, systematic, formal and informal, and shared with families.
5. *Health:* Nutrition and health standards to protect children and staff.
6. *Teachers:* Qualified, knowledgeable, and dedicated.
7. *Families:* Collaborative, culturally respectful relationships with families.
8. *Community Relationships:* Interconnectedness and support for communities served.
9. *Physical Environment:* Safe, healthful, and well maintained indoors and outside.
10. *Leadership and Management:* Policies, procedures, and systems implemented by qualified administrators.

Portfolios benchmark whether a program meets early childhood measurement standards. For a program to be accredited, the director must submit both an overall program portfolio and one portfolio for each classroom. A portfolio is a transportable collection of documented materials such as papers, photographs, and CDs. A portfolio contains all the ways a director or teacher benchmarks or keeps track of a program's progress toward established goals.

Consider the following example. In Standard 7, NAEYC holds teachers to this standard of effectively involving families: "The program establishes and maintains collaborative relationships with the child's family to foster children's development in all settings. These relationships are sensitive to family composition, language, and culture" (NAEYC 2008, 21).

A teacher's classroom portfolio would document in detail what she has done to meet that standard and may include:

1. The **teacher's written description** of her professional philosophy and steps she has taken to involve families.

2. **Photographs** of parents interacting with children in the classroom.

3. **Fliers** inviting families to program-sponsored family activities.

4. **Classroom newsletters** created by teachers with helpful information.

5. **Evaluation forms** for parents to complete on classroom quality.

6. **Lists** of classroom parents who serve on the Parent Advisory Board.

7. **Comments written by families,** including completed evaluation forms.

In these ways, a teacher's classroom portfolio benchmarks progress on effective family involvement.

▶ EXERCISE YOUR EQ   ▨   Select a different NAEYC standard (visit www.naeyc.org/ academy/primary/standardsintro). Develop your own list of portfolio activities that would show the degree to which a teacher has met the standard.

Benchmarking comes more naturally to individuals who enjoy details and order. Professionals with Sensing and Judging as MBTI preferences (see Chapter 4) find that documentation comes naturally. Benchmarking can stress teachers who prefer interactions to record keeping. Rather than hold still to record detail after detail, MBTI Perceivers often prefer to "live in the moment." Supervisors, who know each teacher's strengths and shortcomings, can help staff build on strengths to benchmark their successes.

Practice continuous improvement

"Resting on our laurels" is not part of the TQM equation. Deming's theory instead exhorts us to find ways to better ourselves, especially when we are at our best. How can the best get better? Don't we deserve a break from the rigors of improvement? When we hear from NAEYC that we have been reaccredited, we can take a rest, right?

Practically, yes, we can celebrate and enjoy our hard-earned success. We also can call upon our uplifted spirits to help us take a fresh look at our mission and vision. What is that next step toward our dream? Continuously improving and enjoying our successes need not be mutually exclusive.

Continuous improvement is always looking for and finding ways to grow and change for the better. Leaders who are not only open to but actively seek feedback receive the highest evaluations from their employees. This asking and listening is ongoing.

There will come a time when you believe everything is finished. That is the beginning.

—Louis L'Amour

Imagine a toddler classroom that receives great praise for its innovative curriculum. The teachers in the classroom, however, think that families could be more involved. Continuous improvement, for these teachers, means building on the strength of their innovative curriculum to find more ways to involve families. Continuous improvement brings a dynamic of renewal to the classroom.

Has a definition of quality or professionalism surfaced yet? At least we have clues. Quality is doing our best, within the context of standards that call for us to reach for the stars. Professionalism is continuously making choices to do the right thing.

A wealth of tools to assess early childhood quality

What other sources of quality assurance are available to directors? Fortunately, our profession continues to produce well-researched methodologies for assessing our abilities to provide quality care and education. These processes, called quality rating and improvement systems (QRIS), include but are not limited to:

- NAEYC Accreditation
- Program Administration Scale (PAS)
- ECERS-R (for programs serving children 2 through 5 years)
- ITERS-R (for programs serving children birth through 2½ years)
- FCCERS-R (for family child care programs)
- SACERS (for programs serving children 5 through 12 years)
- CLASS (for early childhood programs and school classrooms)

Each of these assessments takes a unique approach and/or targets a different audience.

The purpose of NAEYC Accreditation is to raise the quality of programs for all children from birth through age 8. The NAEYC Accreditation process targets the entire community affected by the evaluation, from teachers to administrators to families.

PAS (Program Administration Scale) measures the overall quality of a program's administrative practices. Originating at National Louis University's McCormick Center for Early Childhood Leadership, PAS is designed to measure and improve the leadership and management practices of center-based programs (Talan & Bloom 2011). PAS examines the continuum of administrative practices including:

- Human resources development
- Personnel cost and allocation
- Center operations
- Child assessment
- Fiscal management
- Program planning and evaluation
- Family partnerships
- Marketing and public relations
- Technology
- Staff qualifications

Environment rating scales direct their attention to what transpires in the classroom, both indoors and outdoors. The ECERS-R (Early Childhood Environment Rating Scale–Revised), ITERS-R (Infant/Toddler Environment Rating Scale–Revised), FCCERS-R (Family Child Care Environment Rating Scale–Revised), and SACERS (School-Age Care Environment Rating Scale) all originated at the University of North Carolina's FPG Child Development Institute. According to the institute's website (http://ers.fpg.unc. edu), they are "designed to assess process quality in an early childhood or school-age group." The website defines process quality as "various interactions that go on in a classroom between staff and children, staff, parents, and other adults, among the children themselves, and the interactions children have with the many materials and activities in the environment, as well as those features such as space, schedule, and materials that support these interactions." Environment rating scales depend on observations made by a trained outside evaluator.

All environment rating scales assume quality is dependent on:

• Protection of children's health, safety, and well-being.

• The building of positive relationships.

• Opportunities for stimulation and to learn from experience.

The Classroom Assessment Scoring System™ (CLASS) is an observational tool that is used to evaluate the quality of relationships between caregiver/teacher and child. Based on research from the University of Virginia's Curry School of Education, according to the CLASS website (http://www.teachstone.org/about-the-class), the CLASS tool:

• Focuses on effective teaching.

• Helps teachers recognize and understand the power of their interactions with students.

• Aligns with professional development tools.

• Works across age levels and subjects.

Together these assessment tools provide leaders with ample ways to measure the quality of their programs.

Taking a stand for quality and professionalism for all

Quality has many faces. One federal law, the Americans with Disabilities Act (ADA), aims to raise our ethical quality as a nation by requiring equal rights for the disabled. As we saw in Chapter 7, the ADA, as a relatively "young" law, sets a broad standard open to interpretation. Each case that involves an ADA issue furthers our understanding of ethical quality.

The ADA, as amended, does not require employers to hire or continue to employ a person because of his or her disability. The ADA ensures that anyone with a disability is provided with what he or she needs to have an equal chance to be hired, perform the job, and be promoted.

A disability does not justify poor performance. However, employers must make "reasonable accommodations" to enable the disabled employee or applicant to interview for and perform the job. The key question when hiring is, "Can the applicant perform the functional requirements of the job?" Once an employee is hired, the key questions become, "Is the employee performing the functional requirements of the job?" and "Have I made reasonable accommodations to help him or her perform the job?"

Nothing in the ADA condones an employee's violation of a workplace policy or releases the employee from disciplinary processes such as progressive discipline. Directors must determine:

1. Does the employee have a disability covered by the ADA?

2. Is the disability the cause of the poor performance?

3. What reasonable accommodations can we make?

4. Have I documented everything?

5. If I discipline this employee, can I show that he or she violated a workplace policy and knew the consequences for his or her actions?

6. Am I following ethical standards?

▶ EXERCISE YOUR EQ   ▇   With these points in mind, consider how you would approach the following case studies. How would you promote quality, and what is your ethical responsibility as you approach these cases concerning Bonita and Hugo?

Case Study—Bonita

Bonita, head of your school-age program and summer camp, confides she is a recovering alcoholic and member of AA. Bonita asks your permission to call her AA sponsor whenever she feels she is "slipping" into old, unhealthy behaviors like isolating herself or blaming others for her problems.

Bonita cannot predict when she will need to call her sponsor. She is clear she cannot work for you if she does not have this "pressure release valve."

1. What are your responsibilities to the program, children, parents, and Bonita?

2. Is Bonita's disease covered by the ADA?

3. If Bonita were still drinking, would she be covered by the ADA?

4. What steps would you take with Bonita?

5. How will your choices affect the quality of your program?

6. What sections of NAEYC's Code of Ethical Conduct are most applicable?

Case Study—Hugo

Hugo, recently granted U.S. citizenship after serving in Afghanistan, brings bilingual skills and a wealth of cultural competencies to share from his childhood in Guatemala. Children and families adore Hugo for his creative lesson plans, energetic playfulness, and compassion for anyone in need. Hugo is loyal, hardworking, and punctual.

Hugo appears anxious and disoriented at times. He gets red-faced, gasps for breath, forgets where he is, and panics. Hugo dismisses these incidents as "no big deal." He says his ADD helps him understand how to work with Annie and Angel, children in his class with ADHD. You know war veterans can suffer from post-traumatic stress disorder (PTSD). You are concerned for Hugo's well-being and worried he may neglect the children during one of his panic attacks, flashbacks, ADHD moments, or all three.

1. Name the ethical and/or legal issues in this case.

2. What are your responsibilities to everyone involved?

3. What questions can you ask Hugo?

4. If Hugo tells you he doesn't need medical help, what are your options?

5. If quality is your goal, what steps would you take?

If professionalism isn't just a 15-letter word, what is it?

At the beginning of this chapter, I invited you to define professionalism based on your own experiences. I also proposed the following definitions:

- Professionalism is doing the right thing, even when there's an easier way out.
- Quality is providing children with the best of everything we can within our resources.

Remembering Clarence and his sweet, trusting face always brings me to my heart's understanding of professionalism and quality. Who is your Clarence? What brings you back to knowing, with the help of your EQ, that you are doing the right thing?

Reflection questions

1. Choose one experience you have had that helped you deepen your understanding of professionalism. What happened? What issues were raised? What choices could have been made? Was the action taken professional? State your definition of professionalism as you came to understand it from this experience. Consider your definition in light of Feeney and Freeman's comments. Write a paper or create a video with commentary.

2. Do definitions of quality vary from culture to culture? Interview three or more people who share your cultural background by asking questions like "What is quality to you?" and "Can you give me examples of good and bad quality in customer service?" Summarize and assess your findings. Now repeat these interviews with three people whose cultural background differs from your own. Again, summarize and assess your findings. What have you learned about perceptions of quality?

3. Reread the chapter opening case study about Gracie. How do you, the other teachers, the children, and the parents feel about her? Imagine yourself as the director of the program and as Gracie's supervisor. To ensure quality, how would you answer the questions posed by the case?

3. In Chapter 3, you listed your core values. Revisit those core values and revise them into your professional core values. For example, if respect is your core value, you might list "Respect for the cultural differences of families, staff members, and our communities" as your professional core value. Once you have drafted your own professional core values, compare them with NAEYC's core values (*NAEYC Code of Ethical Conduct and Statement of Commitment* 2005, 1. www.naeyc.org/position statements/ethical_conduct).

Team projects

1. Each team member chooses a different profession (law, social work, veterinary medicine, physical therapy, nursing, etc.) to study. Research standards for membership in the profession. Read their code of ethics. Meet again with your team to share and compare what you learned. Select one important section from each professional code of ethics. Share your findings, and discuss what should be included in a universal professional code of ethics.

2. Prepare to visit and evaluate customer service at a nearby grocery store, restaurant, hotel, or other organization after asking permission from the establishment. Using the "stairway to quality," create a checklist of customer service standards and a set of

interview questions for customers and employees. Visit the service provider to assess the quality of its customer service. Pay attention to both external and internal customers. Upon return from your visit as "external evaluators," share your assessment.

3. Read the case studies on page 289 aloud to one another. Discuss your answers to the questions that follow each study. Use either the NAEYC or NACCP Code of Ethics as your guide. Write a team report on pointers for problem solving ethical dilemmas.

Bibliography

Americans with Disabilities Act of 1990, United States Public Law 101-336, 104 Stat. 327, enacted 1990-07-26.

Bloom, P.J. 2005. *Blueprint for action: Achieving center-based change through staff development.* 2nd ed. Lewisville, NC: Gryphon House.

Branham, L. 2005. *The 7 hidden reasons employees leave: How to recognize the subtle signs and act before it's too late.* New York: AMACOM.

Bruno, H.E. 2011. Eliminate whining in the workplace: Moving beyond "grin and bear it." *Exchange* 200: 93–96.

Bruno, H.E., & M.L. Copeland. 2000. Staff retention in child care using an internal customer service model. *Leadership Quest* 4 (2): 5–7.

Butler, T., & J. Waldroop. 1999. Job sculpting: The art of retaining your best people. *Harvard Business Review* 77 (5): 144–52.

Deming, W.E. 1982. *Out of the crisis.* Cambridge, MA: MIT, Center for Advanced Engineering Study.

Feeney, S. 2012. *Professionalism in early childhood education: Doing our best for young children.* Columbus, OH: Allyn & Bacon.

Feeney, S., & N. Freeman. 2011a. *Ethics and the early childhood educator: Using the NAEYC Code.* 2005 ed. of Code, reaffirmed & updated 2011. Washington, DC: NAEYC.

Feeney, S., & N. Freeman. 2011b. Misleading the state inspector: The response. *Young Children* 66 (5): 68–70.

Feeney, S., N.K. Freeman, & E. Moravcik. 2008. *Teaching the NAEYC Code of Ethical Conduct: Activity sourcebook.* 2005 Code ed. Washington, DC: NAEYC.

Hiam, A. 1992. *Closing the quality gap: Lessons from America's leading companies.* Englewood Cliffs, NJ: Prentice Hall.

Hostetler, K.D. 1997. *Ethical judgment in teaching.* Boston: Allyn & Bacon.

Hunt, V.D. 1992. *Quality in America: How to implement a competitive quality program.* New York: Business One Irwin.

Jablonski, J.R. 1992. *Implementing TQM: Competing in the nineties through total quality management.* 2nd ed. San Francisco: Pfeiffer.

Kipnis, K. 1987. How to discuss ethics. *Young Children* 42 (4): 26–30.

Lencioni, P. 2002. *The five dysfunctions of a team: A leadership fable.* San Francisco, CA: Jossey-Bass.

Martin, J. 2007. Do your customers love you? *Fortune Small Business* October: 72–82.

McManus, K. 1999. Is quality dead? *Industrial Engineer* 31 (7): 32–36.

Morgan, G. 2008. Is profession a noun? Unpublished paper. Wheelock College, Boston, MA.

NAEYC. 2008. *Getting started: Introduction to Self-Study and program quality improvement through NAEYC Early Childhood Program Accreditation.* Washington, DC: Author.

NAEYC. 2011. *Code of Ethical Conduct and statement of commitment.* Rev. ed. 2005 Code, updated and reaffirmed 2011. Position Statement. Washington, DC: Author.

Roberts, H.V., & B.F. Sergesketter. 1993. *Quality is personal: A foundation for total quality management.* New York: The Free Press.

Stonehouse, A. 1994. *Not just nice ladies: A book of readings on early childhood care and education.* Castle Hill, New South Wales, Australia: Pademelon.

Strike, K.A., & P.L. Ternasky, eds. 1993. *Ethics for professionals in education: Perspectives for preparation and practice.* New York: Teachers College Press.

Talan, T.N., & P.J. Bloom. 2011. *Program Administration Scale: Measuring early childhood leadership and management.* 2nd ed. New York: Teachers College Press.

Weiss, H.J., & M.E. Gershon. 1992. *Production and operations management.* 2nd ed. Boston: Allyn & Bacon.

Wright State University College of Education and Human Services. 2000. *The conceptual framework: Developing the art and science of teaching.* Dayton, OH: Author. http://www.cehs.wright.edu/main/conceptual-framework.php.

Youngless, J. 2000. Total quality misconception. *Quality in Manufacturing* 11 (1): 16.

Web resources

History of Nursing Profession
www.nursingdegreeguide.org/articles

Malcolm Baldrige TQM Award Criteria
www.tqe.com/baldrige.html

Mind Tools: The Impact of Ethics and Values
www.mindtools.com/pages/main/newMN_TED.htm#ethics

Professionalism: Developing This Vital Characteristic
www.mindtools.com/pages/article/professionalism.htm

Total Quality Management Background Information
www.bpir.com

PART V

Re-Forming

Renewing, Refreshing, Dreaming of What Might Be

> It came to me ever so slowly that the best way to know the truth was to begin trusting what my inner truth was…and trying to share it—not right away—only after I had worked hard at trying to understand it.
>
> —Fred Rogers, *You Are Special*

> Be patient toward all that is unsolved in your heart and try to love the questions themselves.
>
> —Rainer Maria Rilke

16 Leadership Principles to Take with You: Learning to Love the Questions

When I wrote this book and thought about

you reading the first page, I was clear in my intention: Acknowledge and honor the power of emotional and social intelligence in early childhood education leadership. In this book, integrity and loving relationships deserve the same, if not greater, respect that IQ has commanded. My purpose is to affirm that the profession you have chosen, despite low pay and status, is one of the most important professions on earth. Emotionally intelligent leadership in early childhood is a trust, a calling, as much as it is a career, and more than it is a job.

When you "touch the life of a child, you change the world" (teacher and scout leader Forest Witcraft). Likewise, as you help another adult bloom and share her gifts, you enrich the world. Every time you accept more of your true self, that perfect imperfectness, you heal everyone you touch. Early childhood educational leadership makes the world more welcoming for everyone, one child, one family, and one professional at a time. To make a difference, a leader needs to build trusting, respectful relationships, one person at a time, beginning with herself.

▶ THINK ABOUT IT   Stop for a moment to reflect: What affected me most as I read this book? What surprised me? What information will I take away to use in my future? How have I changed my perspective, affirmed my understanding, or both?

From my viewpoint, each chapter has an essential point, or "bottom line," shown below. Your perspective may differ. What key point did you take away from each chapter?

Reflecting helps you go forth as a leader. Now let's look at the remaining principles, data, and theories to further coalesce your knowledge.

Scientists have worshipped the hardware of the brain and the software of the mind; the messy powers of the heart were left to the poets. But cognitive theory could simply not explain the questions we wonder about most: why some people just seem to have a gift for living well; . . . why we like some people virtually on sight and distrust others; why some people remain buoyant in the face of troubles that would sink a less resilient soul. What qualities of the mind or spirit, in short, determine who succeeds?

—Nancy Gibbs

Leadership and the imposter syndrome

▶ EXERCISE YOUR EQ   ▦ Make a list of your daily jobs, functions, and responsibilities. Are you a family member? A teacher? An executive? A student? A breadwinner? A cook or chauffeur? What functions do you serve? Problem solver? Peacemaker? Innovator? Mentor? Devil's advocate? What responsibilities must you meet? Paying bills? Meeting deadlines? Organizing events? Planning the future?

Now, draw a circle. Look back at your list. Make a "guesstimate" of the percentage of time each day you devote to each job, function, and/or responsibility. Divide and fill in the circle like a pie chart, with percentages of time you devote to each piece (job, function, and/or responsibility) of your daily pie. For example, being a student requires what percentage of your time each day? Make that percentage a piece of your pie. How much time do you devote to paying bills and keeping your check register up to date? Make that percentage another piece of your pie.

Gwen Morgan uses this exercise in the management course she teaches at Wheelock College. As she always points out, the pie charts groan with impossible and overburdened percentages. Leaders never have enough time in the day to do everything they must do. For directors who feel they must be all things to all people, the question is this: What matters most? Leaders conduct continuous audits of their work, concentrating on essentials and letting go of inessentials. What does a director do if everything feels like an essential?

John Graden (2008) counsels that we all have the "imposter syndrome" at one time or another. With the imposter syndrome, we see ourselves as far less adequate than others think we are. We live in fear that someday we will be "outed" as imposters, believing: "If people only knew who I really am, they wouldn't think so much of me."

Graden's remedy for this condition is to pay attention to how we help children deal with "failure." We help children talk about what worked, what did not, what they accomplished, and what they learned; then we teach them to move on to the next step without berating themselves.

We adults, Graden observes, have never learned to talk as kindly to ourselves as we do with children—that is, to forgive ourselves (for being human) and move on. Instead, we carry on a repetitive inner dialogue berating ourselves for perceived failures. What does Graden say to himself when he cannot be or do everything he expects? He simply tells himself: "Cancel. Cancel. What's next?" (podcast). "Cancel. Cancel" stops his negative thinking. "What's next?" encourages him to take on a task that can be accomplished. Graden's pie chart may be overloaded. His emotionally intelligent approach, however, is to unload what he cannot do and appreciate himself for what he can do. So much of leading is letting go. As the 12-Step slogan reminds us: "Progress not perfection."

Key Points

Chapter	Bottom Line
1	Know yourself, inside and out
2	Understand how relationships "work"
3	Identify your purpose, direction, and leadership style
4	You have choices about how to make choices
5	Be knowledgeable about your first steps as leader
6	Partner with change and pick your battles
7	Prevent legal and ethical problems
8	Build a team of problem solvers
9	Supervise people to bring out strengths and turn around shortcomings
10	Be proactive and communicative in budget management
11	Create safe, healthy, inspiring environments
12	Understand how to promote learning
13	Spread the good word about early childhood programs
14	Welcome, learn from, and partner with all families
15	Quality is an ongoing quest
16	Expect the best as a lifelong learner and leader

Leader, manager, administrator, all things to all people: What is a director?

Bam!radio
"Feel Like an Inadequate Leader? You're Not Alone"
Interview with John Graden
Heart to Heart Conversations on Leadership
http://bamradionetwork.com.

Leader is a term loaded with meaning. Leaders help others envision what cannot be seen. A run-down building, like the spirit of a team, can be revitalized with visionary leadership. A talented teacher with low self-confidence might discover her strengths when a leader acknowledges them. A family, isolated from others by work, language, or unpopular beliefs, can find a welcoming community. An early childhood program can spring to life from a leader's dream. Leaders have power to make a difference.

In many cultures, standing out or identifying oneself as a leader is unacceptable. Women also sometimes feel uncomfortable embracing leadership roles because of gender expectations. My colleague and AEYC Affiliate leader, Marcia Farris, designs and holds successful early childhood conferences studded with substantive workshops and inspiring presenters. Marcia rarely designates a conference, course, or even a workshop "for leaders." Not many early childhood professionals, in Marcia's experience, identify themselves as leaders.

If not leaders, what then are directors? Some authors distinguish leadership in early childhood from management or administration of early childhood. Let's take a look.

Managers are responsible for putting systems in place and making sure those systems, like supervision and budgeting, proceed effectively. A manager's focus is to run a smooth operation in line with established goals. Management differs from leadership in the amount of vision and initiative required. Managers are more responsible for the operation than for the creation of the vision. Managers have leeway to make changes mainly in their own area. An educational or curriculum coordinator can make supervision decisions, but rarely will make budgetary decisions.

Stephen Covey used a ladder to illustrate the difference between leadership and management in his book, *The 7 Habits of Highly Effective People*. Management is concerned with getting up a ladder in the most effective and most efficient manner. Leadership is making certain the ladder is on the right wall.

—**www.leadershipjot.com**

Administrators are implementers. Administrators attend every day to whatever needs to be done. They follow policies, implement procedures, and take care of nitty-gritty tasks to keep the program on track. Focused on routine duties, administrators rarely have time or feel authorized to make long-term, substantial changes. Someone else sets the vision (the leader) and takes care of putting systems into place (the manager). The administrator orders supplies, deals with complaints, winds weary old clocks, plunges the toilet, and makes sure teachers get paychecks on time.

Leaders "keep their eyes on the prize." Administrators "keep their noses to the grindstone."

Leaders step back to get perspective and step up to the challenge of promoting change. Administrators take care of everyday business. Leaders determine the purpose and future of the organization. Debra Ren-Etta Sullivan (2010), in her book *Learning to Lead: Effective Leadership Skills for Teachers of Young Children*, notes that leaders plan, while administrators carry out plans.

▶ EXERCISE YOUR EQ   ▪ What do you think: If you had to select one of the following three descriptions, would you say an early childhood director is a leader, a manager, or an administrator?

Directors report they are all of these. Directors want more time to serve as leaders and less time putting out fires. Directors long for time to plan and create new directions. This is the dilemma of early childhood leaders—choosing priorities that are true to their purpose.

When we work "on purpose," we lead. When work takes leaders off purpose, they feel as if they are just performing tasks and doing a job. Interestingly, burnout results from the loss of meaning in our work. How can a director deal effectively with all the demands on his time and still make time for "big picture" changes? Keep your eyes on the prize of what matters to you most, and learn to delegate wisely.

Delegation, assigning a task to another and letting go of attempting to control the other person's process, requires EQ and social EQ. When a leader identifies her purpose and priorities, she exercises EQ. When she "reads" her staff well, helping them grow as professionals, she identifies who best will handle delegated tasks. Her social EQ is knowledge of staff strengths, motivation, and blind spots. Knowing what, when, and to whom to delegate is part of the art of leadership. Remember what Jeree Pawl said: "I've been doing supervision for 40 years, and I am just beginning to get the hang of it."

Striving to be emotionally and socially intelligent as a leader—is that enough? Will being a lifelong learner carry leaders through the times when they know little or nothing about a new subject?

New ways of seeing old things
Debating the worth of emotional and social intelligence

The study of the theory of emotional and social EQ sets off passionate reactions, both for and against.

Some critics argue that EQ is unsubstantiated by rigorous scientific analysis and that it is little more than cotton candy. They question the existence and/or value of emotional intelligence. Goleman's work, in particular, has come under criticism. Psychologist Hans Eysenck lambastes Goleman's theories in this way:

> [Goleman] exemplifies more clearly than most the fundamental absurdity of the tendency to class almost any type of behaviour as an "intelligence" . . . the whole theory is built on quicksand; there is no sound scientific basis. (2000, 109)

A growing body of scientific research, however, shows support in favor of EQ theory (Cherniss et al. 2006; Viadero 2007). The data show a strong link between EQ and real-world success, both for kids in the classroom and adults in the workplace. The most successful individuals aren't "solo performers" with a high IQ and internal drive; rather, they are team builders who stay calm under pressure and know how to get along with others. Neuroscience studies also are exploring the neural differences between EQ and IQ behaviors and the dynamic relationship between the brain and social interaction (see Chapter 4).

As you read both support and criticism for Goleman's theory, how does it affect your view of EQ and social EQ? You will have ample opportunities as an early childhood professional to hear about and participate in this ongoing debate.

Throughout this book, I have noted the leadership dilemma of holding two opposite beliefs, often warring theories, one in each hand. You might feel as you attempt this that you are holding two yowling cats back from fisticuffs. On the one hand, EQ is invaluable. On the other hand, EQ is an unscientific fraud. Any new theory, fairly enough, will come under scrutiny and possible attack. Remember the percentage of individuals who welcome change?

I propose we consider both IQ and EQ as a "both...and" rather than an "either...or." Both definitions of intelligence have their merit and their place. One does not have to exclude the other. At times, a leader needs to exercise the "letter of the law" (impersonal, objective, and intellectually critical) approach to decision making. At other times, leaders need to use the "spirit of the law" in managing through relationships, accepting and working through all the unspoken, synaptic (neuron-to-neuron), and emotional communication modes available.

The early childhood profession works hard to earn respect. It documents, assesses, codifies, analyzes, and otherwise applies traditional "hard" scientific approaches to the field. The NAEYC Early Childhood Program Standards and accreditation criteria (2008) exemplify that desire to professionalize beyond reproach. Hard data is persuasive. Rigorous, rational approaches earn respect. "Soft," or nonscientific, approaches remain suspect. Perhaps we could take the best from both approaches, rather than use one to negate the other.

What if we paid attention to this Native American proverb? "Treat the earth well. It was not given to you by your parents; it was loaned to you by your children."

Rediscovering traditional ways of communicating EQ principles

Because theories of emotional and social intelligence have been considered soft rather than hard scientific knowledge, EQ has flourished more outside the university than within the walls of ivy. EQ and social EQ have been the heart of ethnic leadership wisdom for centuries. When we want to "get to the heart" of a matter, we often turn to Native American elders.

Examples of this are plentiful. Black Elk knew that "Grown men can learn from very little children, for the hearts of the little children are pure. Therefore, the Great Spirit may show to them many things which older people miss." Crazy Horse spelled out this core leadership principle: "A very great vision is needed, and the man who has it must follow it as the eagle seeks the deepest blue of the sky." Chief Seattle forewarned, "All things share the same breath—the beast, the tree, the man, the air shares its spirit with all the life it supports."

EQ wisdom is passed down from our elders and soothsayers (truth tellers) through oral tradition, poetry, fables, parables, and song more than through academic textbooks. If you can sing or recite your favorite song lyrics or poem, you invoke that wisdom. "'Beauty is truth, truth, beauty'—that is all ye know on earth, and all ye need to know," wrote John Keats in his poem *Ode on a Grecian Urn* (1819). The quotations sprinkled throughout this book summarize in a few lyrical words the heart of emotional and social EQ.

▶ EXERCISE YOUR EQ   ▪ Recall the message of your favorite children's book. What "life lessons" does that book pass on to children?

Children's book authors create in the realm of EQ and social EQ. *The Velveteen Rabbit* (1922), tattered and aged, is still heartachingly loveable. On Miss Tizzy's block (1993), everyone matters and everyone looks out for one another. *And Tango Makes Three* (2005) reminds us that love makes a family. *Where the Wild Things Are* (1963) comforts us with the message that we all have a wild side and the wild side is nothing to fear. We remember what touches our heart. Facts can fade, meaning remains. *I Love You, Stinky Face* (1997) lets a child know she will always be loved, no matter what.

Wisdom gives rise to courage. Courage gives rise to compassion. Compassion gives rise to wisdom.
—Daisaku Ikeda

"Soft" knowledge can carry us through our hardest times. We remember what touches our heart. Facts can fade, meaning remains.

Nonverbal, nonneural, or both?

Naming something for the first time changes the way we see things. To consider EQ and social EQ, we need to examine assumptions. Consider the well-established term *nonverbal.* Think of what the term indicates: the multitude of ways we communicate without words. Now consider the term *neural.* Neural, or *synaptic,* indicates all the ways our neurons constantly communicate before that communication turns into words.

Mistakes are the portals of discovery.
—James Joyce

The majority (65 to 90 percent) of our communication takes place through neural, rather than verbal, connection. Our most used form of communication is labeled by what it is not (nonverbal) rather than what it is (neural). What if we chisel our terminology more accurately before we "write it in stone"? The term *nonverbal* is, in some ways, backward.

To be accurate, we communicate both neurally and nonneurally. Neural communication, not verbal communication, serves as our first language. We respond neurally in a split second. Since neural communication is the standard communication, other forms of communication should be described accordingly. The term *nonverbal* is not expansive enough to describe all the neural forms of communication. *Nonverbal* conveys what is lacking in neural communication. *Neural* conveys the enormity of what takes place.

Words, rich as they can be, are nonneural communication. Words are the best known nonneural mode of communication. Words matter most when they spark synaptic connections. Otherwise, words "fall on deaf ears." To follow suit, words can be termed nonneural, or verbal, communication.

This difference may sound like semantics—just more words. However, when we accurately name something, that naming communicates meaning. The next time you hear the term *nonverbal,* consider the more accurate term, *neural.* Changing the terms we use is like any other change; resistance is inevitable. Nonetheless, changing the way we look at things opens us to the future.

> People are like stained-glass windows. They sparkle and shine when the sun is out, but when the darkness sets in, their true beauty is revealed only if there is a light from within.
>
> —Elizabeth Kübler-Ross

Leadership principles to take with you

▶ EXERCISE YOUR EQ   ▓   Make a list of the traits you feel a good leader needs to have. Which of these traits reflect your areas of strength? Which of these traits would you like to develop in yourself?

Good boss versus bad boss

In light of the list you just made, see what you think of the **Good Boss versus Bad Boss** list, which outlines the ways effective leaders differ from ineffective leaders (Goleman 2006, 277).

The "good boss" list describes traits of an effective relational leader. The "bad boss" list describes a person who cannot yet bring self-knowledge or empathy into relationships. Consider the following good boss traits as leadership principles.

Tell the truth lovingly

> It doesn't hurt to be optimistic. You can always cry later.
>
> —Lucimar Santos de Lima

Researcher and author Antonio DiMasio (2005) notes that joy, or freedom from stress and worry, opens us to learn more. Joyousness, optimism, and enthusiasm are all neurological "maximal harmonious states" according to DiMasio. Another researcher, Lisa Aspinal (1998), finds that when we are confident and upbeat, we are more able to seek out and take in information, even if the information is difficult to hear.

These principles readily apply to the leader as supervisor. Goleman (2006, 277) notes: "If leaders establish such trust and safety, then when they give tough feedback, the person receiving it not only stays more open but sees benefit in getting even hard-to-take information." Much of leadership is helping others see. Telling the truth lovingly creates trust and safety for change.

> **Bam!radio**
> "Good Boss, Bad Boss: Which One Are You?"
> Interview with Robert Sutton
> *Heart to Heart Conversations on Leadership*
> http://bamradionetwork.com.

Lead with integrity

"Walking the talk," not asking others to do what you wouldn't do, and living on purpose all evidence integrity. A good boss leads with integrity. A good (early childhood) boss spends a good deal of time helping others find their gifts and outgrow their weak points. Shaming, blaming, and threatening are ineffective. Leveling with others, by leveling with yourself first, allows you to exercise your integrity. The difference will be felt and appreciated.

Let's compare the characteristics of good and bad bosses with recent research findings on characteristics of the leader as mentor (DeLong, Gabarro, & Lees 2008). A good mentor:

Good Boss versus Bad Boss	
Good Boss	**Bad Boss**
Great listener	Blank wall
Encourager	Doubter
Communicator	Secretive
Courageous	Intimidating
Sense of humor	Bad temper
Shows empathy	Self-centered
Decisive	Indecisive
Takes responsibility	Blames
Humble	Arrogant
Shares authority	Mistrusts

- Is someone absolutely credible whose integrity transcends the message, be it positive or negative.
- Tells you things you may not want to hear but leaves you feeling you have been heard.
- Interacts with you in a way that makes you want to become better.
- Makes you feel secure enough to take risks.
- Gives you the confidence to rise above your inner doubts and fears.
- Supports your attempts to set stretch goals for yourself.
- Presents opportunities and highlights challenges you might not have seen on your own. (118)

DeLong, Gabarro, and Lees also found that employees "are almost hardwired to smell the faintest trace of negative feedback" (118). Neurons of even the thickest-skinned employees quiver from the message: "You are not getting it right."

However we slice the definition, a good leader inspires, confronts, and supports others respectfully. For the leader to be good, he does all these things in the context of relationships. Otherwise, the tree falls silently in the forest.

Leadership for the twenty-first century

Seeing into the future is both impossible and magical. We cannot know what happens in the next moment, let alone the next year or decade. This doesn't stop us from imagining. Envisioning the way we want to grow as leaders clears the way to our unseeable future. What follows are both leadership principles and findings on how leadership for the twenty-first century is envisioned.

Build partnerships for growth

As I researched views on leadership for the twenty-first century, I found an emphasis on influencing change through respectful relationships. Rost (1993) for example, in *Leadership for the Twenty-First Century*, defines leadership as "an influence relationship among leaders and followers who intend real changes that reflect their mutual purposes" (124). To Rost, the importance of relationships and ethics has been greatly overlooked. Along with influencing through dynamic relationships, Rost foresees adaptability and self-awareness as leadership tools for this century.

The person who has never made a mistake will never make anything else.

—George Bernard Shaw

Be true to your core values

In a *Harvard Business Review* issue devoted to "Leadership and Strategy in the Twenty-First Century," Rosabeth Moss Kanter (2008), in "Transforming Giants: What Kind of Company Makes It Its Business to Make the World a Better Place?" offers this insight:

> Values turn out to be the key ingredient in the most vibrant and successful of today's multinationals. I refer not to the printing of wallet cards but to the serious nurturing of values in hearts and minds. Once people agree on what they respect and aspire to, they can make decisions independently and not work at cross-purposes. When they team up on a project, they communicate and collaborate efficiently, even despite great differences in backgrounds and cultural traditions, because they have a strong sense of business purpose and company identity (45).

Agreed-upon core values, according to Kanter, bring us together when our cultural backgrounds differ.

Foster multicultural communities

Kanter's observation is powerful. Leaders need insight and foresight to foster thriving multicultural organizations. Early childhood education programs need to invite and welcome a world of differences. Our effort as leaders begins within as we ask: "What are my blind spots? My biases? How do I need to grow?" As a leader grows, so grows her program. Denise Scott (2005) asked early childhood leaders: "How do you envision leadership in early childhood care and education in [10 years]?"

▶ EXERCISE YOUR EQ   How do you suppose these leaders responded? If you were interviewed, what would you predict leadership in early childhood will look like in 10 years?

Almost every leader interviewed talked without reservation about global perspective and local activism. "Leaders will require knowledge of myriad cultures and even the ability to speak another language or two," advises Scott Seigfried from Ohio. Luis Hernandez, in Miami, foresees that "leaders will know about various populations, languages, cultures . . . and have a broad view of the world." Davida McDonald, Washington, DC, envisions leadership in the future as "representative, diverse, inclusive, innovative, forward thinking, from the bottom up, not from the top down."

Be as curious as a child

Definition of stress: When your gut says "No way," and your mouth says, "Sure, I'd be glad to do that."
—Sue Baldwin

Hearing from people outside of early childhood on learning from children is refreshing. According to engineer Paul Polak (2008), whose dream is to end poverty by supporting struggling farmers across the world, "There is a simple and direct curiosity in childhood and a love of play that we tend to miss badly in our approach to problem solving as adults. If you think like a child, you can quickly strip a problem down to its basic elements" (32). Polak shares his experience of being as curious as a child when taking on the challenge of designing a cost-effective industrial oven for a rural community:

> In 1996 I was in Cachoeira, an Amazon rain-forest village, trying to figure out how rubber tappers could dry Brazil nuts at the village gathering point so they could increase their income. We had to design a village drier to replace the large industrial driers of big-city plants. When we walked through the villages, I saw that every second house had a *forno de farinha,* a two-foot-high baked-clay surface with an eight-by-ten stove top used to dry manioc flour. When I saw all these ovens . . . I realized that each of them could also become a Brazil nut drier. We just needed to think like children instead of engineers. (32)

Instead of importing, at great expense and effort, large industrial Brazil nut driers, Polak and his local team built a drier from scratch in less than two hours. This "beginner's mind," the curiosity of a child, is a powerful leadership tool.

Take care of you

As Gretta Brooker Palmer once said, happiness may be "a byproduct of an effort to make someone else happy." Altruism, selflessly battling the world's problems while helping others, is admirable. As we discussed in Chapter 6, "Partnering with Change," directors who prevent burnout from overextension take care of themselves first. Self-care is a hard practice to learn.

"Caregiver syndrome," becoming ill from overextension, is a danger for early childhood professionals. Working 12-hour days, taking work home, and trying to "fix" other people and their problems can become habits of self-destruction. Directors need to look guilt squarely in the face and say, "Back off! I am taking time just for me." This act of boundary setting, although awkward for many of us, is essential to restoring our energy.

> How wonderful it is that nobody need wait a single moment before starting to improve the world.
> —Anne Frank

Let go

The other essential dynamic of self-care is learning to "let go" of worry, self-doubt, and beating yourself up for not being perfect. Choose your battles and let go of the others. Manage your energies. Thinking you can be all things to all people is a deadly myth. If you believe this myth, you hurt yourself. Lead "on purpose," take a stand for what you believe in, and let go of thinking you can "make" anyone else change. Let your actions speak for themselves.

The serenity prayer is a director's trusted friend. The one person on earth you can change is yourself. Let go of what you cannot change—other people. Wisdom and self-respect are the gifts you receive in return for letting go. This is especially true about holding onto resentment or worry. Let it go.

> The person who pursues revenge should dig two graves.
> —Proverb

> The gods laugh most when people pray for perfection.
> —Japanese proverb

Ask for help

Directors' support groups can be havens of sanity and humor. There's nothing like hearing that another director has dealt with the same problem you are facing to help you keep perspective. "I don't feel alone!" directors happily tell me once they join or establish a directors' group.

Back in Chapter 6, on page 108, I invited you to complete a chart with the names of people in your support system. If you were to revisit that chart today, would you change anything? Have you met someone while reading this book to add to your list? Have you removed a "high maintenance" person who was draining and not replenishing your energy?

Every time my confidence flagged as I wrote or revised this book, I asked for help—from a friend, a family member, or my spiritual source. You don't have to be religious to have a spiritual source. Spirituality is the belief that there's more to life than what we see on the surface. Every leader has access to her own deeper source of inspiration and comfort.

> My goal is to show my adult children that no matter what my age might be, I can always find ways and time to laugh and have fun with life. Humor is a great coping skill.
> —Sue Baldwin

> Change takes time: [Researchers] found that new neurons continue to mature for six to eight weeks after they are first generated and that the new neurons receive input from higher brain regions for up to 10 days before they can make any outputs. The other brain regions then continue to provide information to the new neurons as they integrate into existing networks.

Find, use, and love your sense of humor

Do you, like me, know you are in trouble when you lose your sense of humor? You may have heard about author Norman Cousins, who believes he healed himself from cancer through laughter. Belly laugh after belly laugh rolled out of him as he watched the

Marx Brothers' slapstick antics on film. Yoga, the meditation practice of breathing and stretching our bodies and spirits, includes a "laughing meditation." Laughing meditation is just that: laughing, even if nothing is funny. I was skeptical about this practice. "It's not funny and I feel silly," I protested. Silly me. I "ha-ha-ha'd" my way into an upbeat place, where I once again found the humor in things. Laughter is a way of getting to the truth.

Your choices from here: Learn to love the questions

Celebrate "the beauty and allure of imperfection: the cozy familiarity of a worn-out pair of jeans, the rustic elegance of an old Italian villa, the faded splendor of well-used china handed down from your grandmother's attic."

—Taro Gold

You and I need to say goodbye. This book is about to end. I am going to miss you. I wrote this book with you in mind and in heart. I appreciate your choice to be an early childhood professional.

As a "recovering attorney," who realized later in life how valuable the early childhood profession is, I mean what I say. Early childhood education enriches children's lives and uplifts their families. As an early childhood educator, you have an impact beyond what you ever imagined. When little ones grow up and seek you out to thank you, you will know what I mean. Perhaps you already do.

Remember the TQM (total quality management) principle of continuous improvement? Are you feeling ready for your next step? No one I know has all the answers. Learn to love the questions, especially the questions that challenge you most deeply. They'll keep you on your purpose.

Please take this gift with you: Fulfilling, happy, and honest relationships are the heart of growth and learning. You can choose how you relate to everyone, including yourself. Choose kindness.

> *Hope is the thing*
> *with feathers*
> *that perches in the soul*
> *and sings the tune without words*
> *and never stops—at all.*
>
> —Emily Dickinson

Reflection questions

1. Without leafing back through this book, reflect on and write about what you most remember learning. Jot down what you recall. Next, reflect on these questions: What do you feel will stay with you? What will be useful? What might you have liked to hear more about? What was not included that you would have liked to have had covered? When you have finished writing your reflection, open the book. Is there anything else you might want to add to your reflection? If so, add that.

2. Consider the definitions of good and bad bosses in light of Robert Sutton's BAM! Radio interview. What would you list as the traits of a good versus bad boss? Sutton maintains that bosses rarely see themselves as their employees see them. He suggests giving employees a "bounty," or monetary reward, for their input about your blind spots as a boss. Do you agree with this practice? How do you think a leader can continuously take stock of her effectiveness? What self-evaluative approaches would you recommend for directors?

3. The title of this chapter, "Learning to Love the Questions," is taken from Rilke, who said: "Be patient toward all that is unsolved in your heart and try to love the questions themselves" (1993, 35). What does this quote mean to you? What are the unsolved questions you feel you could learn to love, particularly about your future as an early childhood professional? Describe which of the leadership principles to take with you might help you the most with these questions.

Team projects

1. As individuals, revisit your response to the "Exercise your EQ" exercise on page 302 when you were asked to answer the question: "How do you envision leadership in early childhood care and education in 10 years?" Next, share your answers with your teammates. Discuss together what changes you expect will take place, and what the greatest challenges will be. In particular, how do you think the eventual demographic shift, from an Anglo majority to a majority of people of color, will affect and be affected by changes in our field? Research other professionals' predictions on these questions.

2. Throughout this chapter, "leadership principles to take with you" are highlighted. As individuals, make your own list of leadership principles. Compare this with the core values you developed as you studied Chapter 3. With your team, share your core values and leadership principles. Together, create core values and leadership principles for our profession. Translate the important points of your discussion into a Power-Point or video presentation.

3. Discuss this statement: "Because theories of emotional and social intelligence have been considered soft rather than hard scientific knowledge, EQ has flourished more outside the university than within the walls of ivy. EQ and social EQ have been the heart of ethnic leadership wisdom for centuries. When we want to 'get to the heart of a matter,' we often turn to Native American elders." What have you noticed about whether EQ, social EQ, and IQ are valued in academic courses? Have the insights of people of color and ethnic groups been included or emphasized in your own studies? As individuals, investigate and select a group or individual whose insights have not been adequately incorporated into academic courses. Share the wisdom of this person or group with your teammates.

Bibliography

Aspinal, L.G. 1998. Rethinking the role of positive affect in self-regulation. *Motivation and Emotion* 22 (1): 1–32.

Baker, B. 2008. How tastes turn into feelings. *Boston Globe* March 24: C2.

Cherniss, C., M. Extein, D. Goleman, & R.P. Weissberg. 2006. Emotional intelligence: What does the research really indicate? *Educational Psychologist* 41 (4): 239–245.

Cousins, N. 1979. *Anatomy of an illness as perceived by the patient*. New York: Norton.

Covey, S. 2004. *The 7 habits of highly effective people*. Rev. ed. New York: Free Press.

DeLong, T.J., J.J. Gabarro, & R.J. Lees. 2008. Why mentoring matters in a hypercompetitive world. *Harvard Business Review* 86 (1): 115–121, 138.

Dimasio, A. 2005. *Descartes' error: Emotion, reason, and the human brain*. New York: Penguin.

Eysenck, H.J. 2000. *Intelligence: A new look*. Piscataway, NJ: Transaction Publishers.

Goleman, D. 2006. *Social intelligence: The new science of human relationships*. New York: Bantam Dell.

Graden, J. 2008. *The imposter syndrome: How to replace self-doubt with self-confidence and train your brain for success*. Bloomington, IN: Xlibris.

Kanter, R.M. 2008. Transforming giants: What kind of company makes it its business to make the world a better place? *Harvard Business Review* 86 (1): 43–52.

Lencioni, P. 2002. *The five dysfunctions of a team: A leadership fable.* San Francisco: Jossey-Bass.

NAEYC. 2008. *Getting started: Introduction to Self-Study and program quality improvement through NAEYC early childhood program accreditation.* Updated ed. Washington, DC: Author.

Polak, P. 2008. Twelve steps to practical problem solving. World Ark March/April.

Rilke, R.M. 1993. *Letters to a young poet.* Translated by M.D. Herter Norton. New York: Norton.

Rost, J.C. 1993. *Leadership for the twenty-first century.* Westport, CT: Praeger.

Scott, D, ed. 2005. Leaders on leadership: How do you envision leadership in early childhood care and education in 2015? *Young Children* 60 (1): 20–21.

Sullivan, D.R-E. 2010. *Learning to lead: Effective leadership skills for teachers of young children.* 2d ed. St. Paul, MN: Redleaf Press.

Sutton, R.I. 2010. *Good boss, bad boss: How to be the best…and learn from the worst.* New York: Hachette Book Group.

Viadero, D. 2007. Social-skills programs found to yield gains in academic subjects. *Education Week* 27 (16): 1, 15.

Wen, P. 2008. Culture gap. *Boston Globe* March 24. www.boston.com/news/health/articles/2008/03/24/culture_gap/

Children's literature

And Tango Makes Three, by Justin Richardson and Peter Parnell. Illus. by Henry Cole. 2005. New York: Simon & Schuster.

I Love You, Stinky Face, by Lisa McCourt. Illus. by Cyd Moore. 1997. New York: Scholastic.

Miss Tizzy, by Libba Moore Gray. Illus. by Jada Rowland. 1993. New York: Aladdin Paperbacks.

Where the Wild Things Are, by Maurice Sendak. 1963. New York: HarperCollins.

The Velveteen Rabbit, by Margery Williams. Illus. by William Nicholson. 1922. New York: Avon Press.

Web resources

Author Bob Sutton: Work Matters
http://bobsutton.typepad.com

Caregiver Syndrome
www.revolutionhealth.com/blogs/michaelrabowmd/caregiver-syndrome-6572

Caregiver Syndrome: Definition, Symptoms, and Tips
www.squidoo.com/caregiver-syndrome

Critical Review of Daniel Goleman
http://eqi.org/gole.htm

Emotional Intelligence: The EQ Factor
www.time.com/time/magazine/article/0,9171,983503,00.html

Leadership Blog
www.leadershipjot.com

Leadership for the Twenty-First Century
www.joe.org/joe/1994june/tt3.php

The Three Rs of Leadership: Building Effective Early Childhood Programs Through Relationships, Reciprocal Learning, and Reflection

Julie K. Biddle

This book redefines the concept of leadership in early childhood education, proposing a model of shared responsibility among school stakeholders. Drawing on her 30-plus years of working in and with schools, the author explores the three Rs of leadership in the context of developmentally appropriate programs that promote and support meaningful learning. *Copublished with HighScope.*

Item #: 365   List: $20 • Member: $16

A Great Place to Work: Creating a Healthy Organizational Climate

Paula Jorde Bloom, Ann Hentschel, & Jill Bella

This book provides administrators with the tools to define and shape the quality of a staff's work life. It helps directors evaluate and improve critical aspects of the organization's work climate and physical setting. *From New Horizons.*

Item #: 262   List: $24 • Member: $19.20

From the Inside Out: The Power of Reflection and Self-Awareness

Paula Jorde Bloom

This book guides readers through a journey to build stronger relationships with others—through self-reflection and connecting to your passions, values, talents, resources, and areas that need more growth. *From New Horizons.*

Item #: 177   List: $24 • Member: $19.20

Leadership in Action: How Effective Directors Get Things Done

Paula Jorde Bloom

This book covers the critical dimension of leadership—from leadership style and behavior to planning for your successor. *From New Horizons.*

Item #: 371   List: $24 • Member: $19.20

For a complete listing of resources on administration, please visit
www.naeyc.org/store or call **800-424-2460**.

Prices are subject to change.